A MOVEMENT'S PROMISE

A MOVEMENT'S PROMISE

THE MAKING OF CONTEMPORARY PALESTINIAN THEATER

Samer Al-Saber

STANFORD UNIVERSITY PRESS
Stanford, California

Stanford University Press
Stanford, California

© 2025 by Samer Al-Saber. All rights reserved.

No part of this book may be reproduced or transmitted in any form or by any means, electronic or mechanical, including photocopying and recording, or in any information storage or retrieval system, without the prior written permission of Stanford University Press.

Library of Congress Cataloging-in-Publication Data
Names: Al-Saber, Samer author
Title: A movement's promise : the making of contemporary Palestinian theater / Samer Al-Saber.
Description: Stanford, California : Stanford University Press, 2025. | Includes bibliographical references and index.
Identifiers: LCCN 2025002592 (print) | LCCN 2025002593 (ebook) | ISBN 9781503642584 cloth | ISBN 9781503643277 paperback | ISBN 9781503643284 ebook
Subjects: LCSH: Theater, Palestinian Arab—History—20th century | Theater—Political aspects—Palestine—History | Theater—Censorship—Palestine—History | Arab-Israeli conflict
Classification: LCC PN2919.4 A78 2025 (print) | LCC PN2919.4 (ebook) | DDC 792.095694/0904—dc23/eng/20250424
LC record available at https://lccn.loc.gov/2025002592
LC ebook record available at https://lccn.loc.gov/2025002593

Cover design: Ann Weinstock
Cover photo: The destroyed Al-Nuzha Cinema when El-Hakawati Ensemble took possession in the fall of 1983. Courtesy of François Abu Salem Archive, Palestinian National Theater/El-Hakawati.

The authorized representative in the EU for product safety and compliance is: Mare Nostrum Group B.V. | Mauritskade 21D | 1091 GC Amsterdam | The Netherlands | Email address: gpsr@mare-nostrum.co.uk | KVK chamber of commerce number: 96249943

CONTENTS

INTRODUCTION	A Movement's Promise	1
ONE	In the Shadow of War, Before 1967 and After	17
TWO	*At the Cross* and a Theater for Many Reasons, 1967–1970	37
THREE	A Movement Is Born, 1970–1973 **Balalin Lights "The Darkness"**	59
FOUR	Wrestling with Commitments, Division, and Arrests, 1973–1977	85
FIVE	A Movement Reconstituted, 1977–1981 **El-Hakawati's Trinity, Sanabel's Cause, and a League of Their Own**	110
SIX	Uncertainty, Censorship, and the Permission to Perform, 1981–1984	140
SEVEN	A Movement Actualized, 1984–1986 **The Building, the March, and El-Hakawati Era**	170

EIGHT	Intifada in the Streets and Crisis in the Theater, 1987–1990	204
NINE	A Movement Transformed, 1990 to Oslo *Al-Kasaba's Star-Crossed Lovers*	232
CONCLUSION	Besieged NGOs and a Movement in Lore	251
	Acknowledgments	261
	Notes	265
	Bibliography	291
	Index	299

INTRODUCTION

A MOVEMENT'S PROMISE

In the existing Palestinian books, period journalism, and in daily speak among Palestinian artists, the theater in Palestine is often referred to as Al-Haraka Al-Masrahiya (The Theatrical Movement).[1] In the Palestinian political sphere and to a great extent, the Arab one, the reference to a certain activity as a *haraka*, a movement, implies an energetic motion toward a particular goal, often liberatory and resistant to an overpowering hegemony. For example, Fateh as a political party was initially referred to as a movement, and so were most Palestinian political parties during their various stages of resistance against military occupation and before their involvement in the Palestinian Liberation Organization (PLO) and participation in governance after the establishment of the Palestinian Authority in the 1990s. The term *movement* also describes efforts associated with a cause, such as the civil rights movement in the United States or, more recently, the Black Lives Matter movement. To call political action a movement suggests an affiliation with a segment of a population that seeks to relieve a specific pressure caused by a shared condition of oppression. By creating a temporary change at the base of a society, "still waters" can ripple into a more influential transformation. To understand contemporary Palestinian theater in Jerusalem and throughout Palestine, specifically in the 1970s and 1980s, it is crucial to examine why the majority of the theater artists of the period saw themselves as part of a movement.[2]

When a small group of individuals call themselves a movement, they create a nonphysical site of attraction for a population that seeks direction. Often, the nucleus of a movement comprises a few leaders and supporters, beginning underground, invisible to the oppressive forces that control their circumstances. From their precarious subject positions and limited resources, they build a larger current, using an appellation that inspires hope and sometimes a pathway to achieve their aspirations. For example, in the Arab public sphere, national movements throughout the twentieth and twenty-first centuries included the Lebanese Naserite movement Al-Murabitoun (Almoravids, connoting resilience and longevity); the Palestinian Abna' Al-Balad movement (People of the Homeland); and more recently, the Egyptian Movement for Change, Kefaya (Enough). These movements rose to manifest substantial change against the brutal realities of occupation, division, and dictatorship. The promise of their formation signaled a necessity for corrective action when a national situation appeared bleak, and a popular belief predominated that the cessation of the status quo deserved some form of collective sacrifice for a higher purpose.

A movement is the vanguard manifestation of an oppressed segment of society and historically but not exclusively an expression of the colonized and a tool of the subjugated. Because an ongoing struggle precedes the formation of a movement that has traction, the founders and followers foresee the influence of their ideas on their immediate community. They quickly become a magnet that attracts local support and participation. Simultaneously, they attract opposition. On the terrain of struggle, a movement faces direct pressure from powerful authorities who prefer to maintain a status quo that serves their long-term goals. In a colonial context, a longer duration of the status quo allows for increasing settlement expansion, strengthening of the colonizer's military control, establishing economic domination, and a slow dismantling of armed struggle and the associated national sentiments within a colonized population. In the case of movements against dictatorships, tyrannical regimes prefer a status quo to deepen and entrench their control within the institutions of the state. Thus, an emerging movement constitutes a primary enemy to a reigning hegemony, which often seeks to settle the movement's cadres by all means necessary as soon as its ripples begin to be felt. Once a movement expands, its cadres increase, and its voice echoes, it initially becomes a formidable adversary: invisible, faceless, and unlocalized. If or when a movement gains material power in the form of economic, cultural, or military force, the reigning regime applies ruthless measures that result in the movement's annihilation or, in rare cases such as the PLO, bureaucratic survival or eventual institutional independence in the form of a known quantity.

What qualifies Palestinian theater makers to constitute a movement? The notion of a movement presupposes a number of characteristics: A movement is not an existing party, faction, or institution; it does not have a recognized set of guidelines; and it springs from ad hoc grassroots action, reacts to a static or absent condition, and seeks to arrive at a particular destination. A movement declares and names itself against a backdrop of rejection, demonization, or diminution by its adversary, which seeks its immediate liquidation at any cost. When the movement achieves its goal, it immediately disbands or transforms into another entity, be it an institution, a party, or an organization. By contrast, when its adversary annihilates a movement without achieving its goal, the movement produces an offspring that continues its mission as a new movement, even after a period of hibernation. In the case of the Palestinian theater movement, which declared itself in the early 1970s, its cadres of performers, directors, producers, writers, and technicians experienced direct opposition to their activity and fought directly against censorship and closures. Some of its cadres were arrested, interrogated, and exiled. Over a period of nearly three decades between 1967 and the mid-1990s, the Palestinian theater makers dissolved the various parts of their movement and reconstituted themselves in order to survive.

In 1979, when Mohammad Anis edited the anthology *The Theatrical Movement in the Occupied Territories*, the term *movement* accurately described theatrical activities in the Jerusalem-Ramallah-Birzeit area, the main geographical focus of his anthology. The theater Anis documented constituted a movement through its activism for Palestine, antagonism toward the occupation and its censorship, and reaction to the absence of Palestinian theatrical institutions. Throughout the seventies and eighties, the theatrical movement in East Jerusalem was dynamic until it came to a halt before springing into action again, as it did, for example, in the early 1980s with the foundation of the Nuzha-Hakawati theater building in Jerusalem. By constantly ending and re-emerging by choice or force, the movement was self-sacrificial, which allowed for a constant stream of new companies and artists to emerge. To a great extent, the movement's inherent nihilism over the divisiveness of the ensembles became a characteristic condition of its continuance. These aspects of the movement were most evident in the quick rise and fall of theater artists and companies on one level but also in the willing dismantling of theater companies in order to create new ones. Most of the continuously operating theater companies in the Jerusalem-Ramallah area underwent several divisions, renamings, and reincarnations by the time they institutionalized their operational standards, thus transforming themselves from members of a movement into recognized institutions.[3]

In East Jerusalem, this movement began with a fertile vigor that characterized its young pioneers. In 1976, Hanan Ashrawi noted, "The most noticeable literary-cultural phenomenon, mainly in the West Bank Jerusalem-Ramallah area, [was] the emergence of theater ensembles."[4] By 1978, there had been fifteen theater ensembles in the Jerusalem-Ramallah-Birzeit area, of which eight were in Jerusalem. In 1979, four theater ensembles (Dababis, Sundouq Al-'ajab, El-Hakawati, and Palestinian People's Theatre) revived the theater committee of the Association for Work and Development for the Arts, which was initially established in 1975 as part of an effort to organize the activities of civil society in the region. They produced a twenty-two-page booklet, summarizing the history of the contemporary theatrical movement in the Jerusalem-Ramallah area. Written in a local Palestinian dialect, this informal narrative told the story of the formation of Balalin, Sundouq Al-'ajab, Dababis, and El-Hakawati. The booklet also explained the reasons behind the latest division in the Palestinian Theatre Ensemble. Emphasizing the continuous desire to unify Palestinian theater under one organized umbrella, the document declared the theatrical movement as an integral participant in resisting the 1967 occupation. Accordingly, theater makers produced political theater because it was collective action, an encounter point for an occupied people, a way to force a population to leave their homes despite massive risks and concurrent social and political transformations. They saw theater as an alternative to the widespread influence of non-Palestinian television, a medium that Palestinians did not have the authority to operate in Palestine until the mid-1990s. Concluding as a manifesto for future collaboration, the booklet promised an inclusive modus operandi: "Dialogue . . . cooperation . . . coordination, joint resources, working programs for the ensembles, for the association, and a candid invitation for the unification of the theatrical movement. We expect a theater season that is rich in productions characterized by quality and commitment."[5]

By the Intifada in 1987, approximately thirteen ensembles had produced plays in East Jerusalem and eight in the Ramallah-Birzeit area. From 1967 to 1987, the astonishing number of twenty theater ensembles had been founded to serve a population of less than two hundred thousand in the East Jerusalem-Ramallah area alone, constituting the overwhelming majority of theatrical activity in the whole of the Occupied Territories.[6] The level of activity and popularity of these ensembles depended on their leadership, their success in circumventing the laws of censorship, and their ability to be financially independent through local donations, partnerships with small businesses, or community volunteerism. In his 1989 study of the theater movement in the West Bank, Mahamid reported: "The ensembles actively working today are concentrated in Jerusalem. They are El-Hakawati, Palestinian Theatre Ensemble, the Theatrical Artistic Group, and Sanabel Ensemble."[7] In this assessment, Mahamid identified the leading founding members of Palestinian theater in Jerusalem in the post-1967 period and to some extent the major theater artists, who continued to be productive into the Oslo period of the 1990s.

The product of this movement in East Jerusalem's theater can be seen in the still-existing theater venues: El-Hakawati Theatre, Sanabel People's Theatre, and Al-Kasaba Theatre. The latter was established in Jerusalem but moved to Ramallah in the late 1990s. El-Hakawati Theatre was the brainchild of François Abu Salem, who was also a founding member of several earlier theater companies, including Balalin, Bila-Lin, and Sundouq Al-'ajab. By the mid-1990s, former members of El-Hakawati established Ashtar Theatre (1992–present) in Ramallah and Theatre Day Productions (1996) in Hebron and Gaza. However, the accomplishments of the theatrical movement can be measured by more than the development of new theatrical spaces since its launch in the post-occupation period. The experiences of the participants in this theatrical movement expanded the horizons of culture makers throughout Palestine. Other members of El-Hakawati established their own production companies in the Galilee, such as Radi Shehadeh's Masrah Al-Seera and Adnan Tarabsheh's Maraia Theater in Mghar, both of which manifested a significant presence for Palestinian collective narratives within Israel. The Palestinian Theatre ensemble and the Sanabel Theatre ensemble emerged from the work of a number of labor-class advocates and explicitly leftist theater artists such as Mohammad Al-Thaher, Ahmad Abu Saloum, and Hussam Abu Esheh, among many others. Since their beginnings in 1973, these leftist artists played thousands of performances asserting the tenets of the Palestinian left and class-conscious theater. El-Warsheh El-Fanniyeh (The Theater Arts Group), which became known as Al-Kasaba in 1989, emerged initially in 1970 to represent the work of George Ibrahim, who excelled at the adaptation of European classics and the development of children's theater for elementary and secondary schools. Ibrahim's early children's plays had inspired many writers, musicians, and theatermakers to pursue careers in theater. For some, employment with Ibrahim signified professionalization and a way forward as artists. All of these artists and ensembles demonstrated impressive continuity on the Palestinian theater scene, beginning in the early 1970s and continuing well into the twenty-first century.

This book narrates the story of the Palestinian theater movement in the 1970s and 1980s and recognizes the immense lore and status that theater achieved in Palestine during this period. *A Movement's Promise* tells the story of Palestinian youth who gathered in the wake of the 1967 war to launch a theater movement and a performance culture that continue to thrive today. The central relationship in this history is a struggle between the theater artists and the Israeli authorities on the one hand and the absence of significant artistic media that tell the Palestinian narratives within historic Palestine during this period. Based on a multiyear ethnography in Palestine and archival research in the Israel State Archive, this history shows how the Israeli authorities inadvertently and unknowingly promoted Palestinian theater as its security forces attempted to suppress Palestinians under occupation and its censorship forced theater makers to navigate its red tape. Simultaneously, the youthful vigor of some of the early artists such as François Abu Salem (figure 1), George Ibrahim, Nadia Mikhail, Sameh Abboushey, Vera Tamari, Emile Ashrawi, Ahmad Abu Saloum, Hussam Abu Esheh, Adel El-Tartir, and Mustapha Al-Kurd, among many others, led to a competitive theater-scape that manifested in the eventual formation of today's Palestinian theater industry, encompassing several theaters, tens of ensembles, and hundreds of workers for such a small population within Palestine, not exceeding six million Palestinians at the time of this writing. This book honors the work of remarkable figures who have not yet taken their rightful place in recorded Palestinian culture and theater history. Despite the significant contributions of the cultural production sector, research in this area remains understudied and under-recognized, paling in comparison to the overwhelming efforts of Middle East and Palestine Studies in the areas of political history, economics, and contemporary affairs, as well as the plethora of works on the countries of the Global South in the areas of theater and performance studies.

Because this book primarily tells the founding story of contemporary Palestinian theater and its movement, the first chapter, "In the Shadow of War, Before 1967 and After," recounts the conditions that influenced the emergence of theatrical activity between 1948 and 1967, including some biographical accounts that shed light on the living experiences of

FIGURE 1 Members of Balalin share a toast near the home of François Abu Salem. Jerusalem, 1971. Courtesy of François Abu Salem Archive, Palestinian National Theater/El-Hakawati.

key artists. These biographies explain the social, political, and psychological states of individuals and thus provide a glimpse of how the Nakba, refugee life, and the eruption of the 1967 war significantly shaped Palestinian performance. The second chapter, "*At the Cross* and a Theater for Many Reasons, 1967-1970," narrates and explains how existing theatrical activities in Jerusalem differed from the nucleus of the theatrical movement, which forms the spine of this book. After describing the theater of the 1960s in Jerusalem as a predominantly community-driven enterprise in shows by the Jerusalem Players and the church-produced repertory *At the Cross*, it tells the story of how George Ibrahim began his professional career as an actor in an Israeli television show called *Sami and Susu*. This chapter shows how theater during the early days of the postwar period existed without a declared national purpose, and in some ways, it was influenced by Israel's developing occupation of Jerusalem. The third chapter, "A Movement Is Born: Balalin Lights *The Darkness*, 1970-1973" recounts a theatrical experiment in the form of the concurrent emergence of several theater companies that self-identified as the theater movement. With the embracing of the movement designation by the Balalin ensemble, the emerging youth also adopted a resistance narrative that situated theater as a necessary social and political action as a result of the 1967 occupation and the expulsion of the nascent PLO's armed resistance from Jordan in Black September of 1970.

The fourth and fifth chapters, "Wrestling with Commitments, Division, and Arrests, 1973-1977" and "A Movement Reconstituted: El-Hakawati's Trinity, Sanabel's Cause, and a League of Their Own, 1977-1981," track the development and reorganization of theater ensembles in a crucial period of self-reflection and increasing production. These two chapters demonstrate how factionalism inside the movement occurred between and within theater ensembles while simultaneously battling against Israeli authorities that rejected Palestinian theater as a living practice in the Occupied Territories. Internal factionalism led to the dismantling and reconstitution of ensembles as well as the emergence of new leadership within the theater movement. The adversarial relationship with the occupation led to increased interruptions, particularly due to arrests and the absence of the permission to perform. Chapter 6, "Uncertainty, Censorship, and the Permission to Perform, 1981-1984," focuses on the strengthening leadership of El-Hakawati Ensemble, which innovated in the areas of international touring and created its own unique aesthetic. Chapter 7, "A Movement Actualized: The Building, the March, and El-Hakawati Era, 1984-1986," begins with the impressive conversion of a derelict cinema into a home for the theater movement, effectively creating a physical address and sanctuary for contemporary Palestinian theater. The establishment of El-Hakawati's new home led to stability and the exponential growth of theatrical production by nearly all existing theater companies. Chapter 8, "Intifada in the Streets and Crisis in the Theater, 1987-1990," narrates the history of division within El-Hakawati, the ensemble's differences with the theater movement, and its local challenges with the Israeli authorities, as well as its censorship in the United States. While Palestinians revolted against the occupation in the streets, the movement entered a period of crisis and necessary self-evaluation. Chapter 9, "A Movement Transformed: Al-Kasaba's Star-Crossed Lovers, 1990 to Oslo," depicts the rise of Al-Kasaba Theater, the establishment of its own venue, and its co-production of *Romeo and Juliet*, while taking stock of the increasing number of active theater companies. The book concludes with "Besieged NGOs and a Movement in Lore," which describes the emergence of Al-Kasaba Theater as the newest leader of the movement and Palestinian theater's march toward a new set of social and political conditions as the ill-fated Oslo Peace Accords (1993) become a potential fact on the ground. Accordingly, the journey of the Palestinian theater movement effectively completes a full cycle of emergence to transformation.

A Movement's Promise intentionally focuses on the period from the 1967 occupation of the Palestinian Territories until the Oslo Peace Accords, specifically in East Jerusalem, for a number of reasons. Palestinian theater flourished in East Jerusalem as part of a Palestinian cultural spring in the 1970s and 1980s. Neighboring Ramallah became a functional capital for the Palestinians after Oslo; however, historically, Ramallah was a small Christian town known for its great summer weather, quality restaurants, churches, leftist intellectuals, and beautiful natural sites. Its economic, educational, and cultural activities were often connected with the influential city of East Jerusalem and its much larger population. Based on their geographic proximity and historical connection, East Jerusalem and Ramallah functioned as a joint cultural center, connected by the social, professional, and familial relationships among their residents. In this critical period of the late sixties and early seventies, the majority of the pioneering Palestinian theater artists of the West Bank lived and worked in Jerusalem, Ramallah, or both. According to the theater makers of the period, productions in these two cities could not be differentiated because many plays and musical performances were rehearsed and performed in both cities, though the lion's share of performances often took place in Jerusalem because post-1967-occupation Ramallah operated under Israeli military laws, while East Jerusalem functioned under the Israeli West Jerusalem's much less draconian civil censorship laws.[8]

This book documents the key theatrical events, ensembles, plays, authors, and players who contributed to the establishment of a vibrant theater culture in the specified period and geography. The narrative, drawing primarily on verifiable Palestinian sources from and about the region, conveys a history of the "center" rather than the periphery of contemporary Palestinian theater. Spanning a period of twenty-six years, the most active theater artists and ensembles take up the majority of this narrative based on their continuity, frequency of production, audience reach locally and internationally, and eventual ability to establish their own theatrical spaces in East Jerusalem or Ramallah. Due to the geographical focus on East Jerusalem, the book does not cover the Palestinian theater of the Galilee, Gaza, and the peripheries of the West Bank. Thus, the works and powerful legacy of the five major Palestinian actors who worked in both Israeli and Palestinian theaters—Makram Khoury, Salwa Naqara, Mohammad Al-Bakri, Salim Daw, and Youssef Abu Wardeh—do not figure extensively in this narrative, despite their occasional appearances in Al-Kasaba and El-Hakawati's productions in this period. Similarly, the famous directors from the Galilee—Antoine Saleh, Mazin Ghattas, Fouad Awad, and Riad Massarweh—appear only in relation to Jerusalemite productions. Most notably, some of the most active Palestinian theaters today—such as Jenin's Freedom Theatre, Gaza's Theatre Day Productions, Bethlehem's Al-Rowwad, Ramallah's Ashtar Theatre, Hebron's Yes Theatre, Beit Jala's Inad, and Beit Jala's Al-Hara Theatre—fall outside the scope of this book due to their date of founding post-Oslo, their location, or both.[9]

This book offers a critical history and an account of the foundations of contemporary Palestinian theater, not an analysis of the theater of the so-called conflict between Israel and Palestine. A theater of the "conflict" narrative would necessarily include a vast global dramatic literature that addresses Palestine through different perspectives. Traditional political narratives of the 'Israel/Palestine conflict' have often overshadowed Palestinian cultural production, which consists of literature, poetry, music, theater, art, film, and performance. In news media reports on the conflict, the saturation of violence presents compelling reasons for an immediate inquiry into ongoing political crises in lieu of the documentation and narration of art and culture, a trend that this book works against. By definition, the historiography of the "conflict" presupposes familiar binaries: peace and war, military forces and civilians, before and after 1948, and Zionism versus Palestinian nationalism. Thus, very often, Palestinian cultural narratives are juxtaposed not only against the political histories of the Palestinians but also with the so-called conflict, effectively forcing Palestine's narrative to exist only in relation to Israel but not vice versa. Although existing conflict narratives may appear to provide a natural home for an emerging field of study such as Palestinian theater, this book presents a "history from below," insisting on the right of Palestinian theater makers to exist on their own merits, without being subsumed by crisis narratives or orientalist motifs. *A Movement's Promise* takes up the challenging task of constructing a cogent narrative from thousands of disparate sources, collating hundreds of key events, and covering a journey of hundreds of key players for nearly three decades. One could say that the book tracks the youth of a promising movement as they evolve, change, and transform as their cause unfolds on the world stage.

By intentionally avoiding the "conflict's" master narratives in secondary sources and relying predominantly on primary sources—ethnography, archives, and period journalism—this book documents and synthesizes the accounts remembered, argued, and reinforced among Palestinian theater artists, whose collective knowledge remains the most comprehensive source on Palestinian theater today. To this end, this book's foremost primary sources are unstructured interviews with artists, witness accounts of Palestinian theater, and biographical experiences on and off the Palestinian stage. Although this ethnography yielded a large number of recorded and unrecorded interviews, a plethora of informal field notes, and long reflections on personal conversations, the book synthesizes the ethnographic evidence to frame the study, contextualize the theatrical events, and narrate the spirited enthusiasm of the period. With each interview, each theater artist presented a personal viewpoint, thus building the evidence for this historical record. During the period of fieldwork (2009-2023), because interviews generated a large set of autobiographical information as well as corroborating evidence for gossip and urban legends, the ethnographic evidence generated further archival materials, leading to new research questions and new quests for historical documents over time. Through committed embeddedness and participation, the lines between evidence, discussion, and memory grew from discrete to nuanced and embodied. In a sense, this book is the result of a long and concerted effort to live and, at times, to work within Palestinian theater until this narrative emerged from deep embodied engagement with the actors on the ground.

Due to the absence of a Palestinian state, Palestinian theater history has not been collected into a centralized archive.[10] During the material collection phase of fieldwork, three types of archives supplemented the ethnography. First, the personal archives of Palestinian theater artists proved to be the most useful. Often, these materials included period journalism concerning the artists' personal work, such as reviews of plays and interviews with newspapers and magazines; original posters, photographs, and brochures of period productions; actor copies of play scripts; and rarely, archival video recordings of original productions. Second, the most comprehensive journalistic records existed in institutionalized archives—namely, the archive of El-Hakawati Theatre Ensemble. In the possession of actor Edward Muallem at Ashtar Theatre, this organized archive includes a large record of the history of El-Hakawati in the form of scripts, posters, photographs, videos, and professionally collected and labeled period journalism. During the period of fieldwork, actor Amer Khalil possessed a similarly comprehensive archive in the form of the estate of the late director and El-Hakawati founder François Abu Salem. Third, the Ministry of the Interior's censorship records included files on the plays evaluated for the Israeli performance permit, a necessary document for artists to avoid closures or arrests. Obtained from the Israel State Archive under the title of each play, a standard file included the application for the permit, two evaluations by different censorship officers, a copy of the submitted script, miscellaneous materials such as related newspaper articles, and a copy of the granted permit. Complex cases of censorship contained related internal correspondence.

In unpublished manuscript form, the plays of Jerusalemite theater are the richest written primary record of the history of the ensembles and the dramatic literary value of Palestinian theater. Unpublished are the majority of the plays of Balalin, the large majority of the plays of Mohammad Al-Thaher, the entirety of George Ibrahim's repertoire of original children's plays and adaptations of European classics, and the full oeuvre of the Dababis theater except for one published play, *Al-Hashra*. In 2021, Edward Muallem edited four original plays by El-Hakawati Ensemble, published in Arabic by the Palestinian Authority's Ministry of Culture; I was honored to write the introduction to this collection. In many cases, the originally composed music became a significant component of the script. In such cases, some artists provided the music. For example, George Ibrahim provided samples of music for a selection of his children's plays. The archival video of El-Hakawati's *Story of Kufur of Shamma* showed how the music originally composed by the legendary radical Egyptian singer and composer Al-Sheikh Imam underscored the mood and stage aesthetic of the production. As primary sources, the scripts reveal the technical abilities of the artists, the choices of topics, the techniques employed to avoid censorship, and, to some degree, the effectiveness of the artists at communicating their grievances to their public under a concerted censorship regime.

Period journalism provides a contemporary record of most theater-related events. Although newspaper articles are sometimes considered secondary sources, they function in this book as primary sources because they often establish basic information, such as dates of performances, names of participants, and locations of presentations. They also corroborate ethnographic evidence through relayed quotations in journalistic interviews. Many articles include photographs that inform the resulting historical account when the original archives of the artists and ensembles could not impart the full picture of the reconstructed incident, event, or performance. In the case of the public battle between El-Hakawati and the theater movement over the Nuzha-Hakawati theater, the debates in the press became a primary source because many articles were written by theater movement artists. Similarly, the European press and Hebrew-language newspapers depicted various attitudes ranging from cautious solidarity to direct and unapologetic opposition (at times racism), which provided a primary source for attitudes directed at El-Hakawati abroad. As a result, a reconstruction of a performance, such as *Mahjoob Mahjoob*, *A Thousand and One Nights*, or *The Story of the Kufur Shamma*, combines the use of period journalism as a primary source of basic information on the presentations and an account of the period's attitudes toward Palestinian theater in Israel, Europe, and the United States.

Preserving the oral history of Palestinian theater—the narration, historicization, and corroboration of undocumented stories based on anecdotes often repeated among the artists—became one of the implicit missions of this book. In the framework of a people's history, personal accounts and encounters fold into this layered narrative that encompasses the circumstances of the creation of theater ensembles and the mounting of theatrical productions under the banner of the Palestinian theater movement. Since the majority of the scripts adapted and created by Palestinian theater artists remain unpublished and, therefore, uncitable in accessible English language books, simple plot summaries are included as part of the performance reconstructions, where multiple testimonies and sets of evidence combine into a single narrative, providing the fullest possible account of this history. In the unfolding of the story, critical analysis and interpretation of texts, events, and performances served as a touchstone to illuminate developing aesthetics and production styles throughout the period.

This introduction aims to situate the history of Palestinian theater within a recognizable scholarly and methodological frame. To respect the experiences of the makers of the theater movement, the first priority of the constructed historical narrative of this book is recognizability by the agents who lived the period. After all, historical scholarship that significantly departs from the realities of its agents, whether it agrees with or rejects their perceptions, fails to represent the legitimacy and heterogeneity of their lived experience. As the first historical account of the Palestinian theater movement based on archival and ethnographic sources, this book enters unique experiences and accounts into scholarly knowledge, making the narrative available for interpretation and negotiation against developing research on other geographies. Thus, *A Movement's Promise* explicitly relays and honors the revolutionary and coming-of-age sentiments earnestly expressed by Palestinian theater makers. In lieu of intervening in the trajectory of the movement and its resultant theater industry, this book documents the journeys of tireless theatrical heroes as they navigate a challenging terrain.

This book enfolds evidence into a story, often drawing from multiple sources at once to capture the theatrical efforts of pioneering artists, who rehearsed, performed, and built an audience under occupation. The throughline is the journey of young hopefuls beginning their artistic practices in a political vacuum after the Nakba had eviscerated the cultural infrastructure of Palestinian life and the 1967 occupation had shackled Palestinian cultural futurity, ostensibly forever. Yet, the performing stars of this movement gathered their energies, intellect, community spirits, and resources to manifest illegal expressions of Palestine in the early 1970s, then grew their operations and practices to establish the foundations of contemporary Palestinian theater today. Without the indispensable work of the theater movement of the 1970s and 1980s, Palestinian theater would not convey its massive cultural force, respected status, recognition, and international reach of today. Renowned theaters such as the Freedom Theater of Jenin, Ashtar Theatre and Al-Kasaba Theater in Ramallah, and the Palestinian National Theatre in Jerusalem, as well as the younger institutions of Khashabi Theater in Haifa, Al-Rowwad Theater in Aida Refugee Camp in Bethlehem, and Al-Harah Theater in Beit Jala all owe a tremendous debt to the individual and collective actions of the theater movement, if not in material lineage, then through inspiring stories, cultural lore, and memorable productions. This book meticulously narrates events, names, ensembles, and productions into a throughline of the emergence of the movement until its decline, not to demonstrate its expiry but to memorialize and assert its durability.

Finally, this book is ultimately about Palestine. The unique historical events that shaped the Palestinian condition, from the initialization of the Zionist project in the late nineteenth century to the tumultuous anticolonial battles of the first half of the twentieth century, the traumatic Nakba of 1948, and the subsequent expulsions and wars against the Palestinian identity, all underlie this theatrical history. As this movement's key leaders and ensembles often stated, the occupation of East Jerusalem and the Palestinian resistance movements sparked a desperate need to act within Palestine. Therefore, every story and conflict in this book expresses Palestine as a place and a people: the collective desperation of the early years, the desire to restore a sense of selfhood after heartbreaking dispossession, the mandatory navigation of the Israeli censorship apparatus, the plays portraying life under occupation, the routine humiliations and violent confrontations with arrests and incarceration, the international tours to share Palestine with the world, the complexity of engaging with one's occupier, the conflicting opinions within Palestine, the divisions and splintering within the theater movement, the symbols with which the artists chose to communicate, and the audiences that attended theater by the thousands. This book is about Palestine's theater movement, which showed promise in the shadow of war, embraced a theater for many reasons, manifested community, committed to the struggle, reconstituted itself when necessary, accelerated toward liberation, self-actualized against enormous odds, and finally self-institutionalized into a new reality.

ONE

IN THE SHADOW OF WAR, BEFORE 1967 AND AFTER

In 1948, the war and expulsion of Palestinians from their homeland annihilated the infrastructure and cohesion of Palestinian politics, society, and culture. The exiled Palestinian elites were located in multiple areas, including the West Bank, Gaza, Jordan, Syria, Lebanon, and Egypt. This fate also afflicted active theater artists. For example, members of Al-Jawzi family ended up in Damascus and Amman, Asma' Toubi in Beirut, Father Estafan Salem in Latakia, and Mohammad Hasan Ala' Al-Din in Amman.[1] In 1966, the Palestine Liberation Organization (PLO) founded the Association of Palestinian Theatre in Damascus, the first known Palestinian theater organization in the diaspora. Ghassan Kanafani—playwright, novelist, journalist, and spokesman for the Popular Front for the Liberation of Palestine (PFLP)—began to produce his novels and plays in the sixties as well.[2] In the West Bank and Gaza, Palestinians were subject to the censorship and governance of Hashemite and Egyptian regimes, which limited the emergence of Palestinian cultural production in general and theater in particular.[3] Nonetheless, conditions in the West Bank became favorable for the creation of theater under the banner of education within the Hashemite Kingdom. This effort resulted in extra-curricular school activities, some radio dramas, and the works of a few playwrights who attempted to fill the immense vacuum in theater production.[4]

When David Ben-Gurion declared the State of Israel in 1948 with the support of nearly all the post-World War II superpowers, Palestinians experienced harsh new realities within the United Nations Partition Line (also known as the Green Line) within today's State of Israel.

Under Israeli military rule (1948-1966), Palestinians found refuge in the Communist Party, the only political institution in which they could voice their demands for basic rights; however, the party influenced literature, poetry, and journalism more effectively than it benefitted theatrical production. From the 1950s to the early 1960s, the Israeli authorities, along with the Histadrut (General Federation of Laborers), sponsored the creation of "positive" cultural activities in Arabic to align the indigenous population with the newly created political establishment. For instance, the play *The Development of the Arab Village in Israel in Ten Years*, crafted in Palestinian dialect, follows two Palestinians who return to their village after a ten-year "willful" absence, only to discover the modernizing influence of the Israeli government.[5] Aside from fairly minor theatrical activities, the theater of Palestinian citizens of Israel in the immediate aftermath of the Nakba was quite limited.

In the Jerusalem/Ramallah area, the 1960s were a period of promise for the Palestinian people, who were just beginning to self-stabilize from the catastrophe of 1948. Families that had been in temporary refugee camps began to find their way into new geographies either as citizens or in better-developed United Nations refugee camps, particularly in Jordan, Lebanon, and Gaza. The cities of East Jerusalem and Ramallah reflected the post-Nakba context in the West Bank, where many Nakba survivors had found refuge. By the mid-1950s, displaced populations dynamically participated in the creation of businesses and offered services to developing Arab governments, particularly in the Arabian Gulf region. Schools in Gaza and the West Bank educated the children of the Nakba generation using Egyptian and Jordanian curriculums. The United Nations Relief and Works Agency for Palestinian Refugees in the Near East (UNRWA) established active educational and health programs to support refugee camps, which produced a generation of well-educated Palestinians. The majority of the refugee population in Amman and Zarqa in Jordan were becoming more stable financially and politically as many acquired Jordanian passports, supporting the growth of the emergent independent Hashemite Kingdom of Jordan. Jerusalem's education system and institutions integrated with Jordan's, unifying core narratives of pan-Arabism and Jordanian nationalism. Socially, Palestinians who suffered the Nakba and became refugees were re-establishing themselves, either in yet-to-be-occupied Palestinian regions in Gaza and the West Bank or in their new host countries as citizens, when possible.

On the theatrical front, under Jordanian law from 1948 to 1967, the basic regulation of theatrical content reflected the Hashemite government's inexperience with this art form. After 1948, the theater was nearly absent from public life in the West Bank, aside from educational initiatives. According to the Jordanian laws of the period, the lawmakers initially perceived the institution of the theater as an endeavor for the government to nurture rather than a medium for potentially dangerous messages against the kingdom. The Jordanian Education Law of 1955, which applied to East Jerusalem as a city of the West Bank, expressed the importance of the fine arts in and outside schools and suggested that educational institutions must encourage the study of acting and music (ch. 1, art. 4). Under the Ministry of Social Affairs Law of 1956, the ministry was entrusted to supervise and "direct" cultural institutions such as theaters, cinemas, festivals, and other sites of entertainment in a "socially positive manner" (art. 4), an early example of governmental attempts to direct and control artistic content. The Laws of the Municipality of Bethlehem (1951 and 1956) and similar laws in other municipalities regulated public entertainments including the selling of tickets and the collection of fees for each seat in cinemas and "acting houses." Cinema houses were given special attention because there were thirty-three in the kingdom; fourteen of them were in Nablus, Ramallah, Al-Bireh, Bethlehem, Jericho, Jenin, and Jerusalem. Classifications by level of service were assigned to these cinema houses, and fees were regulated by 1956 throughout the kingdom. In a 1958 amendment to the regulation, Jerusalem's Al-Nuzha cinema was reclassified from a second-class to a third-class house, a significant fact in the history of the Jerusalemite El-Hakawati Theatre, which converted the failed cinema to a fully functioning theater in 1984.[6]

Although the laws of the Jordanian municipalities did not mention theater apart from the regulation of public entertainments, the Hashemite government gave its municipalities permission to establish new institutions to promote culture and sports such as museums, libraries, schools, and clubs. Along with establishing new buildings for these institutions, the municipalities were permitted to form committees and hire individuals to manage and control (censor) these efforts.[7] In spite of the presence of censorship language in the aforementioned laws, the government was committed to constructing theater buildings. Overall, the fine arts offered opportunities for development in the recently established Hashemite state. The Ministry of Information Regulations of 1966 articulated the kingdom's goals for cultural development to be a national building project directed at making the Jordanian citizen. The tools of the ministry included radio, print publication, the fine arts, and television. Article 3 of the law stated that "the aims of the ministry of information are to plan and execute the process of media, cultural, intellectual, and artistic awareness assigned to the state in Jordan." The ministry specifically noted the goal to develop national sentiment in the Jordanian and Arab citizen. The Press and Publication Law of 1967 documented some of the measures taken by the ministry to control the message to the public. Two copies of all printed materials were to be sent to the Ministry of Information, and the minister reserved the right to confiscate the publication if it was deemed harmful to the public. This law cancelled any previous Palestinian press or print laws, effectively annexing Palestinian culture under the hegemony of the kingdom.[8]

The Hashemite government struggled in its attempts to define Jerusalem's identity in relation to Jordan's political capital, Amman. The lack of freedom in print and in the press proved to be a challenge for Palestinians who wanted to assert their national identity and the unique status of their religious and political capital. About this period (1948–1967), Hanan Ashrawi states that "only the regime's mouthpieces or writers of trashy third-rate literature succeeded in getting their works published, while underground literature remained scarce and did not reach a significant audience."[9] Another factor that deeply affected cultural development in Jerusalem was the Hashemite Kingdom's active opposition to and suppression of the Communist Party, the most significant supporter of Palestinian cultural production at the time. The Resistance to Communism Law, signed by the king in 1953, defined communism as the call to replace the constitution of the kingdom with the communist system that aimed to create a dictatorship of the proletariat. It punished all those who promoted, supported, or participated in the communist cause by any means, including direct financial aid, photography, publication, speeches, or the sale of communist materials.[10]

In contrast, Palestinians in Israel continued to be governed by the emergency laws of 1945, which kept the Arabic-speaking population under martial law until November 1966. As a legally recognized party, the Communist Party of Israel became the only legal political venue for the Palestinians to demand equal rights and to combat the military government's extensive network of collaborators.[11] The legality of the Communist Party in Israel allowed Palestinian poets and writers in the Galilee to publish their work through Party venues such as the Arabic-language newspaper *Al-Itihad*. During this period, in addition to its active suppression of the Palestinian identity, the Jordanian government actively outlawed communist cultural activities and publications. This legal and ideological distinction explains the existence of activist Palestinian cultural production in the press, poetry, and literature in Israel but not in the West Bank and Jerusalem. This historical context sheds light on the location of the fragmented Palestinian people and some of the conditions that affected the development, or lack thereof, of Palestinian theater between 1948 until the 1967 war within the homeland. To further understand the influence of this context, the biographies of the some of the leading artists, who were the children of the Nakba and its survivors, show the deep connection between Palestinian theater and the political traumas of Palestine.

The artists who manifested a theater industry in Jerusalem in the 1970s and 1980s all lived the experience of being noncitizen citizens in the period between 1948 and 1967. The connection between Jordan as a host country and the West Bank cannot be understated as a foundational political circumstance for the formation of the sensibilities of these artists. The figures that founded the theatrical movement in the early 1970s experienced a diasporic existence in the aftermath of 1948, grew up in families that reeled from national, financial, material, professional, spiritual, physical, and incorporeal losses, and sought meaning through artistic expression in an otherwise nihilistic existence. They were influenced by their families' incapacity to reconcile their material existence with their belief in the righteousness of the Palestinian cause, which resulted in tensions between a mandate for armed struggle to liberate Palestine and a desire to survive as unwanted guests under the sovereign control of their host states. The biographical journeys of several of these artists in the 1950s and 1960s exemplify how the roots of contemporary Palestinian theater emerged from the shared colossal collective trauma that continues to echo in their public spheres and personal timelines on this earth.

One of the most representative examples of this phenomenon is George Ibrahim, the founder of Al-Kasaba Theater, which operated under several names from 1970 until 2000 in Jerusalem and then grew into the largest Palestinian theater operation in Ramallah after 2000. The story of Al-Kasaba is unique in its dependence on the efforts and career of one individual. But it is also representative of a complex Palestinian condition, which is characterized by the contradictory daily realities of resistance to occupation and nonstop negotiations with the authorities, whether Jordanian or Egyptian before occupation or Israeli after 1967. To fully comprehend the biographical influence of an individual's journey on the emergent Palestinian theater of the 1970s, the pre-1967 refugee story of the controversial theater artist George Ibrahim Habash serves as an example.

He was born on 8 November 1945 in Al-Ramleh, Palestine.[12] In 1948, his family became refugees and settled in Amman after a series of relocations to Al-Latrun, Ramallah, and Al-Salt. The Israelis had imprisoned most of his uncles during the 1948 war. By the mid 1950s, his first cousin Dr. George Habash—the founder of the Arab National Movement and the Popular Front for the Liberation of Palestine—became a fugitive in Jordan, where King Hussein banned all political organization and invoked martial law.[13] Despite the Habash family's extensive experience with war, politics, and imprisonment, George Ibrahim's parents raised him and his siblings in an apolitical environment. Dr. George Habash had been his family's doctor and a regular visitor to the family home, but news of his expanding political activities remained undiscussed.[14] Nonetheless, his parents always recalled and told the full story of their experience as refugees from one station to the next. Remembering his parents' difficult choices after the Nakba of 1948, Ibrahim recalled: "They concerned themselves with raising us. They didn't tell us what happened.... And the schools didn't focus on our Palestinian identity."[15] In Amman, George Ibrahim studied the Jordanian curriculum and sang the Hashemite Kingdom's national anthem every morning in school. As a fifteen-year-old high school student in the early sixties, he began to learn his Palestinian history from rogue Palestinian teachers and knowledgeable peers.

As a teenager and young adult, he held a number of jobs that served him as a future theater manager and director. While still in school, he participated in productions such as *The Merchant of Venice* and *Othello* in Arabic. These opportunities allowed him to exercise his passion for poetry, which he had developed in poetic contests among peers. He also worked as a carpenter for his uncle. After graduating from high school in Jordan in 1964, he served as a clerk in a small accounting firm in Amman. Then he earned a certificate in business administration from a local college. He also participated as an amateur actor in a community production of the satirical comedy *Al-Beit Al-Sakheb (The Turbulent House)* by the Syrian playwright Walid Marfa'i. Most of the participants, including the director, were aspiring Palestinian youth. He described the crew: "We were young guys, just starting out. There was Hisham Yanis, Hisham Heneidi, Nabil El-Mashini, Musa Ayyoush, and Mohammed Al-Abbadi."[16] Since that time, Yanis, Heneidi, El-Mashini, and Al-Abbadi have become major stars in Jordanian cinema, radio, theater, and television.

In late 1964, Ibrahim accepted the position of assistant manager of warehousing at a British phosphate company in the Jordanian desert. Within a few months of employment, he was fired for damaging a company truck and driving it without a license. When he returned to the family home in Amman, he claimed that the company no longer required his services. Shortly thereafter, his father met the new provost of Jerusalem's Lutheran Church during one of his visits to Amman. Provost Hansgeorg Köhler had just started his new post, which lasted from 1965 to 1971. Mr. Habash asked Köhler for help with his mischievous son. Ibrahim remembered:

> [Provost Köhler] asked me what I studied. I said, "I have a business administration diploma and I speak English well." He said, "All right, come to Jerusalem." So, I worked in the Lutheran Church of the Redeemer in Jerusalem as his assistant and manager of the church hostel. I learned some German, answered the phone, and assisted the principal accountant with teacher salaries.[17]

During this time, Bishop Haddad of the Lutheran Church became his mentor. The Palestinian bishop gave him English-language copies of the works of William Shakespeare and Charles Dickens. He asked Ibrahim to read classics from the Western repertoire, which produced his enduring fascination with Euro-American civilization. Ibrahim remembered: "He taught me the meaning of culture."[18]

From 1965 to 1967, as he began his new life in Jerusalem, Ibrahim regularly travelled back to Amman to act professionally in radio dramas. The Jordanian radio had just begun to air radio dramas in its regular programming. He played small roles in a few short-length dramas, but the brief experience became foundational to his future career as a radio and television actor. He stated: "They used to record the drama. The form caught my attention because it was new to me. When you act for radio, you learn a new skill: the way to interact with the microphone."[19] Simultaneously, starting in 1965, he acted in *At The Cross*, a regularly recurring religious drama that took place in St. George's Cathedral. In 1967, he attempted to mount a production of *Ahl Al-Kahf* (*The People of the Cave*) by the Egyptian playwright Tawfiq Al-Hakim.[20] He found interested actors from the regular visitors at the Lutheran Church. They rehearsed for two months in Jerusalem and Bethlehem but discontinued the project due to the eruption of the 1967 war.[21] To Ibrahim and his fellow actors, the war truncated the real possibility of a milestone theatrical production being a launching pad for contemporary Palestinian theater. He remembered, "We heard the news and thought we were in the midst of political maneuvers, but when the gunshots began and the war started, it was clear that nobody was ready. . . . It was like a cinematic film. . . . I realized that this is what my parents were experiencing in 1948."[22] After the Israeli census of all residents of Jerusalem, he searched for his brother Hanna, who was studying in a boarding school in Bethlehem and had lost contact with the family. Upon his arrival, the school informed Ibrahim that Hanna had been sent back to Amman, so he set out for the King Hussein Bridge (Allenby), searching for his brother. He recalled that at the border, he signed an exit document in Hebrew, a language he didn't speak at the time: "Most Palestinians were required to sign the document in order to escape the war."[23] When he attempted to return to Jerusalem a week later, he was confronted with his signature on the departure affidavit and thus was disallowed reentry at the border that Israel controlled. The experience of the war, his brief departure to Amman, and the Israeli army's refusal to allow him entry back to his home in the Old City would lead to his newfound determination to live and create theater in Jerusalem.

François Abu Salem's story during the pre-1967 period also speaks volumes about the conditions and the personal efforts that led to the establishment of contemporary Palestinian theater. In his case, the biographical events demonstrate how theater became a site for hybridity and solidarity, while maintaining a commitment to the Palestinian identity as portrayed in Jerusalem. On 16 November 1951, François was born to Francine and Loránd Gáspár in Provins, Seine-et-Marne, the home of stunning castles, such as the chateaus de Fontainebleau, de Vaux-le-Vicomte, and de Champs-sur-Marne, as well as the natural beauty of Fontainebleau Forest. When he was a young child, the family moved to Jerusalem, where Dr. Gáspár worked as a surgeon at St. Joseph Hospital. Initially, they lived in Bethlehem but moved to a larger home in Jerusalem's Sheikh Jarah, which became a center for theatrical activity in the early 1970s. Francine Gáspár recalled her life in the 1950s and early 1960s as idyllic. As a visual artist, she was inspired by Palestine's natural environment and felt supported by the Palestinian community that helped her raise three children, Stephane, Patricia, and François.[24]

The family photographs in the François Abu Salem Archive tell the story of elite living conditions. They kept horses, regularly enjoyed family picnics, played European music in their home, and maintained a practice in the visual arts, specifically in painting and ceramics. Dr. Gáspár wrote in French, publishing a poetry book during his time in Palestine. Patricia recalled that François loved leading his siblings in imaginative games, pretending to drive cars and fly airplanes. The children studied in missionary schools, with French and English being their primary languages. Due to the regular absences of Loránd Gáspár, François built a deep connection with their household manager Ali Ahmad El-Abbasi, a figure that connected him to Jerusalem and led to his speaking Arabic better than either of his siblings. The family spoke French exclusively in their home; in Patricia's words, "We were French."

Nonetheless, the Gáspár family developed a deep connection to Palestine through their interactions with the Jerusalemite community. When the 1967 war erupted and during the early weeks of the subsequent occupation, Dr. Gáspár became known for treating Palestinian casualties as a surgeon. His sympathies with Palestinians led to his deportation and the family's departure to Tunis. While Stephane and Patricia remained with their parents, François went to Strasbourg to study theater and eventually moved to Paris to work with Ariane Mnouchkine's company, Théâtre de Soleil. A handwritten draft of a message in Abu Salem's archive shows that the family maintained their Jerusalem home and François continued his connection with Ali El-Abbasi. The message from François to El-Abbasi stated that he was happy to have received Ali's latest letter, asserting that their friendship was perpetual: "Despite my absence from the country I settled in, I am with you all the time, and always.... We must live and reunite for the revolution." He tells El-Abbasi that Loránd Gáspár's book of poetry had been translated and was expected to be published in Arabic by the Syrians, and he suggests that his father's second book would condemn the Israeli government and its politics. François adds that he expects to return to Palestine in the summer, likely referring to his arrival midyear in 1970. As someone who would become a cornerstone of contemporary Palestinian theater, François's return to Jerusalem was charged by the 1968 student protests in France. He channeled the revolutionary sentiment he witnessed into his chosen home and family. He wrote to El-Abbasi: "Not a moment am I far from you all. All day and night, I recall the challenges and problems that face the Palestinian struggle."

Mustapha Al-Kurd was born on 20 December 1945 in the Old City of Jerusalem to a merchant, who co-managed a store near Jaffa Gate. In 1948, his family was expelled from their home in West Jerusalem and became refugees in Jericho. Returning to the Old City in 1951, they reestablished themselves in the Sa'diya neighborhood, where he grew up in his formative years. Al-Kurd inherited his father's voice, who in addition to working as a carpenter, became known for reciting the Quran and attending recitals at Al-Aqsa mosque. He attended Al-Omariyyeh school, which became one of the most frequented sites for theatrical activities in the 1970s. In 1958, after the death of his father, Al-Kurd worked as a blacksmith and discovered his love of music while singing during his shifts. He remembered, "Whenever my employer didn't like my singing, I left him without return." In the 1960s, he found a communist music teacher in Nablus and regularly trained with professional musicians in the Jordanian army to practice playing various instruments, such as the clarinet, saxophone, and trumpet. Before long, he became known as a musician and singer, playing music in salons and moving to Nablus to pursue his musical gift on a full-time basis.

During his time in Nablus, Al-Kurd's teacher, the known communist musician Daoud Hasaneine (Abu Ali), taught him that music carries political connotations. In Abu Ali's library, Al-Kurd found an alternative narrative to his strict religious upbringing: "Starting with access to music, passing through philosophy and intellectual concepts, but not detracting me from the mystical background and Sufi vision that accompanied my conservative and religious approach, he helped me scrutinize the details of the historical events witnessed in our country." The experience with Abu Ali, emphasizing that ideology pervades all aspects of aesthetic practice, became foundational to Al-Kurd's vision as an artist and left a permanent imprint on his musical output. His affinity to both leftist political thought and his belief in the necessity of a spiritual artistic approach guided what often appears as an irresolvable tension in his chords, and yet he embodied both throughout his career. Before long, Abu Ali invited Al-Kurd to be a partner in shared concerts and musical evenings when Al-Kurd practiced his craft by performing popular Egyptian songs by Muhammad Rushdi, Abdel Wahhab, and Abdel Halim Hafez.

When the 1967 war erupted on the fifth of June, Al-Kurd and a group of his comrades went to the Jordanian army camp near Nablus to volunteer, but the officers rejected their service and suggested that they join local civil defense committees. Instead, he decided to return to his family in Jerusalem, where he was most needed. A combination of the impaired transportation network, curfews, and fear of drivers transformed the short trip into a journey of walking and hitchhiking, catching willing drivers for short distances until he reached the post office across the street from the gates of the Old City. Caught in the crossfire, he had the choice to remain outside the gates or to run across the street, hoping that a Jordanian soldier might open the door. He recalled, "I risked it. I ran toward the door and crossed it with the help of a group of guards who opened the door." He volunteered his services to the Jordanian Army, which asked him to participate by transporting ammunition within Jerusalem, only to witness the fall of the city from within its walls. During these crucial days and hours, the calls for the residents to leave reminded them of the 1948 expulsion of Palestinians from their homes. Those who recognized the strategy remained in their homes. One of them was Al-Kurd.

The biographical details of Ibrahim, Abu Salem, and Al-Kurd represent examples that could easily be matched by many Palestinian artists. On the day of the fall of Jabal Al-Mukabber, Ahmad Abu Saloum, whose family had been expelled from the village of Al-Dawaymeh in 1948, remembers his disappointed father coming home when he was a young boy and recounting his attempt to acquire a gun at the Jordanian municipal building but being sent home empty-handed. Ibrahim Jbail, recalling his father's insistence along with other parents in Al-Amari Refugee Camp near Ramallah, remembered crossing the border to Amman on foot with some of his friends due to the destruction of the Allenby Bridge. This decision by parents to send young men to safety parallels refugees' stories of their fear of the paramilitary militias executing army-aged men during the 1948 war. Other future Palestinian theater makers remembered their immediate and extended family and neighbors fleeing on foot from various neighborhoods to safer areas throughout the days of the war. The trauma of occupation and displacement would haunt these artists, each expressing their experiences and family stories on and offstage for the remainder of their careers.

In the aftermath of the war, a new reality had set in. One exemplary encounter speaks to this shift and its consequences. Shortly after the occupation, the communist cultural critic and leftist intellectual, lifelong companion of the period's most prolific Palestinian theater makers, and former editor of several Palestinian leftist newspapers—including *Al-Itihad* (before 1948), *Al-Fajr* (post 1967), and *Al-Bayadir* (post 1967)—saw a car sporting Israeli license plates stop in front of his house, located near the Ramallah prison, which after the Oslo Accords became the center of the Palestinian Authority government, Al-Muqata'a. The building, a Tegart fort built by the British occupation, has long stood as a symbol of colonialism and remains as a memorial to the tumultuous Palestinian struggle for self-determination under the insidious imperialism of the British kingdom. Respecting the military curfew, Mohammad Al-Batrawi stayed in the house and attempted to recognize the middle-aged man, who walked out of the car, past the veranda and toward the main door. The man said, "You're still alive?" Recognizing the Palestinian literary and political figure Emile Habibi, a former colleague at *Al-Itihad* newspaper and a communist comrade, Al-Batrawi exclaimed, "You gained weight, Emile!" The former Israeli Knesset member replied with his signature sarcasm, "We've expanded!"[25]

Al-Batrawi narrated this anecdote with mischievous laughter, crediting Habibi with a quirky sense of humor that could never be imagined during his fiery political speeches on Palestinian rights as a Knesset member. Their demonstrative encounter across the Green Line invokes the spirit of a time often described as a period of reunification, when families and friends were finally able to see each other after a nineteen-year separation. Although the Palestinians in Gaza and the West Bank were indeed physically separated from their counterparts in the territory that became Israel between 1948 and 1967, crediting the occupation for the encounters of the Palestinian people within the homeland would be a historical fallacy. This ability to see each other never led to sovereign reunification, and the separation narrative excluded meaningful efforts to remain connected with exiled Palestinians throughout these years, despite the criminalization of these encounters in the homeland and abroad. When the two men spoke, Habibi expressed his surprise at Al-Batrawi's extensive knowledge of Palestinian politics and cultural production in Israel. For many Palestinian communists in Israel like Habibi, the efforts of intellectuals outside the Green Line were less visible despite the efforts of the besieged Palestinians to remain connected with the Arabic language and culture outside the newly founded Israeli state. The leftist author Salman Natour remembered that he developed his writing skills by reading hand-copied novels by Arab authors, who were banned in Israel. He also remembered hand-copying novels himself in order to disseminate Arab writing within his own community.[26]

Al-Batrawi's poetic explanation of how he remained connected to Arabic communist writings in Israel reveals how some Palestinian intellectuals creatively overcame their isolation at one point during those nineteen years:

> One of the remaining communications of the Palestinian Left was by way of the Palestinian communists in Israel, who threw from the train, near the Tulkarem area, the newspaper *Al-Itihad*. The wind, the air, would carry it into the Arab area. Shepherds of cows and livestock would bring it over. If the Left could employ the wind, couldn't it mobilize a people? He would bring it, so we would get *Al-Itihad* newspaper, full of coal soot and oil from the train. We'd celebrate its arrival and start reading *Al-Itihad*.[27]

According to Al-Batrawi, the educated Palestinian elite never missed an issue of the paper. He told Habibi about his slow and methodical collection of the works of Palestinian resistance poets such as Mahmoud Darwish, Samih Al-Qassem, and Tawfiq Zayyad, as well as his contact with the exiled fellow leftist author, journalist, and PFLP spokesman Ghassan Kanafani, who wrote the landmark literary study *Palestinian Literature of Resistance Under Occupation 1948-1968*. Then, believing that the occupation was soon to end, Habibi browsed through Al-Batrawi's large collection of Arabic language books and borrowed as many as he could fit in his car.

In his book *Six Stories for the Six Day War* (1969), Habibi chronicled the re-encounter of Palestinians across the Green Line, from the Galilee to Jerusalem and Ramallah. Equally important was Kanafani's *Returning to Haifa* (1970), which tells the story of the reverse journey from Ramallah to Haifa in the same post-1967 moment. Although movement across the Green Line became possible, a reversal had taken place. Within less than a year, Palestinians in Israel emerged from oppressive martial law (1966), while Palestinians in the West Bank and Gaza were placed under the occupation government's military laws and regulations (1967). In 1968, Kanafani articulated the meaning of this reversal as an exchange of experience between those who faced Israeli domination and those who had yet to encounter its effects on everyday life. In his analysis of cultural resistance, Kanafani predicted that the experience of cultural producers in 1948-occupied Palestine presented a prophetic historical account of the unknown future of the 1967-occupied Arab areas: the West Bank, the Golan Heights, Gaza, and the Sinai Peninsula. He proposed that Palestinians in Israel had created a model of cultural resistance during the years that Israel had applied military laws to its Palestinian citizens. After 1967, he suggested, this model of resistance could be adapted in the struggle against the occupation in the West Bank and Gaza. Worth noting, both of these authors, the PFLP's Kanafani and the Communist Party's Habibi, believed that the occupation would not last. In fact, the terminology in Kanafani's book referred to present-day Israel as the "occupied land," a reference that is considered radical in the political realities of the twenty-first century. But historically, the Nakba generation's political and artistic literature, especially in the works written between 1948 and 1967, did not recognize Israel as a state and often referred to it as the Zionist Entity, boycotting all the expressions of the State of Israel in culture, commerce, politics, and economy as a matter of principle.[28]

According to Kanafani, who played a role in forming the PFLP's political philosophy, cultural resistance shaped and framed the liberation movement and armed struggle. He believed that cultural production was necessary "to understand the land on which the rifles of armed struggle stand."[29] Habibi, Kanafani, Al-Batrawi, Samih Al-Qassem, Mahmoud Darwish, and the major cultural producers of the period may not have agreed on the exact methods or rhetoric of resistance. Nonetheless, their shared affinity and commitment to the underprivileged classes, their goal of mass popular mobilization, their declared leftist politics, and their belief in the leading role of cultural production inspired Palestinians in the homeland and exile to believe in the promise of Palestinian liberation. Equally so, their ideological and artistic approaches reflected the sentiment and practice of most experienced and emerging cultural producers in the 1967 Occupied Territories.

The writings of the period emphasized relentless hope and simultaneously hid the shame of losing Jerusalem. In June 1967, the painful new geopolitical situation had revealed the reality of the Palestinian condition. The state of Israel possessed the power and the support to assert its military, economic, and political control over the entirety of historic Palestine, crushing the ambition of national self-determination, which Palestinians had attempted to achieve since the Ottoman period. The dream of a unified pan-Arab army liberating Palestine was recognized as a delusion. For the first time since 1948, the Palestinian struggle and its elite leadership lost access to the entirety of the homeland and had to operate nearly exclusively from exile. The Palestinian cultural intelligentsia suffered a similar fate, living and working outside their beloved Palestine, with Jordan, Syria, and Egypt becoming vital sites for producing poetry, literature, and drama. Yazid Sayigh described this transfer of Palestinian nationalism and cultural apparatus into exile as a shift in the struggle's center of gravity, affecting all aspects of Palestinian life and futurity.[30]

On the military front from 1967 to 1972, in what became known as the Palestinian revolution, with both Fateh and the PFLP at the helm, the PLO led a war of attrition from the borders of historic Palestine and in international sites. From airplane hijackings to bombings against civilian and military targets, the guerilla operations brought the Palestinian revolution to the forefront of Western and Arab media. In great measure, however, the news reports associated the cause with terrorist attacks, which undermined modest successes against the Israeli military. Furious debates in various Palestinian leaderships questioned the function of attacks on nonmilitary targets and militia operations on non-Palestinian territories, but these debates paled in contrast to the viral impact of militant operations. In 1970–1971, the Palestinian guerrilla revolution suffered military, financial, and political setbacks in the events of Black September in Jordan, leading to the exile of the militia forces of the PLO from Jordan to Lebanon, a prelude to a series of complex events that eventually led to the Israeli invasion of Lebanon and the expulsion of the PLO to Tunis in 1982.[31]

Returning to the early years of occupation within the West Bank and Gaza, Palestinians became a nonmilitarized society, under the control of the Israeli military and its administrative apparatus. To counter the power disparity under occupation, they reinforced institutions that shaped the cultural and social fronts, particularly through education. They filled the absence of an Arab governing body by "strengthening existing Arab institutions and showing *sumud* (steadfastness)."[32] Raja Shehadeh articulated the concept of *sumud* as an act "practiced by every man, woman, and child here struggling on his or her own to learn to cope with, and resist, the pressures of living as a member of a conquered people."[33] He suggested that perhaps between submission and hate, a third option might be to remain steadfast in choosing to stay present and living. In this alternative shared popular space, which also exists between surrender to the occupation and armed resistance against it, a long tradition of popular peaceful resistance ensured that Palestinian culture and its associated artistic production remained alive at home. The theater was one such expression.

While sumud provided the minimum and most prevalent form of popular resistance, other forms began to take root in the West Bank, particularly in the Ramallah-Jerusalem area, the hub of an emerging intellectual and political elite. In the tradition of the mass nonviolent protests of the 1920s and 1930s in Palestine under the British Mandate and the Palestinian cultural resistance of the 1950s and 1960s in Israel, Palestinians in the Occupied Territories began a process of mass popular organizing that eventually formed the basis for the Intifada of 1987. In the early days after the occupation, the communists led the way in arguing for nonviolent struggle through the formation of grassroots organizations and solidifying relationships with labor unions; other factions eventually followed in their footsteps. The Palestinian Left, which included such factions as the underground communists, the Democratic Front for the Liberation of Palestine (DFLP), and the Popular Front for the Liberation of Palestine (PFLP), is credited with organizing voluntary work committees and establishing the nucleus for the eventual institutionalization of Palestinian civil society by the late seventies.[34] Reflecting on the emergence of a theater of resistance in the post-1967 occupation aftermath, one of the founders of the Balalin Theater Ensemble, Emile Ashrawi, stated, "It was as if all the threads were coalescing for this leap that happened in the seventies."[35]

Ashrawi identifies the threads of a nation stretching back further than 1948 and leading to a robust liberation movement. Although this movement has not borne fruit in terms of political sovereignty, it has produced a massive canon of literature, artistic products, historically relevant cultural events, and an exemplary living tradition of a nation surviving in everyday life against extreme odds. Considering the context and the stories that form the narrative of this chapter—the refugees of 1948, the Palestinian citizens of Israel under military rule, the fedayeen of the Palestinian revolution, leftist writers, Palestinian diaspora, ideologically diverse political factions, Palestinians under Egyptian and Jordanian rule, and individual artists surviving the 1967 war of occupation in the Jerusalem-Ramallah Area and elsewhere—an encyclopedic account of the immense theatrical and performance lives of this liberation movement may be impossible, especially during an analog period. However, these threads have thrived into continuous productivity. They left a historically unique theatrical movement and an artistic spirit, forming institutions, individuals, and ensembles that survived to tell their stories.

In the Jerusalem-Ramallah area, Palestinian cultural producers embraced the atmosphere of sumud and volunteerism, which emphasized the need to build community from the grassroots. After 1967, the proliferation of voluntary work camps in schools and universities set the stage for the development of mass popular and cultural resistance. Reflecting on the spirit of this liberation movement, Mohammad (Abu Khaled) Al-Batrawi considered the Israeli suppression of the Palestinian identity to be "an indicator of the extent of the depth of Palestinian cultural resistance and the extent of the originality and sumud of this second front." Declaring the existence of this robust cultural front, he believed that nationalistic cultural production formed the foundation of the Palestinian spirit:

> In the stage of national liberation for a people, as it is in our case, the culture of the masses becomes a spiritual connector and an embracing fabric to all categories and classes of this people. So it becomes a front of struggle and resistance of more depth and influence than any other form of resistance.[36]

The extensive underground network of leftist-leaning intellectuals set the stage for the mass production of Palestinian culture in the post-1967 era. Their activities in this period can be described most accurately as a cultural front in the battle against the occupation. The experience of *Al-Itihad* newspaper, which documented the Palestinian struggle before and after 1948, served Jerusalemites, as Mattia Nassar, who had previously managed the printing and production of the paper in Haifa, provided technical printing expertise for *Al-Fajr* newspaper in East Jerusalem. The communist Palestinian citizens of Israel Elias Nasrallah, Daoud Khouri, and Tawfiq Abu Rahmeh had moved from the north to Jerusalem and founded Salah Ed-Din publishing house with the technical and production help of Mattia Nassar, whose clothing store Diana was converted for this enterprise.[37] Salah Ed-Din, the most significant publisher in the West Bank at that time, published new and existing works by leading Palestinian communists such as Emile Touma, Tawfiq Zayyad, and Emile Habibi. It also encouraged emerging leftist writers of the West Bank such as Mahmoud Shqair, Hussein Al-Barghouthi, Abdel-Latif Aqel, and As'ad Al-As'ad. The near hegemonic influence of the Left on Palestinian print production may have been most evident in the contributions of East Jerusalem's leftist-leaning editors, journalists, and contributors such as Bashir Al-Barghouthi, Mahmoud Shqair, Mohammad Al-Batrawi, As'ad Al-As'ad, Elias Nassrallah, and Adel Samara. Their efforts to produce culturally relevant newspapers and magazines such as *Al-Bayadir* and *Al-Katib* continued well into the late 1980s.[38]

In this atmosphere of collaboration, political awareness, and shared mission, the liberation movement took on different cultural expressions, or fronts, as Al-Batrawi referred to them. The most distinct and perhaps significant of these cultural fronts was the theater movement. In his description of Palestinian cultural life in the early 1970s, the communist Jerusalemite poet, essayist, and novelist Mahmoud Shqair singled out the theater movement as the most influential cultural producer in the West Bank:

> After the occupation, obvious disparities occurred in the artistic and cultural movement in the occupied land. While a tangible decline appeared in some of the literary and artistic activities, which were comparatively flourishing before June of 1967, the theatrical movement was characterized by growth and maturity to the point that it became the most conspicuous artistic phenomenon on our occupied land. None of the other arts matched it in drawing and influencing the audiences.[39]

This testimony by Shqair, who has just been exiled to Lebanon when he wrote these words, marks the elevated status of the theater movement in Jerusalem during this period. The theater had a distinct flavor as a participatory art form, attracting the attention of Palestinians as both a social activity under an occupation that rejected their assembly and a political action that asserted a forbidden identity. From the depths of daily toils and family obligations, the theater movement had produced a site for free thought and a battleground that did not require forbidden arms, leading a distinct positionality in the Jerusalem-Ramallah area.

To best understand how the theater movement achieved its status, the next chapter documents and recounts the theatrical activities immediately prior to the 1967 occupation and the environment that created limited alternatives to engaging with Israel-controlled institutions. In two parts, the chapter outlines community theater efforts and religiously motivated theatrical programs that predominated in Jerusalemite theater before 1967 and then moves to tell the story of how one of the most significant theatrical figures in Palestinian theater began his professional practice, which led to effectively establishing a model for producing local theater, particularly for children and performing in schools. Although the theater outlined in the next chapter indirectly fed and nurtured the possibility of a rich theatrical enterprise, its trajectory and stated goals, albeit well-intended, manifested a theatrical direction that the Palestinian theater movement would oppose for ideological and political reasons. Nonetheless, to fully capture the complexity of contemporary Palestinian theater and the emergence of the theater movement, the contributions of artists who performed theater for many reasons must be appreciated.

TWO

AT THE CROSS AND A THEATER FOR MANY REASONS, 1967-1970

In historical writing, the conundrum of assigning cause to effect often appears at specific junctures as a challenge couched between the evidence at hand and the phenomenon as expressed by historical agents. No action can be exclusive to a single cause. Direct causes tend to reduce the lives and actions of the agents to known evidence, but the absence of named causes robs a historical narrative of its contextual forces. In the case of Palestinian theater, no history should discount the Nakba of 1948 and the Naksa of 1967 as a direct cause at any given point after their occurrence; however, these massive historical events do not express the complexities of individuals as they strive to create theater. Nonetheless, historical turning points must be understood as macro actualities that explain basic facts, such as time, place, presence, and lived sentiment. In 1948, the war and expulsion of Palestinians from their homeland annihilated the infrastructure and cohesion of Palestinian politics, society, and culture. For the first time, a traumatized Arab Palestinian Diaspora came into existence. With Israeli expansion and the exiling of the Palestinians, a vacuum was created, leaving mostly emerging youth to fill the space of experienced writers, artists, and theater makers. Meanwhile, whenever possible, the former elite struggled to re-establish themselves in their new locations. A similar effect, though to a lesser extent, occurred after the 1967 occupation.

As acknowledged by Palestinian theater artists in the Jerusalem-Ramallah area today, the movement that founded contemporary Palestinian theater in Jerusalem began in the early 1970s with the advent of a determined youth who aimed to express themselves in light of the new realities of the occupation. However, defining the set of individuals, geography, and period that constituted the Palestinian theater movement in the 1970s and 1980s does not negate the existence of meaningful theatrical activity in this region and in historic Palestine parallel and prior to the emergence of this phenomenon. One can look to the activities of Masrah An-Nahid (The Rising Theatre), which was established in Haifa in 1967 and continued until 1977, featuring the work of Sobhi Damouni, Adib Jahshan, Yousef Abdelnour, and Yousef Farah in a truly revolutionary Palestinian theater and forming the foundation for theater in the Galilee region.[1] Further back, in Jerusalem, Nasri Al-Jawzi and his brothers actively produced Palestinian theater that connected to its Arab roots and mythologies, as well as to its local lore. The Al-Jawzi brothers even produced some of their plays for the radio on the Palestinian Broadcasting Station (PBS). Jamil Al-Bahri produced his plays in Haifa in the 1920s. Palestinian newspapers pre-Nakba show a meaningful and reasonable frequency of reviews, announcements, and ads confirming that the history of Palestinian theater and performance has yet to be fully narrated in a grand history that considers the whole of Palestine. This chapter focuses on the transitional pre-1970 period in Jerusalem, which is the central location of this book, to present how the Jerusalemite story of contemporary Palestinian theater and its associated theater movement developed in the post-1967 era. Until the artists declared themselves as a movement with a liberatory mission, theatrical activity occurred for different social, cultural, and religious reasons.

The Jerusalem of the 1960s offered a number of ways to experience theater and performance. The traditional venues that abound throughout historic Palestine continued without meaningful interruptions, suggesting continuity of cultural production since the nineteenth century. In her description of the cultural lives of Palestinians in the first half of the twentieth century, especially during the British Mandate period, Hala Khamis Nassar notes that Palestinian cultural activities, including theater, flourished through the opening of national schools and educational institutions and the increasing local presence of missionary schools, "Christian parish activities, publishing houses, radio stations, newspapers and periodicals, and literary organizations and salons."[2] In the 1920s and 1930s, most of the productions performed throughout Palestine were adapted from classics by European playwrights such as Molière, Shakespeare, Racine, and Corneille. Works by well-known Arab poets such as Khalil Al-Yazijee, Ahmad Shawqi, Anton Al-Jamil, and Father Antoine Rabbat were theatrically produced in this period. In 1936, the Palestine Broadcasting Station was established and became a venue for the production of radio plays. After the Nakba, in the West Bank and Gaza, Palestinians were subject to the censorship rules and governance of the Egyptian and Jordanian states, which limited the emergence of new Palestinian cultural production in general and theater in particular. Nonetheless, the context of education within the Hashemite Kingdom supported extracurricular activities in drama and its related fields. In effect, between 1948 and 1967, one could look to Jerusalem under Jordanian rule as one of the remaining still-living expressions of urban Palestinian cultural life, unencumbered by the Israeli military laws imposed on Palestinian citizens of Israel (1948-1966) and the catastrophic aftereffects of the Nakba.[3]

The Jerusalem Players (1959-1967) was one exemplary product of this Palestinian cultural life that survived the catastrophe of 1948. This cosmopolitan ensemble was composed of Jerusalemites and expats working for foreign embassies, consulates, and institutions in the city. Wassif Daher (1940-) joined the Jerusalem Players when the group initially formed and acted in seven of the eight productions they produced in their short-lived existence. They excelled at producing English language modern classics that had succeeded on Broadway and the West End. Before long, Daher became the vice president of the Jerusalem Players to the reigning president of the company, Haidar Al-Husseini. In 1960, the ensemble performed Noel Coward's *Blithe Spirit* as its inaugural production in English, directed by an American expat known as Mrs. Samuels. Follow-up productions included Reginald Denham and Edward Percy's *Ladies in Retirement*, Edward Percy's *Shop at Sly Corner*, Kenneth Horne's *Two Dozen Red Roses*, and George Bernard Shaw's *Arms and the Man*, all performed in English. Daher directed the ensemble's one and only Arabic language production, a translation of Eugene O'Neill's *Beyond the Horizon*.[4]

The Jerusalem Players operated as a seasonal production company, with one major production per year on average. All their participants were volunteers, but the audience paid one Jordanian dinar for each ticket, which funded the company and its subsequent productions. Taking place at Al-Mutran School, performances were extremely well attended by Jerusalem's elites, including the governor of Jerusalem, who attended every show. Because the plays were performed in English, the shows drew the attention of expats, especially employees of foreign governments in local consulates, making these plays an opportunity for networking, diplomacy, and cosmopolitan interaction among representatives of the international stakeholders. On social, artistic, and political levels, the Jerusalem Players functioned as a meeting place for Jerusalemites to meet and intermingle with the foreign elites and vice versa, essentially turning theater practice into a pathway for intercultural exchange. According to Daher, the performances and the rehearsal process felt like openings into another side of Jerusalem that otherwise might be inaccessible to a local Jerusalemite. It is likely that expats similarly felt that the Jerusalem Players provided a point of access for interpersonal and diplomatic exchange. Based on the titles of the plays they performed, the ensemble clearly aimed to produce light fare with high entertainment value, drawing on popular hits from the English language canon in the first half of the twentieth century.[5]

The visibility and local fame of the Jerusalem Players led the American director Kenneth H. Carmichael to meet with the ensemble to ask about the local theater scene. Between 1962 and 1972, the Commission on Ecumenical Mission and Relations of the United Presbyterian Church U.S.A. sent Carmichael and his wife Sue as communications consultants to the Middle East and Africa.[6] Carmichael held a Master of Arts in Speech from the University of Wisconsin (1930) and a PhD in Theater from the University of Minnesota (1941). Sent by the Presbyterian Church for a ten-year development mission, he focused his efforts on creating Christian dramas in churches and affiliated institutions. He began by expressing interest in creating a series of spiritual plays with local youth and successfully initiated a long-standing performance program in Jerusalem called *At the Cross*, which ran from the mid-1960s until the first Intifada in a collaboration between the YMCA and several Jerusalemite churches. The Jerusalem Players' Wassif Daher was one of a large ensemble of Jerusalemite Christians who worked with Carmichael to create a series of scenes based on the life and death of Jesus Christ in English and Arabic. They drew on biblical stories to write original plays that brought Christian lore to life during Easter holidays and sermons.[7] The majority of the volunteers acted in the production, but some also assisted in preparing costumes and providing input from a local perspective. Sue Carmichael focused her efforts on makeup and wardrobe for the large ensemble, which included Victor Sabella, Marlene Bajjali, Lavinia Jahshan, Wahbeh Wahbeh, Farah Tal Ghraf (headmaster of Mutran School), Vitor Nahhas, William Alonzo, Mario Vinci, Salim Qerri, Youssef Deliani, Jo Kreitem, Majed Kreitem, Nina Thabet, Nadia Mikhail, Tony Abboud, Bassam Zu'mot, and of course, one young George Ibrahim Habash. Some members of this ensemble would continue to work in theater and music throughout the 1970s and 1980s—most notably, Nadia Mikhail as a performer in the Balalin Ensemble and Al-Kasaba's George Ibrahim and Bassam Zu'mot.

George Ibrahim participated as an actor in these religious dramas, all directed by Herbert Kenneth Carmichael, who later worked with members of Ramallah's Theatre Family in 1970 at the YMCA. Ibrahim remembered Carmichael as one of his earliest theater teachers:

> Carmichael, a director from America, used to direct a Via Dolorosa play called *At the Cross* [figure 2]. He came to do scenes of the crucifixion of Christ.... Here was the beginning in 1965. I observed the man and how he worked.... They [the actors] were all amateur, but I took it seriously. They took it as a religious project. For me, it was theatrical and artistic. I observed him. I learned makeup.... This man had surgical adhesives and created mustaches and beards.[8]

Wassif Daher remembered Ibrahim's commitment as unique among the group and suggested that it was clear from these early days that Ibrahim, as well as the actor Bassam Zu'mot, took acting as a professional endeavor. For a few years, Ibrahim viewed his work with Carmichael as an educational laboratory. He observed the experienced director as he worked with large numbers of actors, selecting costumes and staging the play in various churches in Jerusalem. Carmichael instructed his volunteer actors in the basics of voice and movement. Ibrahim recalled: "For them, it was a strictly religious project. They spent a lot of money on the production. That's where I learned that if you want to make beautiful theater, you must spend the money."⁹

Jerusalemite churches paid special attention to theater practice and its inclusion as part of their community-building efforts. In the absence of a functional ministry of culture and sports, as the newly established Arab governments tended to have, the YMCA funded the expensive production as part of its commitment to youth development in culture and sports. The Holy Week events at the end of Lent brought the Christian community together in worship and celebration. Attending these locally written plays became another access point for expats to experience Palestinian Christian cultures. Daher explained that Carmichael directed the English-language version, while the ensemble applied the production elements to the Arabic-language performance. *At the Cross* is remembered fondly by its participants because it provided a group of youth with an outlet for social expression and a learning opportunity to write, direct, and perform in an emerging medium in the absence of an exclusively Palestinian radio or television. To the participants, the spirit of the rehearsal process and performance felt like an artistic and spiritual uni-

FIGURE 2 The ensemble after a performance of *At the Cross* in St. George's Cathedral. Jerusalem, 1972. Courtesy of Wassef Daher.

versity, a place where the young people could develop their interpersonal social life, humorous interactions, performances of identity, and familial friendships. For some, it was an opportunity to read the Bible and bring religious figures to life through embodiment.[10]

When Carmichael left in the mid-1970s, only the Arabic performance survived. The community continued to perform it until the first Intifada. One of the reasons for the survival of this production in Arabic was local authorship. Daher's renditions of *St. Veronica* and *The Human Weakness* continued uninterrupted until political conditions led to the dispersal and immigration of many participants and checkpoints separated Ramallah and Jerusalem's Christian community. The multidenominational event brought Palestinian Jerusalemite Christians together, despite their different calendars of worship. Many Muslims joined in the event preparation, increasing local camaraderie. Although St. George's Cathedral initially hosted the program of *At the Cross*, the YMCA provided it with the necessary longevity into the 1980s, when a new generation of aspiring young actors joined the program. At the YMCA, two future leaders of the Palestinian theater would join: Iman Aoun (performer) and Amer Khalil (technician). Their meeting would lead to Aoun's participation in El-Hakawati Theatre, which set Aoun on a career lasting over forty years in contemporary Palestinian theater.

Concurrent to the years of The Jerusalem Players and the regular productions of *At the Cross*, Palestinian educational institutions used theater as a tool for capacity building and celebration through extracurricular activities. The Teacher's Training Center (Dar Al-Muallemeen) in Ramallah produced two productions a year on average. For example, in the 1966-1967 academic year, the visual art teacher Ibrahim Saba (1935-1993) and the geography teacher Fathi Al-Saber (1940-) collaborated with the aspiring student teachers to produce two plays: *Qahwat Al-Nashat* (Activity Café) and *Al-Darse Al-Awwal* (The First Lesson). The residential teacher's college sought to teach its students performance tools such as public speaking and presence in front of an audience by using these devised plays, which were adapted reenactments of scenes from commercial Egyptian comedies that were playing in 1960s Cairo. In addition, the extracurricular activities provided the students with a pastime in an otherwise regimented and disciplined environment where they lived and studied on campus for two years, waking up at 6 a.m. and retiring to their dorm beds at 8 p.m. daily. After the occupation, Saba returned to work in the fall of 1967 and revived *The First Lesson*, which is credited as one of the first performance activities in the post-occupation era. Saba would continue on a remarkable career as an advocate for theater in education and an important visual artist, leaving behind a significant number of surrealist paintings, which were exhibited and recognized after his death in 1993. He is credited for playing a founding role in establishing the League of Palestinian Visual Artists with key figures such as Suleiman Mansour, Nabil Anani, Rehab Al-Tamri, and Issam Bader.[11]

At the Cross was the only theatrical activity that continued uninterrupted after the 1967 war. The activities of the cosmopolitan Jerusalem Players ended permanently with the fragmentation of its community of locals and expats. Immediately after the occupation, the residents of East Jerusalem and the rest of the West Bank spent the remainder of the year in shock, with many unanswered questions about the future of work, education, worship, governance, and certainly, performance. The threads, or persons, who constituted the potential players for the creation of a theatrical industry were at different places, experiencing similar conditions, but simultaneously considering diverse options for their futures in performance and other professional directions. George Ibrahim, as a twenty-two year old, had sufficient personal life understanding and professional working experience to determine his goal of a life in performance. However, many of those who would become theater artists were still young children or had yet to finish their high school education. The idea of professionalizing in the arts and sustaining one's living through it had yet to occur to many of the young participants in school plays and extracurricular activities. Although *At the Cross* continued and would nurture many future artists for many years to come, George Ibrahim never returned to that program.

As an adult witness to the fall of Jerusalem, seeing a gross disparity in power between the Israelis and Palestinians, Ibrahim launched his theatrical career with the understanding that the post-1967 moment could not be countered with armed struggle alone. After spending a few days with his family in Amman, he was refused entry back to Palestine because of the signed affidavit at the border, which marked his exit as a final one, leaving him with no option to return. To circumvent this technicality, George hired a Bedouin guide who smuggled him across the River

Jordan to the Damia Bridge. The trek took him across the desert between Amman and the river, up the mountains, and then through water. Once he was smuggled without being seen at the Israeli checkpoints, he found horse-and-carriage transport to the first main road, where he took a service car to Nablus. Once there, he took the bus back to Jerusalem. His census number, which he had been given by the Israeli army in the initial days of the war, allowed him a pathway to a permanent-residency (blue ID) card. From then on, he decided never to leave Palestine, committing himself to a life as a Jerusalemite.

In 1968, while suffering the existential dilemmas of life under occupation without professional prospects, Ibrahim responded to a newspaper advertisement for an actor in the Arabic division of Israeli radio. In 1958, the Voice of Israel had initiated an Arabic-language radio station, run by Oriental Jews.[12] Crossing Al-Musrara neighborhood, past the former dividing line at Mandelbaum Gate to Queen Melisande Lane (Heleni HaMalka), Ibrahim arrived at the old building of the British Mandate's Palestine Broadcasting Station in West Jerusalem.[13] He experienced a strange contradiction:

> I am not sure I can explain how I felt exactly. It was strange . . . a strange position. When they spoke Arabic, I felt some closeness. There were an Egyptian man, Abu Fareed, and three or four Iraqis. There also was an Egyptian woman, Leila.[14]

They were Arabs! They asked him to present a performance in Arabic. He performed a poem, which he had memorized, by the Egyptian poet Kamel El-Shinnawi. The five-minute audition included a microphone test, which he passed with flying colors due to his brief experience recording dramas at the Jordanian radio.

According to Ibrahim, the Arabic-language radio dramas seemed to refer to innocuous apolitical daily events. Thus, he perceived his work as both educational and entertaining to Palestinian audiences. He refused to present news-related programming because it often represented anti-Palestinian content. Considering the potential risks inherent in cultural production, he insisted on freelancing and received five to six Jordanian dinars per recording: "I was free. Whenever I wished, I could leave. If I didn't want to do something, I didn't. . . . When I was asked to present political programs or talk shows, I refused. . . . In drama, I was in control of the dialogue and its message."¹⁵ The radio dramas avoided Palestinian subjects and characters. His obsession with Egyptian cinema throughout his childhood served him as he acted with an Egyptian accent, the most common dialect in Voice of Israel's Arabic radio dramas in that period. Despite his rejection of the new political realities and the radio's conscious avoidance of the Palestinian struggle, he took the opportunity to learn skills that he believed were necessary for developing his own work in the future.

The radio job was his first opportunity to learn from professionals. "During this radio period, I learned a lot as a theatrical worker," he told me.¹⁶ When Abu Fareed was asked to write a drama in Palestinian dialect, he asked Ibrahim for help. The experience of adapting plays to Palestinian culture taught Ibrahim new skills. For example, he learned how to analyze and construct dramatic scripts, which required him to expand his vocabulary and to attune his ear to the nuances of the Palestinian dialect. Then he learned to direct for radio, underscore dramatic dialogue, and create musical transitions between scenes. The library of the radio station became an important source of his education about classical and contemporary Western music, as well as the musical scores of Western cinema. By the early months of 1969, he was manually editing audio on quarter-inch tape, thus completing the learning process of radio creation, which included acting, writing, directing and technical production. All these skills became foundational to his understanding of drama. He returned to the books that Father Haddad had given him and began to analyze how Arabic translations of Shakespeare functioned, often disagreeing with them.

While editing a radio series in a Haifa studio, he received a phone call from the Palestinian director Antoine Saleh, who had just accepted a position as the director of a new children's TV program called *Sami and Susu*.¹⁷ Saleh asked Ibrahim to audition for the role of Sami, the presenter of the show. After a successful audition, Saleh offered him the role. At the time, Ibrahim was in a romantic relationship with a Kiwi woman by the name of Marjorie Noel Galvin from Darwin, New Zealand.¹⁸ An Australian newspaper reported Ibrahim and Galvin's love affair, which had started only months before the occupation. It also reported the difficulties she faced in securing a travel visa for "her fiancé," George Habash.¹⁹ Having rejected the prospect of permanent exile in New Zealand, Ibrahim explained: "I decided to stay here. I postponed."[20] Ironically, Antoine Saleh, who had convinced Ibrahim to stay in Palestine, eventually emigrated permanently to Australia and passed away there as an exile. Ibrahim's choice to remain in Jerusalem as a resident, never a citizen of Israel, asserted his subject position as occupied but steadfast on the land. Nonetheless, his choice to work with the Palestinian citizen of Israel Antoine Saleh on an Israeli television production would forever place him in a compromising position. Although Ibrahim was a heroic figure to the Palestinian children who looked forward to his program, he carried the burden of working in a production by the occupying state of Israel. He insisted that his mission was to perform an Arabic-language program with a Palestinian director for the sake of education and language preservation, in effect working despite the occupation, not for it. But for some, he legitimized the occupation. In spite of the norm-defying decision at the time, *Sami and Susu* continues to be remembered with positive nostalgia and deserves its status as a significant milestone in Palestinian performance.

George Ibrahim referred to *Sami and Susu* as a long-term artistic laboratory. He credited Antoine Saleh as his first professional mentor. He remembered: "Israeli television had just launched. They dedicated one hour to Arabic programming and the rest to Hebrew.... Antoine helped me a lot. He taught me a lot, by force... yelling and nervousness."[21] From 1969 to 1977, he worked as an actor opposite the puppet Susu, played behind the scenes by the Jerusalemite actress Labiba Darini. He intentionally adapted his dialogue to the local Palestinian dialect to ensure that children would connect to his character. Over the program's eight-year run, the core Palestinian team remained unchanged; however, different translators worked on various episodes, including Mahmoud Abbasi and one of Palestine's notable writers, Anton Shammas.[22] Jewish Israelis produced the program in all its facets, including script writing, technical production, content development, editing, music, animation, lighting, makeup, set, props, and sound.[23]

The half-hour program often followed a standard format that revolved around educating children on the topic of the day, such as flight, television production, dance, music, or the sea. The opening song depicted a child-friendly animation of marching musicians, a flying child, a car in the shape of carriage, a bird carrying a letter, and young women. As Sami and Susu sing of the folkloric Sundouq Al-ʿajab (Box of Wonder), a boy appears inside the window of the carriage. He pulls down the curtain on the window, which bears the name of the program. The song concludes with the program's motif of education and discovery: "We'll raise the curtain on the box of wonder." The program emphasized child education through storytelling, music, staged theatrical plays, film, animation, and singing.

In one of the extant episodes, the show teaches the process of flight. It begins as Susu chastises Sami for throwing pieces of paper around the room. Sami explains that he is throwing paper airplanes, then proceeds to show Susu and the children at home how to make paper airplanes. They discuss Susu's dreams of flight. Then Sami states, "Children, let's all go to the airport." An educational video appears on the screen. It shows an airport, followed by an explanation of the process of airplane construction, and concludes with an airplane taking off and landing. Throughout the film, Sami and Susu make comments about the images, such as "You see how the airplane is taking off?" After the film, as animation and photographs play in the background, Sami teaches Susu the history of flight from humans wearing wings to hot-air balloons to the invention of airplanes by the Wright Brothers and the creation of rockets for space travel. Following an upbeat song about flying, Sami reads Susu a story about a prince and his invisible cloak; then they watch an animated short film about a youth's attempt to construct a space rocket. The program concludes with an announcement of the names of contest winners: three Jews and three Arabs from Baqa Al-Gharbiyyeh, Karmiel, Haifa, Gaza, Urshalim/Al-Quds, and Tel Aviv.[24]

Two key themes dominated the newspaper reporting on this popular program: artistic coexistence and cultural colonialism. Often mentioned as a successful example of an idealized Palestinian-Israeli coexistence, this top-rated weekly program garnered the attention of Jewish Israelis as well as Christian, Druze, and Muslim Palestinians. Subtitled in Hebrew and spoken entirely in Arabic, it played to a captive audience at 6:30 on Friday evenings, a holiday evening. Aside from Israeli television, only Jordanian television could be picked up by Palestinian and Israeli antennas at the time. Among Jewish Israelis, adults and children, the show became an instant hit. According to one opinion, it may have succeeded among Israelis because "there were no good children's shows in Hebrew."[25] *Al-Itihad* newspaper reported unconfirmed rumors that King Hussein of Jordan watched the show in the 1970s.[26] The article also noted that the show was one of the first to consider the issue of "coexistence between the two peoples."[27] Noting *Sami and Susu* as evidence, scholar Reuven Snir claimed that the Arab section of Israeli television "played a major role in encouraging Arabic-speaking theatrical activities for children."[28] Palestinians in Israel and the Occupied Territories viewed Israel's Arabic-language programming as a tool of Israeli colonialism and propaganda. In describing the Israeli government's early efforts to reach the Palestinian minority through television, historian Ilan Pappé explained the complex context of *Sami and Susu*:

> The Israeli television network opened an Arab section after the inauguration of Israeli television in 1968. While it would soon be seen as a collaborationist arm of the government by many in the community, in the early days it had the opportunity and the means to produce a different visual (if nothing more) reality, which it deserted later on. Particularly impressive was the children's programme *Sami and Susu*, a bilingual Arab-Jewish comic dialogue that had fans in both communities and addressed an audience on the verge of forming negative images of each other.[29]

Pappé regarded the show as a positive way for Palestinians to be seen on Israeli television, but he also recognized that *Sami and Susu* was an exception in a television industry that supported a predominant Israeli public sphere that traded on anti-Arab stereotypes.

Among many Palestinians, the show generated controversy. For some, it was seen as the occupier's tool to dominate Palestinians through cultural production. Although *Sami and Susu* transformed George Ibrahim into a household name among both Arabic and Hebrew speakers, this stardom was accompanied by great admiration and cautious distrust from both audiences. Simultaneously, he was questioned about his career choices and asked for his autograph. Within the Palestinian community, Ibrahim described his television and radio work as purely educational, children-oriented, and apolitical. He believed he could separate his professional work from his political principles, but many Palestinian audiences believed the two were indistinguishable.[30] When asked about his politics in Israeli media, his daring commentaries as a Palestinian earned him a reputation of being a fundamentalist.[31] Although he earned his living as a freelancer from the show, his controversial existence—as

Other within Israeli society and as crossing the boycott line by appearing on Israeli television—burdened him.

In 1973, the prize-winning Israeli broadcaster Edna Pe'er asked him to express his identity crisis on her Hebrew-language radio program, *It Matters Me*. Identifying himself as both a Palestinian and "an Arab you conquered in 1967," Ibrahim continued: "To the Jews I am an Arab. That is obvious. But to the Arabs I am not a Jew; I'm an Arab whom they suspect and distrust."[32] While his capital rose within Israeli society for playing one of the most beloved characters on television, his social capital dwindled among Palestinian theater artists and East Jerusalemite society. In the 1970s, when a group of Jerusalemite artists joined forces in working committees for the development of theater, he was excluded from the Palestinian theater movement because of his involvement with Israeli television. Ibrahim remembered: "The same people, who worked in the [Israeli] post office, the electric company, even the police, blamed me for appearing on television. It was a chaotic period artistically, socially, and politically."[33] The double standards applied to Ibrahim during this period drove him to establish an independent path. He insisted on maintaining his Palestinian identity, working in children's programs even on Israeli television, and making theater as a parallel career.

By the early 1970s, George Ibrahim had built his own community of supporters among members of the Communist Party in Haifa. He never became a member, nor was he asked to become one. Upon hearing a radio interview with him, the Palestinian resistance poet Samih Al-Qassem called him on the phone and asked, "How do you get the courage to make such daring political commentary on Israeli radio?" Ibrahim responded, "That's who I am."[34] During this period, prominent members of the party, Palestine's leading cultural producers, embraced him. He recalls: "The only ones who understood, even the politicians among them, were the Palestinians of the Galilee. I became a personal friend of Samih Al-Qassem, Emile Habibi, Tawfiq Zayyad . . . such a close friendship . . . and Saliba Khamis, God bless his soul."[35] In addition, he gained support among leading West Bank communists such as Mohammad Al-Batrawi and the former head of the Communist Party, Bashir Al-Barghouthi. These Marxist thinkers viewed his work as consciousness-raising and immensely beneficial in preserving Arab language and culture under occupation. The communist roots of Ibrahim's politics guided his ideological approach to artistic production for many years to come. Within Jerusalem and the West Bank, the cultural and political elite understood Ibrahim's position that his freelance work on Israeli television resisted common stereotypes and educated Palestinian children, a worthy goal in the absence of Palestinian media.

George Ibrahim's popularity led to further offers of acting opportunities in Arabic-language television programming. He told Edna Pe'er: "It's true that I am perhaps the best-known Arab in Israel. . . . I am seen as a children's entertainer—Sami."[36] After he overcame the perception that he was only a presenter of children's programming, he was offered only politically offensive Palestinian characters. He refused an offer to play the role of a Palestinian terrorist in the international film *Sabina* because he did not want to appear in a pro-Israeli film "against my own people."[37] By the mid-seventies, he had presented game shows and talk shows such as *2 X 2* and *Nujoom Al-Ghad* (Stars of Tomorrow). He discovered that apolitical programming did not exist on Israeli television: "Television and radio are Israeli media devices concerned with executing their own objectives."[38] In his work on *2 X 2*, he saw the increasing influence of the producers, who attempted to include "political propaganda" in the program. "This event was a wake-up call, though it came late."[39] He found himself in a difficult position: "I worked for the children . . . but a popular show draws audiences to the television, which is ideologically directed."[40] Believing that his popularity was being misused, in 1977 he ceased to accept offers for programs intended for Israeli television.[41] Three months later, his wife, Jackie Ayyoub, left her position as a television anchor for the same reason. The Israeli public fought to prevent the show from ending. The most spectacular attempt to convince Ibrahim to return occurred in the form of a balloon flown in Tel Aviv. It stated: "Bring Back *Sami and Susu*."[42] He never returned to Israeli television, even for interviews, and neither did this popular television show.

Despite his newfound fame, he could never stay away from his first passion, the theater. While working for radio and television, Ibrahim maintained a significant production portfolio for both adults and children. He began by founding his own theatrical enterprise, Firqat Al-Funoun Al-Masrahiyah (the Theatrical Artistic Group [TAG]).[43] In 1971, the TAG produced four productions: *The Turbulent House*, by the Syrian playwright Walid Madfa'i; *The Game of Love and Chance*, by French playwright Pierre Carlet de Chamblain de Marivaux; *The Executor and the Condemned*, by Fathi Radwan, and *Thorns of Peace* by the Egyptian playwright Tawfiq Al-Hakim. From its early days, Ibrahim set the tone of his theatrical body of work with a series of choices. In all four productions, he adapted the dialogue to the Palestinian dialect, Antoine Saleh directed, and the majority of the cast were Palestinian citizens of Israel or Jerusalemites. His casting policy of hiring Palestinians artists regardless of their I.D., city of residence, or citizenship continued throughout his career. During the initial period of development, the recurring ensemble of actors included George Ibrahim, Makram Khouri, Jackie Ayyoub, Youssef Farah, Bassam Zumot, and Marlene Bajjali. The last two also acted in *At the Cross* in the late 1960s.

To avoid legal struggles and maintain his personal commitment to "art for art's sake," George Ibrahim chose published plays, which made it easier for him to receive permission to perform from the Israeli censors. From 1971 until the Oslo Accords (1993), he produced published scripts from the Arab and Western repertoires. When asked to fulfill the censorship requirements, he sent the original published scripts by Jean-Paul Sartre, Marivaux, Molière, Max Frisch, Tawfiq Al-Hakim, Albert Camus, or Alfred Farag. He explained, "I used to adapt the plays. I didn't send in my Palestinian adaptations.... Because it was already available in print, they approved it."[44] Without a doubt, the majority of his early productions would have been accepted by the censors. Directed by Antoine Saleh, Tawfiq Al-Hakim's published play *Song of Death* had been produced and showcased on Israeli television at the same time.[45] Despite addressing issues of the petit bourgeoisie, the marriage plays of Marivaux and Molière did not fit the censors' watch list of originally created Palestinian plays. In production, particularly in the seventies, the Theatrical Artistic Group focused primarily on entertainment value and education.

In the early seventies, during the eight-year run of *Sami and Susu*, Ibrahim made a number of fundamental observations on the state of Palestinian cultural production in general, and theater production in particular. First, the audience was too small to sustain long runs of plays. Most plays were presented in East Jerusalem for a few performances, and then they were closed. Second, locally produced professional children's theater and musicals were nearly absent in Palestinian culture. Third, a theatrical profession could be established in Jerusalem and throughout Palestine only if actors were regularly paid a fair wage. Fourth, a commercially viable play must be presented frequently to nontraditional audiences in nontheatrical settings. Fifth, to increase future theater audiences, Palestinians must be taught theatrical values and conventions from a young age. Sixth, children do not respond to political slogans. Seventh, successful children's theater contains simple plots, folklore, and music. Eighth, children appreciate fully staged productions that include both storytelling and modern technology.[46] He explained:

> I took it as my responsibility to start from the beginning, to work with the children. . . . I would rent the theater of El-Omariyyeh School in the Old City for a month or two. . . . I would bring all the schools of East Jerusalem to El-Omariyyeh. I rented buses and reserved with the headmasters of the schools. At the end of the performance, I was given the shekels in bags. . . . I carried around bags of shekels. At the time, the actors were nearly professionals. They were all paid, but they weren't earning their living exclusively from acting yet.[47]

He took it as a mission to ensure that every performer must be paid for their work, a policy he maintained for the remainder of his career. To achieve his goal of reaching Palestinian children, he typically presented twenty-five to thirty performances in El-Omariyyeh School. Then, he followed the Jerusalem run with tens (and in some cases hundreds) of performances across Palestine.

In the 1970s, the Theatrical Artistic Group produced several popular children's productions and focused on developing musical theater in Palestine. *Adventure in Jerusalem* (1973), by George Ibrahim, was a mobile puppet production, which he toured with actress Christina Abboud throughout the city of Jerusalem.[48] In 1975, the musical *The City of Dreams*, written by Ibrahim and composed by Mustapha Al-Kurd, told the story of the king who disguises himself to investigate corruption among the people. In 1976/1977, the musical *The Happy Shoemaker*, written by Jackie Ayyoub with music by Mustapha Al-Kurd, depicted the story of a poor shoemaker who experiences sudden wealth and learns the value of modesty (figure 3).[49] The fully produced musical received a positive review in *Al-Quds* newspaper, which described it as "a fully integrated musical that introduced the operetta to our country."[50] The production relied on pre-recorded audio for the songs, and the actors lip-synched the

FIGURE 3 George Ibrahim in *The Happy Shoemaker*. Jerusalem, 1977. Courtesy of George Ibrahim.

music. The set successfully represented two locations: the home of the shoemaker and the castle of the rich merchant. When the lustrous court of the castle was revealed, the set change produced "amazement in the audience." Although the reviewer complained of an imperfect transition of one technical cue, he was inspired by the selective isolation of lighting, which successfully revealed the terrifying features of the devil.[51]

The Happy Shoemaker, which played on the stage of Al-Omariyyeh School in the Old City of Jerusalem, exemplifies Ibrahim's early work for children, and it was also presented to adults as an original musical. It tells the story of two characters: a poor shoemaker who dreams of wealth and a wealthy man who has everything. As the parable goes, the wealthy man hears the shoemaker singing on the street, so he invites him to his castle to learn about the secrets to happiness. The rich man concludes that the poor shoemaker is happier because he is living a simple life devoid of material belongings. Seeking to replicate the shoemaker's happiness, the wealthy man convinces him to switch roles for a week. When the shoemaker lives in the castle, he experiences fear for his wealth, always on guard and trying to protect his riches. However, the wealthy man, living the shoemaker's simple life, begins to enjoy his days like never before. The play taught children that wealth cannot be the answer to life's challenges. Instead of running after money, children can seek a life of fulfillment through family, education, and friendship. Ibrahim created the spectacle with a large ensemble, huge sets depicting the castle and the city, and thirteen musical numbers. Because Ibrahim aimed first and foremost to inspire school children to imagine new possibilities, he focused on simplicity in acting and plot. Ibrahim's produceorial prowess manifested in the beauty of the production: colorful costumes, imaginative worlds, and easy-to-follow storylines. Although Ibrahim preferred to write the lyrics, Mustapha Al-Kurd's compositions elevated dramatic moments and coordinated action on stage with musical notes. Al-Kurd's music painstakingly told the play's story alongside the plot by enriching the relationship between the music and dialogue.

One of the primary advantages that Ibrahim had developed in the 1970s over his competitors in the theater movement was a long-standing partnership with his wife Jackie Ayyoub. Her talent as an actress and their consistent efforts to work together allowed him to write significant female roles with complex characters, language, and physical action that many other theater makers were unable to produce due to the lack of full-time female actors in this period. The phenomenon of highly successful theatrical couples would develop over the years in contemporary Palestinian theater, such as François Abu Salem and Jackie Lubeck, Radi and Mounira Shehadeh, Edward Muallem and Iman Aoun, Kamel El-Basha and Reem Talhami, and Firas Abu Sabbah and Christine Hodali, among many others. Like Ibrahim, Ayyoub believed in the role of theater in building the Palestinian character, especially in younger generations of children. Together, they took theater as a way of life. Since their marriage in 1974, they had shared a life fit for a theater family. Despite her nearly complete focus on performing, she designed and built costumes and props for many of their productions as the play and the director required. Together, they hosted performers in evening gatherings, extending the family atmosphere to other ensemble members, including Bassam Zu'mot, Jamal Is'eed, and Mahmoud Awad, among others. The couple became known as exemplary entertainers, often including music as part of their hospitality. To Ibrahim, building a community was as significant as the work on stage.

The primary audience for Ibrahim's children's productions was Palestinian students. Because he understood that schools were the ideal source for this audience, he was confronted with the challenge of the occupation. The West Jerusalem municipality controlled the educational scene in Jerusalem, including elementary schools. Thus, to reach these children, he had to apply for permission to perform for them and to acquire the approval of the school headmasters on the content of the plays. This decision contradicted the common Jerusalemite position to boycott Israeli institutions after the occupation, which created a rift between Ibrahim and the emerging theater ensembles in the early 1970s. Because Al-Omariyyeh School, like many institutions of the Old City and the rest of East Jerusalem, functioned under the umbrella of the West Jerusalem municipality, theater makers were confronted with the conundrum of whether they should perform on its stage. They reached consensus that the Palestinian school and its property were a fair site for performances, but they also agreed that playing to an audience of students who must be approved by the Israeli Ministry of Education and the Jerusalem municipality crossed the boycott line. Ibrahim rejected this argument and believed that he must reach Palestinian children even if he had to negotiate access through Israeli institutions. This disagreement with the emerging theater ensembles of the period led to a significant rift in the theater community in the Jerusalem-Ramallah area well into the 1980s.

After the end of *Sami and Susu* and Ibrahim's departure from all productions associated with Israeli television and radio, theater production became his primary source of income. His productions in the children's repertoire became more frequent. He wrote, directed, and acted in a number of long-running children's musicals: *Aladdin and the Magic Lamp* (1979); *The Moon of the Princess* (1979); *Little Red Riding Hood* (1980); *The Dwarf and the Miller's Daughter* (1981); *The Sultan's Son* (1982); *Ali Baba and the Forty Thieves* (1987); and *The King Went to Sleep* (1989). He also wrote and directed several children's plays: *Uncle Suleiman's Shop* (1981);

My Grandfather Is Not Old (1982); and *Haroun Al-Rasheed and the Shoemaker* (1985). The children's repertoire was characterized by original music, adaptations of *Arabian Nights* stories, classic Western fairy tales, and tales from Arabian folklore. Although he relied on a select number of actors to perform the plays, Ibrahim exerted complete control over the creative process in the majority of the productions. As the productions grew in frequency and actors moved, retired, or changed careers, his regular actors included Basam Zumot, Areen Omari, Siham Ghazaleh, Ahmad Abu Saloum, Mohammad Bakri, Mahmoud Awad, Jamal Is'eed, Hussam Abu Esheh, and Kamel El-Basha. Many of these artists would freelance in what would become an active theater scene throughout the 1980s and 1990s.

The period prior to and after occupation set the stage for a theater industry that focused nearly entirely on entertainment, education, and, in many ways, religiously focused community performances. The Western tradition of theater and its canon influenced how this theater developed, but this effect should not be overvalued or overestimated. Although collaboration with Westerners such as the American Carmichael and the many expats at European consulates provided some human resources and expertise, the majority of the participants, funding, and audience for this theater scene derived from East Jerusalem and its dignitaries. At least, the theater of the Jerusalem Players and *At the Cross* fits the formula of community, diplomatic, and educational theater. At most, the ensembles performed cosmopolitan theatrical events that well-represented the vibrant, culturally curious, and highly educated Jerusalemite population during this period.

George Ibrahim's career as a performer and producer established a production model for the emerging theater industry. This model would survive and operate under several ensemble names: Firqat Al-Funoun Al-Masrahiyya (Theatre Arts Company, 1970), Masrah Al-Shoke (Thorns Theatre, 1984), Masrah Al-Warsheh Al-Faniyyeh (The Arts Workshop Theatre, 1986), and eventually Al-Kasaba Theatre (The Marketplace Theatre, 1989–present). Ibrahim produced plays for children throughout the academic year and for adults in the summer. His productions for adults would eventually become the repertoire he played for secondary school students. His theatrical presentations for students familiarized future audience members with the theater as a necessary cultural activity, effectively achieving his goal of building a theatrical audience in Jerusalem. Nonetheless, his policy to focus on entertainment and avoid politics, combined with his choice to reach students through municipality schools, caused a political rift between him and many of the emerging theater makers of the early 1970s. Although his identity as a Jerusalemite and a believer in the Palestinian cause was never in question, his production model launched many discussions about the identity and practices of contemporary Palestinian theater under occupation. Thus, parallel trajectories in Palestinian theater emerged and quickly became an alternative to both the commercial and religious models of theater production in Jerusalem. A new generation of artists emerged with the aim of producing theater in a movement that declared its primary purpose to resist the Israeli occupation.

THREE

A MOVEMENT IS BORN, 1970-1973

Balalin Lights "The Darkness"

In an interview with the leftist newspaper *Al-Hadaf*, François Abu Salem described the implicit connection between theater and armed struggle. He referred to the events of Black September (1970) as the spark that inspired acts of resistance in many fields of humanistic inquiry in the Occupied Territories. The major shocks and setbacks to armed resistance in 1967 and 1970 clarified the reality that Palestinian liberation cannot be achieved through political parties and military approaches alone. The vacuum left behind after the expulsion of Jordanian governmental institutions would need to be filled through social action and civilian efforts to maintain cohesion. As a result, a narrative of cultural resistance began to take hold on the ground in what Abu Salem referred to as an affirmation of Palestinian national character.[1] Although articulated by Abu Salem, this stated opinion was not unique in Palestine. In the Jerusalem area, Palestinian theater makers from the era mention the Naksa and Black September as formative to the launch of the cultural struggle in the form of artistic practice, with theater and poetry leading the way.

In discussing the state of Palestinian theater in this period, the Palestinian poet Samih Al-Qassem noted the material challenges of creating a vibrant theatrical industry through building creative capacities, audiences, and frequent productions. Nonetheless, he insisted that the roots of Palestinian theater emerged from indigenous sources, movements, and the desire for collective action, not through imitations of Western forms. For Al-Qassem, like many of his contemporaries, Palestine functioned as a site for storytelling in literature, poetry, and everyday life that differentiated its cultural products from European theater. Accordingly, the emergent theatrical practice, while having similarities to internationally recognized styles, never functioned as an imitation of repertoires by Shakespeare, Greco-Roman classics, or avant-garde works like Bertolt Brecht's. Despite factionalism that pervaded the period, the desire to build a national project that expressed Palestinian life against active erasure led many individuals to coalesce into ideologically driven groups that believed in locally constructed theatrical narratives. In writing six plays before the Oslo Accords, Al-Qassem insisted on theater's role as asking questions rather than providing answers because the period necessitated self-examination. His description aligns with the needs of a society that was reeling from sudden loss and desperately attempting to understand its contemporary condition.

Unsurprisingly, one of the earliest production attempts in the post-1967 period was Al-Qassem's play *Qaraqash*, which the poet did not initiate himself. Shortly after Black September, in the later months of 1970, a group of activist youth from Ramallah began their theatrical journey by reading Al-Qassem's play. Calling themselves Usrat Al-Masrah (The Theatre Family) and having an intense desire to build a community of artistic practice, they gathered regularly to manifest their dream of establishing a theater. The core group included Sameh Abboushey, Nadia Mikhail, and Vera Tamari, who respectively had studied architecture, music, and visual art. After recognizing the need for a director to lead the project, they resorted to a familiar name, someone had been regularly producing theatrical activities in the Jerusalem area: the American director Herbert Kenneth Carmichael. Carmichael caught the attention of the young group after they attended his modest staged readings of Western texts at the YMCA in Jerusalem and Ramallah.[2] The fortuitous combination of Al-Qassem's indigenous text, the Theatre Family's desire to create collective action, and the presence of Carmichael's mission produced the meaningful possibility of a theatrical event, especially since Carmichael had successfully staged his production *Eyes Upon the Cross* with regularity around Easter since the mid-1960s.

Simultaneously, in Jerusalem, the brothers Emile and Ibrahim Ashrawi had formed a rock band, Al-Baraʻem. The music combined the spirit of the class-conscious poetry of Ahmad Fouad Najem and the rock and roll music style of Jimi Hendrix.[3] François Gáspár had just returned from a brief stint with Arianne Mnouchkine's Théâtre de Soleil and a year of studying theater in Strasbourg. In 1969, in a private letter to his housekeeper in Jerusalem, François had written of his intention to return to Jerusalem for the express purpose of participating in the revolutionary currents against the occupation through theater. In a culture of peer-to-peer exchange of ideas, the brothers and François built a friendship of kindred spirits. The private schools that they attended, such as El-Mutran in Jerusalem, had produced plays by Western authors as part of their extracurricular activities on a yearly basis. The Jerusalem YMCA presented modest productions of Western texts as well, often under the tutelage of the Palestinian teacher Ibrahim Saba, who taught and produced plays at the teacher's college in Ramallah. This context is reminiscent of the long tradition of uninterrupted performance in Palestine since the late nineteenth century, when missionary schools regularly produced plays for children and adults and a robust tradition of local music and *dabkah* was a mainstay in Palestinian cultural life. By the middle of 1970, Abu Salem had written a play called *Une Tranche de Vie, A Slice of Life*. Emile Ashrawi assisted him in the translation to Arabic and typed the script, but the pair could not yet produce due to the lack of resources and qualified performers. Just like their counterparts in Ramallah, the Jerusalemite youth were inspired to form a theater troupe but the ingredients necessary for production had yet to be fully formed.

In late 1970, The Theatre Family rehearsed at Ramallah's Lutheran Church, in a multipurpose hall that lay empty aside from some columns. Having been approached by the members of a young troupe, Carmichael cast the play and rehearsed it mostly in the afternoons. The young Palestinians had initially considered the project as a thought-provoking youth activity, but after rehearsing and staging it, they decided to apply for a performance permit from the military government to publicly perform it. Upon receiving the troupe's formal application in the early months of 1971, the office of the military governor asked the troupe to return a month later. Subsequently, the request for permission to perform was denied. The troupe debated their available options. First, they could present the play without a permit, which would potentially place them in direct confrontation with the Israeli military. Second, they could accept the production as a valuable community-building educational experience that gracefully ended. The majority of the troupe voted to avoid troubles with the military, therefore Al-Qassem's play, *Qaraqash*, was never performed, marking one of the earliest instances of the Israeli military government negatively influencing the trajectory of contemporary Palestinian theater.

After this initial incomplete experiment, the group investigated possible strategies for continuing their theatrical efforts without having to obtain military permits. They learned that community activities at the Ramallah YMCA did not require a performance permit because the institution did not fall under performance censorship laws, so they embarked on a new project suggested by Sameh Abboushey. Having studied in Turkey, he was familiar with the popular Turkish poet Nazim Hikmet Ran. In his search for a theatrical poem, he found an Arabic translation of Nazim's poem *The Story of the Walnut Tree and Lame Yunus*. Based on his proposal, The Theatre Family decided to produce an evening of poetry at the Ramallah YMCA as their first public performance in 1971. The evening had the nucleus of an emerging theatrical company without the help of the American director: they cast the characters appropriately, divided the stanzas of the poem between them, rehearsed the staging in advance, and underscored the performance with music. In one of the YMCA's empty rooms, the cast spread among the spectators, who either sat on the floor or on low café chairs. Within this simple, private, and familial environment, they read their parts to a captive audience of family supporters, neighbors, and YMCA members.

The performance told the story of young Yunus, who became lame after he fell from the branches of a historic walnut tree. He lives, loves, marries, and loses his wife in the span of the story, but the plot speaks less to the conditions of the performers than the themes and language of the poem. The descriptive language tells of disaster, unhappiness, and death. Still shaken by the occupation, the poem told of how "disaster struck Yunus where it hurt most." The line "Yunus' land slipped from his grasp" recalled the occupation of the territories in 1967. In 1970, the walnut tree that "shed its walnuts in September" stood for a population that had lost thousands of martyrs in Black September. "Ceaselessly Yunus thought about his loss" reflected the state of the population that could not overcome their confounding existence as an occupied people. The performance ended with an inspiring note that "probably the best days of our lives are to come" and acknowledged the "grief in our conversation: of a walnut tree, cut down and sold." In this post-traumatic performance, the youth saw themselves as Yunus, the audience as the walnut tree, and the land as Palestine. The Theatre Family successfully started a conversation about the crises that they experienced in their own homes by performing this poem to a tongue-tied audience that had been silently seeking answers.[4]

In keeping with the family theme, the troupe remained in the space for a personal gathering at the end of the performance. Their audience stayed. Among them were François Abu Salem and the brothers Emile and Ibrahim Ashrawi. Breaking bread over zeit and za'tar, they discussed the performance and the potential of collaboration between the emerging talents of Jerusalem and Ramallah. Abu Salem proposed a union of skills. On the one hand, the Jerusalemites brought Abu Salem's theater training, the brothers' experience in musical composition and performance, and the unproduced script of *A Slice of Life*. On the other, the Ramallah family brought a set of smart performers who had acquired some experience in their recent experiments and community-building efforts. Abu Salem also suggested that they consider performing Hikmet's poem in the garden of his home in Jerusalem's Sheikh Jarrah. Abboushey recalled, "[François] showed us a play called *Slice of Life*, which he had been working on. He had it typed and could make copies."[5] Rehearsals would take place at a location in Jerusalem. "We thought about it. Why not!"[6] As the two groups became familiar and in many ways familial, the proposed coproduction quickly became a merger.

Like many historic ventures, the sociopolitical and cultural environment was ripe for the union to succeed. Palestine had entered a period of social awakening, where collective work filled a massive space in Palestinian consciousness across all social strata. Professor Mounir Fasheh at Birzeit University, a key influencer in this area, promoted communal participation as a method for strengthening the fabric of the West Bank's factionalized population. Voluntary work committees and grassroots community activism played a central role in maintaining the cohesion of Palestinian society in the absence of national institutions and the onset of the occupation. Internationally, the revolutionary protests of French students in 1968 had become an inspiring example of the power of youth to influence political opinion, which took hold in the minds of the group. Similarly, the hippie movement heavily influenced the initiators of the joint project to seek collaborative participants. During these formative years of the newly developed troupe, the atmosphere of openness to international liberatory ideologies and a keen belief in the possibility of a parallel political liberation set the stage for this theater troupe to become a leading model for alternative forms of social development, resistance, and survival. Theater's collaborative nature made the enterprise a candidate for a utopian achievement of these emerging ideals.[7]

In a document found in his archive, Abu Salem described the remarkable serendipity and its context:

> The West Bank was living in an ideological "slump." Aside from a few newspapers, there were very few means of collective expression. The desire to do "something collectively" materialized in the formation of the group into a theater troupe. Against the political repression of the Israeli military government, it seemed like the best way to find a Palestinian cultural identity, distinct from a simple passive acceptance of the Arab culture of other countries, and to be in contact with all strata of the population, by touring throughout the West Bank, in the towns and villages.[8]

His poetic narrative continued to describe the total absence of a tradition of theater in Palestine, a false belief that he maintained until his death by suicide in 2011. Although he contributed immensely as a foundational figure over the years in Palestinian theater, his inability to recognize the theatrical heritage of the region and the contributions of local artists caused a significant rift between him and his collaborators throughout his career in Palestine. Despite this permanent blind spot that earned constant accusations of being a nonlocal orientalist, his astute narrative accurately describes the context of Palestinian theater in the 1970s and the reasons for the emergence of the first post-occupation independent Palestinian theater ensemble in the West Bank, Balalin (The Balloons).

Guided by a utopian ideal of a collective artistic and social life, the troupe rehearsed mostly in François's family home, in East Jerusalem's Sheikh Jarrah neighborhood. The house functioned as a space for communal living, an intellectual center where the group could bond and share ideas, and a place for actors to sleep after late evening rehearsals.⁹ The tradition-free atmosphere was characterized by personal and social freedom. The commune-like environment encouraged a sense of cohabitation, eating and working together for a common goal.¹⁰ As the troupe rehearsed *A Slice of Life* in Jerusalem, additional members joined this work-in-progress. News of this developing project spread in the East Jerusalem-Ramallah area. Local intellectuals and journalists such as Mohammad Al-Batrawi, Fawzi Al-Bakri, and Mahmoud Shqair closely followed the troupe's progress. While taking oud lessons in Jerusalem's Old City, the Ramallah resident Adel Al-Tartir heard of the ongoing rehearsals from the troupe members Ali Al-Hijjawi and Hani Abu Shanab. Arriving at the ground-level villa, which was surrounded by a large grove of grapevines and fig, nut, and almond trees, he participated in the day's improvisational rehearsal and shared the company's sense of commitment and passion for making theater.¹¹

On 22 January 1972, *A Slice of Life* opened in the theater of Al-Omariyyeh School in Jerusalem's Old City. Two days earlier, an advertisement in the *Al-Quds* newspaper had noted that Balalin had secured buses for Ramallah audiences to return home after the performance. One of the major characters in the play was a dictatorial bourgeois man, who lived in a palace surrounded by a garden, stable, and horses. He employed a cook, gardener, and peasant servants. The conflicts in the play addressed the class gap between the servants and the bourgeois class as well as the power struggle between the husband and wife. Abu Salem's description of the play states: "The theme is as follows: in a house of Arab notables, servants play the role of masters and class relations quickly become very conflictual."¹² Emphasizing the philosophical differences between the bourgeois owners and the laboring peasants, the play challenged the traditions and class structures that exerted influence on everyday life. Balalin criticized gender and class norms without fear by staging dysfunctional traditional societal conventions. For example, a woman's desire to become a musician dishonors a family; laborers must not dream of better lives; and a capitalist may mistreat an employee and still demand appreciation for the demeaning employment opportunity. The audience's positive response to these criticisms demonstrated a belief that Palestinian society, at least in Balalin's circle, was ready to confront its failings.¹³

A Slice of Life garnered the attention and support of the community. Reviewer and well-known local Jerusalemite poet Fawzi Al-Bakri complimented the writing and the entertainment value of the script, despite its use of common tropes: "The subject has been done before, but it is never boring because it is always new: the working poor . . . their thoughts . . . imagination . . . and the authoritarian rich, their thoughts . . . philosophy . . . interests." His review describes the atmosphere of the play as a joyous evening, full of surprises. The narrator surprisingly appears from the audience. The elements of production effectively complement the story with lighting and costumes distinguishing characters and scenes. Al-Bakri's enthusiastic review illustrated the audience's engagement with the theatrical form, interpreting costumes, vocal intonations, dialogic moments, and plot points as semiotic references to the various classes represented on stage. While expressing admiration for the writing, directing, the local dialect in the play, and individual performances, he critiqued one performance as artificial and rejected the use of local dialect in the written program, which he referred to as the "performance guide," marking an absence of theatrical vocabulary for the theatrical event among the audience. Most notably, however, the reviewer insisted on distinguishing the theater as a critically needed form in Jerusalem in this period.[14]

The production began some traditions that remained with the troupe. Their marketing style focused on intrigue. On the tickets, various lines from the dialogue were printed, such as "Life without renewal isn't good or fun, and it loses all taste," "Can't we dream? Go dream by yourself!" or "Music? What music! You want to destroy our family's honor? Shut up!" The play also became an opportunity for the troupe to discover their working methods. They improvised to solve staging problems and created discussion sessions to negotiate differences in opinion. They also used improvisation to expand the rough original script and elaborate François Abu Salem's directorial framework.[15] An actor entered at the beginning of every performance with a bunch of balloons to mark the rise of the curtain. Balloons were released into the audience and onto the stage to celebrate the end of the evening. Al-Bakri describes the audience popping balloons together with the performers after the curtain call (figure 4). He states: "I asked myself what does Balalin mean throughout the perfor-

FIGURE 4   Curtain call after a performance of *The Darkness*. Jerusalem, 1972. Courtesy of François Abu Salem Archive, Palestinian National Theater/El-Hakawati.

mance? Then at the end, balloons dropped from the ceiling and I shared the audience's admiration and the performers' ecstasy as they successfully popped them until the hall transformed into a celebratory square."[16]

Because the play had opened in Jerusalem, it was technically outside the purview of the military government and its censorship apparatus. Nonetheless, the record of censorship files in the Israel State Archive in Jerusalem did not list an application for a performance permit, which suggests that Balalin did not attempt to approach any Israeli authorities prior to this performance, essentially managing the production in the same manner as The Theatre Family's evening of poetry in late 1970. When the production moved to Ramallah and Bethlehem, both ruled under military occupation law, the troupe performed the play without a permit. The Israeli military either ignored or was unaware of the performances due to its modest production values and ease of transportation. Abboushey explained, "We treated it like an educational activity at a school. We believed that if we didn't give it importance, neither would [the military]."[17] During this early period of the emergence of contemporary Palestinian theater, the military had not yet fully controlled the population's infrastructure, which allowed for private performances and small events to occur under the radar, but this ability to perform undetected would change quickly as the troupe expanded and their events became more visible.

Balalin's following play, *Al-ʿatma* (*The Darkness*, 1972), became the troupe's most memorable production. The play portrays the challenges of a young troupe as it attempts to perform an original play. After technical difficulties with the curtains and an unresponsive technician (Milad), François performs a well-crafted monologue on death and suicide. Then the lighting system shuts down, leaving the audience and the actors in the dark. The company struggles to fulfill the promise of the evening and to perform the product of seven months of rehearsals. They begin by asking the audience to fix the lighting board. The spectators participate by complaining about the darkness and the waste of their money on tickets. One volunteer, the carpenter Adel, enthusiastically emerges from the audience to help but lacks the necessary skills to repair it. A Western-educated schoolteacher gives a lecture on the history of electricity and theater to help the audience to better understand the situation. In the candle scene, the actors give one candle to each spectator, who must take responsibility for keeping it lit. The onstage experiment fails because some audience members don't believe in the significance of their personal contribution to the overall goal of lighting the room. A female electrical engineer volunteers to fix the board, but traditional social norms and her fiancé's pride prevent her from freely participating until she asserts her right to work. The climax of the play depicts insurmountable conflicts between not only the actors but also members of the audience. Suddenly, the lights switch on; then everyone celebrates and takes credit. Eventually, they realize that the carpenter Adel died in his ceaseless, but successful effort to fix the lighting board. The actors collectively carry him on their shoulders and exit the hall.[18]

Without a doubt, *Al-ʿatma* was Balalin's most successful production. The play's idea emerged from Sameh Abboushey's frequent visits to East Jerusalem's old cinema houses. As an architect and art enthusiast, he knew about the modernist avant-garde movements, including the "happenings" in the United States. Lacking directorial, technical, and playwriting expertise, he approached François Abu Salem with the idea of a play within a play that happens in total darkness. In this theatrical event, the audience and the actors would share the efforts to emerge from the crisis. Abu Salem and Abboushey structured the idea into a series of scenes. Abboushey's original draft was composed of scene titles, situations, and a time frame, as well as a general idea for the staging along with preliminary dialogue. Then, they worked with the ensemble to create the script through improvisations and rehearsal exercises. Abboushey explained, "Most of the scenes developed from the actors. We gave the situation and observed what happened."[19] In the rehearsals, the troupe collectively improvised while Abboushey and Abu Salem edited the scenes and reorganized the play, and Abboushey continually documented it in writing. Although the press coverage from the period credited Abboushey as the author and Abu Salem as the director, the Balalin collective agreed to credit all participants for authorship. This phenomenon of foregoing personal credit for individual contributions for the sake of the collective pervaded Palestinian theater at this time, leading to many interpersonal conflicts in the short-lived existence of various ensembles in the 1970s, including Balalin.

In 1972, the production premiered at Al-Omariyyeh School in East Jerusalem.[20] On the stage, the company set up two platforms. On the first, the troupe presented the main throughline of the play in real time. From the beginning of the play, the actors freely moved between this platform and the audience. Some characters doubled as audience members. In this time frame, the actors strategize to solve their lighting problem, which represents the dark age of the occupation and the struggles of Palestinians in their war of liberation. These realistic scenes represented the internal power disparities in Palestinian society. They demonstrated a large gap between the educated and uneducated, rich and poor, and men and women. On the second platform, the troupe presented surreal flashbacks and dream sequences, which revealed the reasons for the failure to fix everyday problems. For example, one scene presented the female engineer inside a plastic bag as her male oppressor describes her using only the measurements of her body, identifying her physical traits like a sexual object. The party scene depicts dancing, drinking, and expensive gifts, suggesting a gathering of the upper class. Acted mostly in slow motion, the café scene shows men wasting their time playing backgammon and participating in endless discussions about political issues but never taking responsibility for their opinions or engaging in positive action.

The play functioned on two distinct but simultaneous levels. First, it dramatized an immediate problem: the need to repair the lighting for the sake of the performance. On this level, the play realistically illustrates dysfunctional daily life when a community struggles against great odds. The play demonstrated how disagreements, complaints, and personal interests prevent members of the community from achieving their common goals. As the problem of the darkness plays out in real time, the audience shares the common objective of repairing the lighting board. How will the troupe overcome this obstacle? Will the play happen? The moment-to-moment engagement with the theatrical event tricks the spectators into becoming participants.

On the symbolic level, the struggle to end the darkness and perform the play represents the Palestinian struggle to fix its internal conflicts and end the occupation. Community mobilization against the occupation appears as the overriding political theme in the play. The troupe presents collective action as the remedy to the imposed darkness. In the candle scene, the spectators are given candles to carry and keep lit until the darkness ends. Milad, the unhelpful technician, states, "If we don't hold the candles, another audience from the outside will not come to hold them for us, and we could remain in the dark forever. Take care of the candle. It's your responsibility."[21] In the midst of the chaos, François explains: "I have a remedy, here! This young man works and doesn't talk. The remedy is work."[22] The character of François, played by Abu Salem, explicitly calls on the characters to emulate the work ethic of the productive young man, Adel. Implicitly, the play demonstrates the power of mass mobilization. When Adel dies at the lighting board, the worker becomes not only a symbol of resistance but also a martyr for the cause. In a stark parallel to the armed struggle of the late sixties and early seventies, the cast collectively carries the dead worker on their shoulders in the way Palestinian martyrs are carried to their resting place. Emile Ashrawi explained, "It was truly a call for an uprising, but using symbols."[23]

The press covered *The Darkness* with exceptional interest. Reviewers recognized the ensemble's call for cooperative efforts to repair the failed lighting system, suggesting that everyone has a role in Palestinian liberation. Reviewers identified the obstacles to liberation expressed in the production with clarity: the desire to be saved from the outside, the exclusion and infantilization of women, the dysfunctional bourgeois intellectual class, the preference for leisure instead of liberatory labor, toxic masculinity, dependence on religion to solve social problems, conservative regressive politics, and the lack of systematic collaborative planning.

Focusing on women's liberation as the most significant step, every review candidly acknowledged that national liberation necessitated a societal eradication of patriarchal traditions. In a thorough critique, reviewer Najwa Qawar Farah commented that the local feminist tension between seeking women's professional liberation as workers and the struggle for the immediate national liberation is not necessarily the dilemma of the play. She identified with Nadia Mikhail's character and indicated that the play presented Nadia's struggle as exemplary of contemporary women's desire for family planning and social reform. Nonetheless, she complicates these issues by localizing them in specific parts of the Palestinian population and identifies the real struggle in education, healthcare, and poverty.[24]

In Balalin's performances in Jerusalem, Ramallah, Beit Sahour, Bethlehem, and Birzeit, audiences showed their appreciation by large turnouts and enthusiastic participation. Since most audience members were unaware of the production's plot, they attempted to help the actors with the lighting, identifying themselves as repairmen, tradespersons, and engineers. On occasion, professional electricians eagerly walked onto the main platform to offer their services, demanding an opportunity to fix the lighting system. Actors would eventually whisper an explanation in their ears, politely asking them to return to their seats. The audience often delightedly clapped or responded in shock as voices seemed to emerge from anywhere in the performance hall. Abboushey fondly remembered the initial reactions of most audiences: "I think they were scared in the beginning.... 'God save us, is this a trap?'"[25] The audiences responded positively to the troupe's critique of the Palestinian society and demand for reform. The underlying revolutionary messages in the play reached the audiences, which prompted a necessary public examination of the ensemble's political purposes and sources of patronage. When spectators asked which faction or political organization did the troupe really belong to, they answered that they belonged to Balalin.[26]

The tremendous success of *The Darkness* as a truly popular production inspired a creative movement throughout the 1967 Occupied Territories. The humanistic foundations of the play inspired questions about the identity of a potential Palestinian theater industry. The press coverage of the play emphasized the role of performance as a social activity that questioned local norms in Palestinian society. Although the function of theater as national-identity-forming activity and a significant tool of resistance to combat the occupation would be articulated by the mid-1970s, the narrative of cultural resistance had not yet taken hold in the Jerusalem/Ramallah area. The short existence of the Balalin ensemble had led its members to believe in the potentialities of collective action through creative work. Its members had implemented ideas that could only be imagined a few years earlier. Their commune-like environment in François Abu Salem's family home in Sheikh Jarah hosted a living experiment that aimed for personal liberty and gender equality as its primary goals. This utopian prospect became the envy of many creative-minded youth in the area.

Theater artists continued to be the nucleus of the Balalin troupe, but new members brought expertise in music, singing, and dancing. The well-known communist Ilias Nasrallah suggested to the emerging revolutionary singer Mustapha Al-Kurd that Balalin might benefit from his services. Al-Kurd brought his friend Zakaria Shahin, who trained and maintained his own dance troupe, which performed folkloric *dabkah*. The two had been comrades in the union of painters and iron workers in the late sixties. In the first half of 1973, as Balalin prepared for its next major project, the expanded troupe held an outdoor performance of Nazim Hikmet's *The Story of the Walnut Tree and Lame Yunus* in the grove of their center in Sheikh Jarrah, the firsts of what became known as "orchard performances."[27] The variety performance featured music by Mustapha Al-Kurd and expressive frozen tableaus as an integral part of the stage picture. Zakaria Shahin choreographed folkloric dance numbers, expanding Balalin's repertoire into popular dance forms that attracted a larger audience.

A rare voice recording of a company meeting from early 1973 represents the best evidence of Balalin's developing working style and ambitions. The ensemble's discussion revolved around a new script called *Nashrat Ahwal Al-Jaw* (*Weather Forecast*). Abu Salem had written the play and proposed it to the ensemble as a potential follow-up to *The Darkness*. The new play, with significant replication of the style of Theatre de Soleil's production of *1789*, demonstrated Abu Salem's propensity to reproduce avant-garde approaches from the European repertoire. The dramatic throughline depicts the young and naïve Habib, who must battle against the forces of tradition in order to lead a political revolution. The play portrays the world of a population under the spell of religious leaders that he refers to as magicians. They justify their oppressive actions by referring to the will of the great god Shamandour. Using symbolic names, based on a gibberish language of his invention, Abu Salem attempted to create a parallel universe that represented Palestinian society's fears and beliefs. The audience would enter an empty hall and remain standing throughout the performance as actors entered from different parts of the hall to perform on three different platforms.

This 1973 meeting modeled an ideal democratic environment where each member shared their opinion of the script. Testifying to Balalin's successful implementation of gender equality, a woman's voice moderates the conversation, organizing the meeting with the confidence of a respected member of the ensemble and leading the debates without being challenged on her leadership. Abu Salem's script was heavily criticized by the ensemble. Every member of the ensemble rejected the idea that the audience should stand for the better part of a two-hour performance. Some members criticized the limitations of the language, calling it simplistic, unsophisticated, and reductive, and clearly written by a non-Arab Westerner, implying that the writer was an orientalist. Others felt that the quality of the written Arabic did not effectively demonstrate the excellent Arabic of religious leaders or reflect the local characters in the play. One member suggested that the script and its writer hid behind superficial symbolism to criticize Palestinian society and present religious figures as monsters, ignoring all the services that religious leaders and institutions provide to their societies. One male voice on the recording noted that the majority, if not all of the characters were men and asked if this play was going to be performed only by men. The criticisms flow nonstop during the four-hour recording, and occasionally members debate each other, some defending Abu Salem's choices and others asking certain members to show more respect for the work. In one instance, a member proudly expressed that this meeting was a testament to Balalin's power as an ensemble and microcosm of Palestinian society.[28]

By the spring of 1973, Balalin had become a household name in the Jerusalem/Ramallah area and the troupe's efforts to remain under the radar of the military government became impossible. The popularity of *Al-ʿatma*, the increasing size of the troupe, the expanding repertory of performances, and the frequency of events caught the attention of the military governor. After the company remounted a variety show as a small festival of song and theater in Al-Bireh municipality, the military authorities called in the majority of the core troupe members for questioning about their activities.[29] The troupe had consciously been manipulating the occupation's legal system by performing "privately" in churches, municipal halls, and local clubs in the Ramallah, Jerusalem, and Bethlehem areas. To avoid the military, they also performed in Jerusalem's Al-Omariyyeh School. Adel Al-Tartir remembered: "We were allowed to perform in Jerusalem, but not in Ramallah. Therefore, we performed in Jerusalem and our audience came to us from Ramallah, Beit Hanina, and other areas."[30] When the military governor asked them to explain why Balalin performed without a permit, they feigned ignorance and claimed to be producing amateur theater.[31] Feigning inexperience and holding back the ensemble's ambitions worked for a very limited time.

When posters appeared in the streets of Ramallah to advertise the opening of the Palestinian Theatre and Folklore Month in August 1973, all signs suggested that Balalin was creating highly influential popular theater. For example, the Balalin Festival Committee had released a manifesto, entitled *Our Country's Theatre*, announcing the troupe's intention to create an original Palestinian theater and to introduce the Palestinian audience to plays from the "world stage." This manifesto explained their collaborative methodology and commitment to respond to the reviews of the critics and the audiences. Pledging a commitment to the presentation of popular Palestinian culture, the committee also announced the addition of new folklore artists, likely referring to Al-Kurd and Shahin, but it did not mention their names.[32]

To create excitement, Balalin distributed mysterious colorful posters depicting a question mark with the words "Balalin," "Month of August," and "In Ramallah." Advertising the event without announcing the program, these teaser posters suggested that Balalin was actively promoting an upcoming event, but the question mark could be placed after the date, the name of the company, or the name of the city. Black and white posters advertised a three-week program of dance, Palestinian folklore, remounted productions of *Al-ʿatma* and *Qitʿat Hayat*, and three new productions: *Nashrat Ahwal Al-Jaw* (*Weather Forecast*), *Thawb Al-Imbrator* (*The Emperor's New Clothes*), and a musical entitled *Al-Kinz* (*The Treasure*). Events ran four evenings a week starting at seven thirty. The Ramallah Bus Company agreed to run from the hall in the Ramallah municipality building to Jerusalem every night after the performance. Tickets were sold at the Sharbain bookshop in both Ramallah and Jerusalem, the Ramsis novelty store in Jerusalem's Old City, and other sites in Nablus and Bethlehem.[33]

Because there was no dedicated theater in the municipality building, the company transformed the basement into a performance hall (figure 5). In the sixties, the Jordanian government had earmarked the location to be a theater to promote community and educational theater, but the project never materialized. The space remained a hazardous construction zone full of sand, bricks, cement, and stones. The walls were unfinished. The troupe worked together to clean it up, level the ground, and enlarge the existing performance area. They painted the walls and purchased cur-

FIGURE 5 Balalin prepares the Ramallah Municipality building for their festival. Ramallah, 1973. Courtesy of François Abu Salem Archive, Palestinian National Theater/El-Hakawati.

tains to create backstage areas. They manufactured simple "par can" lighting instruments from empty cans of Nido dry milk and in some cases from original materials crafted by a tinker. They also brought chairs in to establish the audience space, turning the hall into a flexible theater, in which the space could be transformed based on each performance. For example, *Nashrat Ahwal Al- Jaw* required multiple platforms, whereas folkloric music and dance were performed mostly on the main stage.[34]

During this period of preparation, construction, and rehearsals, the military raided the hall, collected the identity cards of the artists, and sent official requests for the cast to report to the military governor. Some actors were summoned during the run of the festival. Adel Al-Tartir described his questioning at the Israeli military headquarters in Ramallah as brimming with an "atmosphere of terror." The military governor met him personally. He began with casual conversation and offered him coffee. He questioned him about his activities and personal life: Why do you do theater? Why don't you settle down and get married or travel abroad? What about studying at the Hebrew University? During the interview, Al-Tartir got the distinct impression that he was being offered the opportunity to work as an informant, a feeling several artists mentioned about these encounters. At the end of the interview, he was dismissed with the warning, "Beware because we are watching you."[35] Feeling intimidated by the potential legal consequences, the troupe applied for a performance permit. "We didn't know whether we were going to get it. The tickets were sold and posters were hung. The permit arrived on the opening night of the festival."[36]

The newest major full-length production in the festival was *Nashrat Ahwal Al-Jaw*, which was the subject of the meeting described earlier in this chapter. The play tells the story of a fictional nation called Nitsalaf in a period in the distant past, when the world was polytheistic.[37] A dragon rules the land by destroying neighboring nations. A group of magicians control worship in casinos and communicate with the gods: the Great God Shamandour, the God of Currency, and the God of Catastrophes. Under the dictatorship of the dragon, magicians control the people's level of knowledge. In the school system, they teach children to stop asking questions. The parents rely on the magicians to control the curious minds of the children by using the concept of eternal punishment or pleasure. The magicians maintain a system of religious factions or sects and discourage intersectarian marriage. When citizens living outside Nitsalaf transfer money to family members, the funds run through the magicians, who take commissions. The casinos of worship operate on olive oil, which is donated by the people. In this patriarchal system, law and tradition privilege men over women. Old folks' homes and hospitals are overcrowded and poorly run. The magicians and the dragon maintain strong relationships with wealthy land agents and owners, who control the economy. When peasants and workers complain of poverty and the lack of services, the magicians advise them to pray to the Great God Shamandour. When problems in Nitsalaf increase to unacceptable proportions, the dragon and the magicians agree to begin a great construction project to keep the population occupied. They introduce a new entertainment device called the Talabizion (television), which is sold throughout the land. New entertainments emerge including gambling, ethnic dances, spirits, and wrestling. Then, drought spreads through the land and the economy crashes. The magicians begin ritualistic prayers, but year after year, the people's interest in prayer dwindles. The drought is followed with flood and destruction. The people rise up against tyranny, but the magicians and the dragon succeed in dividing the revolutionaries by nurturing and publicizing their sectarian differences, increasing the presence of the God of Currency by printing more money, and disparaging the image of the educated leadership. The magicians squash the revolution and the people return to their old lives.

After the play ends, an audience member stands up and proposes an alternate ending. Demanding a return to an earlier point in the play, he states, "Let's see now how the people organized themselves in the struggle against those in power."[38] Returning to the flood scene, the people resolve the issue of the flood by using raw materials from the land to build a dam. They claim ownership of the factories because they built them using their own labor. They discover that the dragon's flames were an illusion created by their own oil donations. Unable to accept the new realities, the dragon commits suicide. In their final celebration, the people demand that the magicians entertain them by performing a humiliating striptease, effectively turning the secret society of dictators into a public spectacle.

In addition to the main stage, this collectively created three-hour epic drama was staged on three platforms, expanding the size of the stage space used to produce *The Darkness*. The audience was distributed throughout the hall. The production used Brechtian distancing techniques, which drew attention to theatrical methods of performance to prevent the audience from identifying with the characters. It was also reminiscent of Théâtre de Soleil's landmark production *1789*, which placed several stages in the midst of the audience. Before the play began, some actors consciously spoke with the audience to achieve critical distance; for example, they freely moved on the various stages in costume, but not in character. At times throughout the performance, the actors, posing as audience members, used the aisles. Visible lighting instruments played an important role in directing the audience's focus. The actors set up each scene on the appropriate platform and waited for the spotlight to signal the beginning of the new scene. A narrator began the play by presenting the backstory and announcing the start of the performance. At the end of the play, he created the false ending by announcing the end of the play, prompting the "audience" to demand a new ending. Each character transformed the props as needed throughout the play. For example, functioning like a projected slide, the white blanket from the old folks' home scene became the sign that depicted the word *hospital* in another scene. Pantomime was used to suggest the presence of a radio. The narrator turned it off and on as required in front of the audience. The arrangement and movement of the bodies of the actors shaped the staging to portray the religious classroom, the ritualistic prayer hall, and natural landscapes in the destructive winter scenes.

Although the recorded discussion demonstrated that not all members agreed with the play, Abu Salem successfully convinced them of the value of the script. By renaming or "coding" the place, the gods, the people, and the religious problems, Balalin directly critiqued the difficult issues that plagued Palestinian society. Avoiding the wrath of specific members of the community, the premise of these coded characters was to unmask the conspiratorial relationship between the institutions of religion and capitalism under the leadership of a fascist dictatorship. The play condemns the divisiveness between Palestinian Muslims and Christians, challenging the hegemony of religious ideologues. It claims that sectarianism benefited only the dragon, who already owned all the firepower and the means to suppress the people. Using juxtaposed images, the play exposes contradictions in the social formation. For example, it represents a religious figure as he objectifies the female body during worship. During a serious drought, the magicians eat until they are completely satisfied. Immediately after prayer, a woman smokes a cigarette. While a young man attempts to build his own business, a religious figure sabotages the project by stealing his money.

By presenting coded snapshots of the contradictions in Palestinian society and culture, Balalin called for self-liberation in order to achieve freedom from a foreign power represented through the dragon, whose influence permeates every aspect of daily life. A mix of foreign and indigenous accents suggests distinctions between the locals and the outsiders. In the hospital scene, the nurses, speaking in broken Arabic, botch the birth of a local baby, leading to its death. Using materials from their own land, the people build a massive residential tower that reaches the sky, but they are not allowed to live in it. When the people are close to successfully overturning the oppressive forces, the local collaborating land agent provides insider knowledge to suppress revolutionary sentiments by using a combination of counterfeit money and a plethora of advertising for entertainments and "modern" products. To attain mind control, radio announcements pollute the airwaves and newspapers flood the land, which creates a culture of news addiction. In this dangerously conspiratorial and hopeless situation, Balalin presented a dark ending, then proposed a change of direction.

Like *Al-'atma*, *Nashrat Ahwal Al-Jaw* called for mass mobilization and the organization of all efforts toward personal and public liberation; however, it wasn't as popular. *Al-'atma* told the story of the troupe by using their own lives as the primary source. They told the story of their own struggle to create and present the play in a few months despite their personal differences and against the overwhelming odds. Clearly, the play's struggle was analogous to the Palestinian struggle for freedom. Furthermore, on some level, all the actors played themselves. For example, the enthusiastic actor and craftsman Adel Al-Tartir played the role of the eager carpenter. Emile Ashrawi played the role of the intellectual. Nadia Mikhail played the role of the educated woman intent on offering a major contribution to society. François Abu Salem played the leading actor who drives the production forward.

In contrast to *Al-'atma*'s clarity in plot, structure, and characterization of the Palestinian identity, *Nashrat Ahwal Al-Jaw* presented multiple storylines and characters that were sometimes difficult to follow. Abboushey admitted, "When we started rehearsing it, nobody knew where we were going. . . . The connections were weak and the play was too fragmented."[39] Although the audience clearly understood the symbolism, the overly coded play presented too many alienating names and characters. In performance, the majority of the production was taken up with establishing the world of the play and presenting situations that the audience was already familiar with. In the very end, the late inciting incident of the drought suddenly moves the production from exposition into a conflict between the people and the magicians. While *Al-'atma* offered a clear chronological plot structure in its constant motion from occupation to liberation, *Nashrat Ahwal Al-Jaw* failed to present a story for the audience to follow. Its heavy-handed symbolism permeated the entire script. Despite the lukewarm audience reception to *Nashrat Ahwal Al-Jaw*, the festival's success was unprecedented.

The addition of folkloric dance numbers added an entertainment dimension that attracted audiences from all parts of the West Bank. The rising star Mustapha Al-Kurd as the premier singer and composer of Palestinian heritage music and the most experienced dance choreographer created a popular face for Balalin and allowed new participants to perform without the burden of rehearsing a demanding play. With the help of Shahin, Al-Kurd was able to run separate rehearsals that did not involve the core Balalin ensemble, thus appreciably expanding the offerings for the festival. During this period, Al-Kurd performed his most celebrated song of resistance, "Bring on the Rail," with its famous opening "My country, my country, nothing is as beautiful as you" and its refrain "Bring on the rail, bring on the sickle, never leave your land." The communist motif of the song insisted that the road to liberation would be long, requiring nonstop labor. The song promoted the efforts of villagers who worked in the agricultural sector and emphasized the value of labor as the foundation of Palestinian society. His declared leftist politics matched Balalin's internationalist approach to daily political struggle. Years later, in 2011, at a memorial to François Abu Salem, Al-Kurd reminded the audience: "Let's not forget the internationalist and Maoist currents that inspired his journey and many others who worked with him."[40]

Although Balalin's popularity rose to new heights, personal differences caused irreparable rifts within the company. Perhaps the fragmentation of *Nashrat Ahwal Al-Jaw* as a production and a script signaled the emerging disunity in the collective. In spite of the broadly leftist direction of most Balalin members, the collective creation of plays in the shadow of differing political and intellectual orientations increased conflicts in open discussion sessions. Encouraged by recent successes, some members grew more egotistical and individualistic, demanding credit for their contributions. Others attempted to guide productions toward their own factional, political, or nationalistic goals. Ironically, the ensemble had successfully critiqued division, self-interest, institutional corruption, and division within Palestinian society but failed to remedy these issues within their own ranks. By the end of 1973, Balalin had grown to over thirty-five members, but the core members continued to be overloaded with most of the labor. Despite the popularity of the folkloric performances, the expansion into music and dance diluted the ensemble's focus on creating original Palestinian theater and opened its ranks to the influence of newcomers, who demanded equal representation in the decision-making process.

In the post-festival period, an ill-fated conflict erupted between the majority of the ensemble and François Abu Salem, the initiator of the entire Balalin enterprise. In January 1974, before his separation from the ensemble, Abu Salem called an urgent meeting. According to a document in his archive, he summarized his position on the future of Balalin and set a number of conditions for his continuation as a member.[41] Initially, he described his return to Palestine in late 1970, full of revolutionary dreams and principles, only to find these same principles alive in the people who subsequently constituted the Balalin ensemble. He rejected a position in the French consulate because it conflicted with belonging to the Palestinian people and required noninterference in Palestinian affairs. In the collective (his chosen family as he described it), he achieved his hopes and dreams of a theatrical enterprise. Expressing his personal, emotional, professional, and financial sacrifices, he reminded the members that he offered his home and professional experience to Balalin, even though it meant living on bread and falafel. He said, "I found that the result was loss, sarcasm, doubt, and humiliation. Conspiracies formed behind my back! I was confronted with absolute rejection. Absolute rejection that I should belong to the people I am living with." The speech tells of his feeling used for his work ethic and access to his house, then being discarded. He declares: "I wanted to work with people who accept me as one of them.... Today, I am declaring loudly that as a human being who has dignity and has given everything he has, but received nothing in return, I have the right to a new start." He went on to explain that some members tokenized him as a representative of colonialism and attempted to destroy the roots of colonialism through a single individual who was originally French. He wished that those individuals would challenge real colonialism with the same force they used against him.

Abu Salem expressed his decision to leave Balalin to establish a new ensemble with a fresh beginning unless the current members accept several conditions. Then he revealed the material circumstances that led to his differences with the ensemble in the rest of his speech. François's home, which had become the Balalin center for meetings, socializing, and rehearsals, had fallen into disrepair. The owner of the rental threatened François with a lawsuit and eviction. The February rent, due immediately, had yet to be paid, and he was no longer willing to take responsibility for the financial burden. To keep the house and maintain it as the ensemble's home, it needed a substantial infusion of labor and finances. The ensemble would be required to renovate the kitchen and the bathrooms, as well as repaint the majority of the house. François would have to hire an architect for urgent repairs to the water pipes and the electricity, in addition to replacing the bathtub. The furniture needed cleaning, reupholstering, and repair. He asked for new curtains, pillows, bed sheets, mattresses, and kitchen wares. He estimated that the costs of fixing the damage to the house would run to the sum of 6,000 liras, the equivalent of a year's teacher's salary at the time.

The ensemble rejected Abu Salem's firm set of conditions. Underneath the financial differences, interpersonal differences had been increasingly difficult to reconcile between Abu Salem and his comrades. Given the scarcity of Palestinian plays at the time, he presented and promoted an idealized vision of the collective creation model, which the initial company members had understood as self-erasure and sacrifice in the service of the greater good. They chose to credit the collective for their own individual contributions.[42] Although the Balalin literature proclaimed the collective ideal, Abu Salem played a leading directorial and editorial role for the majority of the productions and often took credit for his directorial contributions in the press. In this, his role was similar in some ways to that of Ariane Mnouchkine, the celebrated director of Théâtre du Soleil in Paris, a company that had inspired Abu Salem. After the festival, François's vision challenged the wishes of the majority of the troupe. Believing in the value of shocking the audience, he wished to break taboos of language, religious values, and conventional physical behavior, using lewd moments of pantomime.[43] As demonstrated in the vehement objections to Abu Salem's simplistic antireligious stance in the aforementioned recording, the performers were often unconvinced by the aesthetic or dramatic rationales behind his suggestions.

Despite these well-documented reasons, one explanation remains understated as "ideological differences" and often underreported by former members in interviews. In the absence of Palestinian television and radio in the Occupied Territories, political parties had become aware of the power of theater to influence public opinion and promote their agenda in both armed and peaceful struggle. The far-reaching influence of *Al-'atma* and the month-long festival proved Balalin's potential to become a significant platform for the promotion of factional politics. Given Balalin's permeable and inclusive membership, it embraced individuals affiliated with Fateh, PFLP, the Communist Party, the Democratic Front, and the emerging National Front, which attempted to be multifactional. One performer explained that various factions encouraged their members to participate in Balalin in order to influence its direction from the inside. As a result, the community atmosphere of the early formative period was replaced by the ideological and philosophical wars that plagued the Palestinian political struggle. Balalin became a battleground for internal Palestinian politics.[44]

The familial, trusting, and liberatory atmosphere—which Sahar Khalifeh, then a young journalist from Nablus who later would become one of Palestine's leading novelists, had described in her article in *Al-Ghadeer* just a few months prior to the 1973 festival—had been broken by irreconcilable artistic, financial, and personal differences.[45] François left the ensemble, believing that his radical politics and commitment to his aesthetic would be better served by working with a new set of collaborators, a pattern that he would repeat for the remainder of his professional career with various degrees of success. Some of the existing Balalin ensemble members attempted to maintain the name of the collective and continue rehearsal and production, but they failed to perform beyond the early months of 1975. The ensemble could not become financially independent and thus was doomed by the audience's expectation of the professional performance standards set by previous productions and the emerging competing theater companies of the period. Balalin could work only on an amateur rehearsal schedule, and Abu Salem's organizing labor proved to be irreplaceable. When the ensemble ceased operating in 1975, it had created only three new small-scale productions that proved to be less popular. At the time Balalin fully disbanded, many of its original members had left the country. Some members were arrested and imprisoned for long periods. Ideological and intellectual differences had continued in full force. The language of sacrifice for the greater good that predominated the early meetings of Balalin had become a burden without a return on personal and professional investment. The battle between the collective creation spirit and authoritarian desires for personal contributions proved to be far greater than the remaining members could manage.[46]

Ultimately, Balalin's story spelled a pattern of emergence and downfall that would plague Palestinian theater in similar ways for the ensuing two decades. The unresolved challenges of establishing durable theatrical institutions would reappear as new groups of artists joined their resources for theater production. With the exception of George Ibrahim's unrelenting and unceasing theatrical output, ensembles would be formed and re-formed as the economic and political conditions of the era necessitated. Against a backdrop of an Israeli occupation that continuously and gradually deepened its military, civic, and administrative control on East Jerusalem and the rest of the Occupied Territories, the theatrical movement that began in earnest in the early 1970s charged forward under increasingly challenging circumstances, not of its own making. The declining sovereignty of the Palestinian people would translate into the declining availability of rehearsal spaces, performance venues, volunteering capacities, and personal security in public assemblies. The strengthening occupation and its censorship apparatus would play a greater role in shaping the experience of making Palestinian theater, despite the increasing desire for artists and audiences to assert this popular form of national self-expression.

FOUR

WRESTLING WITH COMMITMENTS, DIVISION, AND ARRESTS, 1973-1977

In the early months of 1973, the rapid success of Balalin and the hunger of Palestinian audiences for theatrical activity led to the establishment of several new theater ensembles. Balalin had rallied support for its festival by establishing a large circle of friends, creating intellectual salons, gathering the necessary production resources, attracting meaningful press coverage, expanding its repertoire of performed content, managing the charged internal political discourse on Palestinian statehood, implementing an evocative and progressive social mission, and mounting a large, popular month-long festival. The troupe's ability to build the Balalin brand into a recognizable name signaled the possibility that theater was not only an activity but also a potential source of cultural influence in a public sphere that desperately needed local content after being separated from cultural production in neighboring Arab countries. These successes inspired other aspiring hopefuls to attempt similar launches of theatrical ensembles. The efforts that were already stirring in the wings in the early 1970s accelerated to make the period of 1973 to 1977 a watershed of theatrical creativity, in addition to George Ibrahim's ongoing productions. Two concurrent ensembles emerged as Balalin's competition: Dababis and the Palestinian Theatre.

Audiences repeatedly joked that a new ensemble called Dababis (The

Pins) emerged to poke Balalin (The Balloons). Historically, Dababis attained legendary status in Palestine as the premier theater of resistance. Even in recent years, when artists speak of confrontations with the Israeli military, this troupe continues to be discussed as one of the most uncompromising examples of direct antagonism and mass arrests. The ensemble's primary creative force—writer and director Ibrahim Jbail—and its core members were often reputed to be associated with the Popular Front for the Liberation of Palestine (PFLP). Although the story of the ensemble may begin with the personal journey of one individual, its development and growth can be attributed to the volunteer and community efforts of its large membership that extended beyond Al-Am'ari Refugee Camp to Ramallah, Al-Bireh, and Jerusalem.

During the 1967 invasion, Jbail's father sent him from Al-Am'ari Refugee Camp to Amman, where he organized a theatrical troupe in the youth center of Al-Wehdat Refugee Camp. In 1969, he successfully produced and directed a play entitled *Revolution of the Dead*, which addressed the challenges of families of martyrs in the refugee camps. The play became much more significant a few months later with the eruption of the bloody events of Black September (1970), which resulted in many Palestinians losing friends and family members in the battles between the Jordanian Army and the Palestinian guerrilla army.[1] When Jbail returned to the Ramallah area in 1972, he had become deeply influenced by a violent guerrilla war and the class-conscious ideas of Dr. George Habash, the intellectual leader and commander of the PFLP. Upon arrival, he connected with the union of construction workers in Ramallah. By working within the framework of a union, he could avoid the complex legalities of the military laws imposed on all cultural activities. The union referred to its cultural projects as "parties" or "events," but Jbail insisted that his first project with them should be called "a show." He developed the production with a team that combined workers and nonworkers in what became Dababis's first play, *Al-Turshan (The Deaf Ones)*.[2]

Written by Ibrahim Jbail, *Al-Turshan* played in Ramallah in 1973 and set in motion his aesthetic program of proletarian theater, which was dedicated to representing the struggle of the working class and unmasking the ideological claims of the occupation. To a great degree, the play initiated the short yet significant journey of Dababis as a popular theater of resistance. The play adapted a historical event from the Ottoman era to challenge the present-day occupation and the class disparities between landowners and peasants. In the story, Sulaiman Bek attempts to take over a peasant's land and love interest, Aisha. She runs away to avoid Bek and gather support for a revolution against his authority. In the performance of the play, she hides in the audience, blurring the line between theater and everyday life, especially as Aisha feels initially unsupported by the public. When she accuses the audience of deafness and paralysis, Aisha demands action from her fellow Palestinians. The battle transfers from the stage, which represents the authority of a foreigner, to the audience hall, the site of the struggle of an occupied people. At the end of the performance, choral voices in the audience declare that the people will survive and will never leave their homeland or their political struggle. With popular support and protection, Aisha returns to her village and original love interest, a fellow peasant. Throughout, the play draws on folklore to present a uniquely Palestinian aesthetic, with the Palestinian village, traditions, and morality playing crucial functions in the main conflict between the Ottoman occupier and the Palestinian local. The play utilizes the traditional Palestinian dance *dabkah* and well-known local songs to promote the historical Palestinian village atmosphere.[3]

Along with the main event, the company created a performative two-scene companion piece entitled *Da'irat Al-Khawf Al-Dababiyya* (*The Foggy Fear Circle*), which relies primarily on the theme of exploitation. The first scene follows an invalid as he forces himself into the daily life of a bourgeois writer. The invalid attempts to share the writer's space, sustenance, and clothing. When the committed socialist writer is fed up with the intrusion, he becomes the enemy of the lower classes in an act of self-preservation. Written in a symbolic mode, the choreography of the second scene assigns the idea of time to a male actor and the Palestinian cause to a female actor. In this production, Dababis warned that the passage of time diluted the Palestinian cause and suggested it might lead to the demise of the struggle.[4]

As the main event of the union's annual celebration, the double bill appropriately problematized existing power structures by examining the relationship between dominant figures, such as the feudal lord, the bourgeois intellectual, and the stereotypical Arab male, in relation to the oppressed classes represented by the peasant, the homeless, and the traditional Palestinian woman in the domestic sphere. Jbail noted:

> *The Deaf Ones* is a realistic play that deals with the idea of the land and the peasants. *The Foggy Circle of Fear* deals with intellectualism and opportunism in practice. An intellectual thinker and theorist faces problems.... Is it possible to practice ideas in actuality or are they just theoretical...? Overall, the play is a historical treatment of the Palestinian cause. It represented the cause as a woman who is oppressed by history and raped by some elements in this history.[5]

In his expansive description, Jbail sees the Palestinian cause as a battle on several social and political fronts. Can the peasants revolt against land confiscations? Is it possible for the intellectual to enact his theoretical principles? Can Palestine survive its "historical rape?" The questions evoked challenges as the population saw them under occupation. Dababis promoted a radical leftist discourse in a realistic throughline in *Al-Turshan* and a representational performance in *The Foggy Fear Circle*. Jbail confirmed that the audience reacted much more positively to the realism of the class-based conflict in the first play than to the stylized dance, movement, music, and set in the second play.

Jbail's choices as the playwright and director represent a number of widespread trends in the period. To obtain the permission to perform, he approached the union, an existing organization that already possessed the right to assemble as part of its administrative routine. Whether the performance was referred to as a show, a party, or an event, an exclusive performance permit would not be required. (Balalin had similarly employed this strategy in its gatherings at the YMCA.) In lieu of an extensive public process of auditioning and casting, the membership of the union and its extended circle served as a substantial private pool of potential performers. This approach to building the team from an existing membership assured Jbail that his activity would remain under the radar of the military governor and any existing censorship apparatus under both the civil and military laws of the period. Finally, he assured permission to perform from his own community by choosing topics within the consensus of the period about accepted antagonists: the Ottoman feudal lords and the bourgeois intellectual. Both narrative tropes of the peasant against the landowner and the homeless against the bourgeoisie echoed profoundly within the refugee camp and the union's audiences.

The successful performance with the union prompted Jbail and a number of performers to codify their relationship under the constitution of a theater ensemble. Through the Israeli military's civil administration, they applied for a permit to establish a theater company called Firqat Dababis Lil-Funoun Al-Masrahiya (The Pins Troupe for Theatrical Arts). Located in the Ramallah area but also operating in Jerusalem, the troupe defined itself as an interventionist theater company in its mission statements:

> The pin stings, awakens the sleeping, arouses the dull, reveals and blasts the pain, and unearths the root of the problem. Nonetheless, our pin is unusual. It thinks, has a point of view, and puts this point forth to the people. It is ready to cooperate positively with others.[6]

Jbail recalls being summoned by the military governor for interrogation several times during the application process: "They literally asked, 'Who are you going to poke?'" After the rumor of Dababis poking Balalin erupted in the theater community, Jbail remembered fondly with the commitment of a radical artist, "Dababis wanted to protect Balalin from any *other* pokes." After several months, the Israelis permitted the establishment of the troupe on the condition that Jbail would not be a member. They reasoned that Jbail's public association with the PFLP, an enemy organization of Israel, precluded his participation in public events. Instead, he took on a supportive role as an "independent" writer and director.[7]

In the same year, the troupe established its own site of operation in El-Sharafeh, located between Ramallah and Jerusalem. The troupe built a small stage, which on occasion hosted intimate events such as book readings, musical recitals, film discussions, and public lectures. The site also became a rehearsal space, a meeting room, and an office. The original mixed membership of unionized construction workers and amateur performers began to develop into a more stable membership of theater aficionados. Over the following two years, Dababis grew into the organization that supported its existence as "new members entered the troupe and it began to look like a trade union organization or a type of artistic social club."[8] Jbail remembers that becoming part of the troupe was more complicated than membership in political factions: "You had to join us as part of the 'friends circle' for a year before you applied for official membership." The troupe demanded public service from its membership in the form of "raising awareness of culture and the arts." Informally in the ensemble's meetings and rehearsals, he declared their function to be "resistance to the occupation."[9]

The production of *Al-Haq 'al-Haq* (*Blame the Truth*) addressed the absence of municipal services under occupation—most importantly, the absence of fire stations in the Ramallah and El-Bireh areas. The play opens with a report of a fire at the house of a young woman living alone in a refugee camp because her husband works in Kuwait. In their reaction to the tragic event, the characters represent their social and economic classes, such as the peasant who was expelled from his land in 1948 and currently works as a trade laborer; a petit bourgeois who uses higher education as a medium to challenge the power structure; and a bourgeois merchant, landowner, or municipal mayor who can afford to live outside the refugee camps. Throughout the play, a drunkard critiques the various characters in what would become a stock character in the company's repertory. In the climax of the play, the characters hear the horns of a fire truck. Eager to receive the firefighters, the camp residents head to the entrance of the camp only to watch the truck as it passes them by.

According to Jbail, the play was directed at Karim Hanna Khalaf and Ibrahim Al-Tawil, the Ramallah and El-Bireh municipality heads respectively. The troupe wished to provoke them to improve social services. Jbail constructed the production's framework and wrote the script. Before every performance in a refugee camp, village, or major city like Jerusalem, the character names were changed to identify public personalities in the audience. Each audience behaved based on their relationship with the individuals named on the stage. Some reactions demonstrate the significance of the issues posed in the play and the high stakes of performing a socially relevant play during this period. For example, in Al-Jalazone Refugee Camp, the audience physically attacked the actor playing the despicable character of Al-Mukhtar (the Mayor). In Al-Issawiyyeh village, now a neighborhood of East Jerusalem, one elder's verbal objection to his portrayal on stage in the performance prompted the intervention of the audience and troupe members during the show. According to Jbail, this elder was removed from the hall against his will.[10]

This production demonstrated how a theater ensemble could equally challenge members of its own community on issues that did not necessarily target the occupation directly. Although the mayors of Ramallah and Al-Bireh were seen as local heroes, they were not spared the poke of Dababis's pins. By unifying its political and class-conscious social missions, the ensemble engaged its audience with a stage reality indecipherable from the veracity of everyday life, rendering audience reactions not only instantaneous but also vociferous and genuine. Recalling his own performance of "the drunk" in the play, Jbail's vivid memory of this play tells of an active audience living the theatrical event as a social interaction, both illusionistic and veracious, deserving of immediate intervention. This aesthetic of "eventness" that partakes in the characteristic quality of the news of the day invokes the spirit of a time when the happening of the theatrical event rivaled the fast-moving historical realities in the political lives of Palestinians.

Similarly inspired by Balalin's success, the years between 1973 and 1975 witnessed the parallel emergence of the Palestinian Theatre Ensemble in Jerusalem. The Palestinian Theatre Troupe (1973-1996), along with the two splinter troupes Palestinian People's Theatre (1979-1983) and Sanabel People's Theatre (1983-present), probably produced the greatest quantity of performances in Jerusalem since 1973, yet their productions surprisingly remain the least documented of any ensemble from this period. Their combined performances, including their children's theater repertoire in elementary and secondary schools, number several thousand. The original Palestinian Theatre Ensemble produced nineteen productions and presented two hundred and twenty adult performances in their first fourteen years of operations.[11] Focused nearly entirely in Jerusalem, despite their touring and frequent activities in the greater Bethlehem area, the majority of their original productions occurred from 1974 to 1979, when both Mohammad Al-Thaher and Ahmad Abu Saloum were simultaneously active in the ensemble. In Jerusalem, this repertory of adult theater remains unmatched in its variety of originally written plays.

Emerging from intensive discussions among a number of its founding members, the ensemble often produced a theater of everyday life, adopting realism on stage and emphasizing local debates about national issues as they pertained to interpersonal and familial behavior. In their mandate, the company committed to researching the contemporary situation, examining it in rehearsal, and reflecting it to the audience on stage. Concurrently, they hoped to produce relevant theater and high artistic standards of realism on stage. They believed in their productions' potential as documentary evidence and oral history of Palestinian culture. In a shared trend among many theater companies from the early 1970s, the troupe functioned as a cultural club and required its members to pay fees to fund its productions. After evaluating membership applications, the leadership issued identification cards that stated the member's position as director, actor, playwright, or technician. The ensemble funded itself through an ongoing stream of new members, the opening of two new branches in Beit-Sahour and Beit-Jala, internal donations, ticket sales, and cooperation with Palestinian organizations that supported performances.[12] Similar to Dababis, the ensemble was defined philosophically and operationally by the work of one playwright, Mohammad Al-Thaher, who wrote the majority of the plays.

The troupe's inaugural production *Al-Raqqasseen (The Dancers)* targeted a topic that has remained one of Al-Thaher's interests: the role of journalism in Palestinian culture, particularly the abundance of tabloid journalism. In 1974, as Palestinian newspapers and magazines were emerging as a significant voice of resistance, the play promoted a public discussion on the value of local news in the absence of national communications tools such as radio and television. Given the topic of the play and its title, Al-Thaher suggested that the journalists of the period behaved like entertainers, questioning their role as professional communicators of the Palestinian cause. He demanded a principled public stance from local newspapers in the face of occupation. He also promoted the elimination of tabloid journalism in a culture that valued reading the newspaper on a daily basis. The play opens with the character of the Maharaja, who reads aloud the tabloid news of the day. At the end of the play, the same character enters with the same tabloids and makes them disappear in a concluding magic trick.[13] Directed by François Abu Salem, who joined the production as a director in the aftermath of his departure from Balalin, the play was performed before nearly sold-out audiences on the stages of El-Omariyyeh School and the East Jerusalem YMCA. Abu Salem's stylized approach on the avant-garde set presented a stark contrast to Al-Thaher's comedic realism in the text, a difference in aesthetic that continued throughout their careers.

From late 1974 to the end of 1975, the Palestinian Theatre focused its efforts on national themes and the promotion of national unity under the banner of the PLO. Their collectively created and directed play *Hareeq Al-*

Jaheem (The Fire of Hell) portrayed shared political and personal catastrophes as the foundation of the Palestinian nation. Based on the idea of a local celebrity, the poet of the Old City of Jerusalem Fawzi Al-Bakri, the actors improvised the show by representing the political and ideological battles between the various factions of the Palestinian armed struggle. Then the company staged *Majmaʿ Al-Qabadayat (Gang of Toughs)*, which promoted the PLO as the only legitimate representative of the Palestinian people. During this period, the productions implicitly reflected the troupe's alignment with the PLO's mandate for armed struggle. But most often, the themes and discussions in the plays depicted a leftist critical discourse, which consciously and explicitly privileged the base over the superstructure in popular cultural resistance against Israeli hegemony.[14]

At the end of 1975, the production of another original play, *ʿind El-Luzoom (When Necessary)*, launched the Palestinian Theatre into unprecedented popularity as the troupe presented a challenging dilemma: What must a loyal Palestinian do when a family member jeopardizes the national cause? The play tells the story of a brother and a sister who open their family's home as a hotel on the night when three freedom fighters escape from prison. In this fictional account, Israeli radio announces a reward of a hundred thousand dinars for anyone who assists the military's efforts to catch them. Declaring her appreciation for these heroes, Siham challenges the ingratitude that her brother Wadiʿ displays toward those who suffer for the freedom of their people by seeking to help the freedom fighters. For Wadiʿ, the prospects of saving their home from bankruptcy and gaining a comfortable living far exceed a meek attempt to save the fugitives. During the hotel's inaugural night in business, three men rent separate rooms. Mistaken identities provide comic relief, as the audience knows the full story, while various characters remain in the dark about each other's presence in the hotel and the treasonous intentions of the brother. The first act ends as Wadiʿ overhears a conversation between the fugitives about the failure of one of their comrades to remain steadfast against torture. Hamid, the hero and protagonist of the play, tells the traitor Said, "If I forgive you, the cause will not." In the second act, Siham learns of her brother's intention to inform the military of the fugitive's location. She attempts to sway him from collaborating with the enemy. Upon his refusal to change his mind, she decides that she must kill him.[15]

Actor Ahmad Abu Saloum played the role of the resistance leader,

Hamid. Over twenty years later, he remembered that the production played tens of times. Crediting the expansion of the national movement across Palestine and its successes in municipal elections in both Gaza and the West Bank, he believed that the play's ideology matched the politics of the era. The ensemble was celebrated by various institutions, such as the Ramallah Teacher's College, which rewarded the cast with a standing ovation and recognized the quality of the ensemble's performance.[16] The initial production was performed thirty times, one of the longest first runs in contemporary Palestinian theater. It spoke to the anxieties of the period, particularly on the issue of suspected collaboration with the Israelis and the importance of a unified front in the armed struggle. According to Al-Thaher, the play discussed "the necessity for the public to overcome private concerns and to sacrifice all that is dear and precious for the sake of public interest."[17] The play's financial success allowed the troupe to buy the basic sound and lighting equipment necessary to tour the production across the West Bank. The play was officially revived with different casts in 1978, 1984, and 1987. It was also remounted consistently throughout the 1990s.

In the aftermath of the fractured Balalin ensemble, François Abu Salem fulfilled his promise to remain committed to the Palestinian cause and to establish a new theatrical venture in the form of a new ensemble, Bila Lin (Without Leniency).[18] The ensemble existed only in 1974 and 1975 as a vehicle for former Balalin members who wanted to join Abu Salem's production. In 1974, the troupe produced Brecht's *The Exception and the Rule*, a play that Abu Salem was enamored with and directed three times in his career. Carrying on the spirit of its mother company, Bila Lin produced two collective creations in 1975: *Al-'ibra* (*The Moral*) and *Musara'a Hurra* (*Free Wrestling*), which became its most memorable production. *The Moral* receives very little mention in Palestinian theater and left no traces in the press or in Abu Salem's archive. By contrast, *Free Wrestling* is a rarely discussed masterpiece that has left a meaningful archive, including the full text and several expressive images (figure 6), allowing for a reasonable reconstruction of its production.

Free Wrestling opens with a symbolic song by Mustapha Al-Kurd, describing the beauty of an unnamed land that suffers under a capitalist military occupation. A war dance between two opposing teams represents the ongoing battle over it. In the staging, a character named Octopus

FIGURE 6 A performance of *Free Wrestling*. Ramallah, 1975. Courtesy of François Abu Salem Archive, Palestinian National Theater/El-Hakawati.

separates the warring teams "like children," and then all parties meet in a satirical conference resembling the 1973 Geneva Conference on the Arab-Israeli conflict. In overt mockery of international efforts to resolve the conflict after the 1973 October War, the actors represent the warring parties as they violently discuss issues related to the Middle East. These conference delegates play cards, physically fight, and negotiate geopolitical issues such as "separation, the Suez Canal, reconstruction, withdrawal."[19] In the midst of increasing laughter, they begin to agree, open a champagne bottle, and proceed to drink the champagne and shower in it. When the characters leave the wrestling ring, a villager yells to fellow peasants: "They agreed."

After this initial introduction, the atmosphere erupts with the sound of drums of war. Six wrestlers prepare themselves for a grueling match: the imperialist petrol-guzzling Octopus, the fake oily regressive Arab, the shiny bourgeois Palestinian Hyena, the anonymous Angel of the working class with his wife, and the crucified Palestinian from the Galilee. An objective referee judged the match. Other characters in the play included the Donkey Rider and Peasants. The wrestling match portrays the battle between the anonymous working-class Angel against the Palestinian Hyena, who is protected by the regressive Arab, and the petrol-guzzling Octopus. The battle leads to the complete disenchantment of the laborers and ends with a revolution against the entire capitalist system. The peasants repossess their land, imprison the managers of oppressive capitalist institutions in a box, and free the crucified Palestinian from the Galilee region. Finally, they establish a government composed of the rightful owners of the land, the peasants.

In the battle for liberation, the play does not differentiate between the Israeli occupation and the greater capitalist enterprise represented by the Octopus. Staying true to its name, Bila Lin presented an uncompromising vision of the road map toward liberation. The production staged the overthrowing of the local bourgeois class, which represented the interests of the capitalist system. Then, the peasants established grassroots localized governing committees. In their revolt against the Palestinian Hyena, the peasants shut down all institutions of oppression, including education, health, and utility companies.

DONKEY RIDER: What happened? What did you do? Everything is topsy-turvy in the town. Was it you who removed all the electricity poles?

ALL: Of course! Who else?

DONKEY RIDER: Was it you who took apart all the street lamps . . . ? By god, the whole town went dark. . . .

ALL: Of course! Who else? Now, our lives have lit up!

DONKEY RIDER: And the director of the public hospital, was it you who kidnapped him?

ALL: Of course! Who else?! And now we're sitting on top of him. (*All point to the box.*)

DONKEY RIDER: And the director of the school, the director of the electric company and the director of the water company???

ALL: Of course! Of course! Here they all are, imprisoned in the box like monkeys, but don't you worry: We are feeding them and quenching their thirst until we learn from them, then god may have his way with them.

DONKEY RIDER: All good! And now I will inform the other villages to spread the movement.[20]

In their enacted revolution, the people dismantle all systems of control, reducing the authorities' access to the people. They establish that the rights of the refugees and the rights of the crucified Galilean are aligned in their attachment to the land. They declare that land merchants and collaborating agents are traitors. In their rebuilding phase, they discover the lack of necessary tools, equipment, and educated personnel. The characters report the confiscation of the tools and equipment of the rich and the reclamation of their own educated experts working abroad, ending decades of brain drain. Finally, the female peasant announces that she has learned to read and write. In the last moment of the play, she erases a blackboard and "like a child," she writes slowly in a peasant Palestinian accent: "We are the peasant public. The Government!"

Musara'a Hurra signaled a leap in Palestinian theater in terms of the clarity of its message, dramatic structure, and staging methods. The company demonstrated its "no-compromise" policy in the production, which required the audience to make decisions upon entering the performance hall. Suspended signs asked the audience to determine their position within the class system and then sit with their class and support the appropriate wrestler. The familiar confrontational free wrestling atmosphere of the seventies provided the riotous environment necessary for the involvement of an otherwise inexperienced theater audience. The script specifically demands a village-like familial environment. As the drummer accompanies the action of the play, the caricature costumes and stock popular wrestling physical behavior suggest a comedic overtone in the wrestling matches. However, the shadow of the crucified Palestinian looms in the distance and festers underneath the circus-like atmosphere of the wrestling matches. The dramatic structure mirrors the form of the play. The class-based rising action in the ring parallels the class-conscious seating in the audience. Throughout the play, audience members were forced to re-evaluate their sense of identity, class, and community, but it also affirmed the shared state of oppression under occupation. This critical position formed the basis for the vocal audience participation in the mob-like revolutionary action at the end of the play.

In August 1974, a year after the 1973 festival in the Ramallah municipality and subsequent to several popular theatrical offerings, the ensembles in the Jerusalem/Ramallah area founded the earliest serious attempt at coordinating and institutionalizing cultural production in Palestine.

Bila Lin relished in the popularity of *Free Wresting*; the Dababis ensemble had similarly established name recognition and a regular audience; and the Palestinian Theatre had produced three productions between 1973 and 1974. Under the name The Association for Work and Development for the Arts, this formalized voluntary work committee included representatives of the visual arts, *dabkah* dance troupes, and folklore artists, in addition to a support system of writers, intellectuals, and journalists who attended the festival as audiences and participated in press coverage and group discussions in an emerging trend of intellectual salons. Within the association, theater artists formed the first working committee, the Theatre Committee, which became the largest effort to organize Palestinian theater in the post-1967 occupation period.

In February 1975, the leading active theater ensembles in the association—Al-Kashkul (The Notebook), Balalin, Dababis, the Palestinian Theatre, and Bila Lin—collaborated to create the first Jerusalem theater festival. Performed in the theater of Al-Omariyyeh School, two hundred theater workers, musicians, dancers, visual artists, poets, and folklorists participated in plays, sketches, dances, and musical numbers. The festival was a significantly expanded version of the 1973 festival in Ramallah. Audiences from different parts of the Occupied Territories attended, exceeding all expectations.[21] The Palestinian Theatre's production of Ahmad Abu Saloum's play *Marakez Tafteesh* (*Search Centers* or *Checkpoints*) exposed the humiliation of Palestinians at checkpoints and border crossings. Recalling the energetic atmosphere of the festival and the multiple contributions of various theater artists, actor Ahmad Abu Saloum stated: "Despite the cold weather and the snowfall, the shows in the festival continued for a week. Overcoming the cold weather, the audience eagerly followed the plays. It was the first time I participated as an actor, director, and festival organizer."[22]

According to a statement by the Theatre Committee of the Association for Work and the Development of the Arts, Dababis had "surpassed its previous works and solidified its reputation with the Palestinian public. Because it developed an audience that awaited its committed radical productions, Jbail and his comrades felt responsible to continue their artistic journey."[23] They entered the festival competition with a play entitled *Al-Intithar* (*Waiting*). A winner of the second-best play of the festival, it presents a number of archetypes of social classes including the laborer, the peasant, the employee, and the educated intellectual, which was played by a female. As the play begins, the audience finds these characters in an unspecified site awaiting an unidentified character, which represents an absence in their own lives. Based on religious teachings, they believe in the necessity of a "rescuer, savior, reformer, or leader."[24] Yet in the absence or death of a sheikh (religious figure), a drunkard comes along to speak the truth about social and economic disparities. The play stages the battle between blind faith and theoretical ideology. The failure of both options prompts a search for an answer, a truthful path forward for Palestine. The ensemble brings the dilemma to the audience by directly asking attendees for their opinion on the question. According to the playwright, the play concludes as the audience and the characters await an uncertain yet inevitable future, a purgatory that must be overcome for the sake of liberation.[25]

Shortly after this highly successful festival, the association and its theater committee ceased operations but some of its members attempted another major joint project in December 1975 to establish a unified direction for the emerging theater movement: the publication of a fifty-page periodical entitled *Al-Masrah* (The Theatre) and subtitled "An Artistic, Literary, Cultural, Monthly and Comprehensive Magazine." The editor-in-chief, Yehya Abd Rabbo, applied for and obtained the publication permit. Although the mailing address of the magazine situated its activity in Ramallah, it was printed in Jerusalem's Shu'fat neighborhood at the East Cooperative Press. The first issue exemplified the altruistic principles of an idealistic theater movement, and the editor's word was signed "The Editorial Family." In many of the articles, some of which were translations, the authors were not identified. In the inaugural issue, the title of the opening essay asked "Our Theatrical Troupes: Where To?" Signed by "The Editor," the article critiqued the theatrical movement's divisiveness, suggesting that all operate "as if they don't work in the same field," which weakened this artistic community. The editor stressed "Al-Maslaha Al-'amma" (the public good or public interest) and encouraged the sharing of expertise, performances, and actors in order to present higher-quality productions and operational standards. The editor stated:

> But the opportunity has not passed yet! We only issued *Al-Masrah* Magazine to be of assistance to all our theatrical troupes, providing

them with all their needs of direction and instruction. It will be like a library where everyone gathers at the table to nourish their souls.²⁶

Aiming to instruct, critique, and archive, the first issue included articles bearing the following titles: "Amateur Theatrical Direction," "The Constituents of Playwriting," "Audience Psychology," "Theatrical Definitions," "The Art of Comedy," "Theatrical Sets," "The Problem of Dialogue," and "The Movement of the Stage." Other contributions included an interview with the Egyptian playwright Tawfiq Al-Hakim, an article on the Norwegian playwright Henrik Ibsen, a biography of the Egyptian actor Mohammad Tawfiq, and a full Arabic translation of Bertolt Brecht's *The Exception and the Rule*. Although the magazine failed to deliver on its promise of monthly publication, the second issue was published in February 1976.

Under the announced co-editorship of Ibrahim Jbail of Dababis and Mohammad Anis, the third and fourth issues were printed at Al-Nasser Press in Jerusalem. After the long hiatus between the second and third issue, the editorial team expanded the scope of the magazine to include television and the visual arts to appease reader requests. When *Al-Masrah* ceased its operations in the spring of 1977, it had met a number of its declared goals: reviews of Palestinian theatrical productions by its "mobile critic," descriptive snapshots of Palestinian theater in its behind-the-scene accounts, biographies of young theater artists, a historical account of Palestinian theater, and the exposure of local artists to theater practices abroad. In the last two issues, *Al-Masrah* published the remainder of a detailed interview with Tawfiq Al-Hakim, critical articles on Brecht and Ibsen, and translations of one-act plays by Anton Chekhov. It had also matured from its beginning as a primarily instructional theater magazine into a pan-Arab theater and entertainment variety magazine. According to published letters to the editors, from the yet unknown theater makers Radi Shehadeh in Al-Mghar and Fouad Awad in Nazareth, the magazine had found a reading audience outside Jerusalem. A representative of the Center of Middle East and African Studies in Tel Aviv University (Ramat Aviv) sent a letter stating, "We examined the first issue of your magazine and we liked what's in it. We decided to add it to our library; therefore, we ask you to consider us permanent subscribers and to send us issues successively as you publish them."²⁷

At the end of 1975, after the Theater Committee of the Association for Work and the Development of the Arts mounted the first Jerusalem Theater Festival, both Balalin and Bila Lin ceased their operations. Committed members from both ensembles agreed to discuss the prospect of a dedicated collective that would work exclusively in the theater. The members of the collective were Adel Al-Tartir, Mohammad Anis, Mustapha Al-Kurd, and François Abu Salem. In the formative stage, they retreated to Anis's home village of 'Aboud to explore the nature of the collaboration and negotiate the process of creation.[28] Al-Tartir explained, "Although we had previously worked together, we tried to build shared experiences. We lived together." During this retreat, several names were suggested for the ensemble including Al-Hakawati (The Storyteller), but they decided to call it Sundouq Al-'ajab (Box of Wonders) because some members had more vivid memories of this folkloric tradition from their childhood in Palestine. After the initial retreat, they traveled together to Greece to a home owned by François Abu Salem's family to further develop their working manifesto and brainstorm their first original creation. Al-Tartir remembered that the trip was characterized by intense experiences and plenty of arguments. "Yes, we fought, wrestled, and reconciled. It was necessary for us to live these bittersweet experiences in the founding moments of Sundouq Al-'ajab."[29]

According to most Palestinian theater artists, this collective attempted the first significant effort to become fully dedicated to Palestinian theater in the Occupied Territories after 1967. Following Balalin's legacy of collective creation, the ensemble rehearsed on a full-time basis, six days a week. They rehearsed mostly in Jerusalem's community centers and churches but occasionally in private homes or warehouses. They agreed to share all administrative, management, and technical responsibilities in order to avoid too much of the workload and decision-making falling on any single member. Motivated by the desire to create a popular touring theater that combined the vision of *The Darkness* and the mass appeal of *Free Wrestling*, they planned their touring itinerary in advance, reduced their production costs, and minimized their design elements. Since all members had completely abandoned their other sources of income, they borrowed money from personal supporters to free themselves for rehearsals. At the end of 1975, within a six-week period, the original ensemble of Sundouq Al-'ajab had created its first and only full-length play, *Lamma Injanina (When We Went Crazy!)*.

Lamma Injanina follows the transformation of two young men from hopeful dreamers to insane social rejects who fail to find the right medicine for their social and physical illnesses. The play begins with a juxtaposition between 'Antar's happy dream in the first scene and the laborer's muscle market in the second scene. Like bodybuilders, both 'Antar and Abu Al-Janazir display their muscles and physical skills to prospective bourgeois employers. As the potential employer examines them like livestock, a worker likens himself to a mule and another describes his labor as inventory for sale. At the end of the scene, the boss exits, riding his chosen worker. Aside from the difficult life of material labor, the two young men express interest in politics on the radio and in newspapers, football, drinking, and women. They struggle to comprehend the complex politics surrounding them, and they battle against their society's norms on sexuality, especially premarital sex. They are exposed to the fake intellectual, the exploitative merchant, the occupier's physical abuse, and unlawful imprisonment. As these forces accumulate, 'Antar descends into mental instability, his work suffers, his substance abuse increases, and his physical health deteriorates. Eventually, he loses the ability to speak, understand, or interact with others around him. Abu Al-Janazir takes him to different professionals who might be able to heal him, such as the magician, the doctor, and the poet; however, they only exacerbate the situation. Finally, 'Antar and Abu Al-Janazir become insane when they lose their handle on reality and inhabit an alternate world of conspiracy, spies, informants, collaborators, and wars.

Methodologically and artistically, this highly successful actor-driven original production fulfilled the promise of the company. For touring purposes, the staging required basic lighting and transportable sets. To indicate distinct public and private spaces that converge into one larger public sphere, they painted circles on the stage, suggesting different acting areas. The circles collectively created one large circle symbolizing the characters' never-ending cycle of insanity and violence. The company demonstrated the multiple settings of the scenes using physical acting. They mimed carts, tools, weapons, equipment, and various public spaces such as a store, a street, a doctor's office, and a market. Lighting played an important role in isolating characters and signaling the change from one physical space to another. At times, they used a chair or a box to create levels. For example, one scene indicated that the two characters spoke from two different floors of one building. Each in his spotlight, one squatted, looking up and the other stood on a box, looking down. The production was visually enriched by the powerful presence of newspapers, which characters consumed (ate) onstage to literally exhibit two evils: poverty and news obsession. The sound of the transistor radio, as played, spoken, and manipulated by the actors, suggested a culture of news addiction, leading to an unhealthy conspiratorial social formation.

According to the original poster, the initial run was booked and advertised to occur on 22-25 January 1976. The image on the poster depicted a promising troupe of young men. Sitting on boxes, sporting long hair in various styles, costumed in suits and accessorized with hats or mustaches, they appeared confident in their performance and their characterizations. As with many posters from the seventies, the advertising image, name of the ensemble, and the title of the play were printed in ink, while the dates and location of the performances were handwritten, suggesting that posters were printed for multiple uses. After a successful opening at Al-Omariyyeh Theatre in the Old City, the production was temporarily shut down when Mustapha Al-Kurd was arrested. He attributed his arrest to his "theatrical, cultural, and artistic activities."[30] After a few days in custody, he was released, giving hope that the production could continue; however, soon thereafter, he was arrested again and imprisoned administratively for the majority of 1976.

Although the outcome may be similar, Al-Kurd described a clear distinction between being invited for an interrogation or a "conversation" versus being arrested. In the first instance, the police or the military sent a written request to the artist requiring his presence at a particular time in a state-controlled establishment. Most Palestinian artists in the seventies received and fulfilled these requests at one time or another. Many left the meetings with the military with a warning, a sense of intimidation, and the requirement to submit an application for a permission to perform. Others suffered greater consequences. For example, in the case of the Dababis, the invitations to converse eventually led to surveillance, followed by questioning, and ending in arrests. In the case of an arrest, as Al-Kurd described the harrowing process, the military officers used theatrical techniques that constituted a performance of their power:

> They come at night, 2a.m., with a military force like a terror operation.... They wait until your head rested on your pillow to perform this terror show.... Then people start trading stories: "When they arrested him... the stairs... on the roof... through the windows... crossing the streets."[31]

When challenged that cultural production could be a reasonable cause for being arrested. Al-Kurd stated: "I acted and sang. We did *Lamma Injanina*.... Those who were active got arrested." His first arrest happened at two in the morning after a performance of *Lamma Injanina*. On his second arrest, he was brought face to face with an informer who claimed Al-Kurd had attempted to recruit him for a resistance cell. When Al-Kurd didn't confirm or confess to the charge, he was imprisoned as an "administrative detainee."[32] Several lawyers took on his case, including the Jewish Israeli human rights lawyers Felicia Langar and Lea Tsemel, as well as the Palestinian lawyers Walid Al-Fahoom, Mohammad Kiwan, and Ali Rafeʿ. At the end of 1976, given the choice of renewable administrative detention or exile, he left Jerusalem on a journey that took him to Jordan, Lebanon, Germany, and several other countries, where he continued to play his music.[33] He did not return home until 1984, when he performed a concert at the opening of the Nuzha Hakawati Theatre.[34]

Sundouq Al-ʿajab hired the actor Jaber Al-Zubaidi to replace Al-Kurd in *Lamma Injanina*. The troupe toured from the Jerusalem/Ramallah area to Nazareth, the Galilee, Um Al-Fahem, and the Triangle, presenting a total of eighteen performances of the play. Although the production was critically successful and the tour received popular support, Al-Kurd's departure and poor financial revenues paralyzed the ensemble. Since the members frequently disagreed with François Abu Salem's personal and production choices, he was asked to leave. In the absence of his dearest friend and collaborator, Mustapha Al-Kurd, Abu Salem lacked support in the ensemble, and thus, once again, he was ejected from an ensemble that he had founded. By the end of 1976, the production of *Lamma Injanina* closed down, ending the activities of the original ensemble.

During this period, it was not unusual for theater artists to be arrested, detained, questioned, or interrogated by military authorities in the West Bank or the police in Jerusalem. No ensemble exemplifies the antagonistic relationship between the military and the Palestinian theater better than Dababis. In 1976, with the eruption of discussions on the establishment of a Palestinian state in the 1967 Occupied Territories, Dababis produced a highly controversial production called *Khawaziq (Shafts)*. In Arabic, the title refers to the holes that adorned the hats of the Jordanian police before 1967, but colloquially connotes "being screwed" or "getting shafted." After the Israeli military governor explicitly refused to permit the showing of the play, the troupe changed the title to *'imara Min Waraq (A Paper Building)* and showed it exclusively in Jerusalem. The stylized production represented the enemy of Palestinians in the shape of a three-headed monster: "the triad" of Zionism, imperialism and Arab reactionism. Primarily through choreography, the play tells the stories of the catastrophe of 1948, the emergence of the Palestinian revolution and guerilla war of liberation, the opposing forces of the triad, and the proposal of the two-state solution. According to the theater community, it left a lasting impression and a set of unanswered questions on the future of the troupe:

> *A Paper Building* . . . dealt with the subject of the state and raised its pros and cons for discussion. It caused a stir in the hall and on the stage. It was like a people's referendum on the establishment of the state. The play left an impact on the troupe for some gave it a particular spin, which shook up the troupe.[35]

Anis also remarked that during "this work, differences appeared obvious in the viewpoints concerning the proposed subject, which were reflected in production and on the stage."[36]

The play posed a controversial question: Should the Palestinians settle for a state along the 1967 border or continue the guerilla struggle to liberate the entirety of Historic Palestine? Although the playwright and director of the project Ibrahim Jbail clearly objected to the two-state solution, the cast was unable to settle the question in rehearsal. Those who rejected the two-state solution believed that a state under the conditions of the occupation was a house of cards, whereas those who supported this plan believed in its immediate necessity. These internal political differences became public when the question was posed on stage and the choreography of the bodies moved to spell the word *no* in Arabic. In their own act of protest, a number of performers broke the formation, a microcosmic event that captured the conditions and divisions of the time. Militant about staying on message and performing the rehearsed choreography, the senior membership of Dababis evaluated this public objection to the troupe's stance and suspended the dissenters from further participation in the production. Jbail remembered: "At the time, they were tried and suspended for the charge of not adhering to the script."[37]

In 1977, Dababis members had several encounters with the forces of the occupation. During a rehearsal of *Al-Nabʿ Al-ʿali* (*The High Spring*), the military invaded the rehearsal hall at the Ramallah municipality, confiscated the scripts, collected the actors' personal identity cards, and required the members to report to the military headquarters in Al-Muqataʿa. Shortly thereafter, the military invaded the troupe's site of operation, arrested several actors, and confiscated all equipment such as typewriters. Consequently, the performers experienced difficulty in continuing to rehearse. According to Jbail, Dababis "was drained of all its contents and members." Its site of operations was damaged. "Therefore, a state of horror was created. The site symbolized a state of fear. Nobody came to it." The Israeli army had arrested the members for belonging to an enemy Palestinian resistance organization—most significantly, the Popular Front for the Liberation of Palestine (PFLP). Although he acknowledged some members' political activism, Jbail insisted that the troupe maintained its independence from all political factions. Believing in the troupe's revolutionary consciousness-raising theater, he stated: "We were accused of Dababis. . . . They considered the troupe part of the political reality of the time, so they had to diminish it." Whether the cause was their theatrical activities or various members' association with the PFLP, the troupe was not only diminished, Dababis ceased all stage productions in 1977. *Al-Nabʿ Al-ʿali* was never performed.[38]

In May 1979, actors Adel Al-Tartir and Mohammad Anis Al-Barghouthi, who had been original founding members, revived the Sundouq Al-ʿajab by mounting a new work entitled *Taghribat Saʿid Ben Fadel Allah* (*The Exile of Said, Son of Fadel Allah*). The production toured in the Ramallah area and Jordan in 1981. In 1980, under the banner of Sundouq Al-ʿajab, Adel Al-Tartir opened the original production *Ras Roos* (*One Head, Many Heads*). The impressive one-person show told the story of a socially withdrawn worker who creates and interacts with his own ensemble of puppets. The production premiered before a thousand audience members at Sirriyat Ramallah. Afterward, Adel Al-Tartir became the sole representative of Sundouq Al-ʿajab. He mounted productions of *The Blind and the Deaf* (1986) and *The Hat and the Prophet* (1990), based on the work of Ghassan Kanafani. In more recent years, Sundouq Al-ʿajab has focused the majority of its efforts on children's plays, especially intimate storytelling events that take place in its unique center in Ramallah's Old City and tours on demand to various schools and community centers. Al-Tartir continues to operate under the name Sundouq Al-ʿajab, but after the inaugural production, the troupe no longer was representative of the collective creation spirit that originated with Balalin.

Although splintering and discontinuity remained the modus operandi of the theatrical movement during this period, the theater movement existed as a known quantity in Palestinian society and functioned under the watchful eye of Israeli censors, who regularly demanded performance permits and occasionally intervened to prevent performances from taking place. As Mahmoud Shqair stated, the theater of the 1970s drew significant crowds, despite its reputation for being internally divided.[39] Reflecting on the atmosphere of the period, Adel Samara wrote:

> A number of attempts were made to organize and re-organize local theater, in order to avoid some deficiencies on the one hand and to create a state of cooperation on the other. Worth noting here is that each organizational form for local theatre matched the level of theatrical activity in its cohesion and efficacy. For the weak organizational forms, which accompanied limited theatrical activity, there were the active organizational forms during the launch years.[40]

The obfuscating language of Samara exemplifies the unnecessarily complicated writing style of some local intellectuals from the period, but essentially, he describes two common phenomena. The first is the futile efforts of many participants in the theatrical movement to establish an institution that organized the artists into a functioning committee, union, or league. Because of the absence of a Palestinian ministry of culture under Israeli occupation, homegrown laws and policies for cultural production, and any funding bodies that materially assured sustained activities, Palestinian theater makers attempted to coordinate themselves into umbrella organizations that might systematize theatrical activity, often creating rules to govern their interactions. The aforementioned Theatre Committee of the Association for Work and Development for the

Arts was one such example. Samara identifies the second phenomenon as effective organization, as in the case of Balalin during its launch years, which led to a rich repertoire of production and performances.

Despite the emergence of many theater ensembles from 1967 to 1977, the most successful "organizational form" remained Balalin as a community-driven enterprise that embraced music, dance, and the visual arts under its theatrical auspices. It had the longest record of popular theater and the biggest brand name, garnering the support of highly regarded public intellectuals and political figures. Bila Lin had the record for the most popular performance and Sundouq Al-'ajab established the most successful touring circuit between Jerusalem, Ramallah, Bethlehem, and the Triangle area. Even with these impressive successes, the internal conflicts and competition between theater artists throughout the latter decades of the twentieth century did not decrease. Joint projects sometimes resulted in further conflict. For example, the initial Theatre Committee of the Association for the Development of the Arts excluded George Ibrahim on the grounds that he performed on Israeli television. From his vantage point, Ibrahim believed the work of other ensembles to be amateurish because most of their performers labored in day jobs in order to afford working in theater. In contrast to the theatrical ensembles that attempted to create a socially inclusive system of membership and production, Ibrahim insisted on producing his work as an individual, not an ensemble. Even though he worked with a regular pool of actors, he wouldn't form an ensemble, as a roster of paid actors, until the late 1990s.

The tensions between the founder of Al-Kasaba's model of production and the collective creation advocates of various ensembles would continue into the 1980s, with George Ibrahim consistently and frequently producing theater for children and adults. Meanwhile, various ensembles suffered the consequences of their declared anti-occupation missions. In the aftermath of personal conflicts within Sundouq Al-'ajab and the ousting of François Abu Salem due to creative differences with the ensemble, he resolved to create theater as sole producer and a freelance director. Setting his sights on creating and directing a play with mostly Palestinian citizens of Israel, including Bushra Karaman and his dear Jerusalemite friend Talal Hammad, he contacted the Nancy Festival in France about presenting a new production that would later become El-Hakawati's *B'ism Al-Ab w al-Um w Al-Ibn* (*In the Name of the Father, the Mother, and the Son*).

With the initial approval in place, he began rehearsing in Haifa with the assistance of his partner Jackie Lubeck. Because of the Nancy Festival's rejection of the play after evaluating it, the production never materialized with this team. However, the experience generated the nucleus of a script that would later become the inaugural production of El-Hakawati, the ensemble that meaningfully changed the trajectory of contemporary Palestinian theater.

FIVE

A MOVEMENT RECONSTITUTED, 1977-1981

El-Hakawati's Trinity, Sanabel's Cause, and a League of Their Own

From 1967 to 1977, the making of contemporary Palestinian theater depended heavily on community efforts guided by the local leadership of committed theater artists. Two crucial aspects of production led to the successful completion of projects: the existence of a working script and a safe environment to sustain rehearsals under occupation. Projects that came to fruition included a visionary director or playwright who took ownership of effectively organizing the participants toward realizing a fully staged production before an audience. In the early years, these visionaries included George Ibrahim, François Abu Salem, Ibrahim Jbail, and Mohammad Al-Thaher, the first two functioning primarily as performing directors and the latter two being playwrights. The goals of these leading figures were supported by equally driven artists such as Adel Al-Tartir, Jackie Lubeck, Emile Ashrawi, Mustapha Al-Kurd, and Ahmad Abu Saloum, who all became key personalities in Palestinian cultural production in the 1980s. Integral participants such as Majed Al-Mani, Walid Abdel Salam, and Ali Hijjawi, among many others, continued their presence in cultural production in various forms as administrators, writers, and performers but never at the same level of spotlighted participation in making theater as before.

Toward the end of the 1970s, a reshuffling of the main players led to a slow shift in the leadership that became fully visible in the mid-1980s. The undisputed leaders of contemporary Palestinian theater were Abu Salem, George Ibrahim, and Ahmad Abu Saloum. The latter worked consistently with his forever comrade, the talented comedian Husam Abu Esheh; their partnership continued for nearly half a century to the point that Sanabel People's Theatre became equally connected to both artists, with Abu Esheh gaining fame, acknowledged local leadership, and exposure as a social media and television personality. Throughout this transformation of the vanguard visionaries into entrenched leaders, the theatrical movement underwent significant changes in the way theater was produced. The community dimension became less necessary as the recognizable names of the ensembles and their leadership drew audiences to established theater spaces. The artists and ensembles adopted various strategies to sustain their living, such as working for television and frequently producing children's theater (as in George Ibrahim's case) or in gig economies such as photography and journalism (as in the case of Abu Saloum and Abu Salem). George Ibrahim led the way in producing children's theater, regularly filling El-Omariyyeh School's theater with children who paid one or two shekels per performance. As Ibrahim often stated, "The shekels quickly added up."[1]

The communist writer and critic Mahmoud Shqair described the mid-1970s as a powerful emerging movement despite the occupation's influence, but he also pointed out that splintering and divisiveness in the movement led to audience disillusionment.[2] Reflecting on this period, Adel Samara asserted that the root of the struggle within the movement lay in its failure to self-organize: "A number of attempts were made to organize and re-organize local theatre, in order to avoid some deficiencies on the one hand and to create a state of cooperation on the other."[3] He suggested that some ensembles succeeded in organizing their operations better than others, which translated into longevity and higher frequency of production. In his assessment, he describes two common phenomena. The first is the futile efforts of many participants in the theatrical movement to establish an institution that organized the artists into a functioning committee, union, or league. Because of the absence of a Palestinian ministry of culture under Israeli occupation, homegrown laws and policies for cultural production, and funding bodies that materially assured sustained activities, Palestinian theater makers attempted to coordinate themselves into an umbrella organization that might systematize theatrical activity, often creating rules that governed their interactions. The previously mentioned Theatre Committee of The Association for Work and Development for the Arts is one example. Samara identifies the second phenomenon as effective community organizing, as in the case of Balalin during its launch years, which led to a rich repertoire of productions and performances.

Despite the emergence of many theater ensembles between 1967 and 1977, the most successful "organizational form" remained Balalin. It had the longest record of popular theater for adults and the best-recognized brand name. Bila-Lin disbanded after its well-attended performance of *Free Wrestling*, and Sundouq El-'ajab left a significant mark on Palestinian theater history as an incomplete experiment, but Balalin survived as a meaningful milestone. Nonetheless, even with the movement's impressive successes, the internal conflicts and competition between theater artists throughout the latter decades of the twentieth century did not decrease. Joint projects sometimes resulted in further conflict. For example, the initial theater committee of the Association for the Development of the Arts did not find common grounds with the theatrical work of George Ibrahim. Their disagreement with his appearance on Israeli television created a significant rift. From his vantage point, his work in television and theater served Palestinian children. His commitment to high quality professional productions was unparalleled in this period. The fundamental question remained about how theater artists must deal with the occupation.

In the mid to late 1970s, François Abu Salem continued to be a controversial figure despite his committed political ideology in favor of the Palestinian national project. Of Abu Salem's three ventures before the mid-1970s, only Sundouq Al-'ajab endured. Adel Al-Tartir's efforts in Palestinian theater have continued uninterrupted under this ensemble name, primarily through his activity as a traditional storyteller and performer of children's theater. After failing to hold together Balalin, Bila Lin, and Sundouq Al-'ajab, or more accurately upon his rejection from these ensembles, Abu Salem drifted away from the theater community and sought actors to establish a new ensemble by conceiving of a project that later became El-Hakawati's production of *In the Name of the Father, the Mother, and the Son*. With his permanent friend and collaborator Mustapha Al-Kurd exiled, Abu Salem's only theatrical collaborator was a young American technical assistant by the name of Jackie Lubeck. She had supported and toured with the production of *When We Went Crazy* and became his partner in a romantic relationship that lasted the better part of fifteen years. Together, the formidable couple would become a notable force in the trajectory of Palestinian theater. Of note, Abu Salem's skill at recognizing raw talent that required direction to thrive would once again lead to the formation of an extraordinary new homegrown ensemble.

The story of Jerusalem's El-Hakawati begins with Palestinian students at the Hebrew University. In 1977, a group of students supported by the university's Arab Student Union decided to create a play for the yearly Arabic-language cultural event. A number of these students pursued degrees in geography and history while taking classes in the Department of Theater. After exploring the possibility of collaborating with the well-known theater makers Ahmad Abu Saloum, Mohammad Al-Thaher, and François Abu Salem, they selected Abu Salem to lead the development of a play on the topic of freedom of expression. The Palestinian community at the Hebrew University received the short play, *Awwal Manshur (First Leaflet)*, with accolades that inspired many of the students, including Adnan Tarabsheh and Edward Muallem, to pursue acting as a potential career. This success also prompted Abu Salem to discuss with the students the possibility of producing a play outside the auspices of the Hebrew University. From Abu Salem's perspective, he happened upon a group of young upstarts who might allow him the creative freedom he required to achieve his theatrical ambitions.

Already working with his American partner Jackie Lubeck, Abu Salem proposed the foundation of the new ensemble, which included two students from the Galilee, Edward Muallem and Adnan Tarabsheh, and two Jerusalemites outside the university, Talal Hammad and Jamil Eid. During the ensemble's formative period, Muhammad Mahamid from Um Al-Fahem replaced Eid. As with the foundation of most of Palestine's theater collectives, no single person takes full credit for creating or "forming" the ensemble; nonetheless, only Abu Salem had the artistic experience and the potential project to bring the ensemble together.[4] Although they all had participated in theatrical activities through churches, schools, or community centers, the majority of the ensemble members were relative newcomers to theater. Muallem remembered, "I hadn't planned to pursue acting. I wanted to complete a master's degree in geography. . . . But sometimes one encounter changes your whole life."[5] Although Abu Salem was known for his difficult personality, many Palestinian artists expressed their first encounter with him as transformative. Since 1970, Abu Salem had been a leading founding member and undeniable consistent presence in Ramallah and East Jerusalem's most significant ensembles.[6]

For the first time in his theatrical career, nearly a decade after he studied theater in Strasbourg, Abu Salem launched an ensemble that recognized his leadership. El-Hakawati's articles of incorporation named him the director and the sole supervisor of "every theatrical work undertaken by the ensemble."[7] In addition to the "normal rights and authority a director commonly enjoys with respect to the play he produces," the internal bylaws accorded him the privileges of a full founding member and the responsibilities to break a tie vote as well as to appoint a new director if necessary. In the case of group dissolution, the bylaws stated: "The name el-hakawati and the publication rights of the texts of the plays shall be the property of the original Director François (abu salem) gaspar."[8] From its foundation in 1977, through its official incorporation in 1983, and during its golden period in the mid-1980s, the ensemble accepted Abu Salem's creative and organizational leadership. Of note, in 1986, newer members of the ensemble wrote and directed their own productions, which contributed to the eventual fragmentation and demise of the ensemble.

In a period characterized by political factionalism in everyday life, the newly founded El-Hakawati Ensemble perceived the theater as a pluralistic space for the exchange of ideas. The members identified themselves as the natural extension of Balalin, Bila-lin, Sundouq Al-'ajab, and various education-based theatrical efforts from the 1960s and 1970s, but they differentiated themselves from their contemporaries and predecessors by rejecting direct nationalistic slogans and favoring humanistic story lines. In one of their informational brochures, they stated, "El-Hakawati favors the choice of topics, situations, and characters that clearly signify, without compromise, the Palestinian realities as they are presently under the occupation."[9] They attempted to carve out "an unfamiliar path" in a period they described as "frozen according to stereotypes" and "often divided in black and white, heroes and villains."[10] In an op-ed, Edward Muallem noted that El-Hakawati resorted to theatricality, sarcasm, ridicule, stylization, and specificity in lieu of formulaic speeches, tears, complaints, cramming, and description. To promote diligence, research, and analysis, they avoided the ensemble's identification with any specific political factions on and off stage. In their exaggerated stylized characterizations, comedy played a significant role "to combat injustice and oppression." They also adopted the role of the narrator to ensure a clear dramatic structure.[11] Abu Salem, who had developed his stance on the function of theater under occupation by this time in his career, explained how they eschewed popular slogans and representations of heroic characters:

> The minute you create heroes within a national movement, you start to deviate slightly toward national chauvinism and racism. It makes you feel superior to others, more moral and just than others. But it's not true. We have a just cause, it's true, but as people we're just completely normal.[12]

Adopting his approach led El-Hakawati to avoid direct confrontation with the occupation, a necessity that Abu Salem had learned as he watched close friends such as Mustapha Al-Kurd be arrested and exiled. Most significantly, El-Hakawati insisted on asking questions and de-familiarizing everyday situations, without providing answers or promoting a clear plan of action.[13]

Heavily influenced by Grotowski's "Poor Theatre," Bertolt Brecht's "Epic Theatre," and Arienne Mnouchkine's "Le Théâtre du Soleil," they developed their own creative process, which resulted in a series of original plays over the following decade. Similar to many collective-creation-based ensembles, the actors improvised on specific themes and situations while the director conceptualized a throughline, chose the appropriate themes, and guided the development of the play.[14] Usually, each actor played multiple roles and participated in building the set and creating the props and costumes. According to Abu Salem, the ensemble embraced its identity as a popular Palestinian theater in language and aesthetics, choosing to present its messages in easily communicated stage pictures rather than expansive dialogue. When it was used, the dialogue adopted a Palestinian dialect and economical everyday vocabulary because the company's main Palestinian audience resided in the villages and spoke colloquially.¹⁵ During the ensemble's most stable period, 1977 to 1987, they would typically tour their plays for Palestinian audiences in villages, followed by a secondary tour to Europe or the United States for both Arab and Western audiences abroad.

In the early months of 1977, Abu Salem had initiated his production of *B'ism Al-Ab, w Al-Um, w Al-Ibn* (*In the Name of the Father, the Mother, and the Son*) to satisfy an invitation by the Nancy Theatre Festival in France. The original team was composed of a cast from the Galilee, including the actress Bushra Karaman, who played the role of Kharsa. The festival sent a representative to observe the play in rehearsal. According to my conversation with Jackie Lubeck, it is unclear whether the representative was a local in Israel or a French national who traveled for the express purpose of evaluating the play. Based on the representative's assessment, the invitation was withdrawn. The festival's stated reason concerned the poor quality of the play; however, Lubeck remembered that consensus within the ensemble at the time suggested the festival rejected the play for "political reasons." She indicated that the festival did not wish to offend Jewish audiences by presenting a Palestinian play, which was clearly not finished and could potentially be volatile in its last iteration.¹⁶ An article in *Le Monde* on 12 March 1977 reported that "if Zionist propaganda does not derail the project, this remarkable ensemble will perform in the Nancy with the participation of the great musician Mustapha, who has already had to leave the country and the city to take refuge in Vienna to escape the harassment of the occupation."¹⁷ In the end, the invitation was withdrawn. The reaction of the festival representative is better understood in light of the content of the play, which is both anti-occupation and anti-patriarchal.

From October 1977 to April 1978, the newly founded El-Hakawati rehearsed *B'ism Al-Ab, w Al-Um, w Al-Ibn*.¹⁸ Abu Salem had already scripted the play with the original Galilee team; therefore, the new actors developed their characters and scenes in a relatively short period. Rehearsing a few nights a week in Jerusalem at Al-Mutran School (St. George's School), Al- Frères School (Collège des Frères), or the YMCA, the young ensemble discovered their chemistry during the improvisations. In rehearsal, their different personal backgrounds served them in representing the plurality of Palestine in their narratives. Geographically, Muallem, Tarabsheh, Hammad, and Mahamid represented Palestinians from cities and villages in both the 1967 Occupied Territories and 1948 Palestine. Politically, some members may have espoused the theoretical platforms of the Communist Party, the Popular Front for Liberation of Palestine (PFLP), or the Abna' Al-Balad Movement, while others self-identified as leftist liberals. These different leftist schools of thought inspired their focus on educating the masses in a secular atmosphere. One member stated that it was "unnecessary to define such interesting people and company by the religious affiliation of its members." Another noted, "Each of us had his own personal affiliation, but we never became associated as an ensemble with any particular faction." In addition to the indigenous voices, Lubeck provided a necessary female performing voice, theater-making experience, design expertise, and English-language copywriting.[19] Abu Salem's French heritage and upbringing in a Palestinian context contributed significantly to the internationalization of El-Hakawati, while preserving its core values as a popular theater of resistance.

B'ism Al-Ab, w Al-Um, w Al-Ibn tells the story of the male Atrash (Deaf) and the female Kharsa (Mute) as they navigate through their lives between the traditions of the Tamer and the colonial manipulations of the Stranger. Under the supervision of Al-Morawed (the Tamer), Atrash declares his wish to marry Kharsa, who must deny her secret feelings for another man. Atrash tests the skills of his potential wife by asking her to perform menial tasks and demanding a virginity test. After the honeymoon period, the marriage progressively deteriorates as Atrash enslaves his wife to prove his masculinity. The couple plays stereotypical roles as Atrash works every day for an abusive boss and Kharsa stays at home, abused by her husband. When they have a son, they name him Mutee' (Obedient). When their child's exploratory instincts overwhelm them, the parents physically beat him. Meanwhile, the Stranger entrenches himself in the land, builds a colony, and kidnaps the son and then the father, torturing them in his military camp. When released, Atrash becomes paranoid and conspiratorial, accusing his wife of infidelity and his son of plotting his assassination. The Stranger takes advantage of the divided ranks within the family and the weakness of the Tamer, who represents the patriarchal guardianship of this primitive social formation. He buys their home and expands his authority over their land. He then proceeds to brainwash them into believing his own historical narrative. The play ends with the announcement that Arab women must procreate at a fast rate. After undergoing a medical procedure to prevent her from procreating, Kharsa revolts against all the men in the play, foreigners and domestic.[20]

Based on the plot summary, the play may appear didactic, but El-Hakawati plays often contained extensive playful stage directions and short entertaining dialogue, particularly in the early years. The ensemble depended on embodied visual elements rather than the spoken word. The production opens with two vocalists emerging from the audience, asking them to wake up from darkness and chaos. They announce the time has come to tell the story and reveal the truth of their social and political environments. Lights rise to reveal the organizing principle of the world of the play: the marketplace! In the market's hustle and bustle, merchants display their goods. Owners exploit laborers. Merchants hoard inventory to raise stock prices. Lies and manipulation prevail in interpersonal relationships. As the head capitalist, the Tamer monopolizes the market by removing all the petit bourgeois merchants and establishing his own commercial enterprise, which is a circus act with three players: the Father, the Mother and the Son. Like animals, he locks them up in three cages and tames them with a whip and a yell. He speaks in verse, identifying himself as a crafty capable magician who turns wild creatures into servile machines.

Following the aesthetic of a circus, the Tamer initially functions as the master of ceremonies or the narrator of the event, while the actors perform as caged animals, performing tricks for the audience on demand. The characters rehearse the pattern of the tricks by depicting animals as they jump through a ring of fire. The Tamer rewards them with "a little bit of food" and punishes them with his flagellating whip. This pattern of rewarding service and punishing free thought "tames" their basic human instincts and curiosity until they visually behave like unthinking, subservient gorillas on the stage. This technique extends to defining social relations according to the Tamer's vision, which establishes an authoritarian regime within the family unit. For example, he punishes Kharsa for falling in love with a stranger and rewards Atrash for abusing his family. Unlike his overly complex symbolism in Balalin's *Nashrat Ahwal El-Jaw*, Abu Salem's vision in this production betrays clearly structured settings, relationships, visual imagery, and choreography. The world of the play is distinctive from scene to scene as it moves from the public circus to the domestic privacy of the family home.

Abu Salem's anti-capitalist stance that he attempted to exhibit explicitly in *Free Wrestling* matures into an equally potent postcolonial critique with this play, juxtaposing the influence of colonialism outside the home with domestic patriarchal oppression within the family. El-Hakawati's stylized portrait depicts the male head capitalist as the manager of a traditional social formation. The Tamer displays Kharsa as a superior commodity, announcing her measurements, describing her face, identifying her servile qualities, and proclaiming her virginity. He sets the standards for the ideal female and names her price. Accepting these norms, the young Atrash purchases Kharsa in a wedding ritual that satirizes the commercial aspects of traditional marriages. In presenting a grotesque image of a victorious Atrash showing a bloodied handkerchief in the midst of celebratory approval, the play rebukes extremist emphasis on female virginity. The Tamer coaches Atrash on proper male behavior; thus marriage becomes a rite of passage for Atrash to become the tamer of his own social formation, perpetuating the elders' rule of law. Atrash learns to prefer sons to daughters and his wife's servitude to her independence. Before long, a cycle of abuse is established. A bourgeois boss abuses the father, who in turn abuses the mother. Then, the mother and the father abuse the son. In the absence of positive role models in his immediate environment, the son becomes another version of the oppressive father.

The Stranger penetrates this unjust but stable social structure disguised as a lecturer, who explains the close resemblance of Atrash and Kharsa to wild monkeys. He describes their appearance as beastly, their thought process as limited, and their skin color as filthy. By contrast, his own white skin indicates modernization, cleanliness, and nobility. He brainwashes the couple and presents the solution to their "primitive" existence as cosmetic products and procedures. He invites them to strive for his version of beauty and invites them to "taste civilization." He introduces television, which presents the weather forecast primarily in areas of concern such as Judea and Samaria, the East Bank, and the South of Lebanon, never acknowledging them as sovereign. It also shows "civilized" British television programming and greeting shows, where families send letters to be read over the air. The Stranger begins oil (petrol) exploration projects throughout the country. While digging into the ancient ground, he searches for archaeological artifacts to assert his

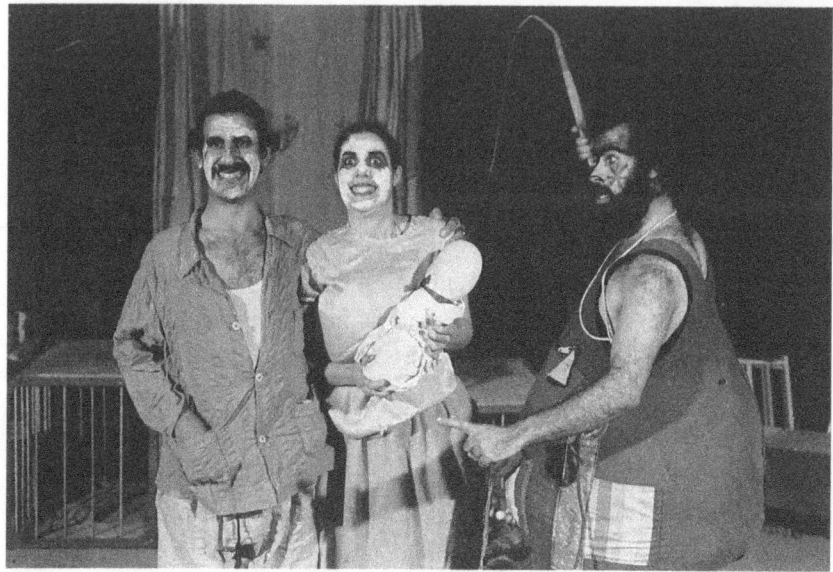

FIGURE 7 A performance of *B'ism Al-Ab, w Al-Um, w Al-Ibn*. Jerusalem, 1978. Courtesy of François Abu Salem Archive, Palestinian National Theater/El-Hakawati.

legitimacy. Criticizing the state of Israel, the stranger ventriloquizes in Hebrew, "We are very small but we must grow." He eventually marches into the audience, expels them from their seats, and sets up a military camp, where he tortures and brainwashes the locals.

An unequal alliance develops between the Stranger and the Tamer through a system of services and bribery. In this arrangement, the powerful Palestinian bourgeois traditionalist becomes a petit bourgeois in the presence of the leading Israeli capitalist. After initially objecting to modern technologies and cosmetics, the Tamer accepts bribes and compromises his traditional values by allowing the Stranger's goods to flood his market. Over time, the Tamer loses control over his population and his influence diminishes on his own land and with his own population. The indigenous domestic sphere is permanently altered as Kharsa and Atrash forget their traditional songs and begin to sing Western nursery rhymes to their newborn. Torn between the intrusions of the Stranger and the traditionalism of the Tamer, Kharsa and Atrash attempt to please all parties (figure 7). They observe their values within their community but they pretend to be Ashkenazi Jews outside it. Accepting their Arabic heritage as a liability among Israelis, Atrash coaches his wife to speak and behave like a Jewish Israeli. In one of the most comical scenes of the play, they test their newly created personas in public:

ABU MUTEEʿ: ... Now let's take the bus to the market. But in Jewish!
(They mime taking the bus. This scene is in Hebrew)
   Shalom Shoshana.
UM MUTEEʿ: Shalom Moshe.
ABU MUTEEʿ: Where are we going Shoshana?
UM MUTEEʿ: We are going to the market.
ABU MUTEEʿ: What are we going to do in the market?
UM MUTEEʿ: I want to buy you avocadoes.[21]

Playing the scene in whiteface, El-Hakawati envisioned the relationship of Palestinians to Israelis as reminiscent of black African slaves to white Americans in the United States. Satirizing the behavior of Ashkenazi Jews, the characters use stereotypical Jewish names and ridicule the purchase of non-indigenous fruit, which was mass-introduced to the Palestinian markets after the occupation. The overwhelming changes throughout the social formation, including the advent of modern technologies and unfamiliar ways of living, prompts the Tamer to retreat from public life. He becomes more religious and more subservient to the Stranger, while demanding more of his patriarchal values inside the family unit and within his community. The result is a complete separation of the political realities from home life, where the Tamer asserts control over his family because he can no longer match the stranger's economic power. Therefore, the play argues that the political battle can take place only after the people overthrow the patriarchy at home.

In *B'ism Al-Ab*, El-Hakawati focused on issues of personal liberation and resistance to Israeli occupation while continuing to critique Israeli colonial expansion inside and outside the Green Line. The play ends with Kharsa as she leads an uprising against Israeli colonialism and Palestinian traditionalism. El-Hakawati's presentation, aesthetic, and content in this inaugural production calls for an uprising against the occupation, beginning with women's rejection of the status quo. This call to action reflected the movement on the ground as Palestinian women's committees led numerous volunteer initiatives and formed a leading front in the struggle for Palestinian liberation. Whether El-Hakawati's production reflected this existing phenomenon or incited it to some degree in its mass viewership throughout its tours across Palestinian villages may be impossible to determine with any certainty. However, the production demonstrated the ensemble's vision of a Palestinian uprising, which it hoped would begin with self-liberation from the Israeli capitalist expansion and the patriarchy of traditional Palestinian society.

When the play opened in the theater of Al-Omariyyeh School on 19 October 1978, it divided audiences into die-hard supporters and absolute rejecters of the play's content and aesthetics. The controversial audience feedback on the play prompted *Al-Tali'a* newspaper to publish a series of articles that displayed a range of opinions. One pointed critique explained that the production exaggerated the position of women in Palestinian society by chaining Kharsa to a cooking pot, marginalized the role of occupation on the lives of Palestinians, and misrepresented men's conception of sexuality; it criticized the play's sensibility as impolite and the director's style as obscene. The critic exclaimed, "Is the production against women's virginity?"[22] A few days later, a follow-up article by the future leading director Ya'coub Ismail countered that the play criticizes economic, social, and political realities, beginning with problematizing marriage and weddings as tools to control women, then critiquing domestic male authoritarianism and condescending patriarchal preference for male offspring, and moving to colonial capitalism that offers superficial "civilization" in the form of clothing and high heels. Ismail compliments the play's treatment of colonial expansion through settlements, describing its effective presentation of checkpoints and barbwire in the audience.[23]

Three days later, *Al-Tali'a* published the third installment debating the play's merits. This time, the Rome-trained director Hatem Al-Dajani acknowledged the skill of the actors and the director but criticized the content of the play. His distinct opinion gestured to Abu Salem being a foreigner who imported production standards that might be acceptable elsewhere in the world but were inappropriately presented in Palestine. First, Al-Dajani suggested that a committed theatrical production should focus on the main issues that plague a society rather than keying in on the details, implying that by spotlighting women's liberation over Palestinian liberation, the play reversed the needs of Palestinian audiences. Second, he criticized the reduction of women's roles in Palestinian society because, by the 1970s, women worked and brought meaningful income to improve a family's economic situation. Finally, Al-Dajani understood how Abu Salem "takes advantage of Western techniques of directing, but he shouldn't borrow the eyes of Westerners to view our problems."[24]

The state of theater in Jerusalem, and more broadly in Palestine, lay at the heart of these debates. Several other articles expressed admiration for the play's achievement of a confrontation with the audience, regardless of the authors' agreement with the play's message or style. The sum of the criticism was a clear rejection of specific exaggerated representational moments in the play: marriage being depicted as a commercial auction of the bride, Abu Mutee' clownishly leaping on top of Kharsa to jumpstart their sexual union on their wedding night, their vocal indication of sexual intercourse under the sheets, Abu Mutee' victoriously showing the audience a bloody red rag to signify her virginity, Kharsa being chained to kitchenware, and Mutee' stylistically indicating masturbation on stage. Although both audiences and critics agreed that these representations had existed and might still exist at the time of the production, they questioned the necessity of constructing a play that depicted these images and social conditions as the norm in Palestinian society. The audiences were clearly both impressed by the theatricality and insulted by the reductive content, a duality of opinion that haunted Abu Salem for the majority of his theatrical career in Palestine. He and El-Hakawati Ensemble were valued for their daring approach and fearless theatricality, but they were also rebuked for their choice to address taboo topics as if they were the roots of the Palestinian struggle, a status that both differentiated them as pioneers and distinguished them as imperceptive and obtuse.[25]

Nonetheless, the humor, circus theme, stylistic ingenuity, skilled performances, and colorful aesthetic catapulted the play into unprecedented popularity. From May 1978 to May 1979, the play toured Birzeit University, Nazareth, the Galilee, the Triangle, and the East Jerusalem/ Ramallah area. Most villages considered El-Hakawati's visit a cause for celebration and an opportunity for civic service. Tarabsheh remembered the atmosphere: "It used to be physically taxing. We would get tired building the stage and mounting the set. Performing used to be the fun part. In the day, you worked really hard because the performance was the relaxing part."[26] For some outdoor performances in the villages, audiences numbered a few hundred and sometimes a few thousand. The residents of the villages assisted with setting up and striking the stage and performance areas. Local organizers sold the tickets well in advance and on the day of the performance. Due to the large audiences, the difficulty of controlling public access to large performance areas, and the ensemble's mandate to create theater for the masses, many audience members attended El-Hakawati performances at no cost, but enough ticket buyers supported the ensemble to regularly compensate performers after each performance.

In 1980, three years after the initial rejection of the play by the Nancy Festival, it toured several European countries and performed at the Nancy Festival. On tour, because they self-identified as a Palestinian ensemble, they struggled with anti-Arab and anti-Palestinian sentiments that emerged through organized acts of sabotage and in some instances physical harassment. Several incidents demonstrated that the majority of their host countries, cities, or organizations took issue with their declared identity. For example, they sold out their entire run in Nancy, only to discover on opening night that there was no audience. An organization or an individual had purchased all the tickets to prevent local people from attending. Their posters were often removed from the streets or vandalized. Most commonly, the words *Palestine* or *East Jerusalem* were replaced by *Israel*. After the opening night at the Nancy Festival, unknown vandals slashed the tires of their rented vehicle.[27]

In contrast to these challenges, the production was well received. Reviews in France, Italy, Germany, the Netherlands, and Switzerland emphasized the predominant qualities of the production's aesthetics and politics. The reviewers recognized the effective communication of the ensemble through the physical acting and visual mise-en-scène. They also highlighted the Palestinian identity of the ensemble, linking it to the Israeli occupation. Simultaneously and unsurprisingly, some reviews tantalized readers with standard orientalist motifs, spotlighting Arab-Muslim culture as backwards and conservative. Appealing to existing perceptions of Arabs and Palestinians, one Italian reviewer promoted the play by declaring it exotic. Although the predominant tone of the reviews throughout the tour was extremely positive, the emphasis on danger, conservatism, women's oppression, distance, and exoticism far outweighed the anti-colonial message of the play. A French press release declared "les hommes sont des cochons" (men are pigs) as the universal theme of the play.[28]

As El-Hakawati were developing into a tight-knit group and beginning to internationalize their operation, other theater ensembles were breaking apart and reconstituting themselves back home. The Palestinian Theatre Ensemble is an example of a group that reconstituted itself into a functional and perhaps more effective ensemble. The members who sympathized with the politics of the Popular Front for the Liberation of Palestine (PFLP) were unable to reconcile their theatrical creations with the communist politics of the Palestinian Theatre Ensemble. Although all members leaned toward left-wing politics, focused on the class struggle, and supported the women's movements, their intellectual affinity to two different political schools of thought created major rifts in the rehearsal process and in the production of the texts. Disenchanted actors demanded "commitment" and the inclusion of their point of view in order to be "responsible" for their own artistic products. Actor Hussam Abu Esheh believed that the ideological differences within the company derived from the way members viewed the struggle for the liberation of Palestine.[29] The Palestine Communist Party explicitly rejected armed struggle and focused on grassroots mass mobilization, worker solidarity, education, and cultural production. The equally Marxist PFLP endorsed and participated in armed struggle as part of a larger social and political program, especially in the 1970s. The theater makers of this period disconnected implicit theorization of the struggle on stage from the explicit staging of Palestinian history and politics, with Abu Saloum and Abu Esheh preferring the latter.

These fundamental political differences appeared in these ensembles' choices of plays during the period of the division. In 1979, the Palestinian Theatre produced *Improvisational Concert for the Sake of the Workers*, which focused entirely on factional politics, class struggle, and the necessity of powerful unions in the marketplace. By contrast, the newly formed Palestinian People's Theatre developed a major staged adaptation of Ghassan Kanafani's 1970 novel *Returning to Haifa*, which not only explicitly represents the wars of 1948 and 1967 but also endorses armed struggle. The prolific novelist and playwright Ghassan Kanafani (1936-1974) was also known as the spokesperson of the PFLP. His novel tells the story of "Said S." and his wife Safiyya, who drive to Haifa after the 1967 occupation in search of the child they left behind in 1948. On the drive, the novel shows Said and Safiyya's intimate connection to Occupied Palestine (now renamed Israel) and their specific knowledge of their own home city, Haifa. Kanafani interweaves the horrific events of the war with the journey to their house, expertly recounting the names of the streets and reimagining the Haifa of 1948.

On the drive, Said S. and Safiyya discuss the stories of the Palestinians who traveled from the West Bank and Gaza to see their original homes, which were now inhabited by Israeli immigrants. Said S. tells the story of a young man from Jaffa's Ajami neighborhood who knocked on the door of his family home. Expecting to encounter a Jewish family, he was shocked when they spoke to him in Arabic. They explained that they chose to live in the house to protect it. At the end of their encounter, Firas El-Libdeh asked to take the photograph of his martyred brother, which still adorned the wall of the living room. When he removed it, it left a mark showing the difference between old and new paint on the wall. He drove away, only to return shortly because of his feeling that the frame should remain in Jaffa. The resident of the house took the photograph back and then stated:

> I felt a horrifying emptiness when I looked at that rectangle left on the wall. My wife cried and my children were in shock. I regretted permitting you to take the photograph back, because ultimately, this man is ours. We lived with him, he with us, and became part of us. At night, I told my wife that if you wanted him back, you must earn back this house, Jaffa, and us. The photograph won't solve your problems, but it is your bridge to us, our bridge to you.[30]

Said S. and Safiyya arrive at their house, where new Jewish settlers, who are Holocaust survivors, live with their son Dov. The Palestinian parents re-encounter their home, intimate belongings, and objects of memorial significance. The story is interspersed with flashbacks and exposition that tell the story of how Miriam and Iphrat, the current residents, came to live at the house that included an Arab child the agency asked them to adopt. Having always known the inevitability of this day, Miriam indicates that upon his arrival, Dov should decide between his Palestinian and Israeli parents. The young man arrives in Israeli army fatigues. In the ensuing argument between father and son, the Zionist narrative collides with the Palestinian one. Dov claims that his parents deserted him in his crib and for nineteen years thereafter did not attempt to get him back. Understanding the futility of his cause, Said S. explains that Dov's first encounter in the Israeli army might be with his son Khalid, a Palestinian freedom fighter. Before they leave the house to return to the West Bank, he states, "You may stay temporarily in our house, for that's something that needs a war to settle."[31]

On 3 April 1980, the Palestinian People's Theatre's adaptation, entitled *Man Is a Cause*, opened with two back-to-back performances at the largest theater house in Jerusalem, Al-Hambra Cinema, which seated eight hundred to one thousand audience members. The performances were sold out and the aisles were full as audience members exceeded the number of seats. In the upstage area was the contested house, with all the details described by Ghassan Kanafani: a window adorned with curtains, a living room set with a rug, a kitchen, and five feathers in a wooden vase. The downstage area was used for the outdoor scenes, the site Abu Esheh described for the scene of the 1948 Nakba, which visually represented the war and expulsion. Approximately thirty volunteers played the roles of expelled Palestinians, carrying their belongings and walking toward exile in a circular formation. He exclaimed, "The scene was comic!" The comedy emerged from the radio messages playing on the theater's audio system, which included mundane domestic concerns of refugees in communication with family in "occupied Palestine" such as "Son, where are you? Be sure to feed the goat. She knows where to go. Just put her in front of the house, and follow her. On the way back, be sure to tie her well, and she'll be full, tired and won't be able to walk."[32] The tragedy and bitterness of these simple details produced intense laughter in the audience members, who still remembered both the 1967 occupation and the 1948 expulsion. The production avoided the common narrative of refugees holding onto the keys to their homes and deeds to their lands. Abu Esheh explained the rationale: The Nakba "had only happened yesterday!" The immediate concerns were urgent matters such as food, clothing, missing family members, harvests, and animals. The messages implied that all refugees believed they were returning home, which starkly contrasted with the realities the audience continued to experience.

From the visual and auditory experience of Nakba, the production took up the details of Kanafani's novel. On stage, the audience sees the life of Said S. and Saffiyya prior to their visit to Haifa. To make their journey to the house, the parents enter from behind the audience heading toward the house. The overflowing aisles forced young men in the audience to clear the way by holding hands, standing side by side to create a long human corridor. Focused on areas of dramatic and visual conflict, Ahmad Abu Saloum's direction and adaptation followed the novel's dialogue, which represents the provocative discussion between the Israeli soldier and his biological Palestinian father. Kanafani's dialogue in the production emphasized armed struggle by presenting an irresolvable and irreversible situation, in which Zionist Holocaust survivors believe in their cause and wholeheartedly embrace the Israeli narrative of cowardly Palestinians who left their homes by choice. In multiple ways, the dialogue establishes that only war will resolve the loss of home and homeland. Kanafani presents examples of characters such as Firas Al-Libdeh and Khalid S., who chose armed struggle with the intention to liberate the entirety of historic Palestine.

The original performances at Al-Hambra Cinema occurred in a tense atmosphere. Since the theater was located at the well-protected high court in East Jerusalem, Israeli forces watched the arrival and departure of the large crowds. Abu Saloum remembered:

> There were clashes, aside from the demonstration atmosphere inside the theater ... the chanting ... I still hear its noise today. There was a very strong reaction. And outside, all you have to do is cross the street to clash with a Zionist institution. There was some friction, especially since hundreds were waiting in line for the following performance.[33]

According to Abu Esheh, any street altercations were probably caused by audience members or passersby. The ensemble avoided all confrontations for the sake of the performances. "If you raised one flag, the show was over and you would have wasted three months' work!"[34] Abu Esheh remembered that buses had come from across the West Bank and Israel for the show, lining the street from the cinema to Herod's Gate. With such a confluence of people, which theater maker and technician Imad Mitwalli referred to as "a river of people," both Israeli forces and the Palestinian public would likely be on high alert. Just a decade after the occupation of East Jerusalem, the area of Salah Ed-din Street, Al-Hambra Cinema, the American Colony, and the Nuzha Cinema had been inaccessible to the Israeli public but heavily watched by the Israeli military, Jerusalem police, and border patrol.³⁵

On 17 April 1980, *Al-Tali'a* newspaper reviewed the performance with a critical eye that allows a glimpse into the performance conditions and demonstrates the limits of theater criticism during this time. The two co-reviewers complained that the production presented too many scenes that took place on and offstage, which split their attention. Their disappointments included the large size of the stage, frequent scene changes, simultaneous scenes, the unexplained kidnapping and killing of a child by Zionist outlaws, and the sudden revelation that the soldier Dov is the son of Palestinians. They found the acting overly dramatic, lacking justification for tears and laughter. Finally, they concluded that the traumatic representation of the Palestinians losing their homes and children was exaggerated. Although the disappointment of the reviewers could be the result of poor production and potentially a failed performance, the lack of familiarity with the source novella clearly shines through the criticism. It also exhibits the infighting between political parties that plagued the period. The reviewers and the communist weekly newspaper appeared to intentionally attack the production and its participants, rather than parse out the qualities of the performance. After all, the leaders of the Sanabel People's Theatre were known within Jerusalem as believers in the PFLP's platform.³⁶

The accusation of membership in the PFLP followed the ensemble on tour to a number of villages in the Triangle Area and the Galilee. In the Galilean village of Kabul, an inciting Israeli newspaper article prompted the police to arrest four actors, which delayed the performance by two hours as nearly a thousand audience members chanted their demands for the show to be performed. In the village of Sakhnin, the police reviewed the ensemble members' identification cards and interrogated them before the performance. On this occasion, they were asked to report to a courthouse in the city of Akka shortly thereafter.³⁷ The Israeli authorities were aware of the ensemble's capacity to attract large crowds to politically charged work, such as Ghassan Kanafani's *Return to Haifa*. Convinced that the production was the primary cause of the repeated harassment, Abu Saloum stated: "In the interrogation in both El-Mascobiyyeh [Jerusalem] and even in the court in Akka, they asked about Ghassan Kanafani, stating that he was involved in an extremist terrorist organization."[38] After a performance in Um Al-Fahem, Israeli police stopped the ensemble's bus, arrested everyone, and confiscated set pieces but kept only Abu Saloum and Hamdi Farraj overnight.

Only a few years after Mossad had assassinated Kanafani in Lebanon and the PFLP had caught world attention with a number of airplane hijacking operations, the presentation of *Returning to Haifa* as the first major production of the Palestinian People's Theatre declared a clear political stance in spite of its undeclared connection to the PFLP.[39] In personal interviews, Ahmad Abu Saloum did not disclose or discuss membership or association with any organized factions, including the Popular Front.[40] Hussam Abu Esheh explained, "People used to say we were Popular Front, and the Israeli Army accused us of being Popular Front."[41] Although it is difficult to confirm or deny this connection, the ensemble gained widespread support among PFLP crowds as well as the watchful eye of the Israeli security apparatus. One local newspaper reported:

> Yesterday, after a four-day delay, Israeli newspapers published the news of the arrest of four young men from the city of Arab Jerusalem and they are the colleague Ahmad Abu Saloum, *Al-Shaʻb Newspaper* sports editor, the lawyer Omar Yassin, the young man Abed Dandis, and the young man Hussam Abu Esheh. They were arrested for the offense of belonging to an enemy organization to Israel.[42]

All the men were involved with the Palestinian People's Theatre in some capacity. The article also reported Dandis's previous arrest for raising a Palestinian flag in a voluntary work camp in Nazareth, a ten-day extension of jail time for the first three men and a fifteen-day extension for Abu Esheh.[43]

From 1980 to 1984, the ensemble did not survive the multiple arrests. Its main members went on a forced hiatus as Palestinian cultural production suffered immensely during the 1980 Hebron Daboya Operation, the 1982 invasion of Lebanon, and their aftermath. Israeli authorities pressured the schools that comprised the theater touring circuit to stop renting out their stages for cultural events. Mohammad Al-Thaher explained that both private and municipal schools could not withstand the threat of legal recourse. During this period, theater ensembles attempted to create their own spaces at workers' unions and one, Al-Amal Al-Shaʻbi, tried to rent out a commercial space across the street from Damascus Gate but could not sustain their efforts. In 1984, El-Hakawati Theatre Ensemble renovated the Nuzha Theatre, which set an example for the rest of the ensembles and provided an independent performance space for the theater movement.[44]

In 1980 and the subsequent few years that lacked significant theatrical activity, one playwright turned to publishing his plays rather than staging them. With the Palestinian Theatre having lost its two most prominent performers Abu Esheh and Abu Saloum, who founded Sanabel Popular Theatre, Al-Thaher crystalized his vision for a predominantly working-class theater in the publication of two plays: *Lawhat Mawlid Thair (Painting of Revolutionary Birth)*—under the title *Al-Mawlid (The Birth)*—and *Al-Luʿba (The Toy)*. The two plays promote worker solidarity and the revolutionary struggle not only against the occupation but also against the capitalists who profit from it. Both plays show the interaction between a bourgeois class and a laboring base. *The Toy* follows the story of a young man who pursues a relationship with a highly educated rich woman. She uses this worker as a "toy" in her tumultuous love affair with a doctor of her own class. During the early phase of the relationship, the worker begins to gain access to the aristocracy. He is promoted at work and tastes a life of leisure. When the novelty of dating a worker wears off, she chooses to return to her high-class fiancé. The play concludes with a violent dance between the bourgeois characters, who wear masks of various animals, such as a tiger, a lion, a spider, a hyena and a serpent. In this surreal scene, the young man attempts to regain power in his relationship with his love interest and her band of aristocrats. When he is rejected and unable to gain dominance in the bourgeoisie, he marches towards his fellow workers in a final image of unity with the laboring class as "The Internationale" blares in the background.

Al-Mawlid begins by painting an image of backwardness. The world of the play is presented as a lost battleground where ideology is prevalent, the revolution is dead, the laboring class has retreated, and words have lost their meaning. A priest-like figure sporting a long beard and a flowing liturgical robe begins the play with the statement, "Glory to God in the highest and on earth the flies," which sarcastically evokes the biblical hymn/verse, "Glory to God in the highest and on earth peace among men." Underscored with the sound of drums and contrasted with a modern dance by a youthful man and woman, the play establishes institutionalized religious messages as a cause for rebellion. The youth express that the old regime nurtures a population of parrots who repeat messages based on the practices of traditional old men. The youth report that language has been co-opted by corrupt authority. They also declare, "I refuse," in an act of civil protest likened in the play to a cannonball shot from "the throats of the revolutionaries."

As they await the end of an era of submission and the birth of a new culture of protest, the young people are confronted by two images: the Statue of Liberty and a worker who enters with a rope around his neck. This hanged man symbolically narrates the plight of the worker, who is executed because his education and words allowed him to resist oppression and to be steadfast in "the face of enslavement." By refusing to eat the crumbs on the rich man's table, to suffocate in coal mines, and to sell his life's labor at the pleasure of the master owners, he pays the price of being hanged. Another hanged man recalls his suffering at the hands of his prison warden and lasher. He tells of his resistance in the form of educating his child. He refused to accept the restrictions of shackles, lawlessness, and humiliation. Despite the worker's belief in the goodness of humanity, the "pirate" hanged him, a sign of imperialism's inhuman practices.

The image of the capitalist as the pirate recurs throughout the play. In the image of slaves rowing the ships of the Delian League in antiquity, Western civilization is represented as pirating human labor. The play depicts worker exploitation in live reenactments of construction workers building skyscrapers and modern laborers operating the machinery of Western modernity. Similar kinds of stark images recur in verse and in staged tableaus, which contrast with the Statue of Liberty in the background. The characters hear the screams of "the tortured" in America, Africa, the Third World, and occupied Palestine. They declare these injustices as a stain on humanity:

> YOUTHFUL MAN: A stain of dishonor on the forehead of Europe
> YOUTHFUL WOMAN: The forehead of the pirate
> YOUTHFUL MAN: On your forehead
> YOUTHFUL WOMAN: Mine ... What did I say?
> YOUTHFUL MAN: Because you are deaf.[45]

The dialogue maintains an accusation against Europe and the United States, whose Statue of Liberty is stained by the injustices against the working class and whose pirate figure stands proudly in the background smoking a Havana cigar.

The play presents the solution to economic and political slavery in the form of the earthquake of "our time," the birth of the revolutionary. From the bodies of the dead victims of capitalism rises a choreographed flower formation, which opens to reveal a woman carrying a baby. The tableau of leadership born of the labor movement is accompanied by quiet revolutionary music, which then becomes Christian music as the stage is emptied of all its contents except the stained Statue of Liberty and a crucified worker. The juxtaposition of the Jesus figure and the Statue of Liberty leads the young woman to express her regret that "we have regressed two thousand years."[46] In an overt critique of religious ideology, the old priest returns to offer his words of wisdom, which amount to a sermon: "Do not interfere! Keep things as they are! Follow blindly!" When the boy attempts to fight against these teachings, he is tried in court for attempting to think or forge his own path. Given the pressures of the political and religious traditions, he fails but declares that a seed of change has been planted. The mobilization of the masses provides the impetus for the youth to throw the first stone of symbolic resistance. The oppressed laborers join in the battle. They use the tools at their disposal: their own bodies, hoes, and stones. The boy celebrates as the "Statue of Hope" replaces the Statue of Liberty. The final image of the play shows the youth and his comrades marching in the same direction, rising to free the crucified.

The late 1970s can be characterized as transitional years in the history of the contemporary Palestinian theater movement. As in any movement, the years of emergence can be full of youthful energy as the main actors respond to difficult conditions, but the spirit of ad hoc organization begins to dwindle when the realities of everyday life begin to set in. The makers of the theater movement of the early 1970s were no longer students and young laborers. Some had completed their higher education and had begun working in unrelated fields; others had emigrated; some had been deported; and many had acquired the responsibilities of marriage and children. If theater were to continue as a legitimate cultural practice, it had to be institutionalized as a functional business. The continuous cycling of artists and companies could not continue as it had been. More importantly, the theater movement had to set an example for newcomers to the art form, showing a new generation of youthful upstarts that producing plays could reward its participants not only politically and socially but also financially.

In 1979, El-Hakawati, Sundouq Al-'ajab, Dababis, and the Palestinian People's Theatre revived the Theatre Committee of the Association for Work and the Development of the Arts. Despite their concurrent theatrical activities in Jerusalem, Mohammad Al-Thaher and the Palestinian Theatre Ensemble were noticeably absent from the committee. The committee reported that a permanent split in the Palestinian Theatre Ensemble was inevitable after the "phenomenon of division and coups in the ensemble became periodical and exceeded the number of performances."[47] The description implies that despite the Palestinian Theatre Ensemble's expansion and frequency of performances from 1973 to 1979, a number of members disagreed with the process and the leadership. In the thick of the crisis, the division was public and at times articulated in negative ways. The "separated" actors cited a number of reasons, such as "dictatorship," lack of a cooperative environment, absence of freedom of speech, absence of political "commitment," and the lack of a forum to express personal points of view. Despite the presence of many of the founding members of the initial 1975 committee, this reconvening failed to produce a festival, but its importance stems from the attempt of several of its members to produce an organized union for theater artists two years later.

In 1981, in the most significant attempt to create an organized theatrical institution, several individual theater artists joined forces to create the Palestinian Theatre League. Examining this initiative and the press surrounding it provides an accurate snapshot of the state of the field and the Palestinian theater movement at the turn of the 1980s. *Al-Bayader* published a detailed interview with the founding members of this initiative: Ibrahim Jbail, Ahmad Abu Saloum, Adel Al-Tartir, Youssef Amin, Anis Mahmoud, Abdel-Aziz Al-Rajabi, and Imad Mizero. Ibrahim Jbail explained, "The league is a comprehensive prospect, where there is space for each committed theater artist. It isn't exclusive to a group that facilitates profits, if any existed, because the existence of a Palestinian theatre is a national responsibility rather than a whim, a product, or a business."[48]

In the interview, the artists recalled the failure of previous efforts to unify the movement. Abu Saloum suggested that these collective efforts often occurred in moments of crisis. Al-Rajabi noted that geographic distance played a significant role in preventing the creation of a comprehensive unifying framework for Palestinian theater. Al-Tartir explained that previous efforts failed in part because of disagreements between working and nonworking artists, crediting the league for including active theater makers. Indirectly explaining the absence of El-Hakawati members in the new league, the artists critiqued the touring of El-Hakawati Theatre Ensemble in Europe. They suggested that the theatrical movement must choose the topics and the individuals representing Palestine abroad.

The founders authored a detailed system of bylaws to govern the league. In the initial three of nine articles, the bylaws stated the league's official name as the League of Palestinian Theatre Artists, declared Jerusalem as its primary location of operations, and detailed its aims, goals, and functions. It aimed to provide material assistance to working ensembles and clubs in the region by supporting performances, holding festivals, providing rehearsal space, and collaborating with national institutions. Second, the members wished to elevate the standards of theatrical activities in the Occupied Territories primarily through finding or writing quality theatrical texts for production, attracting inactive artists at home and abroad, building an inventory of technical equipment, increasing awareness of theater as an art form, providing opportunities for continuing education, and building a library for the arts that included theater. Third, they committed to entrench productive relationships with visual artists, writers, journalists, folklorists, popular poets, and institutions of education. Fourth, they declared a commitment to develop a comprehensive theater ensemble capable of representing Palestinians as their national theater. Fifth, the league would preserve Palestinian theatrical heritage by building an archive to document theater activities. Sixth, it would find financial and moral support for the theatrical movement. Seventh, the founding members intended to create a system for developing and rewarding artistic excellence through full time work opportunities, granting financial rewards, promoting theater as a positive profession, and finding educational opportunities for theater artists abroad. Eighth, the document outlined their plan to create relationships with Arab and "progressive" theaters abroad. Finally, they hoped to organize the relationship between the theater movement and the audiences through the formation of a "friends of the theater" committee. In the remaining articles of the bylaws, the founders outlined the function of the league, the need for a public board, and the regulations for membership.

Unlike the league established in the late 1980s, this significant initiative attempted to create a resistance framework that defined the characteristics of a committed Palestinian theater artist. The document provides insight into how specific artists and companies perceived each other. The comprehensive system of bylaws and rules clearly reflects the ongoing sensitivities among theater artists in this period. For example, the league reserved the right to represent the theatrical movement. By this time, El-Hakawati Theatre Ensemble had pioneered touring in Europe, a de facto representation of Palestine and its theaters abroad. Their initial tour caused intense debates among the artists, especially since most ensemble members were considered to be foreigners to the Jerusalem-Ramallah area. The league also stipulated that members should not be "connected to" or "serve" the institutions of the Israeli authorities, including radio, theater, television, and cinema. The league reserved the right to combat any theatrical works that harmed the national cause and to withdraw support from works that harmed the theatrical profession. To expose the sensitive issue of monetary funding, they would not accept financial support from "suspect" sources, which refers to the Israeli government, the Jerusalem municipality, the Jerusalem Foundation, and institutions with a known Zionist political agenda. This sensitivity to funding sources remains a thorny subject among Palestinians in all disciplines and fields of human development.[49]

Effectively, this proposed league and set of bylaws clearly divided the theater movement into two camps: the committed national companies and everyone else. The founders of this initiative saw themselves as committed to the national cause, often referring to their work as local theater, and their stipulations targeted specific producing companies and individuals, who were technically unnamed. However, the conditions to join the league specifically excluded many theater artists such as Mohammad Al-Bakri, Jackie Ayyoub, Makram Khouri, and George Ibrahim, a group of highly successful Palestinian actors who had appeared on Israeli media. They also excluded François Abu Salem and members of El-Hakawati, who had internationalized their operations and appeared in several European countries as a Palestinian ensemble in *B'ism Al-Ab*, a controversial play that was ostracized and not approved by the members of the proposed league. George Ibrahim had also received a grant from the Jerusalem Fund, a known arm of the Israeli Jerusalem municipality, which disqualified him from joining this proposed league. Finally, a major figure of the period, the playwright and producer Mohammad Al-Thaher, was notoriously absent from the initiative, suggesting that the members had rejected his approach to theater making and managing his ensemble. Despite his occasional productions until 1996, the concurrent publication of his two plays, *Al-Mawlid* and *Al-Lu'ba*, could be regarded as one of his last major public efforts as a key playwright in the theatrical movement. Ultimately, 1980–1981, as Al-Thaher had stated, was an arid period for the majority of theater makers not only because of the lack of theatrical spaces but also, and perhaps more importantly, due to the immense divisions that plagued the theatrical movement in those years.[50] From these divisions, some crucial questions arise: Did those excluded or boycotted from the theater movement wish to be included in it? How relevant were the most vocal representatives of the theater movement? And were they the most productive ensembles?

In contrast to this failed league initiative, the major players of Palestinian theater continued to produce almost uninterruptedly. By creating adaptations of the European canon, George Ibrahim strategically gained free rein to produce his work with the official approval of the Israeli censors. He applied using the already published versions of the plays, not his Arabic language adaptations. He based much of his work on the Russian school of realism and Stanislavski's dramatic theories, seeking consistent progress in his artistic production and setting his sights on elevating his practice to international theater norms, often traveling to see theatrical productions abroad. In 1977, he completely abandoned his career as a freelancing presenter on Israeli television due to increasing demands by producers to engage in politically anti-Palestinian programming. According to Ibrahim, his position of artistic neutrality had become impossible to sustain as Israel's control over East Jerusalem and the Occupied Territories grew more visible and settlement building increased exponentially: "I started to see things as entirely political. The new realities were the opposite of the previous environment. I finally understood that you can't do theater while being neutral."[51] Although George Ibrahim had been excluded by the most vocal representatives of the theatrical movement, he had been the most active theater producer in East Jerusalem for the better part of a decade. With his departure from television and newly declared direction toward a more politically engaged theater, his differences with the movement would decrease.

Reflecting on the advent of the 1980s, theater artists reported a decline in theatrical activity in the Jerusalem/Ramallah area due to the arrest and imprisonment of a number of active theater makers. This period also witnessed a vigorous campaign by the Israeli authorities to prevent the presentation of Arabic plays in schools, particularly in East Jerusalem.[52] Since 1967, the movement had established a standard touring circuit in Jerusalem's private and religious Christian and Muslim schools, particularly El-Omariyyeh, El-Frère, and El-Mutran. Mohammad Al-Thaher recalled:

> 1980 to 1984 was an arid period for nearly the whole theatrical movement.... The Israeli authorities threatened the schools—El-Mutran, Frère, and others—to not give out their spaces to theater artists.... These school headmasters, of course, want to survive, so they stopped renting out. Things froze ... no halls to perform in. Some attempts took place at workers' unions to build spaces, taking matters into our own hands, but it was too difficult.[53]

This suppression of the theater movement in the early eighties set in motion a trend to internationalize theatrical activity based on the model set by El-Hakawati's tour of *B'ism Al-Ab*. It also established that the theater movement had to adopt a more strategic approach in its operations under occupation. Just as George Ibrahim's perspective on theater as an exclusively artistic and cultural preservation endeavor had begun to transform to include the harsh political realities, the theater movement's strategies changed in the following decade to include adaptations from the international repertoire and increasing engagement with Palestinian schools operated administratively by the occupation. Undoubtedly, the differences that shaped the internal relationships within the movement would soon turn into strengths as the formerly hard lines between ensembles, ideologies, political stances, operational standards, and affiliations blurred. Despite these transformations, which led to unspoken recognitions of the necessary and divergent strategies for survival as theater makers, the scars of internal differences would last within the movement, with some artists disappearing entirely from the field and others enduring to struggle for many years to come.

SIX

UNCERTAINTY, CENSORSHIP, AND THE PERMISSION TO PERFORM, 1981-1984

The reconstitution of the contemporary Palestinian theater movement in the late 1970s and the turn of the decade presented theater makers with new obstacles and opportunities in a hostile environment created by both the occupation and the internally divided politics in Palestinian society. On the one hand, Palestinians had shown their undivided position against the Israeli politics of expansion through commitments to the unifying rhetoric of the PLO and the emergent shared understanding of their peoplehood across the Green Line in the massive Land Day marches of 1976. In a sense, the late 1970s affirmed the permanent program of the Palestinian people, which the Palestinian National Council wrote into the mission of the PLO in 1977: the right of return, Jerusalem as the capital of Palestine, the right to resist the occupation, and the right to self-determination. On the other hand, the factionalism that plagued Palestinian politics and cultural production continued to derail the program's unity. The Fateh movement had become the de facto leader of the PLO, and the influence of the Palestinian Left had begun to dwindle. In the theater movement, the rise of national rhetoric overwhelmed the previously dominant communist-leaning production aesthetics and discourse. The influence of unions and political factions on theatrical productions declined as ensembles like Dababis and the Palestinian Theatre reduced or ceased their activities.

To speak of a theater movement in the early years of the 1980s is to reminisce about the years of emergence when Balalin could boast of over a hundred members, hundreds in their friends circle, and thousands of committed audience members. By 1981, the majority of the ensembles that had participated in the 1973 and 1975 festivals no longer existed. The schools and public institutions in the touring circuit that these ensembles had generated stopped accepting reservations, except under unique circumstances and due to established relationships. Between 1981 and 1984, El-Hakawati and George Ibrahim successfully continued their productions by acquiring funding from non-Palestinian sources and gaining access to schools that were controlled by sympathetic leaders. Ensembles composed entirely of West Bank residents boycotted the newly established Israeli administrative structures in the West Bank's military government and the hegemonic West Jerusalem municipality under the Israeli Jerusalem reunification law, but the majority of these ensembles ceased to function because the hostile new facts on the ground drained all their options. Despite the downtrend of production in the theatrical movement, the strategic choices of El-Hakawati and George Ibrahim's production model accelerated the movement's potential and set the stage for a golden production era in the mid-1980s. This chapter focuses entirely on the work of El-Hakawati during these challenging years.

Composed entirely of Palestinian citizens of Israel, Jerusalemites, and international supporters, the star of El-Hakawati continued to rise. Jackie Lubeck and François Abu Salem negotiated the new realities in Jerusalem and Palestine with finesse. Their fellows in the ensemble gathered the necessary support to access Palestinian villages in the Galilee, where the economy had been more stable than in the West Bank. Artistically, following *B'ism Al-Ab*, El-Hakawati had established its rehearsal process and methods for content development under the uncontested leadership of François Abu Salem. He chose the theme, conceptualized the production, and plotted the structure of the script while the team elaborated key concepts in discussions and collectively improvised the scenes in the play. Strategically, the composition of the ensemble fit the political restrictions of the era. Their Israeli, French, and American passports permitted their travel for tours across Europe, which generated cash flow and encouraged the participants to remain in the ensemble. Their connections in Jerusalem and within Palestinian villages and cities in Israel gained them access to present their performances on local tours that proved to be immensely needed in these isolated Palestinian communities and extremely popular due to their commitment to local dialects and entertainment value.

In late 1979, El-Hakawati began rehearsals on *Mahjoub Mahjoub*, which challenged the Palestinian image of heroic characters. In the play, "six characters, in their own spaces on stage and after their own purposes, had been isolated from the world and thus developed their own habits and traditions."[1] The central character in the play, Mahjoub, is a Palestinian antihero who struggles to keep his traditions and nationalistic goals in the face of his desire to survive under occupation. The word *Mahjoub* indicates a person who is covered up, concealed, obscured, or veiled. The title of the play suggests that Mahjoub has been isolated or veiled from reality. Although his naiveté causes him trouble on occasion, he attempts to survive by avoiding conflict. The play begins by introducing each major character in a specific area on stage (figure 8): the bureaucrat Abu Hmayd stamps empty papers; the teacher dreams of creating his own newspaper as he sits behind a makeshift typewriter made of garbage; the merchant Abu Ali cleans his store and shouts for customers to buy cans of goods; Mahjoub cleans a table at his café and attempts to kill flies; Um Mustapha works her land as she reminisces about her home in Jaffa; and the young woman, Lily Asfour, stands on a ladder drawing on a large blackboard. In the opening of the play, the characters intrude on each other by throwing their garbage in each other's working space, thus causing immense disorganization. Meanwhile, a dejected Lily Asfour works diligently to depict "the Palestinian reality" on her blackboard. Breaking the monotony of everyday life, the characters call a meeting to solve the historical problems facing their people. They begin with a ritual election in which Abu Hmayd wins 99 percent of the vote for leadership. To protest the unproductive meeting, Mahjoub decides to die, an action that signals the absurdity of both the meeting and the character of Mahjoub. In the ensuing funeral, the characters place his body in a casket, from

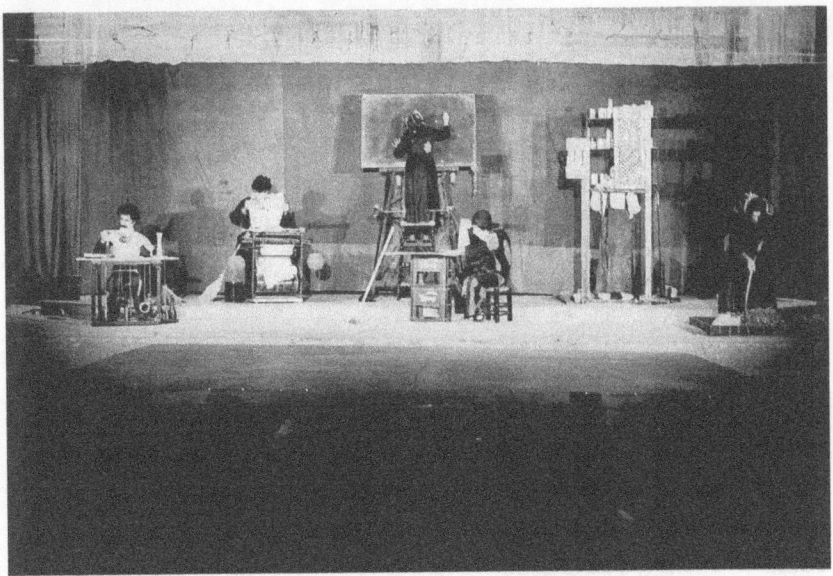

FIGURE 8   A performance of *Mahjoub Mahjoub*. Jerusalem, 1981. Courtesy of François Abu Salem Archive, Palestinian National Theater/El-Hakawati.

which he listens to their account of his personal history. The actor playing Mahjoub, Adnan Tarabsheh, finds his way out of the casket to play in the flashbacks portraying his life story.

In the remainder of the play, each scene depicts Mahjoub's struggle to survive as a Palestinian. Accompanied by the sound of an owl, he is born at midnight on the cursed day of February 29, earning him a birthday once every four years. He also dies on the same date. Because he was dropped on his head as a child, he developed an abnormal gait, with his head swaying sideways to the right. After asking too many questions in school, he argues with his teacher. As a result, he calls his teacher a "donkey" and drops out of school. To sustain his lower-class lifestyle, he attempts to sell water but fails. He also works in his uncle's shop. As a young adult, he demonstrates his love for a girl by unskillfully knitting her a scarf. She accepts his marriage proposal because nobody refuses a request by his patron Im Mustapha, the neighborhood's matriarch. His first struggle against the authorities occurs in Jerusalem before 1967 when he refuses to stand for the Jordanian national anthem. The Jordanian police attempt to arrest him, but like a Tarzan figure, he beats them up to the sounds of admiration from the audience in the cinema. During the 1967 war, Mahjoub cheers the successes of the Arab armies on the radio, only to learn that the Arab victory is an elaborate lie. A few days later, when Israeli soldiers demand his identification in a commuter taxi, none of his fellow Palestinians assist him. Needing sustenance, he works at an Israeli factory but is fired because the police interpret his attire as a depiction of the Palestinian flag. He immigrates to America and works in menial jobs. After he marries an American to obtain a green card, he returns home victorious.

During Jerusalem municipality elections, Mahjoub receives leaflets from various political factions. He joins the Histadrut (General Federation of Laborers in Israel) but leaves when fellow Palestinians call him an apostate and a traitor for participating in Israeli politics. Soon after, based on a condition of employment in the Jerusalem municipality, his friend Abu Hmayd pays him five liras to vote in secret on his behalf. Because he is the only Palestinian in the election site, Israeli television films the event, which would constitute character suicide among the residents of East Jerusalem. With cameras rolling, he pretends to be a janitor, a believable function for an Arab in an Israeli establishment. A series of oppressive events leads Mahjoub to resist the occupation in unusual ways. When he is arrested and imprisoned for attempting to help an activist and then accused of carrying "suspicious packages," he retaliates against this accusation of terrorism and ridicules the police by planting "suspicious" packages throughout the city, which is represented in the production as the audience hall. Toward the end of the play, he meets President Anwar Al-Sadat during Sadat's trip to speak before the Knesset in 1977. They discuss the problem of normalization with Israel and the negative image of the Egyptian president among the Palestinians. When Mahjoub speaks earnestly of the struggles under occupation, Al-Sadat walks away from him, essentially leaving him behind physically and symbolically onstage, presumably heading to the Israeli Knesset for his historical speech. Finally, the cast recalls Mahjoub's feeble attempt to become a police officer, which caused more traffic problems. When the characters complete their overview of Mahjoub's history, he exits the casket, faces their perceptions of his character, and challenges them for their own shortcomings. Together, they decide to resist oppression and exit the metaphorical casket, which represents both the occupation and their own failures. In the last image of the play, the cast leaves Abu Hmayd behind as he carries on his usual pointless drivel in a meeting of that represents the Arab League's ineffective politics.²

In the early 1980s, this production presented a departure for Palestinian cultural production. In a rare depiction, the character of Mahjoub represented the struggles of East Jerusalemites not only with sarcasm and self-criticism but also with indirect satire against occupation. Inspired by timely local issues, the play aimed at challenging the colonial aims of the Israeli government in East Jerusalem. Since 1967, the Israeli government had taken systematic steps to annex the city, occupying it "legally" by extending the sovereignty of the West Jerusalem municipality over the demographically Arab East Jerusalem.³ From the Israeli perspective, this occupation by municipal expansion became a fait accompli by 1980, when the Knesset passed the Jerusalem Law, declaring "undivided" or "reunified" Jerusalem as Israel's capital. The de facto annexation may have functioned administratively at the Israeli state level; however, in the daily lives of the occupied Palestinians, both Christians and Muslims, the new political and bureaucratic realities translated into daily obstacles and questions of self-determination: How would the Palestinians communicate with the Israeli security apparatus? Who collects their taxes and what services do they receive in return? What kind of representation do they vote for in elections, if any? What kind of identity paperwork do they present or honor? How do they preserve their Palestinian/Arab/religious identity in a self-proclaimed exclusive Jewish state? But most importantly, how do they survive a military occupation intent on transforming not only the physical and demographic identity of their city but also the transformation of their legitimate presence as Arab citizens to mere residents of the city?

Mahjoub redefined the character of the typical Palestinian protagonist, which had often been presented as a heroic figure in contemporary poetry and folklore, to an everyman caught between the politics of the Jewish state and the demands of traditional Palestinian society. This naïve post-national antihero strives for normalcy. He yearns to fall in love, get married, start a family, and work peacefully, but he is caught in unusual conditions that force him to behave like an accidental hero. When he fakes his own death, he becomes privy to the interpretations and analyses of his comrades in the struggle. Although his intentions have never been heroic, his people construct a novel posthumous narrative that does not reflect his perception of his own life. In spite of his complex post-national condition, Mahjoub was played with a clearly recognizable Palestinian identity. The production implemented a simplified local Palestinian dialect and common struggles in occupied East Jerusalem. Simultaneously, the narrative situated the character in relation to foreign situations. For example, Mahjoub's journey toward attaining an American green card represents the hopes of a colonized subject to realize the American Dream. His attempt to become a traffic cop shows his desire to earn a living at any cost, even if this employment could be interpreted as collaboration with the occupier's municipality. Thus, this everyman figure becomes a vehicle to represent less of the heroics of armed national resistance and more of the everyday strategies of "making do" in otherwise restrictive and usually unforgiving circumstances.

Local critics responded to the simplicity of the production, which depended primarily on a set composed of chairs, a casket, a table, a writing desk, a ladder, a blackboard, and two platforms in a thrust-stage configuration. In the familiar directorial strategy of *Al-'atma*, Abu Salem staged the events of the present on the main stage and the flashback stories on the second platform. Selective lighting and appropriate accompanying sound effects defined the space for each character. Characters changed costumes throughout the play, which theatrically kept the story moving and created intrigue in the plot development. Jackie Lubeck designed the costumes and wore the most elaborate costume as an American girl, standing tall in a direct allusion to the Statue of Liberty. In overt satire of popular American culture, she carried a torch and wore a costume inspired by the American flag, accessorized with roller skates and large sunglasses. Her darker costumes, primarily in black, gray, and white, differentiate the present-day realities from the colorful dreamy flashbacks in Mahjoub's life. The costume design complements the set in a comprehensive aesthetic demonstrating keen selectivity but careful elaboration in the pieces chosen for the design; thus the audience sees carefully evoked parts of the represented places as a classroom, office, or shop.

On 7 December 1980, based on an application for a performance permit by Jackie Lubeck, the Israeli censorship committee approved the play.[4] In the file is an official's explanatory note indicating that Lubeck provided an English-language summary of the play and suggested that a group of Hebrew University students were to perform it at the YMCA in English. Although the summary describes the events of the play almost verbatim, it intelligently presents a depoliticized text. For example, Mahjoub's retaliation to incessant police searches by placing suspicious packages throughout the theater is described as "Mahjoub has a difficult time throwing out his garbage. In response, he leaves garbage all over town." The play's critique against participating in the West Jerusalem municipal elections is described as "Mahjoub goes to vote and is surprised when he is interviewed by television." Mahjoub's fight against the Jordanian police is described as a fistfight with ushers. His argument over his identity with the Israeli army becomes "he cunningly proves that he is who he is by pointing out his height and the color of his eyes." His interrogation over wearing what resembles the colors of the Palestinian flag becomes "Mahjoub is questioned about the outfit he wears to work one day." Lubeck summarizes the meeting with Al-Sadat as "Mahjoub is flabbergasted when Sadat visits him at work (he worked as a cleaner in a hotel). When Sadat asked him what he can do for him, Mahjoub asks him to get Im Mustafa's wool out of customs." Lubeck's summary also codes the ending of the play by concealing its subtext:

> The play ends with some of the characters demanding a meeting to discuss if Mahjoub is alive or dead, while other characters refuse to join the meeting, and start pulling people out of [their] seats, and asking them to leave the hall.

On stage, the ending inspired revolutionary resistance as the characters provoked the audience to break through the casket of occupation.

Opening in December 1980, the production of *Mahjoub Mahjoub* launched the ensemble to local fame. After opening at the YMCA, the ensemble toured to the villages of the Galilee. In his critical review, Talal Abu Afifeh stated, "The play Mahjoub Mahjoub posed many issues people have lived for many years before or after 1967 under the Israeli occupation. The play showed people's suffering in the street, in school, at work, and at home."[5] However, their successes were short-lived. A few hours before their performance in Nazareth on 16 January 1981, the Nazareth police delivered an order from the Israeli Ministry of the Interior to cease all performances because the ensemble did not adhere to the text of the play. *Al-Itihad* newspaper reported:

The audience of Nazareth, which came to watch the play, transformed the performance into a popular meeting of protest, in which a decision was made confirming that banning the play continues and escalates the policies of suppression in the Occupied Territories, the stalking of male and female students, and political assassinations.[6]

Both the head of the Municipal Cultural Center of Nazareth and theatrical director Riad Massarweh and the former Knesset member and prolific Palestinian author Emile Habibi condemned the ban, expressing anger at the double standards of "Israeli democracy."[7] In his word to the crowd, Habibi stated:

> Actually, the decision to ban the performance surprised us, not because we are naïve, but because we did not realize that the hostility towards democracy had reached this level. To reach the point of banning the performance of a play, a progressive one but still a play, indicates that the deterioration in Israel reached an unimaginable limit.[8]

To appease the crowd's demands for a performance, the ensemble improvised a new scene alluding to the suppression of the censorship. They sat on stage, physically tied to their chairs with their mouths taped shut.[9] Under Habibi's editorship, *Al-Itihad* pronounced that El-Hakawati's alternate scene "served as the funeral of Israeli democracy, which could not handle the play."[10] Without a doubt, El-Hakawati's presence in the city of Nazareth contributed significantly to the spirit of resistance on this fateful night. Since 1948, the city had become a political hub for Palestinian citizens of Israel, also known as the 1948 Palestinians. The Communist Party of Israel, to which the Palestinian political leadership belonged, became the only political platform for Palestinian participation and mobilization at the state level. Furthermore, in the arena of cultural production, resistance poets such as Mahmoud Darwish, Samih Al-Qassim, and Tawfiq Zayyad had produced a model for cultural resistance through their writings in the party's Arabic newspaper *Al-Itihad* and public performances in the Galilee. This model of resistance prompted the cultural critic and West Bank political activist Mohammad (Abu Khaled) Al-Batrawi to declare: "We are all the children of Nazareth," referring to the Nazarenes' assertion of their Palestinian identity during the 1976 Land Day demonstrations.[11] The presence of the Palestinian political and cultural elite at the performance of 16 January 1981 provided the support that both El-Hakawati and their audience needed to resist the orders to close the evening's proceedings. Although the ensemble failed to perform the scheduled play, the series of improvised scenes and speeches of resistance in lieu of the play became a theatrical happening of its own.[12]

A letter dated 6 January 1981 caused the shocking events. Presumably sent by the Ministry of the Interior's censorship office, an official secretly reported on El-Hakawati's performance in the village of Iʿbilin. He analyzed the play in eleven bullet points, each entitled according to the site or his perception of the action in the scene: Checkpoints, Freedom, Colors, House Confiscation, Immigration to the United States, Municipality Elections, Campaign Episode, Coffee Shop, Explosive Materials, Sadat, and Shekels. The description of the production appears sensitive to events concerning issues of oppression, the desire for freedom, the colors of the Palestinian flag, allusions to soldiers and police, satire of security procedures, and all events concerning political matters such as elections and President Anwar Al-Sadat. Although Israel was not explicitly mentioned, this "critic" reported an intention to "disgrace the state." He also noted that the play empowers, incites, and provokes the Arab minority toward hatred and division in the State of Israel through expressions or words, which provoke "uprising." He provides exemplary lines from the play: "Here, forbidden to ask questions" and the radio announcement "We won, we want freedom." After his summary, he states, "In my opinion, there was no justification to give the organizers a permit for this kind of plays."[13]

A series of internal correspondence in the censorship committee suggests that the letter prompted an internal investigation to determine how the ensemble was permitted to perform *Mahjoub Mahjoub*. On 5 January 1981, the responsible committee decided to censor the play, citing a significant difference between the English language summary and the performed text. Believing they were misled by the application, the committee questioned the initial premise that a group of Hebrew University students was going to perform the play at the YMCA. One letter noted that the "secret service agent" who wrote the initial report indicated that the play was full of hatred towards the State of Israel. The events also prompted further investigation of ensemble member Jackie Lubeck and her partner "François Gaspar," who had been reported to be the author of the play. The investigation found an article in *Al-Yassar Al-Arabi* (The Arab Left), in which Abu Salem discusses the theater in Palestine as an integral participant in Palestinian resistance against occupation. Providing an excerpt in Hebrew translation, the investigative report explained that the Beirut-issued weekly magazine was funded by "the terrorist organization of George Habash and Nayef Hawatmeh," referring to the Popular Front for the Liberation of Palestine (PFLP). Based on the article, a member of the council provided his personal opinion that François Gaspar and his wife Jackie, both described as "the motor" behind this company, obtained the permit under false pretenses. By playing in Arab villages, the production realized "the goals of terrorist organizations" that seek "to undermine the existence of the state."[14]

This tangential and inaccurate link between El-Hakawati and the PFLP proved to be a source of concern for the Israeli government and its office of censorship. From the late 1960s until the late 1980s, the PFLP had forced itself on the political scene as a powerful faction that adopted programs of armed, cultural, and social resistance to the occupation. The PFLP spokesperson, novelist Ghassan Kanafani, believed that cultural production was necessary "to understand the land on which the rifles of armed struggle stand."[15] Despite its influential civic engagement in the Palestinian struggle and its declared pan-Arab socialist ideological agenda, the PFLP gained a reputation for being a radical faction after a number of well publicized guerrilla operations, including the hijacking of El-Al, TWA, Pan-Am, and Swissair planes. In Israel and the West, the faction's reputation became synonymous with terrorism, as did that of the PLO (Palestine Liberation Organization), which functioned as the umbrella organization of several Palestinian factions. Meanwhile, some operatives such as the PFLP's Leila Khaled became known as stars of Palestinian resistance, even during their captivity as convicted terrorists. Established connections to the Japanese Red Army and the KGB had made the PFLP and its splinters a significant enemy of the Israeli military apparatus.[16]

In an interview with the PFLP's newspaper, *Al-Hadaf*, François Abu Salem described the implicit connection between theater and armed struggle in the aftermath of Black September, the name given to the battles between Palestinian militias of resistance fighters and the military forces of the Hashemite Kingdom of Jordan:

September of 1970 was the spark that opened up many fields of resistance. When our people felt that armed struggle was struck down in Jordan in 1970, they had to create the conditions to assist resistance in all its forms. The theatrical movement was a facet of resistance, and an affirmation of the Palestinian national character.[17]

Despite the absence of any proven financial or ideological links between the ensemble, the play, and the PFLP, the Israeli censors and their investigators believed theatrical activity posed a dangerous threat. For the censors, to undermine the "existence of the state" suggested an act of treason by a fifth column of Palestinians. Without a doubt, El-Hakawati's critique of the policies of Israel and their open identification with the Palestinian cause of liberation provoked the censors to interpret their commentary in the press to be ideologically directed. In reality, connections between El-Hakawati and the PFLP did not exist in any official capacity beyond their shared goals of affirming the Palestinian identity.

But the allegation of realizing the "goals of terrorist organizations" became an underlying cause to ban *Mahjoub Mahjoub*. According to a Hebrew-language newspaper article in the censorship file, the ensemble requested a "decree nisi" against the censorship decision and provided the council with a Hebrew-language translation of the text for further evaluation.[18] Upon review, a council member determined that the text underwent a special process in order to "look naïve." Noting omitted elements and phrases from the performance in Iʻbilin, the member also questioned the continuity in the dialogue and "illogical leaps" between topics. He summarized the case as a "sophisticated act of fraud" and recommended continued censorship of the play. In a statement dated 26 January 1981, a second member of the council suggested that the full three-hour Arabic language production contained implicit "incitement" and "ridicule" of freedom in Israel and the state's military. He agreed to permit only the Hebrew text, which El-Hakawati had provided as part of their appeal. By the end of January, *Al-Fajr* and the *Jerusalem Post* reported the lifting of the ban and the council's condition for the ensemble to follow the approved text without further changes.[19]

In practice, the censors and the security apparatus could not enforce the restrictions in the permit unless the production was monitored at every performance. The ensemble's improvisational style, coded language, and indirect depiction of local issues presented a difficult interpretational challenge, especially for nonnative informants. El-Hakawati's *Mahjoub Mahjoub* never used any slogans or political symbols. Rather, it represented characters caught in unusually difficult circumstances and their attempts to survive them. This strategic choice not only assured the production's survival under the watchful eye of the censors but also creatively encouraged audiences to root for Mahjoub, the comedic antihero. For example, when Mahjoub is wrongly accused of terrorism, he retaliates by leaving "suspicious packages" in various places in the city. Here, the play ridicules the orientalist stock character of the Arab as terrorist. In addition, the harmless packages represent physical and cultural Palestinian content, which is banned on grounds of "state security." Thus, El-Hakawati satirizes the Israeli censorship's obsessive concerns with Palestinian theater makers, whom the Israeli establishment perceived as propagandists.

With the ban overturned, the ensemble performed the play thirty-six times in twenty-six villages and cities in the West Bank, the Galilee, and the Triangle area.[20] Despite acquiring permission to perform, the ensemble continued to encounter further harassment, suggesting that legal permits did not assure their survival. In various towns, such as Al-Lyd and Majd al-Kroom, they faced interruptions and threats of closure by the police, the secret service, or local municipalities.[21] In the absence of well-equipped theaters, the play often played in the Arabic schools of Palestinian villages in Israel. Recalling this period, actor Edward Muallem noted: "Despite our permit, some school principals received threats. . . . Sometimes they allowed us to play in the school yard, sometimes they didn't."[22] By the end of 1981, they had followed the initial run of the play with a European tour that included sixty-one performances in England, Poland, Belgium, West Germany, Holland, Sweden, Norway, and France.[23] In London, Ned Chaillet of the *Times* reported the uniqueness and purpose of the ensemble: "*Mahjoub, Mahjoub* is a new exception, the work of a Palestinian company called El-Hakawati, a group subject to Israel and Israeli censorship but clearly intent on speaking of that country's occupation of Palestine."[24] The *Jewish Chronicle* reported "a significant police presence outside the theatre."[25] Rosalind Carne of the *Financial Times* explicitly outlined the anxiety underlying the ensemble's presentation of their play in Europe:

> The Riverside Studios, mindful of Jewish backers, has reportedly stated that *Mahjoub Mahjoub* is not anti-Israel. This is bunkum. Nobody mentions the PLO—but their spirit lurks behind the entire production. Mahjoub personifies a population crushed; his two failed attempts to escape from his coffin and his ultimate success can have only one interpretation.[26]

In addition to highlighting the English sensitivity towards the Jewish community, Carne accurately interprets that Mahjoub's attempts to escape the coffin indicate an effort to overcome the imprisonment of the occupation. Accordingly, his ultimate success suggested that the Palestinians liberate their nation. But her clear equation of Palestinian resistance with the Palestine Liberation Organization (PLO) implicitly implied that El-Hakawati functioned as a politically motivated mouthpiece, serving the purposes of the period's leading national representatives, not their own.[27]

Linking El-Hakawati with the PLO placed the ensemble at risk at home and abroad. Especially in this period, the PLO had situated itself as part of a worldwide anti-colonialist movement. In the West, the PLO and its guerrilla army, the Palestine Liberation Army, were synonymous with terrorism. Having taken refuge in Lebanon after the expulsion of Palestinian resistance from Jordan during Black September in 1970, the militarized PLO had established itself as a pseudo-state within a state in civil-war-torn Lebanon. In 1982, Israel named the PLO presence as the pretext for invading Lebanon. Carne's statement that the PLO spirit "lurks behind the entire production" placed El-Hakawati in the context of militarized resistance, contradicting the ensemble's declared intention to present the Palestinian condition and everyday struggles, albeit satirically. Although interviews with members of El-Hakawati suggest that leaders in the PLO were aware of their activities at home and abroad, the ensemble insisted on maintaining financial and political independence during the period of their emergence on the scene in the late 1970s and early 1980s.[28]

Since the Palestinians and their political struggle had not been recognized as a legitimate cause in mainstream international news, El-Hakawati's artistic message caused a crisis for Western journalists, who often responded with sympathy and at times with familiar orientalist tropes. For most critics, *Mahjoub Mahjoub* challenged common stereotypes by presenting the life journey of a defenseless man and performing the everyday struggles of Palestinians under occupation. *City Limits* captioned one photograph "From Jerusalem come the Palestinians of El-Hakawati in Mahjoub Mahjoub," a then radically positive equation of Palestine, Palestinians, and the city of Jerusalem. Positively reviewing the play, Jonathan Keates of *The Guardian* touted the ensemble's performance as vigorous and "sinisterly charming." He wrote: "Put together by the 10 actors, the play blends circus, fable and polemic in the archetypal story of plucky scapegrace Mahjoub giving two fingers to the brass hats, bureaucrats and demagogues before going under."[29] On this tour, El-Hakawati delivered an inspiring positive image of the Palestinian people. They were oppressed but peaceful, poor but creative, and most significantly, occupied but alive.

But underneath the positive reviews, an orientalist subtext positioned El-Hakawati as an exotic foreign presence on the European stage. The majority of the European press insisted on presenting the ensemble not only as accomplished artists with a just cause but also as Arabs arriving from a violent "Orient." Stereotypical framing devices of Islam and the Arab world pervade the European coverage of the ensemble. For example, Ned Chaillet framed his review with the following statement: "Islam is no respecter of the theatrical form. Form in general is unwelcome if it is an artistic representation, particularly where the human form is concerned."[30] A month before El-Hakawati's arrival, the *Jewish Chronicle* published a preview article entitled "Anti-Israel Play Comes to London," a preemptive misrepresentation of the play and the ensemble.[31] In some instances, local papers reached absurd levels of Orientalism. For example, The *Brentford & Chiswick Times* referred to Mahjoub and Im Mustapha as "Widow Twankey and her lazy son Aladdin."[32] The paper further reported: "Drama critics and their friends were being frisked by a muscular heavy at the door of Riverside Studios before being allowed inside," which emphasized the unusual presence of Palestinian Arabs and set up reports of "threats from someone who presumably wanted to stop the show."[33] On the week of the performance, the title of a short announcement in the *Jewish Chronicle*, "Arab Actors in London," accentuated the identity of the ensemble over the content of the production.[34] These articles emphasized El-Hakawati as the "Other," using the stock orientalist framework of Islam as an anti-theatrical religion, the presence of extremists in London, and being "Arab" as a natural enemy of Jews. Taking its cue from the *Jerusalem Post*, the *Jewish Chronicle* reported that the Israeli censorship board passed the play, thus implying that Israel was a mature democracy, while simultaneously suggesting that the play was anti-Semitic. Deeply influenced by an orientalist lens, these articles heightened El-Hakawati's foreignness at the expense of the ensemble's adoption of familiar theatrical tropes and techniques.

Perhaps the Montpellier, France, newspaper *Midi-Libre* best reported the physical and verbal violence against El-Hakawati during the European tour. It reported the overnight systematic erasure of the word *Palestinian* from El-Hakawati's posters, the breaking of the windows and door of their truck, and the breaking of the door of their accommodations at a local school. In the morning of their performance, an "unknown" urinated on the ensemble's flyers, which were on a table at the entrance of the T.Q.M. (Théâtre Quotidien de Montpellier). Strangely, although the contents of the truck were dumped, nothing was stolen. In closing, the unnamed writer of the article exclaimed at the level of intolerance toward Palestinians in Montpellier, suggesting that such actions were a stark reminder of humiliation under military occupation in Palestine.[35]

The *Mahjoub Mahjoub* spirit of survival on and off stage at home and abroad solidified El-Hakawati's position as Palestine's leading theater company in the 1980s.[36] The banning of the performance in Nazareth and the ensuing censorship battle increased the ensemble's popularity among Palestinian audiences and forced the Israeli news media and theatrical institutions to take notice of Palestine's cultural scene. For example, on 22 February 1983, El-Hakawati performed the play in Tel Aviv in a performance coordinated by the Birzeit Solidarity Committee and the leftist Israeli theater Tzavta. The Arabic press referred to the event as the first occasion of a Palestinian theatrical ensemble performing "directly in front of the Israeli audiences."[37] The event presented the ensemble with an unavoidable political question: Should Jerusalemites perform before their occupiers? For El-Hakawati, their mission comprised an educational dimension of "introducing this audience to the truth of Palestinian civilization and culture as comparable to other sophisticated civilizations."[38] At the time, the ensemble saw the Tel Aviv performance as an act of resistance, rather than an act of normalization. After the failure of the Oslo peace process, in the aftermath of the second Intifada, and under present conditions in the early twenty-first century, if a company of the stature of El-Hakawati were to perform in Tel Aviv as part of an Israeli festival, their performance would be attacked as an act of treason.

Building on their local and international successes, El-Hakawati significantly increased the number of their productions and repertoire from 1982 to 1984. They created two new original plays: *Alf Leyleh y Leyleh Min Layali Rami Al-Hijara (The One Thousand and One Nights of a Stone Thrower)* and *Jalili Ya Ali (Ali the Galilean)*. In the first play, also known as *One Thousand and One Nights in the Meat Market*, the ensemble represented the increasing occurrences of kids throwing stones at the Israeli military in the early 1980s. By the 1987 Intifada, this phenomenon had become the quintessential mode of Palestinian resistance to the occupation. The play begins with a satire on the classic folk tales of *The Arabian Nights*. In an unusual military-themed fantasy, actor Radi Shehadeh portrayed King Shahrayar as the violent military governor, who builds his throne on top of a local village and robs the indigenous population of their sovereignty. His Scheherazade is represented as the wise lady of the village, the older Im Mustapha, who attempts to protect her grandson, the young stone-thrower Nassour. As neon lights spell out the word *Shalom* in the opening of the play, the military governor steals the magic lamp from Nassour and takes the throne, entrenching his reign of terror upon the village.[39] Nassour retaliates by throwing a stone at the military governor's forehead, setting in motion a David-versus-Goliath chronicle.[40] The governor orders a curfew to shut down the whole village and demands the arrest and punishment of little Nassour. Will the mighty military find the young stone-thrower? Im Mustapha tells fantastical stories to distract the governor from his manhunt. Finally, when the youth is caught, the governor sentences him to death. In a satirical representation of an action hero, Nassour's grandfather, riding an Arabian horse, saves him from execution at the last possible moment. The epic story takes on the qualities of a fantastical Hollywood action flick while aesthetically adopting the most common tropes of orientalism in the form of a sacred old city that resembles Jerusalem, a palace, horses, knights, kings, magic lamps, and experienced storytellers.

Invited by the French director Jérôme Savary, co-produced with Le Grande Magic Circus, and supported by the artistic director of Théâtre de l'Olivier, Jean-Pierre Comis, the ensemble rehearsed in the spring of 1982 at l'Olivier in Istres, France.[41] Based on the objection of the mayor of Montpellier, Georges Frêche, El-Hakawati was refused permission to play in the festival Rencontres Nord/Sud de la culture that summer. According to journalist Philippe Dauma, less than a year before the Montpellier municipal elections, Frêche and other notables considered the word *Palestinian* to be politically damaging.[42] This rejection of El-Hakawati's identity calls to mind the Nancy Festival's withdrawal of the invitation to present *B'ism Al-Ab* in 1977 and the subsequent challenges that the company experienced in their European tour of *Mahjoub Mahjoub* only two years earlier. It also foreshadows the withdrawal of the invitation to present their work at the Public Theater in New York in 1989, a pattern of censorship that the ensemble battled throughout their existence. In the case of *One Thousand and One Nights of a Stone Thrower*, the patronage of Jérôme Savary successfully altered the balance of power, fending off the objections on the grounds that the performance was humanistic, not propagandistic in its approach. Dauma credited Savary for his militant support of El-Hakawati given the hostile conditions and anti-Palestinian sentiments that the ensemble's presence generated in Istre and neighboring villages. Despite Savary's commitment, the exclusion from the festival after rehearsals and the production process had begun forced a new agreement between Savary and El-Hakawati. The production would open earlier than planned and it would have a single performance before heading to Denmark for several performances in Copenhagen's Festival of Fools.

When the play opened on 11 June 1982, it was not ready for performance. According to several members of the ensemble, Abu Salem's conceptual production required immense technical resources that overwhelmed the ensemble, affecting the storytelling and construction of the play. The memories of the actors resemble those of the Balalin ensemble's recollections of the disjointed *Weather Forecast*, when audiences and performers could not fully understand Abu Salem's obtuse symbolism and the excessive use of sound and lighting cues, combined with insufficient time to explore them during rehearsals. This shared sentiment of audiences, critics, and performers followed the play on its tour after its incomplete run in Istres, despite bright spots that occurred as the play began to find its feet over the course of its performances in Denmark.[43] According to Adnan Tarabsheh, the addition of new cast members for this large cast production played a significant role in creating an unsatisfactory premiere. Years later, in his biography, he questioned the value of producing large-scale productions outside of Palestine and hiring performers who did not have the commitments of the core members of El-Hakawati.[44] Radi Shehadeh described the opening as a three-hour nightmare of a two-and-a-half-hour performance that was plagued by poor transitions and technical challenges.[45]

In its preview of the production, the Copenhagen newspaper *Kristeligt Dagblad* echoed the modern European orientalist trends of the period and confirmed the narrative that El-Hakawati was overtly and unapologetically attacked for its Palestinian identity. The preview opened with the following statement: "When the word 'Palestinians' is mentioned, most Danes see in their mind's eye either a long-bearded terrorist or a ragged pitiful, brown-eyed child." The article goes on to explain how the complexity of the symbolism can only be matched by the realities that Palestinians experience under occupation, including censorship and the need for the military governor's approval to perform in the West Bank. By contrast, a drastically less sympathetic article blamed the production's failures—the absence of a central narrative and the overreliance on visual elements—on the lack of an Arab theatrical tradition.[46] Reporting on the success of the tour and the complexity of the production, Jerusalem's literary monthly magazine *Al-Fajr* conveyed the assessment of the play by the Danish daily newspaper *Politiken* as "an inaccessible play about the most accessible of all dreams: the dream of throwing off the saddle and becoming master of one's own country."[47] Despite the success of the Danish performances and audience appreciation of the production's sophisticated visual amalgam of orientalism and harsh reality of the occupation, reviewers nearly unanimously expressed some confusion at the mix of genres and styles, which included circus, musical theater, tragicomedy, Brechtian alienation, and popular folk culture. Most reviewers singled out the clash of cultures in the pastiche of authentic Palestinian heritage, European experimental avant-garde, and satirical orientalist fantasy.[48]

On 20 July 1982, El-Hakawati's lawyer Jonathan Kuttab requested permission from the Ministry of the Interior to perform the play. Using *One Thousand and One Nights in the Meat Market* as the primary title, Kuttab sent in a thirty-six-page handwritten script that resembles the final script. Although the final production ran for two-and-a-half hours, this shorter underdeveloped censorship copy depicted a class struggle between the people of the village and a nondescript lord or governor who buys weapons and maintains his own security forces. This handwritten copy of the script reduces the significance of key scenes in the production, including the stone-thrower conflict, the stealing of the magic lamp, the establishment of a foreign power overseeing the village, the political satire in the imitation of Egyptian film acting style, and the ruthless self-critique in the representation of the Arab hero. Given El-Hakawati's history with the authorities in *Mahjoub Mahjoub*, the internal evaluation indicated the censors' awareness of the play's potential to cause agitation. In one censor's opinion, some isolated incidents emphasized nationalism and the need to maintain high morale, but stylistically, the playwright failed to adapt the classic folktales to contemporary events. Failing to foresee El-Hakawati's forthcoming local tour and the intent to perform the play before large audiences, he cited his opinion that the play would not be performed "more than once" and thus recommended granting the permit.[49] According to El-Hakawati, the military censorship authorities did not respond to a parallel application for permission to perform in the West Bank.[50]

Upon their return home, the ensemble decided to perform the play in large open-air venues because the set was too large for most existing stages in Palestine. In Jerusalem, the play was scheduled to run at the outdoor terrain of the Ahly Club in Wadi Al-Joz neighborhood on 24-26 September 1982, the secondary school auditorium in Sakhnin on 15-17 October 1982, the Gan Eden cinema in Acre on 9-10 December 1982, as well as in the Triangle area and Nazareth.[51] In reviewing the performance in Acre, the *Jerusalem Post*'s Edward Grossman provided a full picture of how the Israeli leftist public may have regarded El-Hakawati in the early 1980s. His article, in some ways very similar to how European journalists covered El-Hakawati, begins with François Abu Salem as the only leading figure of the ensemble. Grossman shows a liberal Zionist sensibility by acknowledging the legitimacy of the Palestinian struggle and the psychological effects of the destruction of the PLO's resources in Lebanon in 1982. In his accurate reading of the audience response, he questions whether the play's imaginative aesthetics and optimism could lift the spirits of the Palestinians during a particularly traumatizing and

FIGURE 9 A performance of *Alf Leyleh w Leyleh* (*A Thousand and One Nights of a Stone Thrower*). Jerusalem, 1984. Courtesy of François Abu Salem Archive, Palestinian National Theater/El-Hakawati.

hopeless period, describing their repeated disappointments as a result of the continuing failures of the Palestinian armed struggle.[52]

The One Thousand and One Nights of a Stone Thrower developed into a beautifully staged epic saga and a crowd-pleaser after its initial setbacks, but it continued its controversial record (figure 9). *Al-Fajr Al-Adabi* published two reviews of its Palestinian tour that demonstrate its polarising effect on critics.[53] Ghassan Abdallah rejected the "humiliating" characterization of Arabs and Palestinians as playing games as the Israeli expansion in Palestine grew. According to Abdallah, El-Hakawati misused Palestinian cultural heritage, representing Palestinian women as water-bucket carriers in contrast to the modern representation of Jewish women. The play misrepresented national figures as mere talkers and sucking on baby pacifiers. The young men voluntarily leave Palestine; the occupiers perform above the Palestinians on the second level of the set; actors perform Palestinians as exaggerated clowns; and the story line blames the victims for their suffering. Abdallah concludes that committed Palestinian theater must frankly show Palestinians' suffering, and even when portraying their failures, it must show their successes. By contrast, a review by Rustom Dawood presented El-Hakawati's narrative of the Palestinian matriarch as the resistant Scheherazade figure, who potentially sacrifices herself to save her grandson; the governor as a foreign overmilitarized fascist; the saga of the colonized outsmarting the colonizer; and the stone-thrower becoming a symbol of resistance. To this reviewer, the production's complexity, employing a locally modified orientalist aesthetic inspires a culture of self-reflection, collaboration, and faith in the relationships of Palestinians in their neighborhoods and families. Philosophically and discursively, the core of the argument between the two reviewers hinged on contemporary visions of the function of theater. One sought national affirmation, realism, and constructive capacity-building from within. The other sought self-liberation, struggle against the occupation, and complexity beyond everyday life. This debate between El-Hakawati's aesthetic and discursive layering of the Palestinian condition versus the expressed immediate national needs of the audience, against a backdrop of an intensely strengthening Israeli state, would continue until the eventual breakup, or perhaps dismantling, of the ensemble.

From 1981 to 1984, these years of incredible growth and development of El-Hakawati culminated with *Ali the Galilean*, which expands the ensemble's repertoire into a new experimental aesthetic and a deeply personal subject matter, the Palestinian citizens of Israel. In the play, a traditional father from the Galilee disowns his young son, who runs away to Tel Aviv. Once in the big city, Ali must interact directly with Jewish Israelis. At a bar, a Jewish patron teaches Ali to call himself by the Hebrew name Eli. The bartender instructs him to order alcohol, rather than tea with mint leaves. He falls in love with the Jewish Tel-Avivian Eliza, humorously mispronounced 'aleeza. Launched in a sexually adventurous moment in a park, their relationship becomes the foundation of his newly established life in Tel Aviv as a non-Palestinian. After performing menial jobs, he becomes a rising star as the operator of a falafel kiosk. When his Arab identity is discovered, he becomes a fugitive, fights for his life, and gets arrested by the Israeli police. He is then tortured in a mental institution (figure 10). In the final moment of the play, a psychiatrist fails to perform his state-delegated responsibility to erase Ali's identity. Instead, a bomb explodes, destroying the whole establishment.

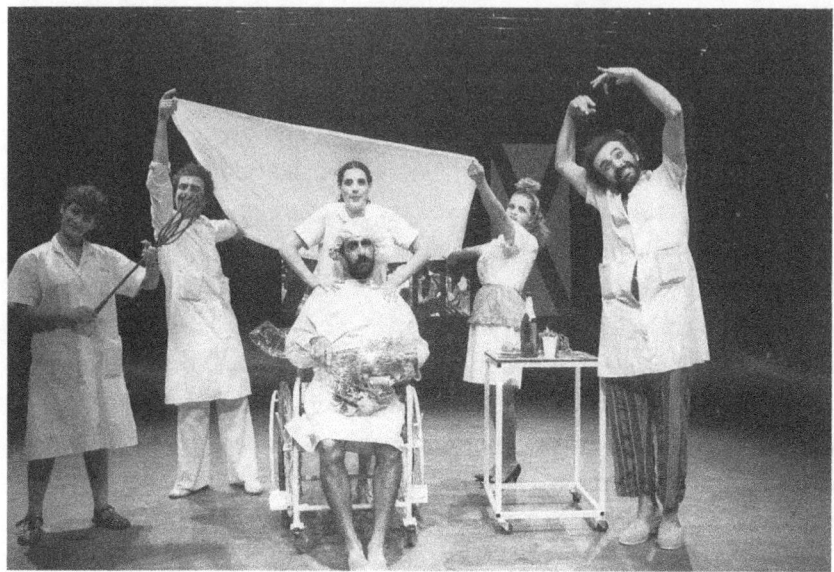

FIGURE 10 A performance of *Ali the Galilean*. Jerusalem, 1982. Courtesy of François Abu Salem Archive, Palestinian National Theater/El-Hakawati.

Similar to the story of the Jerusalemite Mahjoub, *Ali the Galilean* presents a character study of a Palestinian antihero figure. Performed as a series of snapshots closely following his life chronology, the play narrates and analyzes the daily struggles of a Palestinian citizen of Israel who attempts to deny his heritage in order to fit into a hegemonic Jewish-Israeli culture. El-Hakawati's choice to address the Palestinian condition within Israel emerged from discussions within the ensemble, many of whom had held Israeli citizenship since its earliest formation in 1977. The firsthand experience of Edward Muallem, Adnan Tarabsheh, Mohammad Mahamid, Ibrahim Khalayleh, and Radi Shehadeh lent credence to the narration and embodiment of Ali as he attempted to escape the orthodoxies of his village and concurrently failed to integrate into Jewish society. Ali finds success only by adapting his name to Jewish culture, hiding his identity, and selling falafel. When exposed as an "Arab," his Palestinian identity costs him his business, relationship, security, mental health, and freedom. His bitter end at a psychiatric facility echoes the ending of the ensemble's first play, *In The Name of the Father, the Mother and the Son*, in which a state-sponsored establishment attempts to solve the Palestinian demographic growth "problem" by performing an undisclosed surgical operation on the main female character. In *B'ism Al-Ab*, Kharsa revolts against the oppressive state and familial patriarchy. In Ali's case, the doctor refuses to complete the experiment, causing a destructive explosion in the process.

By the time El-Hakawati produced *Ali the Galilean*, Abu Salem had established a production formula that guided the improvisational process and the theatrical event. Similar to all the previous productions, a framing device held the story together, and an overlaid aesthetic conceptualized the visual representation. Whereas the frame story of *One Thousand and One Nights* guided the audience's attention in the *Stone Thrower*, Mahjoub listening to his own story from a casket after his pretended death, and a Palestinian family struggling to survive the circus of life in *B'ism Al-Ab*, the framing device of *Ali the Galilean* is a celebratory festival in honor of Ali, the liberated Palestinian hero. Local theater ensembles represent Ali's story as part of the celebration. The overlaid aesthetic of the production is governed by the style of each theater ensemble participating in the festival. The forefather's company opens with the historical scene of Ali's conflict with his family over inheritance and his subsequent departure. Then the following styles ensue: a children's television episode, murder mystery, cowboy western, romantic comedy, mime, melodrama, Egyptian comedy, and the sloganeering style of the "We Won't Kneel" theater ensemble. Each ensemble performs a unique episode in Ali's life while he watches, extremely dissatisfied by the artistic and political failures in each representation.

On 1 June 1983, Abu Salem applied for a performance permit. Dated 2 June 1983, the internal censorship correspondence and evaluation forms indicate a repeated concern that the script left much leeway for improvisation. Although the script did not offend the evaluators, they were alarmed by open-ended moments such as the MC's improvised interactions with the actors and audiences. For example, early in the play the MC states: "We hope, dear audience, that you understood the mystery of the theatrical movement without talking or explanation," suggesting that choreography played a more significant role than the text. On 8 July 1983, in their final approval of the play, the council objected to the absence of a final script but approved a production that would not stray far from the submitted version. An official letter to the ensemble warned that the council could invoke section 3 of article 4 of the censorship law, which indicates that any additions to an approved performance may nullify the permit.[54] To mount the production in the West Bank, the ensemble applied for permission to perform from the military government. In the process, they supplied the occupation authorities with the text of the play, a videotape recording of the production, and a schedule of performances. After an eighteen-month delay, "the ensemble decided to confront the de facto ban by scheduling a West Bank performance." Taking advantage of the presence of a French television crew, El-Hakawati members prepared a performance at the Jericho Cinema while the ensemble's lawyers pressured the Jericho military governor and the Israeli military government headquarters in Beit El to provide final approval. One hour before the performance, "the permission was finally given verbally by the legal advisor to the military governor in Beit El and relayed to the theatre ensemble's lawyer."[55] The press and several company members reported that the governor presented the one-performance permit in person. Ensemble member Jackie Lubeck remembered the military governor's objection: "We prefer bombs to your intellectual theater-making because we know how to deal with bombs."[56] According to *Al-Fajr* newspaper, the presence of the foreign television crew may have facilitated the process of obtaining this permit.[57]

The play opened at Abrahamic College of Jerusalem on 12 September 1983. Despite the immense popularity of the play with Palestinian audiences, the production caused the kind of controversy that El-Hakawati frequently generated. The critic Ghassan Abdallah continued his unwavering negative criticism, interpreting the celebration framework of the play as a hate-fest against local theater companies. In his view, the play's theatricalization of the original short story by Sharif Kanaaneh fell short and misrepresented the original. Effectively, Abdallah implied that the production served to humiliate the Palestinian spirit with lowbrow language unfit for the stage, exaggerated representations of the flaws of Palestinian society, a nihilistic depiction of Palestinian politics, avoidance of religious persecution against Palestinian citizens in Israel, and sarcastic vignettes against the leaders of national resistance. His review criticized El-Hakawati's portrayal of the Palestinian as sexually repressed, alienated from his identity, naïve, lost, and unhinged. He was also competing with the West in unproductive activities such as drinking alcohol. Comparing the production to Kanaaneh's much-loved and educational original short story, Abdallah found the production manipulative and fundamentally misguided. Antoine Shalhat agreed but with a much less aggressive critique. Shalhat suggested that *Ali* failed to satisfy his literary and political sensibilities in its representation of the struggle of Arab workers within Israel. His main critique suggested that El-Hakawati's improvised play failed to meet the standards expected by Arab audiences: a robust text and a clear lesson at its core. Offended by El-Hakawati's consistent disregard of local norms for sexual representation on stage and frequent use of lowbrow language, Moatassem Sundouqah wrote that even European societies would be embarrassed by some scenes in the play.[58]

Numerous positive reviews and plentiful audiences across Palestine countered the well-written negative reviews, creating a vibrant discussion in the local press. Based on El-Hakawati's tour in the villages of the Triangle, Sakhnin, Arrabah, Majd Al-Kroom, Kabul, Deir Al-Assad, and Kufr Yassif throughout August 1983 and several refugee camps in the Jerusalem-Ramallah-Bethlehem area in December of the same year, the overwhelming critical and popular response to the production suggests that audiences appreciated and understood the satirical performance, text, aesthetic, and story line and left *Ali the Galilean* with a critical perspective on their role as Palestinians under occupation and within Israel. They saw Ali as an everyman figure battling for his place within his society and fighting for his rights against colonization and brainwashing. Satirical condemnation of American cowboy films, Israeli depiction of Palestinians as bombers, Palestinian empty sloganeering, and the Egyptian regime's obstructive politics satisfied the audience's hunger for a complex illustration of the Palestinian reality as an abandoned people, unable to fight for their rights and constantly shrinking as the Israeli state expanded. In defense of El-Hakawati, reviewers represented the performance of Ali as a satirical attack on empty rhetoric and poor commercial television shows for adults and children, not as an attack on the performance qualities of local theater ensembles.[59]

When El-Hakawati performed *The One Thousand and One Nights of a Stone Thrower* in Accra, Edward Grossman wrote in the *Jerusalem Post* that El-Hakawati might tour to Jewish-Israeli majority areas to perform for Hebrew-speaking audiences:

If, however, the negotiations end well, and if Abu Salem and his actors, actresses and musicians decided that to invade Tel Aviv or Haifa is worthwhile, Jewish audiences will have a chance to see some theatre which should be seen.[60]

The possibility of a Palestinian ensemble performing in Arabic in front of a Hebrew-speaking audience seemed to be excessively wishful thinking. After all, El-Hakawati and many of the Palestinian ensembles had been prohibited from performing by both the Israeli civil and military censors. Common sense and the atrocious political conditions suggested that even imagining that Palestinians would accept and Israelis would welcome the prospect was a flight of fancy, not an understanding of Palestinian realities. When the Tel Aviv theater Neve Tsedek proposed the presentation of a Palestinian week of artistic events, including theatrical performances, El-Hakawati initially balked at the possibility, but after discussion, the ensemble deemed the performances a continuation of their declared mission of combating the occupation by creating awareness, even if the performances occurred in Tel Aviv.

From 28 June to 3 July 1983, Hebrew speakers seized the opportunity in Tel Aviv during Palestinian Art Week, held for the first time against local odds. At Neve Tsedek's festival, El-Hakawati performed two plays: *The One Thousand and One Nights of a Stone Thrower* on 28-29 of June and the premier of their new play *Jalilee Ya Ali (Ali the Galilean)* on 1-2 July 1983. The festival exhibited a collection of banned books published in the West Bank and the works of visual artists such as Suleiman Mansour and Nabil Anani. It also included lectures by Palestinian writers such as the short story writer Akram Haniya and the journalist Daoud Kuttab, who was then a member of the ensemble. For the performing arts, El-Hakawati performed on four out of six evenings, and al-Bireh youth club presented an evening of *dabkah* dancing.[61] The Israel Broadcast Authority objected to television coverage of El-Hakawati's performance of *One Thousand and One Nights of a Stone Thrower* because "the news report 'provided encouragement to the rocket throwers to continue and increase' their rocket throwing."[62] In Ma'ariv, after his objection to the representation of Palestinians as "David" and the IDF as "Goliath," Briel Strassman panned the festival as an elitist event at the expense of Jewish taxpayers, declaring it shameless.[63]

By contrast, in her review of *One Thousand and One Nights*, Shosh Avigal praised El-Hakawati's skilled ability to adopt myths commonly employed in Jewish theater: David versus Goliath, weak versus strong, and personal strength against military might. Appreciating the deeper political significance of the play, Avigal's review highlighted connections that El-Hakawati sought to depict, including Jackie Lubeck's Genie representing American support of Israel, Gidi's rockets standing in for the IDF's advanced military, and "Holy Land" tours that warn tourists of mixing with Palestinians. Earnest in her assessment, she admitted feeling embarrassed by the accuracy of El-Hakawati's critique of Israeli positionality: "They adopted all our myths." In her reaction to *Jalilee Ya Ali*, she noted audience whispers that El-Hakawati's expensive professional production, full of well-considered theatrical imagery, must have depended on "hostile" funding sources. Her response was "I am not bothered," explaining that Israelis would prefer that Palestinians made theater rather than war. Avigal described Ali's parody of cultural norms depicted on stage as observant of Israeli materialism, Americanization, addiction to television, and superficial liberalism that ignored Palestinian existence. The Palestinian, a younger-brother figure like Cain, "serves us in restaurants and builds us houses in silence, but he sees, hears, and remembers, and not necessarily forgets." Her perceptive review of both plays reveals that El-Hakawati's Tel Aviv performances connected with a segment of the Jewish-Israeli audience on a deeper level, though it is unclear whether this segment constituted an active majority, especially given the equally passionate rejection that their work provoked. It also reveals an innocent "surprise sensibility," an expression of pleasure and shock at the excellence of the Other that can exist only with low expectations and in a privileged bubble.[64]

Michael Handelzalts of *Haaretz* reported about two hundred audience members attended each performance. Describing El-Hakawati as energetic, he clearly laid out the plot and framed story of the play, complimented Abu Salem's technical wizardry with lighting and sound, and appreciated the talent of the performers. His sympathetic review revealed the positive sentiments of the attendees and the perception of some Israeli audiences that seeing a play by El-Hakawati signaled a condemnation of their own state. Although his review focused on aesthetics, Handelzalts suggested that Arabic-language presentations in Tel

Aviv lacked the prestige of performances in European languages, lamenting that awareness of the occupation did not constitute a status symbol among elite theatergoers. He also recognized from the content of the performances that the target audiences of El-Hakawati were not Israelis but Europeans, a fascinating echo of many of the Palestinian critics of El-Hakawati, who had regularly attacked the ensemble for not respecting local sensibilities in their choices of content, language, and style. In fact, contrary to El-Hakawati's intentions, the insightful reviewer marked the play as a Palestinian self-critique rather than an anti-occupation production, maintaining that witnessing the Arabic-language production was a matter of dutiful political awareness.[65]

The Palestinian Art Week events in Tel Aviv occurred long before the advent of the boycott, divestment, and sanctions (BDS) movement and the concerted political efforts of some Arab nations to normalize relations with Israel subsequent to the Oslo Peace Accords (1993). In this era, El-Hakawati's performances in Neve Tsedek played out as a victory in the Arabic press, declaring that "Palestinian arts cause stir in Tel Aviv." A later profile article in the *New York Times* suggested that El-Hakawati's presentations before Israeli audiences constituted a historic breakthrough: its title declared that "Israeli theatergoers applaud Palestinian play."[66] Against the backdrop of their success, the negotiations to present their work to Jewish-Israeli audiences revealed significant differences in opinion within the ensemble. For most, the choice to work for Israeli theaters differed greatly from presenting a Palestinian performance to one's occupier. One constituted subservience, but the other suggested a breakthrough that could elevate the Palestinian cause and manifest progress on the Israeli political front. Although the ensemble chose to pursue the opportunity, the internal differences of perspective within the ensemble left unanswered questions about the future political direction of El-Hakawati.

While El-Hakawati resolved the struggles of performing by resorting to co-production in France, performing in Palestinian villages in the Galilee, and touring their productions throughout Europe, the theater movement, which constituted the vast majority of theater makers in this period, suffered a major setback between 1980 and 1984. With the exception of El-Hakawati's resourceful touring and George Ibrahim's strategic production model, the well-known figures of the 1970s could not maintain their productivity. During these difficult years, the future of Palestinian theater in the Jerusalem/Ramallah area appeared bleak as the pluralism and complexity of the previously manifested theatrical culture dwindled to two key players. Similarly, the status of the Palestinian cause became increasingly unknown with the Israeli invasion of Lebanon, the expulsion of the PLO to Tunis, and the expanding force of the Israeli military in the Occupied Territories. In the absence of a meaningful political, economic, and theatrical horizon, El-Hakawati Ensemble—namely, under the leadership of François Abu Salem—had to reflect on ways to emerge out of an ongoing crisis that only promised to grow more complex. Despite the international and local successes of El-Hakawati, the struggle for performance permits, the battles with censorship, the regular closure of performances, makeshift rehearsal spaces, and consistent legal negotiations with Israeli watchdogs had created a heightened state and an unsustainable existence for the ensemble and the rest of the theatrical movement. With the acceleration of El-Hakawati's growth, an innovative model for theatrical production had to be established, or else.

SEVEN

A MOVEMENT ACTUALIZED, 1984-1986

The Building, the March, and El-Hakawati Era

While on tour in Tunis in 1982, El-Hakawati spoke publicly about their troubles with the Israeli establishment. Like many theater ensembles, they struggled to rehearse, produce, and present their performances in Palestine. From 1980 to 1984, a period that Mohammed El-Thaher referred to as "arid" of theatrical activity, El-Hakawati toured *Mahjoub Mahjoub* in Europe, produced *One Thousand and One Nights* in France, and presented *Ali* and the *Nights* at Neve Tsedek's festival, thus minimizing direct confrontations with Israeli authorities. Accusing the military of terrorizing their audience, they told the Tunisian newspaper *Al-Sabah*: "Israeli Army Patrols attack us at every performance." In addition to their accounts of encounters with the army, the ensemble corroborated often-repeated stories of headmasters being threatened. On the informal prevention of performances, members of El-Hakawati cryptically explained to *Al-Sabah* newspaper that "they used other ways. For example, they pressured hall owners and schools, who used to assist us in finding places for the performances." Reflecting a heightened security atmosphere, the article concluded with El-Hakawati's concerned statement: "There are many theatrical activities, but the current state of affairs does not permit them [the artists] to state that they have theatrical ensembles."[1] Undoubtedly, the two major forces of production during this difficult period were El-Hakawati and George Ibrahim, who explicitly avoided censorship by producing adaptations of published plays from the Arab and international repertoire as well as adaptations of fairy tales. Ibrahim had also been a known quantity to the Israeli authorities because of his previous work on Israeli television and his well-established program of performing children's plays in schools.

El-Hakawati's struggles with performance venues forced the ensemble to consider building a permanent home. Repeated bouts with military censorship over performances in the West Bank, particularly a two-year delay on the permit for *Jalilee Ya Ali*, suggested that a permanent cultural center would attract audiences to Jerusalem, especially for productions banned in the Occupied Territories. El-Hakawati Ensemble had been rehearsing in churches, clubs, universities, colleges, and alternative open spaces for six years. Their growth, increased frequency of production, and the constant threat of elimination necessitated the creation of a theatrical home. The core ensemble had grown, and grown up, which brought about life decisions concerning marriage, children, home ownership, and sustainable careers. For example, Radi and Mounira Shehadeh already had two children, and François and Jackie were married. Adnan Tarabsheh, who left the ensemble in late 1982, was married, and his reasons for departure included a rejection of the emerging institutionalizing of El-Hakawati, family life, and a desire for a different professional direction. Ibrahim Khalayleh considered a career in social work and could have departed entirely. At this crossroads, Abu Salem knew that these serious questions of salaries, income, professional aspirations, and living conditions could potentially end the ensemble. He believed that a theater building would not only keep the ensemble alive but also encourage them to thrive in Palestine and abroad.

The censorship records at the Israel State Archive show very few requests for performance permits from the Jerusalem/Ramallah area in the first three years of the decade; however, the number of applications increased significantly between 1984 and 1987, with the Intifada being an important touchstone signifying a drop in both theatrical productions and permit applications. Newer theater ensembles attempted to mount small productions.

Having grown up in Sheikh Jarah, François Abu Salem imagined the possibility of converting a local cinema into a theater. Next door to the

FIGURE 11   Nuzha-Hakawati building before El-Hakawati took possession. Jerusalem, 1983. Courtesy of François Abu Salem Archive, Palestinian National Theater/El-Hakawati.

American Colony Hotel in a prime real estate area, the Nuzha Cinema stood as a testament to East Jerusalem's heyday as an emerging cultural center (figure 11). Founded in 1950 by Ali Freitekh, the Cinema specialized in Egyptian popular fair and international second-rate hits from India and China. Before 1967, the Nuzha Cinema was considered a second-class theater, ranking below Al-Quds Cinema and Al-Hambra Cinema. When the Hashemite Kingdom of Jordan regulated prices and established censorship, cinema houses were given special attention because they constituted a meaningful outlet for entertainment throughout Arabic-speaking countries. Egyptian films constituted the largest share of Arabic content throughout the twentieth century, and the Nuzha Cinema benefited immensely from their commercial successes. There were thirty-three cinemas in the kingdom. Fourteen of them were in Nablus, Ramallah, Al-Bireh, Bethlehem, Jericho, Jenin, and Jerusalem. Classifications by level of service were assigned to these cinema houses, and fees were regulated in 1956 throughout the kingdom, which included the West Bank. In a 1958 amendment to the regulation, Jerusalem's the Nuzha Cinema was reclassified from a second-class to a third-class house, which marked its declining status.[2]

During the 1967 war of occupation, according to reports by the Jerusalemite artists, the Israeli army targeted the cinema with an artillery shell and caused a destructive fire, rendering it unusable. The owner, Ali Freitekh, repaired it in the early seventies and resumed playing popular films, but he was also known to play lowbrow and erotic movies, not unlike the films played in the smaller cinemas of downtown Amman during the seventies, eighties, and early nineties. The "immoral" content in conservative Jerusalem did not go unnoticed by the religious elite. Complaints increased as teenage boys frequented it to watch a world repertoire of erotic flicks. Artists and non-artists in Jerusalem confirm the coming-of-age experience of witnessing their first erotic film at the Nuzha Cinema. In the mid-1970s, religious fanatics burned it down to the accolades of Jerusalemite high society and the dismay of the owner and his committed audience. Subsequently, the cinema had lain unused and unattended. One could easily jump over the fence to a world of destruction on the one hand and seclusion on the other. Although the owner attempted to utilize the space for various ventures, including a short-lived printing press, this prime real estate transformed into a known location for invisible illegal activities, from hiding drugs to illicit encounters. Technical director Imad Samara (1950–2023) remembered:

> Before El-Hakawati, this place was deserted. At night, you didn't walk near it. . . . It used to be a spot for drug dealers. The majority of the space around the theater was basically a public toilet. It was one of the infested spots in Jerusalem.[3]

The surroundings of the cinema had become notoriously derelict, a questionable site by all means.

According to Edward Muallem, Abu Salem brought ensemble members to this burned-out cinema. Muallem remembered "François's honey-sweetened words" that cajoled the team to dedicate the ensuing six months to transforming the wreckage of the cinema into their future home. The lawyer Jonathan Kuttab, brother of ensemble member Daoud Kuttab, joined the conversation to explicate the legal dimension of the project and potentially institutionalize El-Hakawati, turning it into the first dedicated modern theater in Palestine. Upon entering the space, essentially a post-apocalyptic war zone, the ensemble initially refused to participate in the Herculean task. While the outside had become a public health risk after the Israeli bombing and the fanatics' arson, the inside had become a jungle of destruction: decayed walls, charcoaled fabrics, destroyed ceiling, unfunctional and ruined seats, damaged electric grid, wrecked orchestra, decrepit loge, broken windows, dilapidated sewer system, derelict lobby, and entirely demolished access points. The battered building appeared to have no hope unless an experienced architect with an extremely enormous budget and a large construction company took on the project of repair and renovation. Abu Salem continued to convince the ensemble with the utmost dream-filled charm. Muallem recalled looking at the site in disbelief: "We accepted. Grudgingly!"[4]

In early 1983, François Abu Salem and El-Hakawati began negotiations to transform the infested site into the first dedicated modern multipurpose theater in Palestine. He closed the deal at a rental price of $15,000 (USD) per year for five years, with a discount of $10,000 each year to repay El-Hakawati for their renovation efforts. Before El-Hakawati took possession of the cinema, the owner of the building received an offer from the American organization Here's Life to re-open the cinema. Founded by the evangelical Campus Crusade for Christ, the organization wished to present an around-the-clock screening of the 1979 *Jesus* film, produced by Inspirational Films and the Genesis Project. The missionary project intended the film to play uninterrupted in forty languages. According to Jackie Lubeck, the competition for the Nuzha Cinema raised the rental price dramatically. Here's Life offered an exponentially larger sum for the rental. Francois and his team could not compete at the level of finances, but they could compete as locals, Jerusalemites, and cultural innovators. They called on Jerusalem's social, cultural, and political leaders to facilitate the negotiations with the owner, who eventually caved to the will of the public, the dignitaries of Jerusalem, and El-Hakawati's determination to turn his derelict building into a Palestinian cultural landmark.[5]

On 30 October 1983, El-Hakawati signed a five-year rental agreement for the building. The *Jesus* film distributors found a theater in Bethlehem, hoping to establish their imperial and ironic missionary project of teaching Christianity to Christians. *Al-Fajr* reported that the film opened to an audience of Bethlehem's dignitaries in February 1984. In a bizarrely sardonic turn, the Bethlehemite audience was shown local hospitality by the foreigners: "During the intermission, Arab viewers were given tea, coffee and cookies with a napkin with 'Enjoy It' written on it in Hebrew." Mayor Elias Freij complained that "he was unaware of the literature being used to promote the film before seeing it." A booklet distributed at the screening depicted the film's original poster, which was modified to include the sentences: "israel is a spiritual experience" and "jesus is a life changing experience." The film played four times daily. Bethlehem residents explained they were not against a Christian film depicting the life of Jesus, but they opposed the propaganda surrounding it.[6] Although this mission failed to achieve its goal, it is remembered in the theater movement as the colonial American project that almost cost Jerusalem one of its premier cultural sites and a contemporary landmark of East Jerusalem's Sheikh Jarrah.

Between October 1983 and May 1984, El-Hakawati members labored continuously to transform the space into a world-class theater, as Jackie Lubeck recalled:

> The company stood strong together. We rented the old burned-out shell of the Nuzha Cinema after difficult negotiations. The company of actors became a company of builders, and as people passed by the building site, the most common comment was "impossible. . . ." El-Hakawati Theatre Company hand-built the theater that opened under the name of the Nuzha/El-Hakawati Theatre.[7]

Al-Awdah magazine described the spirit of the improvised construction process:

> Aided by an architect and engineer who donated their time, armed with a "how to build it" book purchased at a local store, and supplied with more than a modest share of wholly unrealistic, wildly optimistic ideas of what is possible, seven professional actors donned scruffy, tattered work clothes, raised axes, shovels, drills, and embarked on a project which any sane man in the street wouldn't attempt for the memory of his departed mother.[8]

Edward Muallem remembered that they lacked construction equipment and experience: "We initially worked with hand tools, hammers, axes, rakes, and wrenches." The ensemble members lived in the same house during the renovation in order to afford this period of unpaid labor, which began with demolishing the existing structures inside the building. In the initial ninety days, according to Muallem, there were occasional moments of support when individuals or organizations would show up for a few hours or a day to help, but throughout the process, the core ensemble worked alone. They were François, Jackie, Edward, Radi, Daoud, and Ibrahim. Fellow travelers included François's mother Francine, Radi's wife Mounira, and François's friend Amer Khalil. One young man from Nablus ran away from his family to live and volunteer with the ensemble during the initial phase, but his mother appeared at the theater one day and forced him to come home. He is remembered by the ensemble for his short-lived but significant contribution for the better part of the first phase of the process.

Within two months of beginning the project, the company had gutted the old building, turning it into a shell (figure 12). This phase required hauling all the building's contents outside and saving reusable materials for their future El-Hakawati Theatre. Then they methodically proceeded

FIGURE 12 The main stage area of El-Hakawati Theatre after the ensemble gutted the interior, in preparation for building the auditorium and the stage. Jerusalem, 1984. Courtesy of François Abu Salem Archive, Palestinian National Theater/El-Hakawati.

to even out the slated audience floor by digging as far as two meters into the ground. They intended to divide the audience hall. In the main theater, the loge area would continue to the ground, creating a four-hundred-seat raked auditorium. Underneath the auditorium, they would build a small exhibition and rehearsal space. But reality struck and crashed their dreams when the ensemble ran out of money. They had been working manually, using common household tools, until the work ceased entirely in February 1984 because they lost confidence in their ability to fund the more significant portion of the project: the actual construction inside the gutted shell. Muallem recalled: "It was as if a working motor suddenly shut off." Under the threat of declaring their dream a failure and walking away from the Nuzha Cinema, François and Jackie began contacting funding organizations in the United States and Europe; meanwhile, local dignitaries were informed of El-Hakawati's inability to continue the project.

Abu Salem traveled to Switzerland to meet the Welfare Foundation's leaders, who responded with an emergency grant that allowed them to resume. Amal El-Nashashibi successfully acquired individual donations from Palestinian dignitaries in Jerusalem, Gaza, Ramallah, and Nablus. Once the inside structure of the building and the stage were constructed, businessman Thafer Al-Masri loaned El-Hakawati the funds to buy all the theatrical equipment for production. When treasurer Edward Muallem contacted him after the opening to begin a repayment plan, Al-Masri forgave El-Hakawati for the loan. Often these donations arrived in cash that was immediately used for purchases and contracting. Jackie Lubeck installed a desk with a typewriter in the lobby and became the company's fundraiser, sending hundreds of applications and letters to international foundations and supporters. Her application to the Ford Foundation led to a grant of $100,000 (USD) for El-Hakawati Ensemble's operations and programming, which became the seed grant of the theater and the largest single performance grant in the history of Palestine until that date. As the ensemble's treasurer, Muallem remembered that these emerging streams of local and international funding allowed them to hire construction professionals to take the project to the next level: blacksmiths, masons, electricians, and plumbers.[9]

With trickling funding and hired professional contractors came the equipment: scaffolding, lift, loader, truck, hauler, cement mixer, compactor, and electric jackhammer. Even with these construction professionals,

El-Hakawati could not afford to hire sufficient laborers, so the ensemble became construction workers, learning on the job. They discovered that the ceiling contained asbestos and holes from years of neglect and poor repairs following the 1967 artillery attack. François and Edward began the ceiling repair, eventually joined by technician Imad Samara, who left his day job as a lathe operator and machinist to work on the project full-time. To install a new wooden ceiling inside the theater, Edward and Imad worked daily for two months, up in the air on the scaffolding from morning till night. Contractor Mubarak Awad, a relative of ensemble member Daoud Kuttab, volunteered to repair the roof, plugging the holes to assure safety. After an acoustic evaluation deemed the space unfit for theatrical performance, they installed new acoustic boards throughout the walls and the ceiling over a period of several weeks before the May 1984 opening.

The details of the demolishing and constructing of El-Hakawati's home boggle the mind, deserving of their own long-form study, especially concerning the individual contributions of each ensemble member, but clearly, the themes of the operation were the hope for a better quality of life and for self-determination under an occupation that denies both. The building was entirely redesigned to include a costume shop, a carpentry workshop, a box office, dressing rooms, an entirely new electric system, and an inviting lobby with a traditional café. They installed the new raked auditorium and a stage with a "working floor," a theatrical name for a flexible wooden stage that allows designers to fasten freestanding sets and protects performers' bodies from the hardness of a concrete floor. El-Hakawati also equipped their new theater with the latest audio and lighting equipment. Although the ensemble members performed nearly all the renovation, working alone 90 percent of the time, they acquired support from some community volunteers on occasions that necessitated massive numbers of workers, particularly toward the final stages of completion.[10]

The core vision for this performance venue belonged to François Abu Salem, who managed the improvisational process like an extended backbreaking rehearsal, but two principal streams of input supported the team as they moved forward. First, the members of the ensemble had toured their plays to Tunis and many European festivals. Having experienced challenges of performing internationally and locally, they had acquired a superb sense of performance architecture and the needs of actors on stage. Their input played a meaningful role in identifying the crucial internal architecture that led to El-Hakawati Theatre's aesthetic and practicality. Second, a local architect, Yousef Sabbagh, consulted on the project and provided support and expertise for the design of the new auditorium, backspace, and carpentry shop. Renovation ideas flowed from various sources according to their experience. Francine Gáspár's visual art background in ceramics led to the choice of local tiles, some of which were saved from the original cinema. Jackie Lubeck's design artistry influenced the construction and scheme of the costume shop. Imad Samara and Imad Mitwalli, who became resident technicians, designed the storage, electric grid, and final layout of the carpentry shop with the help of Abu Salem and Muallem. Wasif Dandis, who once acted in *Mahjoob Mahjoob*, donated his time as a carpenter to install the stage floor in the backspace under the auditorium. The combination of incoming expertise, ensemble needs, spatial necessities, financial constraints, and improvisational flexibility led to a locally specific architectural design that still remains in use.

On 9 May 1984, the Nuzha Hakawati Theatre opened its doors to the public, effectively establishing a home for El-Hakawati as its founding resident company (figure 13). The *Jerusalem Post* described the new theater as a "place for raising consciousness," after a quote by the ensemble's lawyer Jonathan Kuttab, who saw the new center as an "encouraging sign in the midst of trouble."[11] The festive opening celebrations included a Bedouin tent experience by Al-Farafir theater ensemble; an exhibition of artworks by Kamal Boulata; and *Clowns*, a play by the Friends Girls School drama group. El-Hakawati presented an original choreographed sketch, depicting the story of the building's acquisition and their competition with the *Jesus* film as a Palestinian wedding joining El-Hakawati as the groom with a Palestinian girl named Nuzha in marriage. *Al-Fajr* reported:

> Actors, dancers, and scouts posing as a groom marched to a stand where another actor was posing as the bride's father (the theatre owner) and asked for the hand of his daughter, Nuzha. The request was granted only to be interrupted by a rich American who tried to bribe the father.[12]

After a battle between the local artist and the wealthy foreigner, the story ended with a traditional celebratory *dabkah* dance that included

FIGURE 13 The lobby of El-Hakawati Theatre at the time of its opening. Jerusalem, 1984. Courtesy of François Abu Salem Archive, Palestinian National Theater/El-Hakawati.

the spectators and the celebrating local theater community. The weeklong celebration also included an evening of poetry by the leading resistance poet Samih Al-Qassem. Starting on 10 May 1984, El-Hakawati presented a remount of its production *One Thousand and One Nights of a Stone Thrower*, an aptly chosen spectacle demonstrating the technical capacities of the theater.[13]

Inside the theater, the two most anticipated events of the opening were the performance of *One Thousand and One Nights* by El-Hakawati and a musical concert by Mustapha Al-Kurd, who had been in exile since his arrest after the opening of Sundouq Al-'ajab's *Lamma Injanina* (*When We Went Crazy*). Al-Kurd had been a mainstay of the Palestinian cultural scene in the late sixties and early seventies. He had gone on an eight-year journey through Lebanon and eventually to Germany. From his new home base in Europe, he performed concerts for Arab audiences abroad, singing a combination of his own classic resistance songs and newer songs from the Muslim Sufi tradition and the Palestinian resistance poetry canon. He often described his exile as a musician's dream and nightmare, carrying his oud on his back and performing for the Palestinian cause. But his connection to François Abu Salem had never ceased, emerging dynamically when he joined El-Hakawati at Istres to compose the music for the *Nights*. Abu Salem convinced Al-Kurd to attempt a return home for the theater's opening. Al-Kurd arrived at Ben Gurion airport on May 3, only to find that his oud had disappeared in transit. His arrival had alarmed the Israeli authorities because of his previous arrest and administrative imprisonment under the generic cause of being a "security risk." After a search, his oud was released from the lost-and-found office, but it had been broken. With the assistance of the Israeli lawyer Leah Tsemel, Al-Kurd returned to his beloved city and regained his status as a Jerusalem resident. According to Al-Kurd, the broken oud portrayed a clear message by the authorities that he was being observed.

At El-Hakawati, the formerly struggling production of the *Nights* thrived. The spectacle's intricate set finally had found a home that fit its largesse. The complexity of set changes and frequent entrances and exits were resolved with ease as the ensemble successfully experimented with their new space. Instead of the makeshift spaces for actor preparation that they had creatively established while on tour, they effectively got ready for their performances in a comfortable dressing room, spacious wings, and organized backstage area. The successful remounting of the *Nights* at El-Hakawati demonstrated one of the crucial challenges in Palestinian theater: the unstable environment of production due to fluctuating political and economic realities as well as the lack of long-term security forces theater makers to make extremely difficult aesthetic and operational choices and thus deeply affects the end product and the viewing experience. The establishment of El-Hakawati Theatre marked a qualitative leap in the history of Palestinian theater as it promised to provide an oasis, a home for artists to thrive.[14]

Thousands attended the festivities and performances in an unprecedented turnout. Thanks to consistent coverage by the Palestinian press, the lead-up to the opening had begun over a year earlier, creating phenomenal engagement by the Jerusalemite community and Palestinian theater artists. El-Hakawati's truly humongous undertaking had seemed untenable in the beginning, especially considering the small size of the ensemble and the massive size of the vandalized building, often referred to as a ghost house or ruined wreck. Hundreds of articles in Arabic, English, and

Hebrew lauded El-Hakawati's foolishness with enthusiasm. When the funding dried up, the press covered their campaign, creating a supportive foundation, adding legitimacy to the project, and producing excitement about whether the project would succeed. In turn, El-Hakawati publicly announced their commitment to the development of a vibrant theatrical culture in Palestine and emphasized the national significance of the project. On the local level, the ensemble expressed that they wanted to ease the burden of finding rehearsal and performance space for budding theatrical companies. They promised that the new center would be available to the community without distinction and serve its part in the national struggle against Israeli policies. El-Hakawati stated that their mission was to elevate the quality of theater practice and access in Jerusalem, the West Bank, and within the Green Line, indicating a wide scope of influence stretching across the entire population in historic Palestine. Repeatedly, members of the ensemble spoke to the press about their intention to open the theater to local ensembles. For example, Muallem noted: "I hope that the other ensembles feel that this project is for all theater workers and not exclusive to El-Hakawati Ensemble." Although they worked tirelessly and often alone, their inclusive narrative created community enthusiasm, and when they struggled financially, many came to their aid. During opening week, all stakeholders appeared for the celebration: fans, committed audiences, theater ensembles, local dignitaries, donors, journalists, critics, cultural elites, visual artists, musicians, politicians, board members, writers, poets, and public intellectuals.[15] In theory, the building would be considered the home of the theater movement and the frontline institution in Palestinian cultural resistance to Israeli hegemony in Jerusalem.

The opening celebrations caught the attention of the Israeli authorities. On 14 May 1984, the day of Samih Al-Qassem's presentation of a night of resistance poetry at the theater, François Abu Salem was arrested and interrogated for two hours by Israeli police at the Mascobiyya detention center. *Al-Fajr* newspaper reported that he was asked "provocative political questions." Historically, Palestinian theater artists reported that such questions often included inquiries about their sources of funding, political affiliations, family history, connections to Palestine, and stances concerning the state of Israel. The police released the uncooperative Abu Salem on the condition that he returned the next day with his lawyer.

In the presence of his lawyer, Johnathan Kuttab, the police's questions centered on whether the theater had a license to operate, despite El-Hakawati's registration as a non-profit organization in Israel, its regular procurement of performance permits, and a building owner's license to operate as an entertainment venue.[16]

The construction and operation of the theater served to establish a home for theater production and a site of assembly for local organizations, which drew the ire of an Israeli security apparatus mandated to prevent Palestinian congregation and political events. On 4 August 1985, *Al-Fajr* newspaper reported that Radi Shehadeh, Ibrahim Khalayleh, and Edward Muallem were questioned by the police in Mascobiyya, where Shehadeh was physically beaten by an officer. According to Shehadeh, the officer screamed at him "I will teach you what democracy is" as he attacked him. The performers, all Palestinian citizens of Israel, were initially summoned from rehearsal on 1 August 1984 because the police suspected that the theater regularly rented its space for political activities. The usual interrogation questions aimed to associate El-Hakawati with political, resistance, and militia organizations, but the performers denied any connection with such parties and demanded the presence of their lawyer. *Al-Fajr* stated: "They said interrogators ignored their rights and tried, instead, to interrogate them without their lawyer present. Two were beaten when they failed to answer questions."[17]

The dramatic events and regular summoning of El-Hakawati members, as well as the occasional temporary closures of the theater, demonstrated that the theater movement finally had a functional and known address. The ensemble had developed a regular site of confrontation with Israeli authorities. Whenever the censors wished to question their practices, they knew when and where to find them. The covert practices of sending informants, as had been done for the production of *Mahjoub Mahjoub*, became more accessible, and sometimes the evaluation of the texts took place in plain view. During a special performance for Hebrew University students at the Nuzha Hakawati Theatre, the council sent a team of six examiners to review the production of *Ali the Galilean* to ascertain the ensemble's compliance with the original script. Jackie Lubeck remembered that they sat in the front row, notepads and pens in hand, taking notes on the production. Heavily coded with Palestinian humor and indirect references, the censors were unable to revoke the permit or to recommend any cuts to the script.[18] Nonetheless, the newly founded theater allowed for the surveillance of the theater movement and El-Hakawati in particular. In the game of cat and mouse, which the makers of the theater movement had excelled at in the past, their ability to disappear until further notice was no longer possible. As their activities and influence grew, so did the attacks on their sovereignty.

During these initial two years, El-Hakawati Ensemble rehearsed and produced their first original production since *Jalilee Ya Ali*. According to the script found in the censorship file of the Israel State Archive, *The Story of the Eye and the Tooth* alludes to traditional customs and biblical stories to critique the political conflicts in Palestine (figure 14). At an ancient spring, two women are washing clothes when they both have contractions and each gives birth to twins. At birth, the families arrange for the future marriage of the boys to the girls. Fifteen years later, neither boy is willing to marry the ugly girl, Afifeh, setting in motion a family feud. As per tradition, the village council begins a process of reconciliation, which ends with forcing Khaldun to marry Afifeh in order to keep

FIGURE 14 El-Hakawati ensemble in their costumes for *The Story of the Eye and the Tooth* in the auditorium of El-Hakawati Theatre. Jerusalem, 1985. Courtesy of François Abu Salem Archive, Palestinian National Theater/El-Hakawati.

the peace. The first act ends with a celebratory wedding. The second act begins forty years later. The original generation remains frozen on stage in the form of human-size puppets. The families have grown, traveled, and feuded in the intervening years, but love always finds a way. Two of their teenagers, Sarah and Tanza', fall in love upon their first meeting. They decide to marry, leading to a temporary stop in the feud and the bloodshed between their families. During their wedding, the war restarts for an inexplicable reason. The parents kill each other. In the last moments of the play, the spirits of the parents look down on the battle with remorse and see the effects of their violence.[19]

On 20 February 1985, plainclothes policemen broke into the theater and arrested members of the ensemble during rehearsal. According to *Al-Fajr* newspaper, the men of the ensemble, dressed in their memorable female-drag costumes from the play, were taken to Jerusalem's Macobiyya detention center for a "ten-minute talk." All six founding members of the theater were accused of planning to host an illegal event the next day and asked to sign a pledge to reject the rental. After clarifying that the ensemble did not manage the hall rentals, which they left to the administration's discretion, they were released. A celebratory convention for the Working Women's Association was held on 21 February 1985 at El-Hakawati under the watchful eye of the authorities. The Hebrew-language newspaper *Kol Ha'ir* reported that a "large police force and border guards" checked the identity cards of each attendee before they entered the theater and questioned the legitimacy of a women's solidarity event in which 90 percent of the attendees were men chanting national slogans. Although the event and the association indirectly represented Fateh and the PLO, two illegal organizations in Israel, Radi Shehadeh told *Al-Fajr*: "We will not act as censors and policemen, checking every word to be said and investigating each group," a policy that El-Hakawati maintained throughout the ensemble's residency in the building.[20]

Unintimidated by these recent events, El-Hakawati insisted on continuing their rehearsals for *The Story of the Eye and the Tooth*. On 26 February 1985, ensemble member Radi Shehadeh applied to the Israeli Ministry of the Interior for a performance permit. The submitted seven-page script presented a very similar dialogue to the production version, but it omitted the majority of the production's stage directions and any references to Zionism or indications that some characters were Jewish.

It also omitted significant pages of dialogue that contained references to land and colonial aspirations. For example, the production version of the first act included the following stage directions:

> Youssef Salameh takes out a gun ... fires in the air ... the dancers get scared ... they transform to dummies ... they retreat to the back ... they congregate center stage ... they sit to the sound of bullets ... they sit frozen ... Youssef Salameh starts to sing a Zionist song ... His voice disappears slowly with the blackout ... announcing the end of the first act.

By contrast, the censor's copy read as follows:

> The storyteller transforms to a dancing dummy and hears the sound of Yarghul.[21] Enter the rest of the characters as dummies, dancing to the sound of the Yarghul. Then the dance ends as they transform into statues sitting on chairs in center stage. Blackout.

These careful modifications throughout the script inoculated the play from any possible censorship critique by the Israeli officers who evaluated the play. The censor described the play as a critique of the old Arab custom whereby families arrange a marriage by promising a particular boy to a specific girl at birth. He saw the play as a chronicle of the complications that ensue from the refusal to consummate the agreement. On 4 March 1985, within one week of the application, the Ministry of the Interior officially permitted the performance of this apparently benign, boring, and absolutely incomprehensible traditional play.[22]

When the play opened in 27 March 1985, the audience witnessed a nearly three-hour performance with sparse dialogue and exceptional stage imagery, composed of extensive choreography and physical action that presented a markedly more compelling theatrical experience than the censorship script. While the plot of the story remained similar to the censor's copy, the internal dialogue, choreography, movement, and silent communications in the play told the story of a people living on their land and celebrating their culture, only to be interrupted by a family feuds and subsequently a colonial project. In the second act, their infighting takes on a political dimension when some members of take control of the land within forty years. During the wedding that ends the first act, Youssef Salameh claims to have inherited the land from his forefathers.

Although leaving room for interpretation, the production identifies the bourgeois Salameh family as Zionist: Youssef the patriarch, Sarah the matriarch, and their daughter Layla. The modest peasant Rustom family, Arabs or Palestinians, are represented by the patriarch Abu Rustom, his wife Afifeh, and their son Tanza'. All the characters in the first act remain on stage in the form of dummies, always watching the activities of their progeny. The play ends with a bloody war that makes the innocent love of Layla and Tanza' impossible to culminate. Well-armed, Salameh terrorizes the families until they are physically unable to move, turning into dead bodies or dummies on stage. The cousins fight a bitter war over the land, one led by Salameh and the other by Abu Rustom. Dissatisfied with the bloodbath, the wives and children of the leaders object to the war but fail to change the outcome, even after asking the forefathers for help. The story could have ended in a full circle with a wedding that leads to assimilation and reconciliation, but El-Hakawati ends the play on a dark note of continuing war with blood that "reaches the knees." Youssef Salameh crashes the wedding of Sarah and Tanza', kills the groom and mistakenly shoots his wife Layla, then collapses during the escalation of the war. In the last moments of the play, Rustom begs his wife to burn the books of the past in hopes that the feuding parties might have an ambition for a better future.

Reviews of the production at El-Hakawati Theatre lauded François Abu Salem's aesthetic choices and directorial concept, while praising the stylized acting of the ensemble. However, nearly all reviewers complained about the ambiguity of symbols in the play. While celebrating the ensemble's skill in presenting grotesque characters and the production's technical excellence in design and music, communist critic Mohammad Al-Batrawi saw the play as an examination of an unidentified type of war. He asked whether it is a war of liberation. Ahmad Abu Saloum described the play as excellent, but then he sarcastically stated, "If I could comprehend its content, I would have called it a well-integrated theatrical work." Rateb Awawdeh suggested that one could read it through multiple political lenses: the Arab/Israeli conflict, the Palestinian/Zionist struggle, an internal Arab struggle, or a universal struggle of any people. These commentaries, while positive in many respects, allude to the controversy that surrounded this production in Jerusalem. They also demonstrate that El-Hakawati had given into surrealism and visual staging to an extent that distanced them from their core audience: a public that demanded clarity in their opposition to occupation and bias for the Palestinian struggle.[23]

Despite the relatively positive reviews by well-educated elites and artists, some critics assaulted the production as a fabrication against the Palestinian political struggle. The negative critique of the *Story of the Eye and Tooth* recalls similar previous critiques of El-Hakawati concerning the choice of topics, the representation of Arab culture, and the selective representation of Palestinian history. Nabil Al-Joulani complained that El-Hakawati insisted on representing old customs, such as arranged marriages and communal breast-feeding, as if they remained prevalent in Palestine. He railed against the simplification in representing Palestinian women, who had proven themselves as progressive and educated. Then he accused El-Hakawati of calling for normalizing relations with the occupation by presenting a love story between a Palestinian boy and a Jewish girl as a potential solution for conflict. His greatest indictment against the play was that the early family feuds and battles in the play showed Arabs as anarchic barbarians with a superficiality that he deemed expressly violent and purposeful. Al-Joulani saw a play that depicted Arabs as dancing and holding onto folklore while Zionists colonized their land. They didn't resist; they fled. They were susceptible to their sexual desires and easily manipulated with alcohol and corruption. He interpreted Abu Rustom's ripping books at the end as an erasure of history that confirmed the play's insidious intentions.[24]

The provenance of the play explains the strikingly different interpretations of the play. When El-Hakawati began their improvisational process, they intended to produce a story that examined internal feuds within Palestinian leadership in a period marked by factional politics. In 1985, the PLO's presence in Tunis was tenuous and the future of Palestinian resistance was uncertain. The fedayeen movement and resistance operations that marked the Palestinian struggle throughout the 1960s until the early 1980s were in decline as they progressively lacked a military presence on the ground, first after Black September in Jordan and subsequently after the Israeli invasion of Lebanon. In Palestine, the 1980s witnessed a reformulation of the struggle on the ground through elevated factional activity in workers' unions, educational institutions, civic organizations, clubs, and national committees. The factional divisions reached their height by the late 1980s, when many workers' unions split into separate organizations led by various parties like Fateh, PFLP, and DFLP. El-Hakawati chose to address the meaning of these increasing divisions within Palestinian society in *The Story of the Eye and the Tooth*. Their improvisations around the idea of family feuds aimed to represent conflict between Palestinians.

As the play grew progressively more complex, the team struggled to make sense of the story. The potency of the layered characters and the comedic scenes they created through improvisation overwhelmed any potential meaning or plot. In his memoir, ensemble member Radi Shehadeh recounts some of his dialogues with the other actors. His detailed representations of the discussions demonstrate spirited discourse during rehearsal and the elevated intellectual negotiation of potential possibilities for the play. They also clearly show El-Hakawati's struggle to produce a meaningful play with the extensive content they had created. In these published dialogues, actors Hussam Jowaylis, Iman Aoun, Radi Shehadeh, and Amer Khalil all state that they did not understand the play or its aims well into the rehearsal process. Their critiques of the process and the content matched the concerns expressed by the aforementioned critics. Simultaneously, they expressed the presence of the point of view that the play represented contemporary reality in Palestinian society: strong-willed leaders, complex tradition, struggle for self-determination, a just national cause, and larger-than-life characters that deserve to be seen by Palestinian audiences. According to Shehadeh's memoir, Abu Salem solved the crisis by settling on a first act that began prior to 1948 in Palestine, where all the characters are Palestinian but of different religions. Then, the second act would represent the separation of the Zionist movement, symbolized by the character of Youssef Salameh. In theory, this solution would appease the concerns of the team and find its echoes with Palestinian audiences.[25]

The ultimate representation on stage reflected not only factionalism within Palestinian society and the battle between Palestinian nationalists and Zionists but also the philosophical predilections within El-Hakawati. This production demonstrated that two ideologies operated within El-Hakawati, one tending toward prioritizing the Palestinian national cause and one toward a post-national Western and universal philosophy. Abu Salem's directorial concept and overall vision endorsed a multiplicity of perspectives, appealing to a wide range of non-Palestinian audiences and leaving space for interpretation that facilitated Western concerns which privileged Arab-Jewish dialogue and deprioritized contemporary constants of the Palestinian identity, such as the unnegotiable need for a Palestinian state and the right to armed resistance. Although improvisations emerged from the ensemble, Abu Salem's keen editorial eye left clear traces of meaningful historical signifiers such as a people being displaced for forty years, characters named after Judaism's founders, Zionist music ending the first act, and parallel staging between "Arabs" and "Jews." The diametrically opposed discourse among cast members and the directorial as well as editorial vision of Abu Salem demonstrate a conflict larger than mere dialectic. Directorially, in practice, Abu Salem constructed a production that valued Western discourses of equal Jewish rights to Palestine.

Radi Shehadeh formed the most vocal opposition within the ensemble, arguing against Abu Salem's liberal and post-national approach. On one hand, Abu Salem believed in a universal humanity that surpassed nationalism and the quest for statehood. He perceived value in dialogue, which could potentially end the war and occupation but preserve Israel's statehood and Jewish claims in Palestine. After all, according to this viewpoint, the progressive trajectory of the human race can only eventually lead to internationalism, fraternity, and liberty, a quintessentially French post-national viewpoint. Challenging the Marxist and socialist roots of Abu Salem's argument, Shehadeh insisted that even theoretically, within the Marxist tradition, a people cannot leap beyond immediate national and class concerns into the sphere of humanist universality. Shehadeh believed that the Palestinian cause must be addressed and resolved before Abu Salem's sought fraternity could be achieved. In practice, this debate of a battle between Abu Salem's structure and the ensemble's content manifested in the choreographed aesthetics of the production. Abu Salem choreographed the second act as a series of passes along two parallel lines upstage and downstage. Thus, Palestinians and Zionists cross the stage multiple times along their established track, but they never cross each other's paths. In practice, the stunning visual aesthetic serves the argument of an equal conflict in claims to land and strength of military power. The internal dissension inside El-Hakawati also appeared on stage in the form of the conflictual approaches to resolving the play's ending. Should the play end with a wedding that joins Palestinians and Israelis in newly formed blood ties? Does the bloody war tragically annihilate all the characters? Who survives the destructive war?

Unresolved, these questions left Palestinian audiences unsatisfied with El-Hakawati's representation of their cause in Jerusalem, but they were equally impressed by the brilliant theatricality of the production and the ensemble's capacity to produce such visuality and complexity of discourse in their city. The audience's exhibition of critical distance and evaluative wisdom between content and aesthetics demonstrated that El-Hakawati had nurtured its community's capacity for theatrical discourse along multiple evaluation metrics. *The Eye and the Tooth* provided a forum for examining notions that Jerusalemites had been grappling with, such as the need for collective narratives, the question of political dialogue, the cost of armed resistance, the role of recent and ancient history, and the merit of peace talks. The tension between aesthetics and content had appeared strongly in El-Hakawati's production of *In the Name of the Father, the Mother, and the Son*, but the audience critique tended toward one-dimensionality, either detesting the production's focus on domestic "dirty laundry" or relishing in its postcolonial critique through the character of the Tamer. The maturity of audience critique and reviews in the press, aside from few direct attacks on the company and the production, showed that El-Hakawati was not only developing its own performance tools, social status, and theatrical home but also the community that it chose to embed itself within. The play may have been controversial at home, but it served many higher purposes.

On multiple tours, Abu Salem's risky concept of multiple significations reaped the attention of international audiences. In the initial tour to Europe, the production played throughout May and June of 1985 at El Festival de Sitges in Spain, the Tempodrom in West Berlin, the Munich Theater Festival, the Monty in Antwerp, Luxor Theater in Rotterdam, and VHS Hietzing in Vienna. In long engagements, El-Hakawati also presented *The Eye and the Tooth* at London's Almeida Theater 2–18 January 1986 and Paris's La Maison des Cultures du Monde 21–31 January 1986. Throughout their presentations on tour, critics and audiences compared the play to Shakespeare's *Romeo and Juliet*, often construing the play as a Palestinian cry for political peace talks with Israel, an interpretation that El-Hakawati vehemently denied. Nonetheless, the persistence of this view suggests that Abu Salem's conceptual wizardry as a director and the European audiences' predisposition to interpret Jewish characters as essentially sympathetic overwhelmed the intention of the majority of the acting ensemble to present Palestinian suffering as a direct consequence of Zionism's colonial expansion. As the tour progressed, Abu Salem and the ensemble attempted to modify scenes to avoid these misinterpretations, but the structure of the play, especially with the parallel and equal blocking between the two feuding families, created an unavoidable equivalent with the Montagues and Capulets.

El-Hakawati's success in obtaining the censor's approval for *Ali the Galilean* did allow the production to avoid a confrontation with the Israeli authorities. To publicize their performance of the play at the Akka (Acre) Festival, which opened on 1 October 1985, Ibrahim Khalayleh marketed the play by attaching a special poster to a donkey that roamed the city. The poster stated: "I am not going to see the Palestinian el-Hakawati Theatre Troupe because I am a donkey."[26] The police arrested Khalayleh and the donkey on the grounds that the word *Palestinian* was offensive to the residents of Akka. Meanwhile, the ensemble engaged in a heated negotiation with the festival organizers because the venue had an Israeli flag flying above the stage. El-Hakawati insisted that the Israeli flag must be removed or a Palestinian flag must fly beside it during the performance. Because the Akka municipality hosted the festival, the organizers escalated their complaint to the Israeli mayor of the city. With an audience of twelve hundred Palestinians and Jewish Israelis in attendance, the mayor conceded to the ensemble's request to avoid the performance's cancellation. Due to the illegality of the Palestinian flag in Israel, the mayor decided to remove the Israeli one.[27] Both incidents concerning the ensemble's Palestinian identity, running concurrently on the day of the performance, threatened a failure to perform the play. Although the police released Khalayleh in time to perform, many ensemble members could not ascertain the fate of the donkey that the actor left behind. But they did remember that the donkey did not watch the play.

Within two years of its opening, the theater hosted thirty-six different productions by local ensembles, nine exhibitions, fifteen lectures, thirty-six festivals, forty-one films, and several workshops. It had also become the rental site of choice of political organizations and unions for yearly celebrations and public meetings. The café in the lobby (see figure 13) functioned as a meeting place for local artists, playing a major role in bringing the community under one roof and encouraging interdisciplinary work. At any time of day, a visitor to the theater could find a known writer, poet, visual artist, or performer sitting at the café with a journalist or an aspiring mentee. Book clubs, writer's leagues, and cinema aficionados scheduled regular weekly and monthly meetings at El-Hakawati. At the front door of the theater, actors and directors were often seen in heated discussions about the latest production or an upcoming project. When political organizations rented the theater, new audiences learned of El-Hakawati, constantly adding to the public status of the theater and expanding the reach of theater companies that regularly presented their work. Within the first two years, the theater printed five thousand copies of its monthly calendar and distributed them by mail, effectively publicizing the works of local theater companies and events by musicians and visual artists. Between 1984 and 1986, the Nuzha-El-Hakawati Theatre became a Jerusalemite landmark known simply as El-Hakawati.[28]

As El-Hakawati Ensemble was building its new home and establishing this enviable cultural center in the early months of 1984, other theater ensembles were emerging from the extreme conditions that prevented their productions from coming to fruition. After the arrest of the leading actors of the Palestinian People's Theatre in August 1980, the ensemble had frozen all their theatrical activities. Upon their release and when conditions became appropriate, the two leading men of the ensemble, Ahmad Abu Saloum and Hussam Abu Esheh, sought to rebuild the previous glory of the landmark production of *Man Is a Cause* (1980), the adaptation of Ghassan Kanafani's *Returning to Haifa* and the primary cause of their arrest. The dynamic duo reestablished themselves as the new theatrical entity Sanabel People's Theatre and announced its foundation on 11 December 1984. They stated their mission as the expression of the Palestinian popular struggle, as exemplified by the working class. Unapologetically, the dynamic duo became known for their sympathy with the revolutionary program of the Palestinian Front for the Liberation of Palestine (PFLP), resulting in immense popularity with declared and undeclared members of this political faction in Jerusalem and in historic Palestine, as well as in their future travels abroad. They also garnered the attention of working-class audiences, who counted on Sanabel to present their plight. Jamil Salhout wrote in *Al-Katib*, "From this standpoint, they present plays that carry a revolutionary message in its nature; therefore, the working people respond to their popular theater and the auditorium is filled with the children of the working people and revolutionary intellectuals."[29]

Opening in March 1985 at El-Hakawati Theatre, their first play, *Al-Mahrajan (The Festival)* addressed political differences among Arab countries. Author Ahmad Abu Saloum set the play in a school. He also acted in the production and recalled that he played the role of the school's custodian, who is well loved by the students and the community. The premise of the play is to prepare a graduation celebration in a school that serves two neighboring villages. Humorously, he called the villages Tuna and Sardine, which are easily consumed by greater powers, a direct critique of the weakness of Arab and Palestinian leaders. In a comic scene, the local leaders argue over minor details: Who will sit in the first row? Who will make a public statement? Eventually, the whole event falls apart due to self-interest and lack of a cohesive program. Abu Saloum ridicules the state of Arabs, suggesting that Arab leaders and their followers are vehement in a discussion or a television program when they argue for the front-row seat, but in reality, they are beaten and dominated politically and militarily by Western hegemony, colonial powers, and the Israeli occupation. Overtly critiquing the Arab League, the play represented Arab conferences as inefficient and driven by the personal interests of authoritarian regimes. With the goal of raising popular consciousness, Sanabel challenged Arab neighbors to place priority on their involvement in the Palestinian cause. Referring to Palestine as the prelude to future land losses and eventual domination by the State of Israel, the play famously states: "He who gives up the rooster gives up the cow. And he who accepts minor losses certainly accepts major ones." The Sanabel ensemble expressed disenchantment with the state of Arab nationalism and suggested that Palestinians must affirm their national rights of independence and self-determination, even if the Arab regimes have not. The ensemble presented fifteen performances of *Al-Mahrajan* in Jerusalem, Bethlehem, and Beit Sahour, becoming a mainstay at El-Hakawati Theatre and expanding their reach to neighboring cities.[30]

In the same year, the ensemble followed *Al-Mahrajan* with a production by director Hayyan Ya'coub entitled *Sayyidi Al-General (The General Sir)*. Opening in October 1985 at El-Hakawati, the play was inspired by and adapted from three plays: *The General* by the Iranian playwright

Gholam Hussein Saidi, *The Dictator* by the Lebanese playwright Issam Mahfouz, and *Blood Melody* by Mustapha Mahmoud. The satirical take on the never-ending cycle of military coups reflected the ensemble's identification with the oppressed classes in the formerly colonized nations of the "third world." The play presents a conversation between a general and a sergeant, played by Hussam Abu Esheh and Ibrahim Othman Eliwat. The insane General oppresses his underling in unreasonable ways, explaining that reaching positions of power requires the willingness to kill. The production aimed to depict the notions of peace and war as they relate to repetitive military coups, particularly in the Global South as represented by Arab and African nation-states. By the end of the play, the General learns that his office is his prison and the Sergeant is his jailer. The play ends with a reversal, showing the collapse of the General as the Sergeant walks out of the room in a sign of the ensemble's commitment to the revolutionary struggle through popular unity, not the constant overturning of leadership in never-ending military coups.[31]

On behalf of Sanabel People's Theatre, director Hayyan Ya'coub applied to the Israeli censorship board for a performance permit on 22 October 1985. He sent in a partial text made up primarily of the Mustapha Mahmoud script rather than the complete adaptation that he had prepared for performance. The censor evaluated the work as "very banal" and "a completely childish attempt without content and without message."[32] Although internal censorship policy stipulated a requirement for two evaluations of each script, a handwritten note in the file indicates that only one Arabic-speaking reviewer was available. The brief evaluation demonstrated a lack of interest in critically evaluating the play or a possible difficulty in analyzing the subtext. A deeper evaluation might have revealed that the play offered a Palestinian call to Arab dictators to review their priorities and to Arab soldiers to challenge their superiors. For example, the General demands a meeting with all his staff only to find out they all went on a trip. The ensuing comical interplay suggests the soldiers were at a club or on vacation, an allusion to Egyptian pilots partying on the eve of the 1967 Israeli attack on the Egyptian air force. The brevity of the script may have misled the censorship officer as Ya'coub sent in only part of the source materials for the production and not the final script, a tactic that theater makers often used during this period.[33] Because the script was not examined with the necessary expertise, Sanabel's permit was printed on 4 November 1985, and the production gained final approval of the censorship committee in a plenary meeting on 11 November 1985.

Opening their next production, *Kilab w Arqam* (*Dogs and Numbers*), in late March 1986, with the permit obtained on 17 March 1986, Sanabel targeted the silent majority in Palestinian society. Inspired by two plays by Sa'dallah Wannous, *The Tragedy of the Poor Molasses Seller* and *Corpse on the Pavement*, the production adapted the context of the small-town seller and the police state to the Palestinian context, where the people struggle to survive the military occupation and its informants. In *Dogs and Numbers*, Abu Saloum addresses the necessity for Palestinians to unsilence themselves and revolt against the occupation, using the suffering of Sa'dallah Wannous's characters as cautionary tales: the molasses seller ends up in a torturous and perpetual prison, and the corpse on the pavement becomes food for the bourgeoisie's dogs. Based on El-Hakawati's event calendar for May 1986, the play was advertised with the tagline: "Is patient waiting a form of challenge . . . or does it turn us into mere numbers . . . ?"[34]

Simultaneous with the opening of El-Hakawati, the return of Sanabel People's Theatre added to the theatrical scene a frequency of performances that included many popular recurring events. Their regularly programmed Ramadan Nights proved immensely popular and became a model for collaborative entertainments with local theatrical ensembles, sketch troupes, poets, solo shows including mimes, and musical acts. Their most popular collaborations with Ramallah's Firqat Al-Funun Al-Sha'biya (Ensemble Folk Arts), Mustapha Al-Kurd, and the Sabrin musical ensemble led to packed houses and further popularized their theatrical offerings. The combination of comedy sketches, variety performances, and a concert atmosphere became a hit formula that kept their audiences flowing and interested. The dynamic duo of Abu Saloum and Abu Esheh—the first playing the oud and singing popular nationalistic fare and the second engaging in satirical popular stand-up comedy and interview numbers—hit a chord for local audiences.

Sanabel were not the only ensemble to step up their offerings. The monthly calendars of the theater demonstrate that a theatrical revival had taken place in Jerusalem. Some plays from the 1970s and many artists that had not shown their work in the early 1980s returned to the scene with full force. The Palestinian Theatre remounted their popular production of *'ind El-Luzoom* (*When Necessary*), recapturing the attention of their audiences in Jerusalem. Mohammad Al-Thaher reappeared in full force as a playwright in a new production called *La'nat 'atrees* (*The Curse of Atrees*). The two-actor play is a parable that depicts a discussion between a powerful priest, who seems to have lost his will to live, and a young woman, who attempts to save herself before she is sacrificed to the gods. Existential in discourse, the dialogue tracks the young woman's challenge to a God in his own place of worship as she repeatedly asks the priest the cursed question "Why?" Why must the sacrifice be a virgin girl? Why do curses exist? She attempts to dismantle a systemic structure of injustice—namely, women's oppression. The absurd representation of religious power leads to nonsensical questions about the nature of curses, their punishment, and their market price. Over the course of the play, the young woman sarcastically and logically disassembles the priest's belief system until he begins to ask similar questions. Eventually, his newfound freedom leads to his decision to attempt suicide as the ultimate choice of free will, but she convinces him to resist this impulse. They end the play in a tableau, moving together in lockstep.

Al-Thaher applied for a performance permit on 26 February 1986 and received it on 17 March 1986. Two factoids are of most interest in this file: Al-Thaher did not name his ensemble as the Palestinian Theatre, and the file refers to the application by his name and a generic reference to a theater in East Jerusalem. This choice indicates that Al-Thaher had become a sole producer, no longer operating with a regular ensemble, but more significantly, his hiding the theater name illustrates that the open declaration of Palestinian identity in Jerusalem had become increasingly unsafe. Second, the evaluation of the text seems to have occurred on the same day as the approval of the play and the plenary meeting of the evaluators of the council. Only one evaluation appears in the censorship file. The long and verbose text submitted by Al-Thaher could not have easily been evaluated on the day of the plenary meeting, but the evaluator's comment stated that the play should be approved for the purpose of "boring the audience."[35] The dialectical text openly depicts a desire for personal and political liberation, calling on the audience to privilege logic over blind spirituality and tradition. According to Al-Thaher, *La'nat Atrees* (*The Curse of Atrees*) caused controversy because of its call to think and critique "all that is accepted." Based on listings in El-Hakawati's archived calendars, the Palestinian Theatre presented several productions between 1984 and 1992, including Al-Thaher's successful plays *Man Al-'aqer (Who's Infertile?)* in 1985/1986 and *Al-Sarkha (The Scream)* in 1987.[36] Although Al-Thaher had returned to the scene, his productions did not attain their previous status and the Palestinian Theatre no longer stood as a leading theater company.

Perhaps El-Hakawati's most significant competitor on the contemporary Palestinian theater scene in Jerusalem was George Ibrahim. Since the emergence of El-Hakawati as an itinerant ensemble and well into their growth as a frequent presenter of original productions in Palestine and abroad, Ibrahim was continually developing his craft and his audiences in a distinguished career, producing plays for both children and adult audiences. Throughout the 1970s and early 1980s, he operated under two company names: Masrah Al-Shoke (Thorns Theater) and Firqat Al-Funoun El-Masrahiyyah (Theater Arts Company). His repertoire for children continued to be influenced by Arab and international canons, focusing on children's experiences and showcasing educational content, fairytales, and light musical fare. The most popular of these were *Happy Shoemaker* (1976), *The Broken Jar* (1978), *Little Red Riding Hood* (1980), and *Uncle Suleiman's Shop* (1981).

When El-Hakawati Theatre opened, George Ibrahim frequently presented children's plays, which filled a significant gap in the ensemble's repertoire. His repertoire of *The Dwarf and the Miller's Daughter* (1981), *The Sultan's Son* (1982), *My Grandfather Is Not Old* (1982), *The Emperor's New Clothes* (1983), and *Haroun Al-Rasheed and the Shoemaker* (1985) found a home beyond the touring circuit that he had established throughout the 1970s, which typically started at Al-Omariyyeh School in the Old City of Jerusalem and continued to schools throughout Palestine, crossing to the West Bank, Gaza, and the entirety of the Galilee. Ibrahim saw the opening of El-Hakawati as an opportunity to liberate his work from the bureaucracy of the West Jerusalem municipality. For El-Hakawati, Ibrahim's well-constructed plays, especially the children's musicals, filled the seats, promoted the theater, and provided much-needed rental income.

By the 1980s, George Ibrahim's choices of adult repertoire expressed his desire to produce politically engaged theater, which was a departure from his entertainment-focused productions of the 1970s and his professional children's productions. In 1986, he established Masrah El-Warsheh El-Fanniyeh (the Artistic Workshop Theatre), which reflected his transition from traditional well-made plays into more experimental scripts and adaptations. In 1986, Max Frisch's *The Fire Raisers* told the story of arsonists who destroy the homes of unsuspecting citizens (figure 15). Originally produced in the aftermath of World War II, the play presented the actions of the arsonist occupiers as a metaphor for fascism. In the same year, he adapted and directed Albert Camus's *Caligula*, which told the story of the Roman emperor's revolt against the natural order. The play depicted the ultimate failure of immoral revolution and absolute freedom. Presented on the stage of the Nuzha Hakawati Theatre, *The Fire Raisers* and *Caligula* critically analyzed the relationship between individual choice and absolute power. In Jerusalemite theater, these two productions gestured toward a new departure for George Ibrahim and El-Warsheh El-Fanniyeh. His previous focus on entertainment and education had begun to give way to the rising consequences of the occupation. He set himself on a different path, one that maintained his trend-setting children's theater productions and simultaneously experimented with adaptations of foreign dramatic canons for political conditions in Palestine.[37]

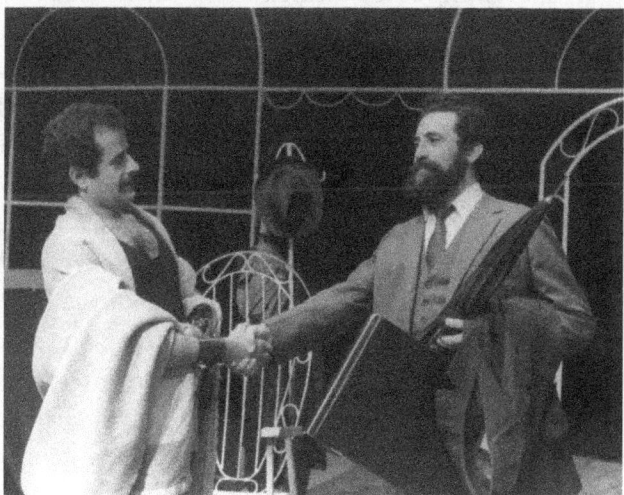

FIGURE 15 A performance of Al-Kasaba's production of *The Fire Raisers*. Jerusalem 1985. Courtesy of George Ibrahim.

By building and opening a new theater, El-Hakawati created a home that highlighted the massive artistic and cultural activities taking place in Jerusalem during the mid-1980s. Many of the activities would otherwise go unnoticed and undocumented, but their presence under one roof and advertising in the monthly calendar of El-Hakawati showcased the theatrical activities, illustrating how the movement had developed and was progressing effectively. In a single month, El-Hakawati Theatre would host numerous workshops, such as children's theater and puppet theater by George Ibrahim, musical lessons by Mustapha El-Kurd and Emile Ashrawi, and pantomime by Fateh Azzam and Emile Ashrawi. Jerusalemites enjoyed dance performances by many local troupes throughout Palestine, including Birzeit's Sharaf El-Teeby Dabke Troupe and Al-Funoun El-Sha'biyyeh. Local audiences and supporters of civil society organizations attended musical concerts and variety evenings of folklore by Mount of Olives Youth Group, Yu'ad Group: Rameh Youth Troupe for National Song, the Artistic Committee of the Voluntary Work Committee, Fawzi Al-Sa'di and Wafaa Dafrawi's Nazarene Evening, Firqat Zahrat Al-Mada'in, Birzeit's Sanabel Singing Troupe, and the General Union for Expressive Arts. Local organizations and unions such as the Committee of the Working Palestinian Woman or Silwan Club would often host local troupes for their own celebrations, adding a collaborative and political dimension to most evenings at the theater. On occasion, the theater hosted musical concerts from the world repertoire. For example, the European Quatour group played an evening of baroque music at El-Hakawati.[38]

In 1985-1986, smaller and emergent theater companies also benefited immensely from the opening of this cultural hub. The Jerusalem Al-Jawal (Itinerant) Company, led by Saqer Al-Salaymeh, presented several productions, including *Al-Harah Al-Mukhtarah (The Chosen Neighborhood)*, a satirical play that depicted daily Palestinian struggles through the battles between two neighborhoods. They also produced the hilarious *Jannanouny (They Made Me Crazy)* to satirize the life of a single individual under occupation. Al-Rahala Theatre (*The Travellers*) presented *El-Mazbaleh (The Garbage Dump)*, *The Dictator*, and *Al-Rijal Lahom Ru'us (Men Have Heads)*, directed by Ya'coub Ismail, who would become one of the outstanding avant-garde directors of the 1980s and 1990s. The recently formed Beit Anan Troupe offered a small production of *Zilzal Fi Al-Ard (Earthquake on Earth)*. This inaugural play is a parable of a young man experiencing a conundrum when an external force attempts to dispossess him from his land through manipulative games of financial enticement and temptation. Sundouq Al-'ajab returned to the scene with an adaptation of Ghassan Kanafani's *The Blind and the Deaf.* Productions and availability of performances to Palestinian audiences had never reached this high frequency before this period in the mid-1980s.

To celebrate two years since the opening of El-Hakawati Theatre, the ensemble prepared a unique mega-event that would never be repeated in contemporary Palestinian theater. The brainchild of company member Ibrahim Khalayleh and the product of the ensemble's collective ingenuity, the celebratory parade would function like a caravan inspired by Arab tradition and the historic Palestinian festival of Nabi Musa, gesturing to the wedding atmosphere that Jerusalemites adore. Once at the theater, the grounds would be prepared in the form of the historic Souq Okath, the most famous pre-Islamic market of the Arabian Peninsula. The souq was known as a performance forum for poets, musicians, and singers. To re-create this phenomenon, El-Hakawati invited local performers to join in the celebration. They advertised it as a variety event for the whole family, urging all Jerusalemites to participate in the celebration, which would include "everything that the spirit desires artistically." Coinciding with the start of the holy month of Ramadan three days later, the inspired marketing event combined Jerusalemite pride in the Holy City and the artistic spirit of a vigorous theatrical movement that proved its merits since the opening of El-Hakawati Theatre.

On Thursday 7 May 1986, at noon, the majority of performing artists in Jerusalem and the West Bank began congregating on Musrara's lush grass near the Damascus Gate. The staging area became a carnival in itself as musical troupes played local tunes on their instruments, dance troupes led audiences in *dabkah* circles, performers busily painted their faces and prepared their makeup, film crews moved between participants, and Sufi troupes beat their drums. Before the start of the parade, the yaghul players stole the show with their recognizable traditional music. Banners identified the parade as the second anniversary of the opening of El-Hakawati Theatre. Effectively organized and publicized, the promised track was lined up with audiences. El-Hakawati had received a permit for their planned parade, which included a request for the closure of streets during the afternoon of the event.

The caravan of hundreds of artists departed from the Damascus Gate, heading along the Old City walls and turning onto the commercial Salah El-Din Street, past the Israeli District Court to the theater (figure 16). El-Hakawati's red banner and two horsemen in traditional Levantine costumes led the caravan, followed by the cast of Radi Shehadeh's children's production *Sharshouh*, who were carrying a beautifully constructed puppet of a white-winged horse from Arab mythology. Then Jerusalem's Al-Jawwal Troupe promoted their production of *The Chosen Neighborhood* by playing scenes from it as they moved forward. Gaza's Al-Amal Troupe for Art and Theater performed a tragic scene, reminding the audiences of the Palestinian struggle in the midst of the celebration. Mustapha El-Kurd's musical ensemble elegantly played local popular music and Sufi anthems and encouraged the audience to sing along. Handheld signs identified each artistic troupe: Al-'idda Sufi Troupe from Nablus, the Mount of Olives Equestrian Troupe, Jabal Al-Mukkaber Theatrical Troupe, Shu'fat's Zahrat Al-Mada'in Performance Ensemble, Gaza's Al-Amal Troupe, Hebron's Charitable Candle's Association, Jerusalem's Musical Orphanage, and members of Jerusalem's Music Institute. A marching band held the attention of the spectators lining both sides of

FIGURE 16 Celebratory marchers on the second anniversary of El-Hakawati's opening. Jerusalem 1986. Courtesy of François Abu Salem Archive, Palestinian National Theater/El-Hakawati.

the streets and kept the rhythm of the parade. The roofs and windows of buildings along the way were full of watching eyes and waving hands acknowledging the impressive accomplishments of the Palestinian theater and artistic movement. Once they arrived at the grounds of El-Hakawati, the parade continued the celebration with events inside and around the theater.[39]

The second-anniversary celebration demonstrated El-Hakawati's leadership within the theater movement and proved the viability of a popular theater in Jerusalem and Palestine more broadly. With the establishment of a dedicated theater building in Jerusalem, the theatrical movement believed it had found a home as well. Since 1967, Palestinian theater artists in the Jerusalem area had sought a framework to hold the theatrical movement together in different ways. Many frameworks, such as the Committee for the Arts, several attempts at creating a theater league, and the informal touring circuits, had sustained the growth of the movement, but no structure could form the necessary launching pad to accelerate the movement. Theater artists operated under similar conditions, which forced the creation of temporary joint efforts to self-organize as joint cultural associations and festivals between the early 1970s and the mid-1980s. Most of these efforts at institution-building failed due to the influence of the occupation, the absence of stable funding sources, and internal disagreements within the movement. Despite its dysfunction and the frequent dismantling of its most successful ensembles for the better part of two decades, the theatrical movement succeeded in creating highly popular productions, leading the city's struggle to maintain its Palestinian identity, sense of community, and the establishment of El-Hakawati Theatre as a symbol of the golden era of contemporary Palestinian theater. Nonetheless, without question, two decades into the 1967 occupation, the movement's successes were often short-lived. After the 1986 celebratory parade that effectively reinvigorated ownership of Palestinian streets in Jerusalem, the Nuzha Hakawati Theatre became a symbol of national pride and provided the most successful framework to unify the movement. In those two years of bliss after the opening of the theater, this one-of-a-kind movement and its theatrical efforts under occupation had finally found their footing.

EIGHT

INTIFADA IN THE STREETS AND CRISIS IN THE THEATER, 1987-1990

The Nuzha-Hakawati Theatre became a center for public assembly. On the anniversary of the launch of resistance movements, workers' unions, and political parties, organizers prepared major events and political rallies. This mainstay tradition of Palestinian politics became a contentious challenge and the Israeli authorities regularly attempted to shut down these events. An organizer for the Democratic Front for the Liberation of Palestine (DFLP) remembered playing a game of cat-and-mouse with the Israeli authorities. When his party hosted a public event that was likely to be shut down by the IDF or the Israeli police, the announcements would state a location in the press and on flyers, then on the day of the event, the location would be changed to avoid confrontation. "We once had a launch announced at Al-Quds Cinema but a small circle in the local leadership of the DFLP knew that I had booked El-Hakawati for the same time," he recalled. "We placed guides at appropriate locations to reroute participants. When the Israelis attempted to shut down the event, Al-Quds Cinema was empty."[1] By the time the authorities had investigated the situation, the event at El-Hakawati had concluded. Because the organizers' strategies were often successful, the theater had become a target of closures and regular investigations by the Israeli police. Regular demands for the theater's administration to explain their rentals to civil organizations associated with political parties were aimed to intimidate the theater into refusing to host such nationalistic events.

To some, 1986 was a year of hope in occupied Palestine because political organizing on the ground had reached an apex. To others, it was a year of fragmentation because political parties competed for the attention of workers' unions and civil society. Many organized unions split into two or more factions associated with different political parties, such as Fateh, PFLP, and DFLP. The press paid close attention to this fracturing because each newspaper maintained its own associations with these parties and was mandated to celebrate the successes of its cadres in the field. Outside Palestine, the PLO had developed relationships with Tunisia, its host country, and its prime partners Jordan and Syria in potential peace negotiations with Israel. Factionalism reached a nadir when three Fateh leaders, Abu Nidal, Abu Jihad, and Al-Za'yim, feuded separately with Yasir Arafat on multiple issues, including the managing of the camp wars in Lebanon and the PLO's relationship with the Jordanian regime under the Amman Accords, which excluded Syria from their bilateral covert negotiations with Israel and aimed to separate Palestinian self-determination from larger Arab conflicts with Israel. By late 1987, political fragmentation, divided loyalties, attritional camp battles in the Lebanese civil war, and a de-prioritizing of the PLO's position in the Arab League characterized this period of uncertainty. By contrast, the Jerusalem/Ramallah area reached what many felt was a boiling point, and the verb associated with the word *Intifada*, "to rise up," was in common usage.[2]

When theater artists remember the period leading to the 1987 Intifada, they often describe it as having "a different flavor." Roughly two decades after the occupation and four decades after the Nakba, the Palestinian cause remained alive with consistent multilateral efforts in the homeland and abroad. The idea of a Palestinian state did not feel so distant as confrontations with the State of Israel continued on a daily basis. Many of the active Palestinian theater artists in the mid-1980s had experienced the 1967 war, the aftermath of the Nakba, and direct clashes with the Israeli military. Many had experienced arrests, imprisonment, and forced exile. The connectedness of the theater makers to the roots of the struggle formed a foundation for their movement across Palestinian urban life and informed their cultural production in conscious and unconscious ways. Equally, their connection to the high-level feuds of the

PLO and the emergent daily news of the battles in occupied South Lebanon fueled and inspired theatrical events. For example, El-Hakawati regularly held events in solidarity with the Palestinian struggle abroad and memorial events for local tragedies at home, most notably for the Sabra and Shatila massacres.

Theater productions acknowledged and addressed pressing issues of the Palestinian cause directly in this period, with each ensemble exhibiting its ideological beliefs through the topics of examination and choices of aesthetic. El-Hakawati's *The Story of the Eye and the Tooth* began with a clear attempt to address the leadership rifts within the PLO with a universalist aesthetic that functioned like a historical parable about feuding families, with the rift between Arafat and Al-Za'yim being a crucial starting point. Sanabel's *The General Sir* questioned the value of dictatorship and direct support for absolutist leadership using realistic staging. The Jerusalem Al-Jawal ensemble questioned internal divisions within a cohesive society with a satirical approach. Ya'coub Ismail's Al-Rahala took on a magic realism and absurdist style to question the existentially precarious reality of the Palestinian people, especially as they age and manage a semblance of normalcy in a nihilistic political environment. George Ibrahim's El-Warsheh El-Fanniyeh adapted Max Frisch's *The Fire Raisers* to examine anarchism in a crumbling society and lack of unified vision or rule of law. Al-Thaher's the Palestinian Theatre repeatedly asked "why" in the *Curse of Atrees*. Sundouq Al-'ajab staged Ghassan Kanafani's incomplete story *The Blind and the Deaf*, which humorously brings together two differently abled bodies to discover that miracles can be achieved only by the living and through cooperation. With each production in the mid-1980s, the theater makers of the 1970s emerged as thinkers, public intellectuals, and known figures in Palestinian society. Their movement was no longer hypothetical. It was active and its home address was El-Hakawati Theatre.

Against this backdrop of creativity and the Palestinian cause's political uncertainty, a duel lurked within the theater movement. Surrounding the period of its construction and opening, a question arose about the ownership of the Nuzha-Hakawati theater building and its potential users. In their idealistic and inclusive vision, El-Hakawati members replied that the theater would be available for use by the theatrical movement, to which El-Hakawati Ensemble belonged. By 1986, a debate raged in the Palestinian public sphere. Said Al-Ghazali of *Al-Fajr* noted: "It is not yet clear whether Hakawati is a private or public center, an argument which intensified as the Hakawati Ensemble celebrated last May its second anniversary." After promoting El-Hakawati since its foundation in 1977, the Palestinian English and Arabic press gave voice to this public debate in articles such as "Originally constructed to serve all the artistic groups... Has this slogan come true?" and "El-Hakawati and its politics." The debate in public forums only amplified an existing rift within the movement, to which El-Hakawati not only helped create but also magnified and logistically supported.[3]

Two months after the massive second-anniversary celebration parade, which was lauded for its spirit and panned for presenting Western numbers such as a Russian snake charmer from Tel Aviv, *Al-Fajr* published Al-Ghazali's long exposé about the crisis surrounding El-Hakawati's theater.[4] According to its opponents, El-Hakawati received grants to serve Palestinian cultural production, but local artists were required to pay rental fees for each rehearsal and performance regardless of box office revenues. The board of directors, composed of community leaders and the six founding members of the theater, did not include representatives from local theater ensembles, which meant that the needs of the theater movement could not be voiced in administrative meetings. Local artists claimed that El-Hakawati had created a theatrical monopoly, and they rejected the composition of the board and the preferential treatment El-Hakawati embedded for itself in the theater's bylaws. They argued that El-Hakawati received funding from Palestinian sources in the name of the theater movement to build the theater but then functioned as a gatekeeper that monopolized the theater's calendar and its production resources. Some community members directly attacked the chair of the board, the well-loved Jerusalemite political leader Faisal Al-Husseini, for allowing these injustices to continue.

The attacks on El-Hakawati's management of the theater continued for the better part of 1986 and 1987, mirroring the state of national fragmentation in many institutions in Palestine. The ensemble attempted to address many of the concerns through clear distinctions. They explained that El-Hakawati continued to function as an ensemble within the theater. The Nuzha-Hakawati Theatre functioned under the leadership of its managing director, Anis Al-Qaq, and the head of the board of trustees,

Faisal Al-Husseini. And the theater administration began to function at arm's length from the ensemble, often signing contracts and announcements with the signature "The Palestinian Cultural Center." But these distinctions did not appease the critics, who insisted that El-Hakawati's access to the building far exceeded that of any other ensemble. One of the crucial points of contention included El-Hakawati's access to technical support by virtue of their permanent presence in the building and close contact with the center's staff, most of whom had assisted the ensemble in the later stages of constructing the theater. Local ensembles complained that El-Hakawati prepared their productions over a longer period because they were not required to pay for rehearsal time and technical preparation. Opponents suggested that the quality of El-Hakawati's performances and their ability to perform world-class plays in Palestine and abroad can be attributed to many of these unfair advantages. Inherent in their argument was the steadfast belief that the local ensembles did not lack talent, intellect, skill, or content, but resources and access to the building.

In turn, El-Hakawati responded to these criticisms. They explained how they built the theater and funded it from grants they diligently acquired. Their fundraising efforts exclusively addressed the needs of their ensemble, which indeed served the audiences and the Jerusalemite community, and established a theater that the theater movement could utilize, but the theater was never intended to be a public community center. El-Hakawati functioned as a resident company by virtue of their relationship to the space, which had been derelict prior to their intervention. El-Hakawati insisted that in the first two years, all theater ensembles that requested to book the theater had succeeded in doing so, as evinced in the calendars of performances. In fact, frequently, the theater charged only nominal fees, and at times, they waived them for both rehearsals and performances. Between 1983 and 1986, El-Hakawati had not received funding from national organizations such as the PLO for the construction of the building. On the contrary, they obtained their primary funds from international funding agencies such as the Ford Foundation. Although they sought donations from local dignitaries and the Welfare Foundation (Palestinian founders), these funds were comparatively minor and given to El-Hakawati based on its reputation, personal relationship with donors, and its known ability to complete projects.

But the attacks continued, often behind the scenes and unconfrontational. From the perspective of some local theater ensembles at the time, El-Hakawati Ensemble became a foreign implant, leeching off the community but not supporting its needs. According to local gossip, the ensemble was primarily composed of foreigners to Jerusalem: a Frenchman, an American, and three Galileans. The objectors witnessed El-Hakawati members entering and exiting the theater as they pleased; sometimes, they perceived them to be bumping a local ensemble using their preferential status as the founders. If El-Hakawati booked a rehearsal or performance based on emergent needs, the availability quickly dwindled. Drawing a modest salary from their work for the center as a resident company, they were effectively benefiting even when they did not have a running production. Other ensembles felt that they couldn't compete for El-Hakawati's audiences. Furthermore, all productions that occurred at the theater were perceived to be by El-Hakawati, thus expanding the fame of the ensemble, while the new ensembles received very little credit for their productions.

The controversies expanded dramatically when some members of El-Hakawati Ensemble wished to produce their own productions. Radi Shehadeh had written and produced his own plays since the early 1970s in the Galilee. During the controversial production of *The Story of the Eye and the Tooth*, he had begun to conceive potential productions and wished to utilize the immense resources of the theater for his own work as a playwright and director. His desire to produce his own work led to significant dissension within the ensemble because the internal bylaws necessitated that El-Hakawati's brand would be attached only to productions directed by François Abu Salem. Shehadeh's ambitions threatened Abu Salem's leadership and the structure of El-Hakawati. Ibrahim Khalayleh supported Shehadeh's ambitious plans, as did the administrative leadership of the center. By contrast, the other original founding members of the ensemble, Abu Salem, Lubeck, and Muallem, preferred to maintain the aesthetic and tradition they had deeply believed in. The administrative leadership of Anis Al-Qaq and Fateh Azzam, with the emergent presence of the young Jamal Ghosheh, supported the potential of multiple productions, particularly as local objectors continually expressed concerns about Abu Salem's and Lubeck's foreign status and perception that their influence on cultural production led to Westernized theatrical aesthetics and content.

At the apex of El-Hakawati's success, after nearly a hundred performances of *The Eye and The Tooth* in Palestine and abroad, as well as the massive second-anniversary celebration, these criticisms and dissensions bubbled to uncontrollable levels. Abu Salem had a strong leading position with many members of the company, including Jackie Lubeck, Edward Muallem, Amer Khalil, and Iman Aoun. Emerging performers dreamed of performing in this locally and internationally successful ensemble. But in order to maintain the integrity of El-Hakawati, Abu Salem and Lubeck insisted on specific criteria that progressively became less acceptable to some members. For example, only Abu Salem and Lubeck were initially allowed to speak with the press. Some ensemble members felt that this rule reduced their contributions and aggrandized Abu Salem's position as the omniscient leading figure, especially since El-Hakawati had become a de facto representative of the Palestinian theater in international media and the local Hebrew press. Although Abu Salem and Lubeck had successfully managed the brand and its narrative, Palestinian members of the ensemble felt that their personal stories were being obscured. If the local theater movement and the press had not fanned the fire of conflict, such internal disagreement would not have loomed large, but El-Hakawati's successes and celebrity status heightened disagreements.

During this period of theatrical factionalism, starting initially in 1985 and continuing through the Intifada of 1987, the Nuzha-El-Hakawati Center presented many significant productions. Abu Salem's El-Hakawati produced Brecht's *The Exception and the Rule* (1986-1987), a centennial celebration of Chekhov's one-act plays (1986-1987, including *The Bear* and *The Proposal*), and Dario Fo's celebrated one-person performance of *Mistero Buffo* (1986), starring Youssef Abu Wardeh and directed by François Abu Salem. Simultaneously, the close-knit and committed team of Abu Salem, Lubeck, and Muallem had begun preparing for a new creation in the original spirit of El-Hakawati under the title *The Story of Kufur Shamma* (1987). Although the founding members of the Nuzha-Hakawati Theatre all participated in the initial rehearsals and improvisations for this project, Jackie Lubeck had taken the lead as playwright. In the same period, Radi Shehadeh was specializing in working with children and puppets. He wrote, directed, and produced the children's plays *Sharshouh* (1985) and *Yoya* (1989-1990). Ibrahim Khalayleh researched the work conditions of Palestinian laborers in Israel and led the process to produce the play *Slaves Go West* (1986–1987), which Radi Shehadeh directed. Khalayleh also produced *The Birds* (1988), directed by the Nazarene Fouad Awad. Shehadeh wrote and aimed to produce a play inspired by the pre-Islamic black Arab poet Antara, which he called *Antara in the Courtyard* (1988–1989). This simultaneous process of producing and performing multiple plays under the roof of the Nuzha-Hakawati Theatre created an energetic atmosphere that enlivened Palestinian theater in Jerusalem, but it also weakened El-Hakawati members regarding a wave of objections against their residency in the theater. The strength and frequency of the tide of criticism guaranteed the drowning of the fragmented ensemble sooner or later.

The various productions in this period spelled out the aesthetic and substantive directions of the artists involved. Khalayleh's *Slaves Go West* addressed the question of factionalism within the labor movement, examining whether unions should fight for improvements in laborers' salaries and working conditions immediately or after the end of the Israeli occupation. Relying on his expertise in social work, he performed ethnographic fieldwork with Gazan workers specifically for this production. This timely play spoke to urgent debates that exploded as unions factionalized and produced parallel unions according to partisan Palestinian politics.[5] Between Khalayleh's commitment to leftist politics and his intense satirical style on the one hand and Shehadeh's directorial experimentation and powerful writing skills on the other, the play hit a chord with Palestinian audiences, who had grown tired of the factionalism that broke down the unified national struggle. The production relied on less trained performers who had the experience of laboring under Israeli rule but did not possess the acting and improvising technique that El-Hakawati Ensemble had developed over the better part of a decade. Thus, the well-received popular production generated extensive discussions that continued within contemporary Palestinian theater. Should the theater movement focus on nationally urgent content or the aesthetic development of theater practice? This question will remain open as long as the Palestinian liberation struggle continues alive and unresolved.

Shortly thereafter, Shehadeh's *Antara in the Courtyard* (1989) exhibited his fascination with poetry, storytelling, Arab mythology, puppetry, and traditional Arab music. He labeled the play a love poem for Palestine, spoken in local dialect and structured like a folktale. This one-person performance was supported by François Abu Salem and Fateh Azzam as movement coaches. The Jerusalemite visual artist Suleiman Mansour painted the set, and Bethlehemite artist Adnan Zubaidi designed the horse puppet, while Jackie Lubeck designed the costumes that Mounira Shehadeh built. Onstage, Antara's partners were his puppet horse and the musical compositions of Mustapha Al-Kurd. Played like a heroic figure, he was the opposite of the Western Don Quixote. The play toured locally in schools after its successful opening at the theater. In keeping with El-Hakawati's tradition, Shehadeh also toured the play to Tunisia, Egypt, and Japan. By producing and performing this play, he set in motion his theatrical aesthetic, focusing on local lore and placing Arab and Palestinian cultural heritage at the center of his future endeavors.

Simultaneous to the rising conflicts in the saga of El-Hakawati and their theater, many theater companies produced some contemporary classics relying on local experience and the repertoire of world theater. The two most notable productions running in parallel to El-Hakawati's *The Story of Kufur Shamma* were *Natrin Faraj (Awaiting Salvation)* and *Mawta Bila Qubur (Men Without Shadows)*. In 1987, Sanabel People's Theatre created and mounted *Natrin Faraj*, their most significant production since *Returning to Haifa*. Inspired by Athol Fugard's South African play *Woza Albert!*, the play tells the story of two laymen arrested by the authorities. After a humiliating process of body searches and personal interrogation, they are imprisoned. While in custody, the peaceful, soft-spoken one tells the other of the news of the coming Messiah. The play explores perceptions about the coming salvation as a journalist interviews tradesmen and merchants about their wishes for the miracle-performing Messiah. When the Messiah is finally spotted walking on the surface of the sea, the government identifies him as a foreign object and nukes him.

The Sanabel production kept the frame of *Woza Albert!*, but increased the number of actors in the play from two to four and drew on the local experience of the occupation. Although the original play was inspired by apartheid South Africa, the company of Palestinian actors discovered that the frame story and plot structure fit the Palestinian experience: "We not only shared aspects of it, but it was also as if the situation was the same in Palestine and South Africa. There was the idea of identity. 'Blacks' lived in ghettoes they couldn't leave without permits, etc., and it was the same [in Palestine] and continues to be: Blue IDs, Green IDs, Orange IDs, and permits."⁶ Under the direction of Hayyan Ya'coub Al-Ju'beh, for a period of three months, the company improvised the situations in the play to produce an original Palestinian production. They asked, "Since the Muslims, Christians, and Jews all had been awaiting the Messiah, what would happen if he appeared in 1987 in occupied East Jerusalem?" Sanabel suggested that the Messiah would be killed. The irony of Sanabel's answer is that the Holy City is sustained by the Messiah's legacy, but the balance of contemporary power led to his annihilation.

A few months before the Intifada of 1987, the Sanabel People's Theatre started rehearsals at the house of actor Hussam Abu Esheh in Al-Sa'diyeh neighborhood of the Old City, the home of Sanabel at that time. Focusing on three main topics—salvation, prison life, and exploitation of Palestinian labor—they performed fieldwork at two sites not far from the walls of the Old City, Al-Musrara and Damascus Gate. For ten days, they followed the routine of Palestinian laborers, who worked on Israeli projects to feed their families. They woke up before dawn, headed to one of the labor pick-up sites, and participated in the process of impressing potential Israeli employers. Upon the arrival of an employer's vehicle, two common scenarios occurred. If chosen from tens of thousands of workers in this muscle market, the Palestinian would earn a day's living working on a settlement or a labor-intensive project in Israeli territories. If the worker failed to impress the potential employer, he waited for the next vehicle and repeated the process until he gave up and returned home. This experience set the tone for the play as a labor-class satire about the poor and the oppressed as they await salvation on a daily basis in the form of the bourgeois employer, freedom from administrative detention, or the end of the occupation.⁷

The company interwove their research from fieldwork, personal stories in Israeli prisons, and the Palestinian desire for salvation from a seemingly never-ending cycle of oppression. They established a critical distance by undoing theatrical illusion from the first moment of the play. The play begins with a satirical representation of the laborers' muscle market, where each actor displays his muscles like a wrestler or a body builder; then they identify themselves by their real names, tell Sanabel Theatre's history as an ensemble, and situate their production in its South African context. They state, "We liked the play because it depends principally on two colors, black and white. The events you'll see today, you've seen before, and got used to it."⁸ By revealing the theatrical apparatus, the actors invite their audience to question their own behavior under occupation and their desire for salvation by an external force.

The play and the production prevent the audience from accepting the theatrical illusion, which is typically achieved by using traditional acting and staging techniques. The four actors collectively play over fifty characters that change from one instant to the next. The suggestive set functions as a train, a prison cell, a helicopter, a barbershop, and various outdoor street scenes. Throughout, the satirical representation of the Israeli and Jordanian media along with constant references to the audience's reactions, including an accusation of boredom, keep the audience engaged as the actors fulfill their promise to present events that the audience are habituated to. For example, when workers are asked about what they hope for from the soon-arriving Messiah, their stereotypical wishes include the preservation of Palestinian ownership in the Jerusalemite Electric Company, dinner for one night with family members in the diaspora, the gathering of brothers in one prison to facilitate family visitations, protection from settler attacks and house demolitions, and the refugee right of return. These familiar demands are followed by the more satirical challenge for the Messiah to save his own life from the occupation or to obtain a permit to build a church.⁹

Director Hayyan Ya'coub and the company of actors understood the fine line between situation comedy and sacrilegious satire. In the scene depicting the arrival of the Messiah at Ben Gurion Airport, he is described as he descends the stairs, lands on the ground, and begins his conversation with an eager journalist. The depiction of a prophet dressed in seemingly ancient attire and appearing to both a predominantly Muslim Sunni majority and a significant religious Christian minority of various sects presents a potentially dangerous conflict for a Palestinian audience. Just as the faithful audience is about to say, "Stop this ridicule," the scene reveals the identity of the individual as a new immigrant who is mostly interested in visiting his aunt Rachel in Tel Aviv. In his reflection on the production, Ya'coub admired the audience's sense of humor and their ability to play along.¹⁰ However, the censors, who banned the play shortly after its opening, did not share the Palestinian audience's enthusiastic reception.

Although incomplete scripts usually misled the censors, Ya'coub's public admission to a journalist that the censor-approved script and the public performance were vastly different prompted a new confrontation between the censors and the Sanabel People's Theatre. After three performances, the Israeli authorities shut down the production, citing controversy and insensitivity to Christians as the primary reason.[11] The well-known Israeli Jewish lawyer Leah Tsemel took on the case of freeing the production by citing a loophole in the censorship law. She argued that the law typically allowed for a number of experimental performances before "official" theatrical openings.[12] Private communications between the censorship office and the Ministry of Religious Affairs showed that a fundamental difference in Palestinian and Israeli viewership probably played a major role in the decision-making process. An official at the ministry explained in his evaluation that there are two types of Christians in Jerusalem. The liberal-minded thoughtful Christian type would see the play as an enlightening artistic reflection on the role of religion and the Messiah in our lives. The second type of Christian in the Holy Land, the average or conservative one, is the narrow-minded fundamentalist, who would likely be offended by the play's lack of reverence to Jesus and his impotence to help people in crisis. The official noted: "Most of the Christians in this country in my opinion belong to the second category I mentioned above." On the same evaluation, a second handwritten note confirms the first opinion and opposes giving a permit due to the high sensitivity about such issues in a religious community.[13]

The show's popularity and notoriety as an unapologetic satirical drama earned the ensemble a United States tour organized by Palestinian students in American universities and supported by Clergy and Laity Concerned (CALC). Officially endorsing the tour, the executive committee of CALC sent a letter to the US consulate in East Jerusalem facilitating the visa process. CALC stated: "Knowledge about the peoples of the Middle East and familiarity with their cultures is essential to creating an environment conducive to peace. A US tour of Assanabil Ensemble would, we feel, be a positive step in that direction."[14] The letter cited thirteen performances in thirteen cities across the United States for a period of one month. After the ensemble's arrival in New York in July 1988, the tour grew to twenty performances in sixteen states. Controversy followed the production on the tour to the California State University in Sacramento (CSUS), where the Jewish Community Relations Council complained that the show was anti-Semitic: "These groups always say that they will be putting on a cultural show, but the message of the show is always anti-Semitic, and you can be sure that the hate literature will be out in the lobby."[15] Dennis Bates of the Israeli consulate in San Francisco stated:

> It is a very fine and usually invisible line that divides something that is anti-Israeli, something that is anti-Zionistic, and something that is anti-Semitic. For the audience drawn to this type of show they all mean the same thing.[16]

According to the CSUS student newspaper, *The State Hornet*, Jewish community leaders complained that nearly $5,000 of student money was being spent on a "blatantly one-sided political play that helps incite anti-Israeli feelings."[17] On 17 September 1988, CSUS University Theatre hosted the event, which also included several nationalistic songs by the actor Ahmad Abu Saloum.

At the conclusion of the tour, director Hayyan Ya'coub stated to the *Washington Report on Middle East Affairs* that the tour had been successful on two accounts. First, the Sanabel People's Theatre established that Palestinian theater "developed its own methods and has come of age." Second, the ensemble had been able to show that "the real Palestinian problem is in the fact that the US government supports Israeli occupation." Author Pat McDonnell summarized Sanabel's American tour:

> If the ensemble returns to the United States for future tours, and translates its script into English so that Americans are made aware of the humor and bravery of the Palestinian people, it is likely that non-Arabic speaking Americans would turn out to give the same warm welcome Sanabel received this time by the Arab-American community.[18]

To their credit, Sanabel People's Theatre was the first contemporary Palestinian theater ensemble to embark on a theatrical tour of the United States, a country that fully supported the State of Israel and lacked resources for Palestinians. In line with their grassroots mandate, the organization of the tour relied on Palestinian and Arab students on university campuses, using relatively small budgets. According to Abu Esheh, committed students who believe in the message of the PFLP and the Palestinian cause made this tour possible, as did the growing Palestinian diaspora. In the absence of an official agent or spokesperson and occurring during the height of the initial full year of the first Intifada, the troupe encountered extreme resistance at the institutions where they played, but their Arabic-speaking audiences attended in droves, countering the predominant orientalist trends of 1980s America. Sanabel's choice to perform the play in Arabic substantially assisted their cause of reaching Palestinian audiences, but it also significantly reduced the number of English-speaking attendees. Nonetheless, this first major encounter between contemporary Palestinian theater and the United States set a precedent to be followed by many theaters since the late 1980s.

Of note, censorship followed this production into the 1990s and post-Oslo. On 17 May 1999, four days after Bethlehem's Al-Ro'at TV station aired a video of the production, the Palestinian Authority's Ministry of the Interior shut down the station. One representative explained that the Ministry of the Interior clearly understood the danger of provoking sectarian sentiments and claimed that a team from the ministry watched and evaluated the play, deeming it offensive to the Lord Jesus Christ. Another representative denied the Palestinian Authority's involvement. In spite of the mixed messages, the order submitted to the director of the station, Hamdi Farraj, cited President Yasser Arafat as the source. The closure caused a stir in the religious community and the theatrical movement. According to actor and ensemble co-founder Hussam Abu Esheh, representatives of Sanabel People's Theatre and Al-Ro'at station met with heads of the churches at the Latin Patriarchate, watched the play with them, and answered their questions. Shortly thereafter, churches and institutions of civil society in the district of Bethlehem sent President Arafat messages demanding the reopening of the station and reprimanding the use of Christian sentiments as an excuse for the ministry's actions.[19]

During the period of El-Hakawati's slow and painful fragmentation, George Ibrahim's star was on the rise. He had successfully resolved a long-standing conflict between him and the theater movement when he presented his children's productions at El-Hakawati Theatre instead of El-Omariyyeh school. This move politically aligned with the position previously preferred by the majority of theater artists in Jerusalem to boycott the West Jerusalem municipality and all institutions it funded.

His productions in the later 1980s engaged with the Palestinian politics of the era even though they still did not take the direct approach clearly witnessed in the works of Sanabel People's Theatre, the Palestinian Theatre, and other local ensembles. In 1988, Jean Paul Sartre's *Men Without Shadows* (*Mawta Bila Quboor*) became El-Warsheh El-Fanniyeh's most memorable production of the decade (figure 17). Directed and adapted by Mazen Ghattas (1954-2005), the production indirectly but clearly constructed a parallel between the occupation of France in World War II and the occupation of the Palestinian Territories in 1967: "The events occur on the eve of the end of the German occupation of France, when one of the French Resistance groups falls in the hands of the Germans. Its members face brutality and death for their cause, freeing France."[20] The audience received the production, staged during the period of the first Intifada (1987-1993), as a representation of ongoing events. For example, theater critic Ghassan Abdallah contextualized the performance as an event occurring "in the shadow of hundreds of fallen martyrs and thou-

FIGURE 17 A performance of Al-Kasaba's production of *Men Without Shadows* at El-Hakawati Theatre. Jerusalem, 1986. Courtesy of George Ibrahim.

sands of injured individuals." He described the crux of the production: "What is death? Do we die to live or the opposite? Do we draw life from our own death?"[21]

On 1 September 1988, George Ibrahim applied to the Ministry of the Interior for the performance permit. The process of evaluation began on 7 September 1988. On 16 September 1988, the first evaluator approved the production, and a second evaluator approved it two days later. On 22 September 1988, the final permit was printed.[22] The quick approval process can be attributed to the European origins of the text, its availability as a published play in Israel, and the association of the play with resistance to the Vichy regime in World War II. One can imagine that an Israeli censor might have difficulty fathoming the potential of the play in Palestinian hands, rendering the approval easy and simultaneously ironic. Needless to say, director Mazen Ghattas's concept was absent from the application. Ghattas focused his production on depicting the torture of the resistance fighters at the hands of the Germans in the shadow of numerous scarecrows that populated the stage.[23] Ibrahim played the role of Clochet, whose sadistic interrogation techniques were expressly drawn from the oral accounts of Palestinian prisoners. To indicate the parallel between the French and Palestinian resistance, the French prisoners spoke in Palestinian accents. The German interrogators spoke in accented classical Arabic, the dialect sometimes used to depict Hebrew speakers on the Palestinian stage. Even if the Israeli censors had seen the production on stage, they would have been unlikely to understand the play as the Palestinian audiences did. To Ghattas's credit, without comprehending the equivalency of classical Arabic to Hebrew, the play suggests a museum piece from the Western theater tradition, not a production that equates Palestinian resistance to French resistance and the state of Israel to the Vichy regime. Had the censorship officers seen the production, they likely would have banned Ibrahim and Ghattas's liberal adaptation. In the set design, scarecrows standing throughout the stage represented the occupation as a dominant figure, always watching but hollow. In his review of the production, Carl Vitale of *Al-Fajr* newspaper described the success of the adaptation: "The situation is all too real for the Palestinians in the Occupied Territories, right down to the army taking over schools and turning them into military posts."[24]

The play's local spirit appears in the first act after a band of revolutionaries is imprisoned and their torture by an illegitimate government begins. They spontaneously sing the words of the Arab anthem "Ya Thalam Al-Sijn" ("Oh, Darkness of Prison") by the anti-colonial Syrian activist, journalist, and intellectual Najib El-Rayyes (1898-1952), who wrote it while exiled in a colonial French prison in 1922. After it was set to the Ottoman tune of the "Osman Pasha March" ("Plevna March") by the Lebanese composer Mohammed Flayfel (1899-1986), the anthem became the rallying cry of prisoners across the Arab world. The actors on stage committed to the tone of the music as performed and popularized by the Palestinian musical troupe Al-Ashekien, who were formed in Damascus in 1977 and specialized in singing the resistance poetry of Mahmoud Darwish, Samih Al-Qassem, and Tawfiq Zayyad. The anthem challenges the darkness of prison and promises that the dawn of glory will rise. It tells of the revolutionaries' commitment not to betray their oath, urging the guards to listen to the revolutionaries' truth. The idealistic principles and utopian horizons of the anthem inspired thunderous applause in an audience thirsty for communal assurance in a time of mass arrests during the first Intifada (1987-1993).

The production highlighted the value of sacrifice for the sake of the national cause. After Clochet's torture of the revolutionary Sorbiet (Kamel El-Basha), the Palestinian audiences cheered and whistled in excitement when Sorbiet chose to commit suicide by jumping out of a window after informing on his comrades in the struggle. A similarly oversized reaction took place when another prisoner chose to kill her own brother to prevent him from talking. These audience reactions revealed the influence of the production on the Palestinian audiences in Jerusalem. Because the Intifada had been raging for over a year, many of the Fateh, PFLP, and DFLP cadres that actively guided the Palestinian street through flyers and strategic announcements through word of mouth had been imprisoned. Confessions by party members had become a clear sign of treason. One leading figure of the Intifada, DFLP organizer Mohammed Al-Labadi stated, "When one of the cadres got caught, it was a domino effect, and they would start catching the others. Sometimes because of collaboration and sometimes because finding one person led to another by mistake."[25]

The power of *Mawta Bila Quboor* emerged from its representation of an immediate condition in the lives of Palestinians without explicitly stating the location as Palestine. To a non-Palestinian watching the production, critical analysis would easily reveal the parallels; however, the depth of the performance resided in the messaging and characterization of Israeli interrogators by George Ibrahim and Siham Ghazaleh. The production effectively folded performers' lived experiences into character work. For example, actor Kamel El-Basha had served two years in Israeli prison. The remainder of the company members and the director clearly understood and well represented the Palestinian view of the occupation through this adaptation, which also became a departure for George Ibrahim as an artist committed to political theater. On the heels of this production's success and during the frequent strikes, closures, and acts of civil disobedience of the Intifada, Ibrahim saw fit to create his own theater space that would become one of the most recognizable names in the history of contemporary Palestinian theater: Al-Kasaba.[26]

During the emergence of Sanabel and El-Warsheh El-Fanniyeh as frequent producers with rising stars, El-Hakawati's growing fragmentation led to a temporary increase in production for a limited period. At the doorstep of the first Intifada in the last half of 1986 and in 1987, it could be argued that El-Hakawati's heightened productivity could be attributed to a last effort by various members of the ensemble to extend the duration of their reign in Jerusalem. While Ibrahim Khalayleh and Radi Shehadeh pursued their individual projects and sought to sculpt their identities as artists, the original El-Hakawati Ensemble proceeded with their newest original creation. Authored by Jackie Lubeck with the support of the acknowledged conceptual leadership of François Abu Salem, *The Story of Kufur of Shamma* (*The Story of the Village of Shamma*) proved to be the ensemble's longest-running production and perhaps, its most controversial with Israeli and Jewish audiences. The play tells the story of a fictional village, a stand-in for the Palestinian villages destroyed in 1948 (figure 18). After the death of the village mayor and an undisclosed catastrophe, the narrator of the story, Walid, returns from his studies abroad to find Ka'wash, the village fool. Ka'wash describes the desertion of the village as a strange race in all directions. Walid convinces Ka'wash to join him on a journey to find the people of Kufur Shamma and to bring them home. During their search, a cast of characters joins them. They are Nijmeh (Star), a fifteen-year-old girl originally from a village near Yafa; Karim,

FIGURE 18   A performance of *The Story of Kufur Shamma*. Jerusalem, 1989. Courtesy of François Abu Salem Archive, Palestinian National Theater/El-Hakawati.

an eighteen-year-old Palestinian fighter from a refugee camp in Lebanon; Hijleh, a divorced matchmaker from Yafa; and Abed, a merchant and poet originally from Nablus but residing in the Gulf. A series of scenes depict the cast's reactions as they encounter the fragmented Palestinian population. Upon seeing the Palestinians dressed in traditional Arabian Gulf attire, the group determines that many Palestinians in the Gulf States may have lost their sense of belonging. In America, the people of Kufur Shamma cannot or will not necessarily return home, but they preserve their traditions in exile. Finally, Walid and his company return to the village, only to discover that it has been completely erased. The grave of the mukhtar (mayor), a tree, and a stone remain as the only reminders of the pre-1948 village. Kaʿwash suggests that Walid's story must not disappear like Kufur Shamma. Kaʿwash concludes the play by saying, "Tell them."[27]

On 1 March 1987, the censorship office approved Jackie Lubeck's application for the permit to perform the play. In his evaluation on 1 February 1987, the censor summarized the play as a boring and unsuccessful attempt inspired by *Roots*, the 1977 American television miniseries about the African diaspora. He described the play as a take on the story of Palestinian Arabs, who had reached as far as the United States and still preserved their traditions. He approved the play because, in his opinion, it was as long as "exile" and a form of "punishment" in and of itself. In a sarcastic tone, he proposed to permit the play to increase Palestinian/Israeli misunderstanding and he expected the audience to receive it by "clapping with their feet," suggesting that audiences would simply leave the production.[28] The play proved to be El-Hakawati's longest touring production in Europe, playing in English, French, and Italian. It was also the ensemble's first production to tour in the United States.

In their presentation in the Acre Fringe Festival, referred to in Arabic news outlets as "Theater of the Other" and in Hebrew as "The Alternative Theater," El-Hakawati faced their most aggressive encounter with the Israeli government and right-wing extremists. On 6 October 1987, *Al-Itihad* newspaper reported on a series of pronouncements by the Herut Party's Acre representatives, calling for the ban of three anti-Israeli plays and the cancellation of El-Hakawati's performance of *Kufur Shamma*.[29] On 9 October 1987, the *Jerusalem Post* reported: "Police reinforcements are expected to help supervise a demonstration by Herut supporters at the opening of the Acre fringe theater festival tomorrow night."[30] The police had approved the protest in advance while members of the Citizens Rights Movement announced their intention to hold a counterdemonstration. Failing to ban the three Israeli scripts, which had been approved by the censorship board, "the Herut councilmen subsequently shifted the focus of their attention to the East Jerusalem theater ensemble, which refused to perform with Israeli flags flying in the background when the group last appeared at the festival."[31] Herut councilman David Bar-Lev announced that he expected the Herut demonstrators would raise the Israeli flag, but did not expect them to cause trouble.[32] Palestinian and Jewish supporters demanded the cancellation of the Herut demonstration's permit on the grounds that it provoked racial hatred in a mixed city. The three Arab councilmen in the Acre municipality officially objected to the demonstration as well.[33]

On 10 October 1987, the initial demonstration at the festival's opening passed without incident. Under the banner of Arab-Jewish coexistence, *Al-Itihad* reported a carnival atmosphere within Acre's Old City walls.[34] On 12 October 1987, the day of El-Hakawati's performance, a number of right-wing groups, including Likud activists and Kach/Kahane Chai extremists, showed significant presence outside the Auditorium Theatre in Acre. Well-armed and prepared to control potential disorder, large numbers of local police and border guards searched audience members as they entered the theater through metal detectors.[35] Despite El-Hakawati's agreement with the festival that they would not perform under Israeli flags, flags were raised outside the hall, but not inside the auditorium. Ten minutes before the performance, the head of the Acre municipality and a Likud member entered the hall and placed two flags on each side of the stage. When ensemble members objected to playing before the Israeli flags, the head of the municipality asked them to choose between respecting the flag and preventing hundreds of audience members from seeing the play.[36] In their tradition of collective decision-making, the ensemble deliberated to evaluate their options. Entering stage left, François Abu Salem responded to the crisis with the following announcement in English:

> You are most welcome. We have decided after a long talk between each other that we are going to perform *The Story of Kufur Shamma*, despite very heated atmosphere and some very unfortunate and childish provocations that have fallen upon us all day long.

Then he repeated the announcement in Arabic with slight variations:

> Welcome! We decided to show the play of Kufur Shamma despite the anxious atmosphere and the buildup of childish provocations that we faced all day long. But in spite of it, we felt that maybe you came here to see a play and our connection is primarily with you as our audience. We hope that you'll share our sentiment that we made the right decision.[37]

To the audience's rhythmic applause, the actors began the performance. In the dark, technical director Imad Mitwalli removed the flags before the first lighting cue. Nine minutes thereafter, a band of unknown individuals stood up in the front row, opened their shirts to reveal the Kahane Chai emblem, raised an Israeli flag, and chanted racial slurs: "Arabs out!" and "Death to Arabs." An unidentified voice shouted in Arabic, "You shit!" Shocked, confused, and unable to see into the dark auditorium, the actors stopped the performance. While observing events, actor Amer Khalil exited stage left, actress Iman Aoun moved upstage, Jackie

Lubeck and Imad Mizero observed from stage left. Actors attempted to see into the darkness to evaluate the source of the interruption. Mitwalli raised the house lights as the majority of the audience stood up and young Palestinians engaged the intruders in a physical fight. Amidst screams and murmurs, the audience united its response by rhythmically applauding and collectively chanting a traditional leftist slogan in Hebrew: "Fascism won't pass." According to *Al-Itihad*, the "Arab-Jewish audience" beat up the "hooligans" until the police and the border guards "saved" them:

> Voices were raised to protest the actions of the police and the border guards. They demanded the punishment of those responsible for the entrance of Kahane's riffraff to the performance hall. The protesters asserted that the police had the first and last responsibility for what happened. The voices insisted to continue watching the show.[38]

Armed with light machine guns, border guards reentered the hall along with the audience members who had participated in the altercation. After a short discussion, the actors returned to their positions on stage to the sound of applause and whistles in the audience, who shouted encouraging words such as "We're here!" to pledge the actors' safety. At the end of the second act, forty minutes into the performance, a high-ranking police officer took the stage to announce a ten-minute break and an order to evacuate the auditorium because an anonymous caller had informed the police of the presence of explosives hidden in the theater. The audience complied. The police and border guards physically searched the premises, but did not succeed in finding the reported bomb. After the actors and the audience returned to the theater, the performance continued without interruptions. When they departed the theater, the ensemble members found the tires of their vehicle had been slashed.[39]

The incident in Acre foreshadowed the atmosphere of the first Intifada that erupted in December 1987, the subsequent rise of right-wing Israeli politics, the dwindling power of the Israeli left, the collusion of Israeli security forces with the settler movement, and the years of popular struggle against increasing intolerance of Palestinian existence on their historic homeland. The play's representation of the Nakba as the foundation of the Palestinian struggle and the insistence of the Kahane faction on physically preventing the ensemble from performing in a pluralistic environment at any cost embodied the rising tensions in historic

Palestine. The point of contention, to play before the Israeli flag, became the "straw man" for an altercation far larger than the theatrical space. At the heart of the confrontation was the rejection of Palestinian performance and ultimately existence by a then-fringe ideology that would later become the determined political direction of the Israeli state, sidelining any potential for coexistence. It is essential to read this event as part of an ongoing timeline where Israel grows out of an immigrant community in the first half of the twentieth century into a Zionist movement of armed militias that established a state in 1948, then self-organized into a military that occupied the Palestinian territories in 1967. In other words, the 1987 events leading to the Intifada had been only twenty years away from the 1967 occupation. The extreme Israeli-settler expansion using its disproportional economic and military prowess had not reached its apex. Therefore, with the asymmetry of population and rootedness in Palestine not yet being so disparate, the ability of El-Hakawati and their audience to fight against this attack was still possible. Similarly, on the Palestinian street, the Intifada's eruption as a popular movement was equally still possible as the hostile environment was reaching a boiling point.

During the Intifada, Palestinian theater was arrested, nearly in its entirety. Throughout 1988 and 1989, closures of roads, theaters, schools, and universities prevented theater makers from performing. To perform in any public environment placed performers and audiences at extreme risk. While general labor strikes pervaded Palestinian public life and violence erupted throughout the Occupied Territories, El-Hakawati toured *Kufur Shamma* internationally, becoming one of the few cultural exports that survived the violence in the homeland. While on tour, in an unprecedented event and for the first time in its history, El-Hakawati played directly in front of the Palestinian leadership. In Tunis, the leaders of the Palestinian Liberation Organization (PLO) attended *Kufur Shamma*. Although it is difficult to ascertain whether Yasser Arafat attended the performance, the ensemble received his invitation to meet him in person. François Abu Salem and Jackie Lubeck were led to an undisclosed location, where the leader met them in person. He said: "This play must go to America." Based on this meeting, the PLO donated $20,000 to fund El-Hakawati's tour to the United States. According to interviews with all living members of El-Hakawati, this donation was the only time that a

Palestinian political faction contributed to El-Hakawati's existence as an ensemble.

In 1989, El-Hakawati embarked on its first tour in the United States with an English-language production of *The Story of Kufur Shamma*. Represented in North America by John I. Patches of International Arts Consultants, the ensemble booked performances in Lexington, VA; Woodstock, NY; Vancouver, BC; Seattle, WA; Pittsburgh, PA; Atlanta, GA; and New York, NY.[40] On 30 June 1989, the *Philadelphia Inquirer* broke the shocking news that Joseph Papp had cancelled El-Hakawati's booking at the Public Theater. The article related that Papp discussed the issue with his rabbi, who expected the play would incite strong feelings in the Jewish community. In a phone interview with the *Inquirer*, Papp stated:

> I was thinking that we do have an enormous number of supporters who are very sympathetic to Israel.... Jews constitute a high proportion of the theater audience in any city, but especially in New York. I didn't want to offend those people. They're my people and they're part of my audience.[41]

Describing his discussion with Papp, the ensemble's US representative John Patches stated in the same newspaper article:

> I knew that he had come under pressure from individuals in the Jewish community. He said something to the effect that he'd never been in a position where he had to cancel something he had agreed to do. He said he felt very bad about it because he had heard so much about El-Hakawati, but he could not jeopardize the institution that he represented.[42]

According to the *Philadelphia Inquirer*, Papp insisted that his board of directors did not pressure him to make the decision: "Papp said he began rethinking the engagement upon receipt of a letter from a 74-year-old Jewish woman who had lost relatives in Israel's long conflict with its Arab neighbors."[43] The woman criticized him for booking El-Hakawati. In the American press, Papp's argument became more elaborate over time. He provided several reasons for the cancellation. Since he had never addressed the Arab/Israeli conflict in his theater, he did not wish to make a political statement. He suggested that if he had programmed an Israeli play to perform in the same season, he would not have canceled the booking. Upon seeing El-Hakawati's production, Papp feared his audience would misconstrue the Palestinian political position as his own. He also stated that El-Hakawati had failed to provide their portion of the financial agreement; thus no contract was signed, a claim that El-Hakawati and their agent denied. Most often, the press primarily reported that the cancellation stemmed from Papp's desire to present a balanced representation of the Israel/Palestine conflict.[44]

On the evening of 1 July 1989, the ensemble made their American debut at the Painted Bride Art Center in Philadelphia.[45] In his review, the *Philadelphia Inquirer*'s theater critic William B. Collins commented on the unusual circumstances surrounding the production:

> This is not an ordinary show checking into a downtown theater. It is an event of political as well as theatrical implications. We see it through eyes blinkered by years of conditioning against the Arabs. We go knowing ahead of time that already one door has been slammed in the face of these Middle Eastern visitors. A tentative booking at New York's prestigious Public Theater fell through when producer Joseph Papp backed out, saying he did not want to offend Jewish theatergoers.[46]

The Painted Bride Art Center received one letter of complaint regarding the booking.[47] While his review clearly outlined the political implications of the production, his critique of the performance merely mentioned the use of diverse production elements, such as masks on refugees and a mix of live and taped music. He also described the Palestinian actors' English as heavily accented and the writing as flat and self-conscious.[48] Wondering "where offense might be taken," Collins described the play as nonconfrontational and nonbelligerent. He suggested it was "political only in the inevitable sense of being told from the perspective of the Arab side rather than the Israeli."[49]

Determined to present the play in New York, Patches arranged for a run of the play from 26 July to 1 August 1989 at the Dance Theater Workshop (DTW). As a contributing financial sponsor through its Suitcase Fund, the theater had been involved peripherally in the United States tour.[50] The Papp cancellation prompted DTW to book El-Hakawati in its theater in Lower Manhattan's Chelsea neighborhood. Although he suggested the play required "serious editing," *New York Times'* Wilborn Hampton positively reviewed the performance:

> The physical production, however, is a small marvel, especially considering that the company is on tour. Set and costume changes are woven seamlessly together, using a few doors, curtains and rugs, robes and scarves and some old jerrycans, and fit the workshop's space as if they had been tailored for it.[51]

Unlike Collins of the *Philadelphia Inquirer*, Hampton did not shy away from declaring the underlying source of the Papp controversy:

> Of course, one would have to be more of an idiot than Ka'wash not to know that someone flew the planes and fired the guns that dispersed nearly a million Palestinians. But "The Story of Kufur Shamma" is about those refugees, not the armies that put them to flight, and El-Hakawati tells it with humor and skill. One should be grateful to Dance Theater Workshop for giving them a stage from which to tell their story.[52]

In his account of the New York opening, John Simon of *New York Magazine* concluded by describing the spirit of El-Hakawati: "Above all, there is no hate in the play, and the Israelis are barely touched upon. There is sadness and sorrowing, but rather more endurance, childlike humor, stoicism, fortitude, and hope."[53] He continued: "As for Joseph Papp, though I did not see him applaud, he was there in the opening night audience."[54]

During the tour of *Kufur Shamma* in the United States and Europe, El-Hakawati Theatre celebrated five years in existence in a far less triumphant atmosphere. Negotiations were fully underway to reach a final status agreement between El-Hakawati Ensemble and their own theater administration. The five-year contract that François Abu Salem had signed for the building, which included a temporary reduction in rent for the renovation work, had expired. The pressures from the local theater movement, the administration, and within the ensemble had reached the level of a final ultimatum: El-Hakawati Ensemble as represented primarily by François Abu Salem, Jackie Lubeck, and Edward Muallem had to either take on the full responsibility of managing the building and take on its financial responsibility in its entirety or relinquish its status as a resident company and the founder of the theater. Although the board of trustees included many supporters of El-Hakawati, the vote leading to this decision fell on the side of the ensemble's opponents and technically fulfilled the quorum requirements in the bylaws of at least two founding members and one-third of the board of trustees. While they toured their tremendous sixth unique creation, the original founding ensemble members had to confront a painfully difficult choice: to dedicate their time to managing and funding a theater building on their own or to give up their home and function as an itinerant ensemble once again.

To best understand the complexity of this historical moment in contemporary Palestinian theater, one must comprehend the transformations occurring simultaneously for the Palestinian cause. The first Intifada exported images of Palestinians struggling for freedom of occupation without arms. The popular uprising that came to be associated with child stone-throwers drew the sympathies of the international political stage. The divided factions within Palestine united as a single front of mass unarmed resistance. The PLO, which had been marginalized in the mid-1980s, was exiled in Tunis after its involvement in the Lebanese civil war and resistance against the 1982 Israeli invasion of Lebanon and sought a new function as the political representative of the Palestinian cause. In 1988, Yasser Arafat announced the independent Palestinian state in a well-respected historic declaration. The resistance of Palestinian civil society and the near unification of political factions on the ground, as well as several demands by the international community for Israel to withdraw its 1967 occupation forces, promised a real possibility for the liberation of the Palestinian Territories and the establishment of a permanent Palestinian state in the West Bank and Gaza. Under all these conditions, the Palestinian elite within the homeland had begun to prepare for the establishment of state institutions. Jerusalem's El-Hakawati had been understood as the premier contender for a potential national theater.

In 1989, a local desire to transform the theater from an implicitly private enterprise to an explicitly public one necessitated the departure of the resident company, even though it had founded this theater. If El-Hakawati had chosen to continue to manage the building, the board and its chair Faisal Al-Husseini had considered the possibility of establishing a future national theater in a building two blocks away in Sheikh Jarah.[55]

Ultimately, the protests of the theatrical movement and its supporters on the board of directors of the Nuzha Hakawati Center, as they referred to it, forced a difficult dilemma, to which El-Hakawati Ensemble had to respond. Given the political and economic uncertainty of the moment, as well as their diverging paths, the founding members of the theater chose to accept the board's offer of minor monetary compensation, and their relationship with their namesake theater was forever severed. Claiming victory over the "monopolizing" ownership of El-Hakawati, the theatrical movement and its supporters intended to transform the theater into a publicly run enterprise, available to all Palestinian cultural producers. In preparation for the oncoming peace accords, and since 1990, the theater was colloquially renamed the Palestinian National Theatre, though Jerusalemites consistently continue to informally call it El-Hakawati.

NINE

A MOVEMENT TRANSFORMED, 1990 TO OSLO

Al-Kasaba's Star-Crossed Lovers

In 1989, after a series of highly successful long-running productions for children and adults, especially the critically acclaimed *Men Without Shadows*, George Ibrahim desperately needed his own theatrical space for rehearsals and performances. The Nuzha Hakawati Theatre, aka El-Hakawati, had become a hub for Jerusalem's theatrical community and a growing number of patrons, proving the presence of previously untapped audiences. El-Hakawati contained a single rehearsal space and one large theater with over 350 seats, an auditorium too large for many smaller productions like the majority of locally produced plays in Jerusalem. As an alternative to the heavily used and occasionally unavailable El-Hakawati Theatre, Ibrahim believed "it was necessary to establish new performance halls to accommodate the increasing growth of national culture."[1] In the midst of the first Intifada, the feeling of potential statehood had increased in the promised future Palestinian capital of East Jerusalem. Unprecedented revolutionary sentiment, community participation in the struggle, and cohesion among political factions under the United National Front, the designation adopted by most Palestinian political factions on the ground during the first Intifada, had instilled the desire to continue building the institutions of the potential Palestinian state.

Al-Kasaba Theatre, which would become the largest theatrical institution and the most important Palestinian cinema for the better part of two decades, emerged during the height of the first Intifada. George Ibrahim had produced a track record of uninterrupted production since the 1970s. Like many theater artists of the period, he dreamed of owning his own rehearsal and performance venue. During the 1980s, he attracted many local artists to work with him, especially when he began to present politically engaged plays at El-Hakawati to wide acclaim and wider press coverage. Without referring to his regular actors as an acting ensemble, he intelligently gathered a group of actors who became associated with Al-Kasaba due to the frequency of their casting: Jamal Is'eed, Bassam Zu'mot, Hussam Abu Esheh, Georgina Asfour, Kamel El-Basha, Khaled El-Masou, Makram Khoury, Salwa Naqqara, Areen Omari, and Mohammad Bakry, among many others. This pool of actors represented performers from the West Bank and Palestinian citizens of Israel, but Ibrahim identified his work as Jerusalemite, insisting on the significance of the city, which he had adopted as his home since his arrival in 1965. When El-Omariyyeh School ceased renting to theatrical productions, El-Hakawati's availability became increasingly less reliable, and Ibrahim's house no longer satisfied his need to rehearse with larger casts, he searched for a theatrical home of his own.[2]

The proprietor of the Nuzha Cinema, Ali Freitekh, owned a property across the street from El-Hakawati that, strangely enough, was burned down just like the Nuzha Cinema. Freitekh operated the basement property as a restaurant and a party venue, often renting it out for weddings, special occasions, and Christmas parties. During the Intifada, the space was burned because local fanatics perceived it as a nightclub. It frequently hosted late-night entertainments that were misread as sinful by a handful of religious radicals. According to Ibrahim, it was never a bar or a nightclub, despite the common perception. In 1988, Freitekh offered Ibrahim the opportunity to rent the space for US$5,000 annually. The opportunity would at least satisfy Ibrahim's need for consistent rehearsal space. The $5,000 price tag is noteworthy because Freitekh had successfully rented the damaged Nuzha Cinema to El-Hakawati nearly five years earlier for the same price and under the identical condition that the tenant took responsibility for repairs and renovation. At least from the perspective of the property owner, theater revived the block between the Salah El-Din and the American Colony in East Jerusalem, and as a result, he wished to repeat his successful experience with another theater venture.

From his travels visiting theaters abroad, Ibrahim assessed that restaurants provided a generative outlet for audience development and an ongoing business for income between productions. It also satisfied the need of audiences to gather before and after the performances. Freitekh's offer intrigued the commercially minded theater producer. A reasonable business venture, a novel strategy for income generation, and a potential solution for Ibrahim's rehearsal space problem across from the highly successful El-Hakawati planted the roots for a potential theater district in the elegant urban geography between Sheikh Jarrah and the Old City of Jerusalem. Due to the heightening political tensions of the Intifada and increased closures of businesses, schools, and institutions, theatrical production and tourism showed significant signs of decline, providing an ideal time for a major renovation project that would likely take months to complete. By accepting the offer, Ibrahim took on a risk that very few individuals in Palestinian theater could muster at the time. This risk laid the foundation for a theatrical space that would casually and lovingly be referred to as a beehive, indicating the frequency of its productions.

In 1988, he registered his company as Al-Kasaba Theatre, a non-profit organization that operated his new commercial space. Interestingly, he adopted a "don't ask, don't tell" approach to the business; the new theater company operated without a food, alcohol, or performance license, relying on Freitekh's existing license of the space as an entertainment venue. For the entire duration of Al-Kasaba's operations, Ibrahim maintained a status similar to that of a nongovernmental organization and a non-profit association. To establish this new space, he executed the renovation and repair process slowly over the better part of a year, costing approximately fifty thousand dollars in total because, just as El-Hakawati had done, he took on the responsibility of construction himself with various contractors and actors aiding him. The lighting and sound equipment, carpets, seats, and the auditorium were the largest investments. With the support of hired workers and, on occasion, regular company actors, he led the process of transforming the burned-down basement into a small theater and entertainment complex. The newly opened theater contained three halls. The main hall functioned as a fully equipped ninety- to one-hundred-seat theater, which contained a raked auditorium and a slightly raised stage. Ibrahim bought the seats from a bankrupt cinema through a local scrap-yard merchant. The second hall functioned as a front lobby and a permanent exhibition hall for the visual arts. The third area was designed as a meeting space for artists. It contained a cafeteria, which became one of the most commercially successful spaces in the theater (figure 19). Auxiliary areas included a business office, dressing rooms, a control booth, a workshop, a kitchen, and bathrooms.[3] Describing an evening at Al-Kasaba, the resistance poet Samih Al-Qassem stated, "Al-Kasaba Theatre . . . is a new kind of social and cultural frame."[4] He expressed admiration for the integration of the visual arts, the theater, and fine dining. He was particularly impressed by the ability of the Palestinian people to create such a "civilized" space during the violence of the Intifada. By the end of 1989, Al-Kasaba was open for regular business.

The crucial difference between El-Hakawati and Al-Kasaba during this period was their mission and operational standards. Al-Kasaba aimed to function as an entertainment venue, not only as a theater. Because of its private ownership, Al-Kasaba did not owe any explanation for its programming or financial sources to the local Jerusalemite community, whereas El-Hakawati intentionally aimed to create a space for public ser-

FIGURE 19 Al-Kasaba Theater opened in Jerusalem in 1989. Courtesy of George Ibrahim.

vice as a theater. In contrast, Ibrahim created a small venue that clearly operated as his own while hosting artists and the public for dialogue and discussion: "I believed that growing the industry required connection with the audience on a daily basis." The economically constructed theatrical space generated significant income for Ibrahim and employed many actors in Jerusalem for the weekly and sometimes nightly entertainment events, in addition to theatrical productions. Al-Kasaba generated revenue from its frequent productions and performances for adults and children. The latter often toured outside Jerusalem, particularly in schools, maintaining Ibrahim's production business model from the early 1970s.

Al-Kasaba's restaurant, which the theater movement referred to as "the cafeteria," maintained regular business hours, offering coffee, snacks, sandwiches, lunches, and dinners. Tourist groups to the Old City frequently arranged visits with the hired restaurant manager. Patrons for the restaurant became the audience for theater and vice versa. Across the street, El-Hakawati maintained its position as a theatrical venue and, at times, a space for political activism. Al-Kasaba aimed to create a cultural entertainment venue in Jerusalem that could be frequented for food, gatherings, and entertainment, as well as theatrical performances. With entertainment being its primary function, Al-Kasaba's most important contributions to the cultural life of Jerusalem became its Sunday-evening variety performance and its regular business hours as a meeting place for the cultural elite. Cultural and political figures like Fadwa Touqan, Yehya Yakhlof, Yasser Abed Rabbo, a young Syed Kashua, and Faisal Al-Husseini frequented the venue outside the context of theatrical performances. For many Communist Party figures from the north, such as Samih El-Qassem, Tawfiq Zayyad, and Emile Habibi, who had been key supporters of Ibrahim's cultural work since its beginnings, Al-Kasaba was an essential stop during their stays in Jerusalem. Some even participated as performers in evenings of poetry at the venue.

From the opening of Al-Kasaba (1989) until the Oslo Accords (1993), Ibrahim integrated himself into the theatrical movement, bypassing many of their differences. His adult repertoire had also transformed significantly from its earlier entertainment-focused mission to include a more critical approach, as exemplified in his productions of Camus's *Caligula* (1986), Frisch's *Fire Raisers* (1986), and Sartre's *Men Without*

Shadows (1988). Simultaneously, Ibrahim had been elected as the head of the Palestinian Theatre League, and de facto, Al-Kasaba became the premier site for related professional meetings with him and events hosted by the league. As the elected president of the league, Ibrahim represented the theatrical movement during the artist strike of 1989, in which many political leaders participated in a sit-in and a hunger strike at the Red Cross for fourteen days, demanding the release of Palestinian prisoners and cessation of Israeli military violence. The strike attracted regular international visitors to the Red Cross to demonstrate their solidarity with the Palestinian people. It included public readings of Palestinian demands for liberation during the Intifada and created an opportunity to educate visiting diplomatic delegations about the Palestinian struggle. By participating in this sit-in and making Al-Kasaba available for Intifada-related activity, Ibrahim and Al-Kasaba built their profile as a national institution during this critical period of the Palestinian struggle in Jerusalem.

Al-Kasaba innovated significantly in the field of children's theater. Ibrahim continued to adapt stories from the Arab and world canons of children's stories for the stage, often producing the same plays with new twists, aesthetics, and actors. He would initially produce the plays with live actors, sometimes presenting them at El-Hakawati in their initial run or as part of El-Hakawati's programming for children. Then, he adapted the same performances to be puppet productions that toured schools. He found it was easy to transport and tour puppet performances with a maximum of three performers. His longest-running puppet productions of *Layla Al-Hamra (Little Red Riding Hood)*, *Al-Samaka Al-Thahabiya (The Golden Fish)*, *Qamar Al-Amira (Princess Moon)*, and *Aladdin* were all performed with live actors initially, then toured as puppet shows in schools throughout Palestine, including Gaza and the West Bank. The main touring actors for these performances were Hussam Abu Esheh, Jackie Ayoub, Georgina Asfour, Bassam Zu'mot, Jamal Is'eed, Mahmoud Awad, Ahmad Abu Saloum, and of course, George Ibrahim. After El-Hakawati Ensemble disbanded, Edward Muallem acted in Al-Kasaba's production of *Qamar Al-Amira*, an acknowledgment of the emergent leadership of Al-Kasaba. As a talented producer, Ibrahim cast the actors according to their discipline and fit for a particular role, rejecting the idea of a permanent ensemble. He saw tremendous talent in Hussam Abu Esheh as a comic and improviser. Children loved Abu Esheh's local knowledge and his ability to play multiple characters, as well as Ahmad Abu Saloum's singing voice in musicals and sing-alongs. The rising star Georgina Asfour captured roles of young ingenues and presented a model for young girls in her performances for children. Ibrahim also maintained a close friendship with the composers Jameel Al-Sayeh and Bshara Al-Khil, who became his most frequent collaborators in children's musicals well into the subsequent two decades.[5]

As a stylistic innovation in children's theater, Ibrahim removed the distinction between actor and puppet in his touring productions, opting for pauses within a performance for the actors to step out from behind the puppet to speak with the children. They would begin a performance as themselves to prepare the audience for the puppets and the characters in the play. Then the actors returned backstage to play the puppets. As the play's story developed and reached pivotal moments, actors returned on stage to discuss the various options for the character's journey with the audience of children. Ibrahim's directorial choice to frequently shift between suspension of disbelief and discussion maintained the relationship between the human actors and the children, consistently teaching the theatrical form as they told the story. By reacting to the actors and puppets separately, children understood the theatrical technique and absorbed the moral embedded in the story. The back and forth developed the spirit of discussion in the audience, allowing children to critically encounter the theater as a mode of storytelling. Al-Kasaba's close connection to education served its longevity and became a crucial factor in its survival even during the crises of the first and second Intifadas.

Perhaps Al-Kasaba and George Ibrahim's greatest contributions to contemporary Palestinian theater and Jerusalemite culture between the occupation of 1967 and the Oslo Accords (1993) were the extensive repertoire of children's theater and the development of an audience that appreciated the possibilities of performance from a young age. This focus on children included nontheatrical events such as the yearly Christmas parties that included games, gift giving, sing-alongs, entertainment, and a family atmosphere for children and parents. The theater annually hosted events for Catholic Christmas on December 25 and Orthodox Christmas on January 7, leading to community building for a dwindling Christian population in Jerusalem and the West Bank under occupation. Similarly, it hosted entertainment events for Ramadan and Eid based on the lunar calendar, insisting that the theater served the Palestinian population regardless of religious affiliation. The roster of actors that Al-Kasaba regularly employed held a pluralistic variety of religious beliefs, which also assisted in the reception of the theater as a truly local Palestinian theater despite Ibrahim's preference to produce adaptations from the world repertoire.

Ideologically, the newly reformulated theatrical operation by Ibrahim held a peculiar position as an institution under occupation that insisted on also serving Palestinian citizens of Israel. As a commercially viable theater, it offered acting employment for Jerusalemites, West Bankers, and Palestinian citizens of Israel, who sought to work outside the auspices of Hebrew theater as a political stance against the Hebraization of Palestinian culture. Unlike El-Hakawati, which occasionally hired outside their ensemble for larger productions, Al-Kasaba cast actors based on the needs of each play, even though Ibrahim often exhibited a preference for his frequent local collaborators and a roster of Palestinian performers from the Galilee. His insistence on maintaining the identity of a Palestinian from Ramleh, a city currently under Israeli sovereignty, while being under occupation with a Jerusalemite permanent residency (blue) ID led to his affinity with Palestinian performers within the Green Line. Although he refused to apply for or hold Israeli citizenship, he did not separate his operations from Palestinian citizens of Israel as audiences or performers. This ideological distinction explains his consistent choice to present his plays for children in municipal schools despite the cultural boycott that many theater makers of the West Bank insisted on during the 1970s. Another explanation for Al-Kasaba's ideological position is Ibrahim's leftist affinities based on his deep connection and affiliation with the leading figures of the Arab faction of the Israeli Communist Party, including Palestinian national treasures such as Emile Habibi, Tawfiq Zayyad, Hanna Abu Hanna, Samih Al-Qassem, and Saliba Khamis, the father of the late Juliano Mer Khamis.

The rise of Al-Kasaba, the decline of El-Hakawati, and the reformulation of the Nuzha-Hakawati Theatre into a public institution initially sparked growth in theatrical production in Jerusalem between 1990 and 1993. The theater movement that rejected El-Hakawati's leadership saw an opportunity in the increased availability of rehearsal and performance space. Meanwhile, El-Hakawati Ensemble contended with divisions within their ranks. After the highly successful tour of *The Story of Kufur Shamma*, François Abu Salem, Jackie Lubeck, Edward Muallem, Amer Khalil, Nabil El-Hajjar, and Jan Williams formed the core ensemble for Abu Salem's newest production *In Search of Omar Al-Khayyam*, which was rehearsed in Paris and Basel in the spring of 1990. During rehearsal, personal and creative differences led to the departure of Lubeck and Williams from the project. Shortly thereafter, Edward Muallem permanently exited El-Hakawati over creative differences that included Abu Salem's insistence on constructing a large, expensive, and complex set for a show that the ensemble had agreed to tour. During this period, Abu Salem and Lubeck's impending divorce and the loss of the Nuzha-Hakawati theater had taken a toll on the psyche of Abu Salem, who suffered from panic attacks and emotional instability during that difficult year. The decisive split of Muallem and Lubeck from Abu Salem's enterprise effectively ended El-Hakawati as it had been known until 1990, despite Abu Salem's continued use of the name until his death by suicide in 2011.[6]

In Search of Omar Al-Khayyam reflected Abu Salem's state of mind and preoccupations in 1990 and 1991, when he attempted to hold onto his dream ensemble, and the so-called clash-of-civilizations politics were on the rise in the Middle East amid the American war against Iraq. Several performers in the production described him as extremely difficult to work with and the production environment as toxic. The play depicts the poet and scholar Al-Khayyam at the cusp of the Crusades in the year 1095 CE, time-traveling to the present and engaging with a theater ensemble in the throes of attempting to tell his story. Although Lubeck and Abu Salem initially collaborated on the early draft of the production, Abu Salem continued the development of the text and the production after her departure. The aesthetically pleasing production failed in its final version to capture the lofty ideas of its inception as a clarification of the civilizational rift between the East and West, beginning with the Crusades through the eyes of Omar Al-Khayyam. A review of its performance in London panned its failure to distinguish between symbols of the past and the conflicts of the present. The reviewer identified two main problems in the production, placing the responsibility primarily on Abu Salem's directing. First, the production attempted to "say everything" and, therefore, did not present a theatrical experience in a focused dramatic action for the audience to follow. Second, the production's predetermined statement on the conflict between the East and West prevented the creation of a narrative of discovery linking the Crusades' past to the contemporary war in Iraq in 1990–1991. In other words, the reviewer suggested that El-Hakawati's foregone conclusion of indicting the West appeared in the early scenes, leaving the performance without intrigue for the audience. Other complaints included a fractured throughline, excessive melodrama, and overextended monologues, including some performed by Abu Salem.[7] Needless to say, *In Search of Omar Al-Khayyam* represented El-Hakawati's demise as the unstable ensemble lost its leading figures, leaving Abu Salem without his artistic support system. The play's failure demonstrated that Abu Salem could not replace his ensemble by writing, directing, and performing his own productions, at least not at this stage of his career. Abu Salem successfully performed monodramas over a decade later, showing his capacity and the necessity of reformulating one's career to fit the changing context in Palestine. Ultimately, he never recaptured the world-class successes that he had attained with his golden-era ensemble in the 1980s.

In Jerusalem, the theater movement filled El-Hakawati's vacuum with a steady stream of productions and press coverage in the first three years after their departure. The Nuzha-Hakawati Theatre took on the name the Theatre for Palestinian Culture and Arts and produced plays in collaboration with local artists. In 1990, it produced *Ansar*, a play depicting the experience of Palestinian prisoners. The documentary production, starring Nidal Al-Khatib and Ismail Al-Dabbagh and directed by Fateh Azzam, tells the story of two characters, Kifah and Zahran, depicting the details of arrest, prisoner transport, arrival to prison, and life's limitations within the prison cell. The play represents the activities of resistance during incarceration, including learning Hebrew, writing smuggled notes in Arabic, lectures among prisoners, critique of prison circumstances, refusal to work, and striking to achieve simple demands like watching television or hearing the radio for limited hours. The popular production relied on its original text, documenting realities known only to former prisoners, and on expressive movement visually highlighting the day-to-day struggles of incarcerated men in Israeli prisons. The play continued as one of the longest-running plays of the 1990s, and its main producer, Tantura Theatre, presented it well into the 2000s with a cast change, but Nidal Al-Khatib remained as its main performer. As Kamel El-Basha stated in his review, *Ansar* demonstrated a pivot in contemporary Palestinian theater in this decade by representing gritty conditions and direct documentary encounters with the Israeli occupation without embellishment.[8]

The new management of the Nuzha-Hakawati Theatre buttressed its new mission of open access to theatrical ensembles by producing the First Jerusalem Festival (1990) in collaboration with the Palestinian Theatre League under the leadership of George Ibrahim and Al-Kasaba Theatre. This festival has the distinction of operating in two theatrical spaces simultaneously and presenting fourteen performances by local theater ensembles, films, lectures, and roundtables about the development of the theater movement. With former technician of El-Hakawati Imad Mitwalli serving as the head of the programming committee, the theater movement rose up in full force, performing new productions and recent popular successes, including Al-Kasaba's *Men Without Shadows* and *Ramzi Abu El-Majd Died*, Al-Rahhala's *The Case of Mr. X* and *Men Without Heads*, Al-Jawwal's performance for children *I Must Light Up*, and Al-Rowah's *The Garbageman*.[9] These plays exhibited the range of theatrical offerings in the period, as Al-Rahhala specialized in experimentation under the guidance and leadership of Ya'coub Ismail, Al-Rowah's Ismail Al-Dabbagh focused on storytelling and solo performance, Al-Jawwal's Saqer Al-Salaymeh shone as a superb comic actor, and Al-Kasaba led the way with politically charged commercial productions. As a direct product of the theater movement's campaign to oust El-Hakawati and generate a theater culture that allowed equal open access to the Nuzha-Hakawati Theatre, this festival successfully demonstrated the prowess and productivity of local theater artists and ensembles. Despite this initial success, many of the leaders of the discourse against El-Hakawati have regretted their campaign and wished that the founding ensemble of the theater had remained.

Despite the Intifada's persistence into the early 1990s, a local understanding that official peace talks had begun between the PLO and the State of Israel generated excitement about the possibility of ending the occupation and establishing an internationally recognized State of Palestine. The trustees and management of the Theatre for Palestinian Culture and Arts once again changed its name to prepare East Jerusalem and the theater movement for the oncoming changes in the political arena, calling El-Hakawati's former home the Palestinian National Theatre (PNT). Starting in 1991, the PNT became a public site and a podium for political expression as press briefings occurred openly at the theater when Palestinian delegations returned from official negotiation duties, particularly from the publicly declared Madrid negotiations, as opposed to the secretive Israeli/PLO meetings in Oslo. On 24 December 1991, *Al-Fajr* reported on a press briefing at the PNT, where Dr. Hanan Ashrawi and Faisal Al-Husseini accused Israel of ignoring previous commitments to dialogue and refusing to discuss substantive aspects of the peace process with the Palestinian delegation. Throughout the Oslo period, highlights of the theater's politically charged programming included frequent open meetings and public talks with local leaders and leaders of the Palestinian delegation to peace negotiations, such as Faisal Al-Husseini, Dr. Hanan Ashrawi, Dr. Ghassan Al-Khatib, Samir Abdallah, and Sami Al-Kilani as well as leading community, journalism, and academic figures such as Dr. Nabil Al-Khatib, Na'im Tobasi, Hamdi Farraj, and Dr. Sari Nuseibeh. Discussion titles at such public events included "Us and the Israeli Elections," "The Press League between Difficulties and Challenges," "Our Stance on Multilateral Groups," "Assessing Political Action," and "The Economic Situation during the Transition Period." This open program also extended to meetings between Israeli and Palestinian organizations like Women in Black, There Is a Limit, Red Line, and the Israeli Communist Youth Union. The formerly attacked yearly celebration of the Union of Palestinian Working Women Committee convened publicly without Israeli intervention. The transformation of the Nuzha-Hakawati Theatre into a site for open political discussions with mass popular participation marked a political shift that fit the emerging national theater's new political mission.[10]

The development of Al-Kasaba and the PNT into public assembly sites increased the number of unique nights at the theater in Jerusalem, with both institutions hosting evenings of variety shows, film screenings, school festivals, and visiting performances by Palestinian citizens of Israel. In the absence of major galleries and conference centers, all of which would develop rapidly in the post-Oslo period, the theaters hosted exhibits for book festivals, visual artists, poster competitions, and youth writers. The PNT stepped into the role of an acting ministry of culture.

It created specialized festivals that the local community rallied behind, sometimes volunteering in-kind donations. For example, the PNT organized a theater festival for local schools, a literary festival to memorialize the twentieth anniversary of Ghassan Kanafani's assassination, and the themed Festival of Covenant and Continuation," which included concerts of national songs by Mustapha Al-Kurd.[11] Al-Kasaba shouldered its share of the national responsibilities of cultural institutions. It hosted meetings between local politicians and international delegations, as well as national celebrations. On 11 December 1991, it was the site of Faisal Al-Husseini's public encounter with a German delegation of diplomats and citizens about the future of Palestinian statehood.[12] On 15 November 1992, on the anniversary of the Palestinian Declaration of Independence (1988), it held a festival that joined the Palestinian Writer's Union, the Theater League, the Journalism League, and the Visual Artists' League. With the participation of the leading cultural figures of the era, Ibrahim Qara'een, Al-Motawakel Taha, Abdel Latif Aqel, Ibrahim Jowhar, and Radi Al-Jara'i, this celebration under the auspices of the Palestinian Council of Culture and Media emphasized the theater's local leadership and the rising possibility of achieving the long-awaited Palestinian state.[13]

From 1990 until shortly after the Oslo Peace Accords of 1993, the PNT's dedication of resources beyond a single resident company cleared the way for new productions and the theater movement to access wider availability, spotlighting artists from the margins, such as Hussam Abu Esheh, Kamel El-Basha, Ismail El-Dabbagh, Saqer Al-Salaymeh, and Ya'coub Ismail, all moving to the center of theatrical activity. This younger generation of performers and artists would become leaders in theater, television, or cinema in the following decades. By the early 1990s, Al-Salaymeh, who had performed in El-Hakawati's *One Thousand and One Nights*, had performed three monodramas and adapted stories for popular children's performances. Ismail El-Dabbagh, from his emergence as a leading performer in El-Hakawati's *Kufur Shamma* and Al-Kasaba's *Men Without Shadows*, starred in his well-received monodrama *The Garbageman* and established Al-Rowah as his own theater company. Abu Esheh established a career beyond his partnership with Ahmad Abu Saloum and Sanabel People's Theatre, building on his successful performances with Al-Kasaba, creating his own path as a stand-up comedian, presenting television programs after the establishment of Palestinian television, and growing his standing within Jerusalem as its premier local storyteller. Kamel El-Basha, who credits El-Hakawati with his professional start in *The Exception and the Rule*, performed as a popular freelancer for Al-Kasaba and other local companies, but his regular appearances in Ya'coub Ismail's experimental plays and adaptations would capture his imagination as an actor and director. El-Basha would eventually attain worldwide stardom after winning the Best Actor award at the seventy-fourth International Film Festival for his performance in Ziad Doueiri's *The Insult* (2016).[14]

In 1994, after a five-year absence, François Abu Salem returned to Jerusalem to direct and produce *Jericho Year Zero*, co-written by Abu Salem and his mother, Francine Gáspár.[15] In the immediate shadow of the Oslo Peace Accords, the play interrogates the meaning of a new beginning, peace, that bypasses trauma and avoids the necessary process of reconciliation, compensation, and accountability for the Palestinian condition. The story follows a French tourist who encounters a militant former prisoner, his siblings, his cousin, his grandfather (a guide), and his mother. The tourist follows the militant, who searches for a buried treasure, later revealed as old weapons and remnants from war, in order to perform a suicide operation against the occupation. The journey leads to a magical night, where the play's characters encounter ghosts and fairies, hear marvelous music, and see secret lovers in a delirious reality. The play ends with an announcement of amnesty in Jericho, and the population begins to plan for a normal life, but the militant refuses to surrender to a false peace. Although Abu Salem produced, directed, and presented the play at the PNT under the name El-Hakawati, no founding members of the original 1977 ensemble nor the 1984 Nuzha-Hakawati Ensemble acted in the play. Amer Khalil, Abu Salem's collaborator and confidante for many years to come, was the only cast member who had acted for El-Hakawati previously.[16]

Simultaneously, Al-Kasaba addressed the question of peace by co-producing *Romeo and Juliet* with the Israeli Khan Theatre, directed by one Israeli (Eran Baniel) and one Palestinian (Fouad Awad). In late 1992, Baniel had initiated the prospect of collaborating with Awad on Shakespeare's *The Tempest* in an "Arab-Jewish" project as a vehicle to strengthen the relationship between the two primary ethnicities in Israel. Because of the Khan's geographical location between East and West Jerusalem,

Baniel viewed such collaboration as a national responsibility for his theater during the Intifada. Having met Baniel as the artistic director of Acre's politically engaged Alternative Theater, Awad responded with interest, but rejected *The Tempest* because the play ended with a reconciliation that did not reflect the conditions of the Intifada and the continuing occupation of the Palestinian territories. Awad responded with a suggestion to direct *The Night and the Mountain* by the Egyptian Abdel Ghaffar Makkawi to begin the proposed collaboration between Palestinians and Israelis. This starting point would explore the possibility of collaboration in a less expensive project while diversifying the Khan's offerings. The directors also set their sights on developing the fully co-produced *Romeo and Juliet* in the following year. During Awad's production, which opened in late 1993 to reasonable reviews in the Hebrew press, Baniel successfully fundraised for *Romeo and Juliet*. After several meetings with Jerusalemite theaters and ensembles, including the PNT, the Khan found their ideal partner in Al-Kasaba.[17] With the blessing of the leadership of the PLO, Al-Kasaba agreed to join the project.

This co-production necessitated massive resources (figure 20). With an artistic team exceeding fifty, including twenty-one salaried actors during the rehearsal process and the initial run, the collaborating theaters and directors insisted on equality between Palestinians and Israelis. The process of achieving this undertaking required equal rehearsal time, design, and access to resources for both participating ensembles. Pre-rehearsal preparations began in early 1994. Al-Kasaba hosted the first full company read-through in the second week of February, and rehearsals started shortly thereafter in late February, with the shadow of the Goldstein massacre in Hebron (25 February 1994) looming over the early days of the joint venture. Rehearsing at Al-Kasaba, the Palestinians played the Montagues and spoke their text in Arabic, translated by the distinguished novelist, poet, and academic Hussein El-Barghouthi. Meanwhile, the Jewish Israeli ensemble played the Capulets, rehearsed at the Khan, and spoke their text in Hebrew, written by the celebrated translator Ehud Manor. Eran Baniel established a network of funders, co-presenters, and supporters that included local commercial companies, the Israeli Jerusalem Foundation, France's Lille Festival, the Land Nordrhein-Westphalia Festival of Germany, and France's lighting specialists Mazda Eclairage.[18]

FIGURE 20 A performance of Al-Kasaba Theater's co-production of *Romeo and Juliet*. Jerusalem, 1994. Courtesy of George Ibrahim.

Despite its impressive theatricality, successful presentation, beautiful aesthetic, and frequent enthusiastic standing ovations after its opening on 16 June 1994, this co-production became known as the ultimate failed peace project in contemporary Palestinian theater. As a concurrent theatrical mirror to the Oslo Peace Process, the production appeared to present a utopian present or future that Palestinian stakeholders rejected in light of contemporary events. An exposé by Laura Blumenfeld of the *Washington Post* described several challenges accompanying the production: Fouad Awad and Palestinian members of the ensemble being threatened at gunpoint or excessively held at checkpoints, Eran Baniel receiving death threats from Jewish extremists rejecting interracial marriage, actor Ghassan Abbass feeling like a hypocrite performing in a joint project while Israel banned his brother from entry at the border because of his political activities in the PLO, three Israeli actors dropping out of the play during rehearsals, and Khaled El-Masou's permit to enter Jerusalem being revoked mid-process and before the opening week. Blumenfeld ends her article on a note of visceral truth, commenting on actress Orna Katz's attempts to catch the attention of Palestinian cast members while they sing an angry nationalist tune during a rehearsal break: "she hears the pretty Eastern notes, but she cannot understand," implying that a dark cloud of instability and incomprehension hanged over the production. Although Palestinians could understand Israeli existence, the Israeli ensemble struggled to comprehend Palestinian realities.[19] After seeing the performance of the play in Jerusalem, Professor Freddie Rokem of Tel Aviv University aptly wrote that the production reified existing stereotypes of Palestinians and Israelis, disregarded the real imbalances in power on the ground, failed in its choice to perform the play in the non-neutral space of a warehouse owned by the Israeli Electric Company, and disappointed in its choice of historical European theatrical design including costumes that "smelled" of European costume storage. Effectively, the production appeared to maintain the play's European heritage but offered ethnic casting as a symbol of conflict without connection to contemporary Jerusalemite realities in its aesthetic concept and style. Rejecting the production's subdued representation of the intifada and the hegemonic Hebrew influence on spoken dialog, he states: "The performance says nothing about this and about the Palestinian struggle for independence and the official Israeli reaction to the struggle."[20]

Al-Kasaba's George Ibrahim remembered an omen that haunted the opening and performances of the play. He and the ensemble confronted an issue that El-Hakawati had faced in 1985 with their production of *The Story of the Eye and the Tooth* at a festival by the Alternative Theater. Israeli flags adorned the theatrical space. The Palestinian ensemble refused to perform under the flag of their occupier unless the Palestinian flag flew beside it. While symbolic, the flag incident demonstrated that despite their best efforts, the ensembles that worked together for months could not truly be equal unless the peace accords actually bore fruit with facts on the ground: a Palestinian state, the right of return, and East Jerusalem as an unoccupied and free Palestinian capital city. According to Ibrahim, the Israeli partners on the theatrical project successfully removed the flag to achieve symbolic neutrality for the performance space; however, the incident demonstrated that the Israeli theater and its ensemble lacked the power to offer their Palestinian partners the political and theatrical sovereignty they deserved. When the production toured European partner cities, Ibrahim stepped in front of the audience after the standing ovation to deliver a message from his theater and ensemble that this co-production of *Romeo and Juliet* did not represent contemporary Israel and Palestine. Rather, the promise of peace had yet to manifest itself on the ground. He recalled the content of his frequent speeches after performances:

> This play is a tribute to the Oslo Peace Accords, but the Israeli occupation of Palestine endures. As a Palestinian under occupation, I don't have freedom. The checkpoints continue, and the Israeli military is everywhere. Our actors don't rehearse and perform freely. The conflict isn't resolved. Until now, peace is just on paper and doesn't exist in our reality.[21]

Before long, within both ensembles, enthusiasm for the production fizzled. After fifty performances, the Khan and Al-Kasaba agreed to cease the production despite regularly sold-out performances.

In his memoir, Fouad Awad recalled this production with mixed feelings. Proud of the production, his artistic partnership with Baniel, and the performances of his Palestinian ensemble, Awad reminisced that the production successfully addressed the gap between contemporary horrors in Palestinian life and fictional theatricality in *Romeo and Juliet* by ending the play before the reconciliation of the Montagues and Capulets, insisting that the death of the lovers better represented the region's realities. Nonetheless, in hindsight, he believed that the framework of a theatrical play prevented the Palestinian ensemble from representing their struggle on stage because of the actors' mandate to perform their fictional characters as written. The disparity between the performers' lives and the concerns of Shakespearean characters progressively burdened the Palestinian ensemble during the critical historical juncture of the promised transition from colonial occupation to freedom and peace, neither of which materialized as facts on the ground. Furthermore, the absence of a reconciliation process that addressed the Nakba, years of occupation, and historic dispossession of Palestine left a plethora of unanswered questions in the production. Awad rightly pondered in his biography whether Palestinians could forget the past. Ultimately, as represented in Anat Even's subversive documentary film depicting the project, the Palestinian ensemble answered no.[22]

The *Romeo and Juliet* collaboration set the stage for the chaotic post-Oslo period of Palestinian theater, which ultimately mirrored the harsh Palestinian realities for the ensuing three decades. Whereas the Palestinian theater movement of the seventies and eighties knew and recognized its role as an inseparable participant in the Palestinian struggle for liberation, *Romeo and Juliet* functioned as a potential opening for a peaceful coexistence that never arrived and a promised ending to an occupation that became more entrenched. For the better part of two years, the massive project consumed cultural visionaries, who imagined a sovereign Palestinian state that could begin to address the psychological and material traumas of the nearly fifty years since the Nakba by representing the Palestinian people. Committed to their craft, the Palestinian ensemble of performers, writers, musicians, and technicians willingly entered the experience with the hope of manifesting the possibility of equality and mutual respect in their historic homeland, but progressively, the vision dissipated over the following decade as Israeli checkpoints and settlements fragmented the existing geography. The post-Oslo political and economic chaos and this production of *Romeo and Juliet* had much in common: international funding, illusory peace, focus on psychological trauma over material circumstances, larger-than-life empty rhetoric, perceptions of equality, and an increasing sense of paralysis as false peace endured.

CONCLUSION

BESIEGED NGOs AND
A MOVEMENT IN LORE

In the mid-1990s, nearly three decades after the emergence of the Palestinian theater movement in the Occupied Territories, the theater artists in East Jerusalem produced more productions than ever before in two state-of-the-art venues and toured many simultaneous plays to schools and nontraditional venues throughout Palestine, including Gaza. The break-up of El-Hakawati generated smaller companies such as Radi Shehadeh's Al-Seera Theater (Mghar, 1989), Edward Muallem and Iman Aoun's Ashtar Theatre (Ramallah, 1992), and Jan Williams and Jackie Lubeck's Theatre Day Productions (Jerusalem/Hebron in 1994, then Gaza). In the Beit Jala/Bethlehem area, starting in 1987 but with increasing productivity in the 1990s, Khaled El-Masou and Raeda Ghazaleh operated Inad Theater to address audiences in the southern West Bank with productions for children and local communities. Local Jerusalemite companies such as Al-Rowah, Al-Rahhala, Al-Amal Al-Sha'bi, Al-Kashkul, and the Palestinian Theatre continued to produce, albeit at a much less frequent pace than the Palestinian National Theatre, Al-Kasaba, and the newly founded rising star, Ashtar Theatre. Ramallah's Sundouq Al-'ajab occasionally produced single productions and storytelling events under the leadership of Adel Al-Tartir. Hayyan Al-Ju'beh, Sameh Hijazi, and Ya'coub Ismail made their names as leading local directors, thoughtfully experimenting with aesthetics and dramaturgy. Despite this productivity, the theatrical terrain of contemporary Palestinian theater and its movement transformed fundamentally in the aftermath of Oslo.

In the shadow of the ineffective Palestinian Authority, the declining influence of the PLO, the encroaching occupation economy, and rising anti-Palestinian politics within Israel, the theater movement that emerged as a cultural arm of the Palestinian liberation struggle confronted a new reality. On the surface, an influx of cultural aid primarily funneled by the United States International Agency for Development (USAID), EU's European Commission, the Swedish International Development Cooperation Agency (SIDA), cultural offices of European and North American consulates, associations such as the Goethe Institute and Institut Français du Proche-Orient (IFPO), and international foundations like Stiftung Mercator, Open Society, Ford, and Rosa Luxemburg allowed for significant development opportunities for the theater movement to institutionalize itself in the form of independent and professional non-governmental organizations (NGOs). The ensembles of the theater movement could finally sustain their operations as they raised the profile of the cultural sector in Palestine from the status of surveilled outlaws to professionally engaged organizations. They could also inaugurate new theatrical spaces, establish offices, and pay salaries to administration, marketing, and box office professionals. Fundraising emerged as a crucial skill and profession throughout Palestine because the position generated subsistence funds for theaters, cultural institutions, and NGOs more broadly. As international experts and politicians insisted that institution-building and civil society must form the bedrock of the future Palestinian state, the grassroots theater movement transformed into a cluster of disparate funding-based institutions and income-generation vehicles.

Underneath the surface, this transformation led to the marginalization of many individual artists who constituted the dynamic and pluralistic collective spirit of the theater movement of the 1970s. By writing successful grant proposals that appealed to foreign funders, Palestinian theater artists and specific companies such as the PNT, Al-Kasaba, Ashtar, and Theatre Day Productions raised significant funds that elevated their production values, financed capital projects, paid substantial salaries, and increased the quality of life for all their participants. Similar to *Romeo and Juliet*, which emerged as an issue project of "Arab-Jewish coexistence," the first caveat for production became the successful Palestinian appeal to foreign sensibilities according to the assessment of the funding bodies and their declared priority issues in any given year. Networking and contacts with international personalities and diplomatic bodies, as well as the education and language skills necessary for communicating with employees at foreign funding sources, separated the theater movement into two categories: employed owners of professional theaters and precarious part-time freelance participants. In this period of contemporary Palestinian theater, the movement ultimately paid the price of this transition. It transformed from a movement for the liberation of Palestine through theatrical production that prized collective material resistance against occupation, direct confrontation with the Israeli surveillance apparatus, national community enculturation, and insistence on steadfast identity preservation to a collection of separate theaters that competed for the same funding sources to sustain their existence in equally challenging circumstances.

The transforming grounds of the struggle mirrored the physical fragmentation and ghettoization of the cities and population of the Occupied Palestinian Territories. From the mid-1990s until the present, the emergence of the Israeli colonial Wall, the proliferation of military checkpoints, and the rapid pace of settlement growth detached East Jerusalem from the West Bank, reducing audience access to the PNT as the preferred theater for performance presentations. Within a few years, most of the population of the West Bank could no longer visit Jerusalem without a permit, which geographically besieged the PNT from its largest audience base and separated Jerusalem from its artistic twin, the Ramallah area, effectively limiting many familial, artistic, and professional relationships that had led to the emergence of the theater movement in the early 1970s. The ghettoization of the major West Bank cities of Ramallah, Hebron, Bethlehem, Tulkarem, Qalqilia, Nablus, Jenin, and Jericho locked cultural activities into these cities, forcing theater makers to tour to their audiences instead of expecting a freely moving population to bus into Jerusalem for a performance at the theater. Although theater makers compensated for this access problem by founding and nurturing theater companies in Hebron, Bethlehem, Beit Jala, and Jenin, each theater confronted the problem of limited audience growth as the military-constrained movement continued to restrict their geographical reach. Freelance Palestinian artists holding Jerusalemite residency identity cards (blue IDs) or Israeli passports could work in and tour many different cities, but West Bank identity-card holders (green Palestinian Authority IDs) could rarely work across the dividing lines of the post-Oslo geography without the highly prized and hard-to-acquire Israeli checkpoint permits.

The mid-1990s witnessed the growth of Ramallah as the de facto Palestinian cultural and political capital. The Palestinian Authority founded a ministry of culture that provided limited encouragement for theater makers due to its extremely limited financial resources but supported the foundation of local cultural institutions and museums—often in cooperation with the Ramallah and Al-Bireh municipalities—their largest capital project being the Ramallah Cultural Palace established in 2005. Nonetheless, institutions supported by private, local, and international funding along the NGO model far outweighed the influence of the Palestinian Authority. For example, Khalil Al-Sakakini Cultural Center (established in 1996) and Al-Qattan Foundation (established in 1993), hosted frequent public talks, cultural events, and performances that may have been far smaller in size than the events at the 750-seat Ramallah Cultural Palace, but the frequency and specialization of their offerings built a loyal audience base and provided a venue for local intellectuals and artists to disseminate their work. The cultural divisions of foreign embassies and consulates, such as the French-German Cultural Center, the British Council, and Goethe Institute, similarly provided forums for "politically friendly" events and collaborations, hosting international scholars and artists for well-attended public presentations. With increased visits by solidarity activists, international politicians, business entrepreneurs, politically motivated tourists, expat NGO staff on rotations, and international artists seeking collaboration with Palestinians, Ramallah transformed into an active space of public discourse and debates on the future of Palestine. The vibrant internationalism and abundant culture-centered programming also opened new horizons and possibilities for Palestinian theater. In particular, Ashtar Theatre and Al-Kasaba operated in Ramallah before and after the second Intifada, both taking advantage of the city's rising liberal values and cosmopolitanism. By effectively adopting the NGO funding model, they re-created the theatrical energies and creativity of the golden era of 1980s Jerusalem, albeit in Ramallah and within the issue-play limitations of this new period. Although Al-Kasaba and Ashtar operated primarily in Ramallah, they maintained a limited presence in Jerusalem, including occasional presentations at the PNT.

The new political terrain transformed with Israel's changing strategy from direct to indirect occupation in the form of controlling and surveilling from the peripheries, instrumentalizing the Palestinian Authority for local policing, and creating Palestinian "Bantustans" (typically not exceeding ten to thirty square kilometers) that functionally reduced the Israeli military's influence on quotidian life. A new generation of Palestinians born in the 1990s no longer had to learn functional Hebrew to survive the occupation's civil administration and daily encounters with Israeli soldiers. Especially within the city limits of Ramallah, it became possible to openly produce and perform Palestinian plays that directly addressed the occupation and expressed the desire for Palestinian self-determination. Within Palestinian Authority-managed cities, symbols of the Palestinian struggle—such as flags, resistance poetry, representations of the Nakba, anti-occupation rhetoric, national parties, and iconic images of resistance—no longer formed the basis for immediate arrest and Israeli incarceration. In this new reality, a play based on Ghassan Kanafani's *Returning to Haifa* could be produced in Ramallah without an ensemble being arrested, as had been the case with Sanabel's People's Theatre's production of *Man Is a Cause* in 1980. Al-Kasaba ventured into producing devised plays that directly and unapologetically addressed the occupation, such as *The Wall* (2006) and *Alive from Palestine* (2001). Ashtar took on the mantle of August Boal's Theater of the Oppressed techniques and produced forum plays that emerged from Palestinian communities, speaking of everyday struggles in plain, unconcealed language. Inside the illusion of safety in the Bantustans, Palestinians could be Palestinian in a way that characters like El-Hakawati's Mahjoob and Sundouq El-'ajab's Abu El-Janazir could not have expressed openly on stage two decades earlier. Within the Bantustan, the Palestinian flag and identity became legal.[1]

By the mid-1990s, although the Palestinian theatrical movement actualized many of its declared goals—a functioning Palestinian theater league with stable membership, performance and rehearsal spaces, frequent representation in international festivals, and consistent touring circuits—few original movement participants continued as theater makers after Oslo. The passionate collective, altruistic, and volunteer spirit that inspired and sustained the movement in its early years declined dramatically with the avalanche of institution-building practices that pervaded the whole of Palestine. The period required the movement cadres to surrender the mantle of resistance in favor of a "nation-building" agenda that never materialized a sovereign state. The new terrain demanded that individual leaders, who could represent a coherent social mission in lieu of the original movement's national liberation mandate, become visible personalities behind each theater. These leaders, being the funders' trusted partners, spoke the language of community service, capacity building, intercultural dialogue, and self-critique in order to communicate awareness of the challenges of the Palestinian people, exclusive and separate from the Israeli occupation. Communicating the rhetoric of dialogue and coexistence accompanied declared public missions to elevate cultural production and educate the Palestinian people on priority issues such as gender, childhood, LGBTQ rights, religious pluralism, and democracy, to name a few. To access the necessary aid from the representative offices of foreign countries, known individuals became faces of friendly theatrical brands, not theaters of resistance or a liberation movement. The leaders who survived the Oslo transition understood the necessities of the period, managed funder expectations, or believed in the Oslo peace project. The leaders who disappeared from the theatrical scene rejected or were ill-equipped to play the new compulsory performance of reform.

Nonetheless, the Palestinian theater movement survived in some fashion among all those who participated in it. The lore of the early days of the movement remained an essential gateway into contemporary Palestinian theater. As a result, many young theatrical hopefuls in Palestine today often ask questions that many of their predecessors asked in their youth: What is the theatrical movement? Do we have a theatrical movement? Is Palestinian theater in crisis? How can we transform the movement? Until today, the words "Al-Haraka Al-Masrahiyya" continue to echo among emerging and established performers alike, often with the mention of the movement's leading ensembles: Balalin, Bila-Lin, Dababis, Sundouq Al-'ajab, Sanabel People's Theatre, Al-Kasaba, and El-Hakawati. Although this book does not cover the ebbs and flows of these words and the significance of the movement in the ensuing three decades since Oslo, one final story may demonstrate how the transformation of the movement with the advent of Oslo did not lead to its demise.

When François Abu Salem committed suicide in Ramallah on 2 October 2011, news quickly spread across Ramallah, Jerusalem, and the rest of Palestine. On the day of his burial, Ashtar held a funeral in his honor at its theater in Ramallah, and then the casket was moved to his church in Jerusalem for prayers. Afterward, several busses followed François to his burial site on Mount Zion in Jerusalem, where it was adorned with a Palestinian flag before it rested in its final place. Theater makers surrounding the grave site gave Abu Salem one last round of applause and a standing ovation as his casket descended into his beloved Jerusalem. In attendance throughout the program, which started at Ashtar hosted by former El-Hakawati Ensemble members Edward Muallem and Iman Aoun and ended at the PNT/El-Hakawati, were many of the core members of the Theatrical Movement. At each site, his mother, Francine Gáspár, took condolences from Mustapha Al-Kurd, Adel Al-Tartir, Emile Ashrawi, Vera Tamari, and Nadia Mikhail from the Balalin days; Radi Shehadeh, Jackie Lubeck, Edward Muallem, Imad Mitwalli, Wassif Dandis, and Iman Aoun from El-Hakawati days; and George Ibrahim, Ahmad Abu Saloum, Hussam Abu Esheh, Kamel El-Basha and many other longtime comrades and adversaries of the theatrical movement. These pages would not suffice to name everyone who participated in the ceremonies and shared in the grief of Abu Salem's passing; however, the hundreds of attendees at various sites and the thousands of consoling parties exhibited his influence as an essential founding member of a movement that outlived him. Against a backdrop of differences, disagreements, and a perpetual crisis, the story demonstrates a continuing sense of collectivity and belonging.

This book narrated the story of a group of theater makers and their context from the late 1960s until the early 1990s. They declared themselves a movement as Palestinians were founding political counterparts for the liberation struggle throughout the sixties and seventies. While the theater makers' goals of liberation were not achieved, they successfully established the grounds for a robust and thriving theater culture. When examining Palestine's theater industry today, lineage can be drawn directly to this movement through key players in this book. For example, these are a few connections: Al-Kasaba fostered and employed the emerging director Nizar Zu'bi and the star actors Khaled El-Masou and Georgina Asfour as members of its ensemble. In Bethlehem's Aida Camp, Al-Rowwad's Abdelfattah Abu Srour fondly remembers being inspired by the work of El-Hakawati and Al-Kasaba in his youth. In Hebron, Yes Theater's Ihab Zahdeh and Raed Shyoukhi initially began their professionalization with Jackie Lubeck's Theatre Day Productions. After his incarceration, Jerusalem's best-known star actor, Kamel El-Basha, credits François Abu Salem with restarting his theatrical career in El-Hakawati's production of Brecht's *The Exception and the Rule* in 1986. Both Ashtar and Al-Kasaba established very different training programs for aspiring actors, who became integral to the continuity of contemporary Palestinian theater. The connections between the movement and contemporary artists, theaters, performances, and practices continue to be a topic of conversation among the new generation of Palestinian hopefuls. Certainly, the ensuing thirty years of theater production utilized the foundations initiated by the movement.

The legacy of the Palestinian theater movement cannot easily be enumerated; however, the established theatrical spaces in the Jerusalem/Ramallah area directly emerged from the ceaseless efforts of its participants to create performances for Palestinians under occupation. At this book's publication, Amer Khalil helms El-Hakawati's former home. He renamed it the Palestinian National Theater/El-Hakawati. Al-Kasaba continues its operations in Ramallah. George Ibrahim continues to serve as the artistic director and seems to always find a project. Ahmad Abu Saloum and Hussam Abu Esheh continue to work together, with the latter becoming a social media influencer, well-known comedian, and television personality. El-Hakawati's Adnan Tarabsheh and Radi Shehadeh published biographies detailing their lives in the theater and maintain their theatrical activities in the Galilee. Ashtar's Iman Aoun and Edward Muallem handed the reins of their company's artistic directorship to the emerging actor and director Emile Saba and began a cultural village project in Birzeit. After a twenty-five-year odyssey, Jackie Lubeck and Jan Williams passed Theatre Day Productions to company members in Gaza and retired in Amsterdam, where Jackie paints, writes, and crochets. Adel Al-Tartir continues to operate Sundouq Al-'ajab as a storytelling enterprise in Ramallah. Emile Ashrawi operates workshops and various cultural projects with the Ramallah municipality. Imad Mitwalli runs Qafila

Theatre, which performs on an eighteen-wheeler truck that transforms into a touring theater. Although space does not allow for an update on all the now-familiar personalities of the movement, it is necessary to mention the passing of Mustapha Al-Kurd in Jerusalem in 2024, shortly before the completion of this book

The questions surrounding the movement and its efforts cannot all be posed and answered in a single book. And yet, one question must be addressed: does it still exist? According to this author, the answer is affirmative. The movement has generated durable artifacts and professionals; however, its more significant offering is its persistent mythical lore, which this book narrated, not comprehensively but expansively. The memorable stories of this disparate, diverse, and determined movement include El-Hakawati's battles with the censors and with Joseph Papp in the United States, their tours throughout Europe, and the construction of their theater; George Ibrahim's bags of single shekels, his closure of the production of *Romeo and Juliet*, and his departure from television work; the arrest of the entire company of Dababis; the divisive politics within Balalin and the Palestinian Theatre; El-Hakawati's exit from their theater; the legendary stature of *Al-'atmeh* (*The Darkness*); the radical leftist politics of communists and nationalists; Sanabel's productions of Kanafani and Athol Fugard; the movement's intersection with renowned figures like Emile Habibi, Tawfiq Zayyad, Faisal Al-Husseini, and Mohammad Al-Batrawi; and the national aspirations of each ensemble. The lore of the movement sustained two generations of Palestinian theater artists, who are deeply influenced by the stories decades after its golden era. Even during war, genocide, and uncertainty, the movement is alive in its lore and lineage, promising and delivering a richly diverse theater industry. Despite the immensity and brutality of the present fragmentation and destruction, at the very least, the collective spirit of the Palestinian theater movement appears emergent through storytelling. If, at times, it seems dormant, its history has shown that it may simply be under the radar.

ACKNOWLEDGMENTS

The first and last thanks go to Kate Wahl and the staff at Stanford University Press.

This book emerged from many years of immersion in academia, various artistic communities, and intellectual circles, but my most significant gratitude goes to Palestinian theater artists who generously told their stories to me in formal and informal interviews over nearly two decades. Over the years, influential Palestinian artists, friends, and/or colleagues have included Abdelfattah Abu Srour, Abdel-Salam Abdo, Adel Tartir, Adib Jahshan, Adnan Tarabsheh, Ahmad Abu Saloum, Ahmad Tobasi, Ashtar Muallem, Amer Hlehel, Amer Khalil, Bayan Shbib, Daoud Kuttab, Edward Muallem, Eid Aziz, Emile Ashrawi, Emile Saba, Fida Zidan, Francine Gáspár, François Abu Salem, Fuad Awad, Ghada Al-Madbouh, George Ibrahim, Gina Asfour, Hamdi Taweel, Hanin Tarabay, Hiam Abbass, Hussam Abu Esheh, Ibrahim Jbail, Ibrahim Muzain, Ihab Zahdeh, Iman Aoun, Imad Mitwalli, Imad Samara, Jackie Lubeck, Jamil Eid, Jan Williams, Juliano Mer Khamis, Kamel El-Basha, Lina Ghanem, Lutof Nuwayser, Majed Kreitem, Majid Al-Mani, Marina Barham, Marriam El-Basha, Marwa El-Basha, Milad Kidan, Mirna Sakhleh, Mohammad Al-Batrawi, Mohammad Al-Labadi, Mohammad Mahamid, Mohammad Al-Thaher, Mohammed Bakri, Mona El-Basha, Muaz Jubeh, Mustapha Al-Kurd, Mustapha Sheta, Nadia Mikhail, Nicola Zreineh, Nizar Zuabi, Petra El-Barghouthi, Radi Shehadeh, Rajai Sundoka, Ramsey Sheikh Qassem, Ramzi Jubeh, Reem Talhami, Riad Masarweh, Saleh Bakri, Salim Daw, Salman Natour, Sameh Abboushey, Samih

Al-Qassem, Sayyed Kashua, Shaden Salim, Talal Hammad, Uday Jubeh, Wassif Daher, Youssef Abu Wardeh. I also thank the cast of A Midsummer Night's Dream, which I directed at Al-Kasaba in 2011: Milad Knebe, Moaiad Samad, Amjad Hashem, Yasmin Qadmany, Hazem Alsharif, Firas Abu Sabbah, Yasmine Sameer, Shams Assi, Husam Alazza, Majdi Nazzal, Mahmoud Shawish, Muayad Odeh, Jihad Al-Khateeb, and Ramzy Hasan.

I am thankful to the academics who have been a significant and meaningful part of my journey, including Thomas Postlewait, Sarah Bryant Bertail, Barry Witham, Odai Johnson, Michael Vincente-Perez, Terri Deyoung, Freddie Rokem, Gibson Cima, Michelle Granshaw, Jyana Brown, Lisa Jackson-Schebetta, Mimi Kammer, Elizabeth Coen, Lezlie Cross, Sarah Nash-Gates, Ted Ziter, Carol Martin, Patrick Mckelvey, Elizabeth Osborne, Kris Salata, Clint Sleeper, Adam Gaiser, Aline Kalbian, Matthew Goff, Will Hanley, Zeina Schlenoff, Joseph Hellweg, Zafer Lababidi, David Levenson, Rebecca Joubin, Sharon Green, Mark Sutch, Scott Denham, Chris Alexander, Sophia Stamatopoulou-Robbins, and Caroline Weist. Published a year after my arrival to Williams College, this book must also acknowledge the kind welcome and support of my colleagues Amy Holzapfel, Shanti Pillai, James Pathica, Omar Sangare, and Robert Baker-White. I thank the staff at the Department of Theater and the wider faculty community at Williams, including Sarah Keys, Atiya Husain, Armond Towns, Mejdulene Shomali, and Sohail Chichah.

As an academic, institutional support has furthered my career and the writing of this book. I am indebted to the University of Washington, Davidson College, Florida State University, Stanford University, Williams College, Mellon Foundation, Harvard Mellon School, and the Palestinian American Research Center (NEH-PARC). Other institutional access and support includes the British Library, British Archives, Israel State Archives, Hebrew University, and Birzeit University. The majority of this book was written while I was on faculty at the Theater and Performance Studies Department (TAPS) at Stanford. I thank my colleagues at TAPS, including Jennifer Brody, Harry Elam, Aleta Hayes, Branislav Jakovljevic, Diana Looser, Peggy Phelan, Michael Rau, Matthew Wilson Smith, and Young Jean Lee. I am especially thankful to Jisha Menon for her consistent and unwavering intellectual and institutional support. I am also eternally grateful to Aileen Robinson for her partnership, friendship, collegiality, and limitless positivity, as well as her never-ending personal and emotional support.

In the wider Stanford community, I am grateful to all my colleagues at the Abbasi Program and the Center for Comparative Studies in Race and Ethnicity. I also thank Lisa Blaydes, Vaughn Rasberry, David Palumbo Liu, Zack Al-Witri, Ali Yaycioglu, Priya Satia, Kelda Jamison, Kabir Tambar, Anna Bigelow, Denise Gill, Bissera Pentcheva, Ramzi Salti, Khalil Barhoum, Abiya Ahmed, Paula Moya, Roanne Kantor, Marci Kwon, Asad L. Asad, and Usha Iyer. Nora Barakat, Alexander Key, Betty Shamieh, and Jisha Menon were the earliest readers of this book. Thank you for the notes and the words of encouragement. During his fellowship at the Humanities Center in 2022, Salim Tamari gave me the first set of notes on my manuscript. Suhaila Meera supported this project as a graduate student and now as a colleague. Marina Johnson has been an incredible interlocutor, draft reader, and researcher.

Arab theater scholarship in English is on the rise because of the work of these amazing colleagues: Roaa Ali, Sahar Assaf, George Potter, Sarah Youssef, Hadeel Abdel-Hameed, Katherine Hennessey, Margaret Litvin, Kate Wilson, Amir Al-Azraki, James Al-Shamma, Khalid Amine, Marvin Carlson, Hazem Azmy, Samar Zahrawi, Hala Baki, Yasmine Marie Jahanmir, Hadia Mousa, Daniel Potenza, Malek Najjar, Samy Selim, Rand Hazou, Mona Marhi, Sarah Fahmy, and many others. A growing community of scholars, who write about Palestinian theater, has inspired me: Hala Nassar, Rania Jawad, Ruba Totah, Gary English, Mahmoud Abusultan, Rayya El Zein, Najla Nakhle-Cerruti, Gabriel Varghese, Rashna Darius Nicholson, and Ben Rivers. Certainly, Hala Nassar has led the way in this arena.

Some colleagues and friends are forever intellectual partners. They stick with you even when distance makes connection difficult. The "Seattle School"—Jacinthe Asaad, Sahera Bleibleh, Anjali Vats, Ziad Zaghrout and Amal Eqeiq—remains a permanent rock and always will be. They make imagining many brilliant paths in and after academia possible. Ibrahim Muhawi has always had a profound influence on my work. Aileen Robinson, Nora Barakat, Alexander Key, Anna Bigelow, Usha Iyer, Freddie Rokem, and Jisha Menon have shown me that academia can be an inspiring place. Betty Shamieh has been a real friend and writing angel. Amal Eqeiq's friendship and commitment to the cause have sustained me.

The journey of this book was only possible because of logistical and personal support in Palestine provided by meaningful friendships of people who have become family over the past decade. The following have contributed materially to this book: Amal Eqeiq picking me up at the airport; Beesan Ramadan's ability to make anything happen; Lina Ghanem's transcriptions; Jackie Lubeck's heartfelt care, generosity, and impeccable storytelling; Edward Muallem's stunning perspective, attention to historical detail, and organization; Iman Aoun's openness, fairness, and criticism; Salim Tamari's beautiful home and long interlocutions about Palestinian culture; Emile Ashrawi's enthusiasm and archival wizardry; Adel Al-Tartir's living monument to Balalin; Reem Talhami's compassion and friendship; and George Ibrahim's permanent familial welcomes and deep, uncensored interviews. Amer Khalil shared his impeccable memory, princely spirit, and love of Palestinian theater, becoming a stand-in for the departed François Abu Salem. Kamel El-Basha welcomed me into his work and home life and spent long hours with me in crucial debates. Salim Abu Jabal created a home base for me throughout my fieldwork, fixed many challenges, and shared the research experience through road trips, archival visits, lengthy phone calls, videography work, translations, personal disasters, formative epiphanies, and critical discussions.

My immediate family—Fathi, Hedaya, Rami, and Enji—has always been the only constant in my life and work. Both my grandmothers, Marriam and Moyassar, would have been proud. My family made me Palestinian.

NOTES

Introduction

1. See Muhamad Mahamid's book, *Masirat Al-Harakah Al-Masrahiyah Fi Al-Diffah Al-Gharbiyah*, and the anthology of Mohammad Anis, *Al-harakah Al-Masrahiyah Fi Al-Manatiq Al-Muhtallah*.

A general note on transliteration: I used the symbol ʻ to indicate the Arabic letter ʻayn and an apostrophe for the hamza; discrepancies in spelling are often the result of disagreements between sources or the problem of transliterating colloquial and classical Arabic; and where possible, I used existing English language spellings of names, places, and titles. Whenever an artist's name is spelled in different ways, I used the artist's preferred spelling. Citations of Arabic newspaper articles are inconsistent due to the variety of sources and locations where I found them; however, I provided at a minimum the name of the publication and the date. Whenever possible, I provided the name of the author, page number, and/or an English transliteration of the Arabic title.

2. For a general discussion of what constitutes a "movement" in the artistic sense, see Renato Poggioli's review of the term in *Theory of the Avant-Garde*, 25–27.

3. Poggioli, *Theory of the Avant-Garde*. My description fits the suggested definition.

4. Hanan Ashrawi, *Contemporary Palestinian Literature Under Occupation*, 1976, 8. My translation.

5. Theatre Committee, *The Association for Work and Development for the Arts* (booklet), 22. My translation from the original Arabic.

6. See Schedule 1 in Mahamid, *Masirat Al-Harakah Al-Masrahiyah Fi Al-Diffah Al-Gharbiyah*. For various breakdowns of theatrical activities in the Occupied Territories, see this comprehensive study. It outlines the activities of these ensembles from 1970 until 1993.

7. Mahamid, *Masirat Al-Harakah Al-Masrahiyah Fi Al-Diffah Al-Gharbiyah*, 89.

8. Since they are fifteen miles apart, Palestinian residents of both cities behaved as if they lived in the same city. In interviews, this relationship was explicitly stated by most theater artists, including Adel Al-Tartir (Ramallah), Emile Ashrawi (Ramallah-Jerusalem), Kamel El-Basha (Jerusalem), Majid Al-Mani (Jerusalem), and George Ibrahim (Jerusalem-Ramallah). Today, a clear distinction is often noted between Jerusalemite artists and West Bank artists due to the forced separation created by the Wall and the Qalandia Checkpoint, which now prevents West Bank artists with Palestinian Authority IDs from traveling to Jerusalem. This separation began with the Oslo Peace Agreements in 1993.

9. I state these absences to indicate a dire need for focused research on specific regions, ensembles, cities, and artist biographies. Because they discontinued their operations, significant Jerusalemite ensembles such as Firqat Al-Amal Al-Shaʻbi (People's Hope Ensemble), Jerusalem's Al-Jawwal Ensemble (The Touring Theatre), and Al-Kashkul Ensemble (The Notebook) are deserving of examination in a study that focuses on less frequently producing ensembles.

10. Since its establishment in 1916, the Palestine Museum in Birzeit has begun the collection and digitization of materials related to Palestinian theater. This is the first archiving effort that has produced a tangible and accessible outcome.

Chapter 1

1. See Nasri Al-Jawzi's various sections on the fate and work of these personalities. They had various levels of contributions. Al-Jawzi labels them, among others, as some of the pioneers of Palestinian theater. The biographical portions in his book show the noted cities as places of residence.

2. See Nassar, *Palestinian Theatre: Between Origins and Visions*, 43; and Snir, *Palestinian Theatre*, 77–81.

3. Nassar, "Palestinian Theatre," 1032.

4. Al-Mallah, *Safahat Matwiyat*, 96–120; Nassar, *Palestinian Theatre: Between Origins and Visions*, 40–43.

5. Israeli scholar Snir Reuven describes the conditions imposed on Palestinian citizens of Israel: "The years of severe economic hardship that followed, the disruption of all cultural life, but not least the silent hand of the Israeli secret service that made itself felt everywhere, made it impossible for artists, writers, poets and dramatists to work freely." Snir, *Palestinian Theatre*, 51 (from his chapter "Annihilation and Re-Emergence" in *Palestinian Theatre*, 45–84). Snir provides a critical and historical assessment of "positive" activities, as well as an excerpt of the aforementioned play in both Arabic and English. He concludes that the play is "pure propaganda," *Palestinian Theatre*, 73. See also Nassar's chapter "From 1948 to the War of 1967: The Palestinian Uprooting, Decline, Isolation and New Beginning" in *Palestinian Theatre: Between Origins and Vision*, 39–46.

6. The Arabic-language version of all these laws at http://muqtafi.birzeit.edu/.

7. For an example of this, see ch. 11, arts. 105–108, in El-Bireh Municipal Bylaws of 1957, http://muqtafi.birzeit.edu.

8. See also the previous version of this law, the Press Law of 1955, which was enforced by the Ministry of the Interior.

9. Ashrawi, *Contemporary Palestinian Literature Under Occupation*, 3.

10. An earlier version of the Resistance to Communism Law was passed in 1948.

11. Note that the Palestinian Christian and Muslim populations were the only ones within Israel to be governed by the 1945 emergency laws during the period of 1948 to 1966. See Hillel Cohen's chapter "Communists vs. the Military Government, Collaborators vs. Communists" in *Good Arabs: The Israeli Security Agencies and the Israeli Arabs, 1948-1967*.

12. From here on, I refer to George Ibrahim Habash (the artist) as George Ibrahim or simply Ibrahim. I refer to his cousin George Habash (the political leader) as Dr. George Habash.

13. During this period, Jordan feared the existence of a plot to overthrow the king. For a concise biography of Dr. George Habash, see Bernard Reich, *Political Leaders of the Contemporary Middle East and North Africa: A Biographical Dictionary*, 213-220. See also the entry on Dr. George Habash in Reich, *An Historical Encyclopedia of the Arab-Israeli Conflict*, 409-410.

14. George Ibrahim stated: "If anything, his influence was that my family tried to distance us from politics. Life was difficult. The ideas of George Habash influenced me only after I grew up. He sometimes visited us, but all I knew was that he was a doctor, a relative, and my family were treated by him." George Ibrahim, personal interview, 8 January 2011.

15. George Ibrahim, personal interview, 23 October 2010.

16. George Ibrahim, personal interview, 23 October 2010.

17. George Ibrahim, personal interview, 8 January 2011.

18. George Ibrahim, personal interview, 8 January 2011. The church had two bishops, one Palestinian and one German. George Ibrahim saw Bishop Haddad as a father figure and considered the bishop's family as his own.

19. George Ibrahim, personal interview, 8 January 2011.

20. For a translation of the play see Ḥakim, *Plays, Prefaces and Postscripts of Tawfiq Al-Hakim*.

21. Ibid.

22. George Ibrahim, personal interview, 23 October 2010.

23. George Ibrahim, personal interview, 27 October 2023.

24. These biographical details are found in the François Abu Salem Archive at the Palestinian National Theater/El-Hakawati Archive in Jerusalem. They were confirmed in my conversation with Francine Gáspár. François acquired the name Abu Salem during rehearsals in 1970. His friend Ibrahim Ashrawi is often credited with giving him the name.

25. Personal interview, 24 October 2010. My translation.

26. Salman Natour, personal interview, 2010. My translation.

27. Mohammad Al-Batrawi, personal interview, 24 October 2010. My translation.

28. Kanafani, *Returning to Haifa*, 45. "The literature of resistance in occupied Palestine is characterized by its deep vision, which is why it fights on multiple fronts. It'll be truly marvelous for the scholar to see in the literary production of the occupied land, the early recognition—through poetry, story and drama—of the givens of the situation, which Arab literary producers discovered or are about to discover in various Arab countries in general after 5 June 1967." My translation.

29. See Kanafani's introduction, *Returning to Haifa*, 9. As a member of the Popular Front for the Liberation of Palestine, Kanafani embraced both armed struggle and cultural resistance, together and separately.

30. Yazid Sayigh, *Armed Struggle and the Search for State*, 173. "The centre of gravity in Palestinian nationalism moved into exile and with it the locus of political and social activity, military command, decision-making, and institution-building. Strategies of civilian resistance and mass mobilization in the Occupied Territories were obscured, marginalizing the local political activists and social forces in Palestinian decision-making. The balance was not to shift significantly until the eruption of the intifada in December 1987, twenty years later."

31. For a detailed history of Palestinian Armed resistance, see Yazid Sayigh, *Armed Struggle and the Search for a State*.

32. Qumsiyeh, *Popular Resistance in Palestine*, 116.

33. Shehadeh, *Journal of a West Bank Palestinian*, viii.

34. For details on Palestinian peaceful resistance in the twentieth century, see *A Quiet Revolution* by Mary Elizabeth King and *Popular Resistance in Palestine* by Mazin Qumsiyeh.

35. Emile Ashrawi, personal interview, 11 January 2011. He refers to a theatrical leap, spring, or emergence.

36. *Samid Al-Iqtisadi*, 157.

37. See article by Elias Nasrallah, http://www.palpeople.org/atemplate.php?id=2631 (last accessed on April 2, 2012). Al-Batrawi and Adel Samara echoed much of this information in personal interviews. Hanan Ashrawi also emphasized the influence of leftist, particularly communist literature in her 1976 study.

38. See Allah 'Abd's detailed account of the Palestinian press from 1967 to 1987.

39. Mahmoud Shqair, *Shu'un Filastiniyah*, no. 47 (July 1975): 239.

Chapter 2

1. For theater in the Galilee, see Haddad, *Al-masrah Al-Filastini Fi Al-Jalil: Bahth Wa-Tahlil*.

2. Nassar, "Palestinian Theatre," 1030-1032.

3. On the period 1918-1948, see Al-Jawzi, who provides a survey of the most influential theater artists, playwrights, and companies in the major Palestinian cultural centers, particularly Jerusalem, Haifa, and to a much lesser extent Jaffa. See also Al-Mallah, *Safahat Matwiyat*, 96-120. Nassar, "Cultural Activities Within Palestine," 40-43; and Nassar, "Palestinian Theatre," 1032.

4. Wassif Daher, personal interview, 24 August 2023. Daher provided the entirety of the source materials for the Jerusalem Players.

5. Wassif Daher, personal interview, 24 August 2023.

6. McKim, *The Presbyterian Hymnal Companion*, 62.

7. Wassif Daher, personal interview, 24 August 2023. The majority of the information about the Jerusalem Players is based on this interview.

8. George Ibrahim, personal interview, 18 January 2011.

9. Wassif Daher, personal interview, 24 August 2023; George Ibrahim, personal interview, 18 January 2011.

10. Wassif Daher, personal interview, 24 August 2023. Daher and Majed Kreitem provided the majority of the source materials for *At the Cross*.

11. For a biographical account of Ibrahim Saba in Arabic, see https://www.alwatanvoice.com/arabic/news/2015/09/16/777545.html (last accessed October 23, 2023). My father, Fathi Al-Saber, originally from Jaffa, could not return to his job because he was not counted in the post-occupation Israeli census, leading him to a teaching career in Jordan, Saudi Arabia (Mecca), and Kuwait. He retired from teaching after his immigration to Canada.

12. Jamal, *The Arab Public Sphere in Israel*. See chapter on media and the Arab minority in Israel, 39–60.

13. For a scholarly history of the PBS during the British Mandate, see Stanton, *This Is Jerusalem Calling*. For a personal account of the history of the station, see Edwin Samuel, *A Lifetime in Jerusalem: The Memoirs of the Second Viscount Samuel*; or Nasri Al-Jawzi's history of Palestine Radio, *Tarikh Al-Idha'ah Al-Filastiniyah*.

14. George Ibrahim, personal interview, 8 January 2011.

15. George Ibrahim, personal interview, 18 January 2011.

16. George Ibrahim, personal interview, 18 January 2011.

17. From Nazareth, Antoine Saleh was known as a leading Palestinian director at the time. According to George Ibrahim, Saleh studied at the Sorbonne. By the early 1970s, he had directed several productions for Al-Masrah Al-Nahid (The Rising Theatre), including Goldoni's *The Servant of Two Masters*, Strindberg's *The Father*, and Suhail Abu Nuwwara's original production of *Zaghrudat Al-Ard* (*The Ululation of the Land*). When George Ibrahim was operating his own theater company, he asked Saleh to direct many of his productions.

18. The only public record I could find on Galvin is her 1982 MA thesis in political science, "New Zealand and the UN Partition of Palestine 1947-49," at the University of Canterbury.

19. The article, entitled "Man 'Without Identity' Hopes to Come to Darwin: A Girl Who Loves Him Works on Immigration," was found in the personal archive of George Ibrahim. The 1968 article identified the date as his birthday. The newspaper and the author are not identified on the clipping.

20. George Ibrahim, personal interview, 18 January 2011.

21. George Ibrahim, personal interview, 8 January 2011.

22. Shammas held a post as professor of Comparative Literature, Near East-

ern Studies, and Modern Middle East Literature at the University of Michigan. He is known for translations from English to Arabic and Hebrew, as well as between Arabic and Hebrew. He also produced his own creative works as a writer and poet.

23. I based this information on the credits of four existing episodes in the personal archive of George Ibrahim. During the period of my fieldwork, Israel's Channel One did not respond to my request for archival material on this show.

24. This description is based on my analysis of several episodes in George Ibrahim's personal archive. To provide a model of the structure of the episodes, I described one episode in full.

25. Swedenburg, "Sa'ida Sultan/Danna International," in Armbrust, *Mass Mediations*, 108. Swedenburg correctly describes the show as a "cross between Sesame Street and Mr. Rogers"; however, in his paragraph on the show, he relays that Ibrahim lost his job during the Intifada "when he started to express his political views openly." Ibrahim resigned in 1977 by choice. I discuss his reasons in this chapter.

26. *Al-Itihad*, press clipping found in George Ibrahim's personal archive. Date is not indicated on the article.

27. *Al-Itihad*, press clipping found in George Ibrahim's personal archive.

28. Snir, "Palestinian Theatre: Historical Development and Contemporary Distinctive Identity," in Urian, *Palestinians and Israelis in the Theatre*, 35.

29. Pappé, *The Forgotten Palestinians*, 103. Pappé describes this program (and the initiative of the Arab section in Israeli television) as "an attempt from above," meaning a state-level initiative.

30. George Ibrahim, personal interview, 23 October 2010.

31. George Ibrahim, personal interview, 18 January 2011.

32. *Jerusalem Post Magazine*, 24 August 1973.

33. George Ibrahim, personal interview, 18 January 2011 and 23 October 2010.

34. George Ibrahim, personal interview, 23 October 2010.

35. George Ibrahim, personal interview, 23 October 2010. Ibrahim names the foremost leaders of the Communist Party in that period. Saliba Khamis is the father of the assassinated theater director Juliano Mer Khamis (1958-2011).

36. *Jerusalem Post Magazine*, 24 August 1973.

37. *Jerusalem Post Magazine*, 24 August 1973.

38. George Ibrahim, personal archive, scrap of a newspaper dated 9 July 1989. The interview in the paper was conducted by Mohammad Zebdah and Ahmad Mashharawi.

39. George Ibrahim, personal archive, scrap of a newspaper dated 9 July 1989. The interview in the paper was conducted by Mohammad Zebdah and Ahmad Mashharawi.

40. George Ibrahim, personal interview, 23 October 2010.

41. George Ibrahim, personal interview, 18 January 2011.

42. George Ibrahim, personal interview, 18 January 2011.

43. Al-Kasaba Theatre, *30 Years: Al-Kasaba Theatre 1970-2000*, 5.

44. George Ibrahim, personal interview, 18 January 2011.

45. George Ibrahim, personal archive, scrap of a newspaper dated 9 July 1989. The interview in the paper was conducted by Mohammad Zebdah and Ahmad Mashharawi.

46. This list is compiled from informal discussions with George Ibrahim and personal interviews with him on 23 October 2010, 18 Nov 2010, 8 January 2011, and 18 January 2011. In addition, Mohammad Al-Batrawi informally explained that George Ibrahim's "beautiful work with the children" had a significant impact on Jerusalemite theater and gave him similar credit in a personal interview, 24 October 2010.

47. George Ibrahim, personal interview, 23 October 2010. Ibrahim insisted on charging each child at least one shekel per performance to teach them from an early age to buy a ticket for a theatrical experience. In a personal interview, 26 January 2011, Mohammad Al-Thaher stated that George Ibrahim started his theatrical career as a professional and paid his actors.

48. Al-Kasaba Theatre, *30 Years: Al-Kasaba Theatre 1970-2000*, 37.

49. *Al-Quds*, 4 April 1977.

50. *Al-Quds*, 4 April 1977.

51. *Al-Quds*, 4 April 1977. According to Ibrahim, Ahmad Abu Ghannam continued with musical composition after Al-Kurd's arrest and exile in 1976.

Chapter 3

1. François Abu Salem interviewed by Hussam Abdel Latif, *Al-Hadaf*, 6 February 1982, p. 48.

2. Sameh Abboushey, personal interview, 11 January 2011. According to Abboushey, the Palestinians working with Carmichael at the time included Rima Nasser Tarazi and Tanya Nasser. Today, the hall has now developed to host parties and receptions, but at the time it basically was an empty room.

3. It may be difficult to name all the participants in Balalin because the troupe grew quickly, especially after the 1973 festival. According Sameh Abboushey (personal interview, 11 January 2011), the Ramallah group included Sameh Abboushey, Nadia Mikail, Saheer Abdel Hadi, Adel El Tartir, Walid Abdel Salam, and Jabr Al-Zubaidi. The early Jerusalem group included François Abu Salem, Emile Ashrawi, Ibrahim Ashrawi, Milad Kidan, and Ali Hijjawi.

4. Nazım Hikmet, *Beyond the Walls*, 165-170.

5. Sameh Abboushey, personal interview, 11 January 2011.

6. All details aside from information on Carmichael are from my interview with Sameh Abboushey on 11 January 2011.

7. Combined account from Sameh Abboushey, personal interview, 11 January 2011; and Emile Ashrawi, personal interview, 11 January 2011.

8. François Abu Salem Archive, Palestinian National Theatre.

9. Emile Ashrawi, personal interview, 11 January 2011.

10. Majid Al-Mani, personal interview, 13 October 2010.

11. Adel Al-Tartir, personal interview, 24 October 2010.

12. François Abu Salem Archive, Palestinian National Theatre.

13. I have been unable to obtain a copy of *A Slice of Life*. This description is a reconstruction based on brief mentions in interviews by Adel Al-Tartir, Emile Ashrawi, and Sameh Abboushey as well as an email exchange with Al-Tartir on 22 June 2012.

14. Fawzi Yasin Al-Bakri, *Al-Anba'*, January 1972 (newspaper clipping in the François Abu Salem Archive, Palestinian National Theatre).

15. Combined account from several sources: Sameh Abboushey, personal interview, 11 January 2011; Emile Ashrawi, personal interview, 11 January 2011; Majid Al-Mani, personal interview, 13 October 2010; and Adel Al-Tartir, personal interview, 24 October 2010. Adel Al-Tartir framed and hung the tickets and posters in the center of Sundouq Al-'ajab in the Ramallah, Old City.

16. Fawzi Yasin Al-Bakri, *Al-Anba'*, January 1972. Newspaper clipping in the François Abu Salem Archive, Palestinian National Theatre.

17. Sameh Abboushey, personal interview, 11 January 2011.

18. For an alternative discussion and analysis of the play, see Snir, *Palestinian Theatre*, 108-116; Nassar, *Palestinian Theatre: Between Origins and Visions*, 91-104.

19. Sameh Abboushey, personal interview, 11 January 2011.

20. According to press clippings, the first reviewed performance took place on 28 September 1972 on the stage of the Friends School in Ramallah. Another meaningful date is on the poster advertising a Ramadan evening performance on 21 October 1972; however, a press clipping announced the cancellation of this performance due to a car accident involving performers. The production was initially performed five times in Jerusalem, Ramallah, and Qalandia. Source: François Abu Salem Archive, Palestinian National Theatre.

21. For the Arabic script, see Anis, *Al-harakah Al-Masrahiyah Fi Al-Manatiq Al-Muhtallah*, 41. For an English language translation, see Jayyusi and Allen, *Modern Arabic Drama*, 196. This quotation combines both.

22. Jayyusi and Allen, *Modern Arabic Drama*, 211.

23. Emile Ashrawi, personal interview, 11 January 2011.

24. Najwa Qawar Farah, *Al-Quds*, 3 October 1972 (clipping in François Abu Salem Archive, Palestinian National Theatre).

25. Sameh Abboushey, personal interview, 11 January 2011.

26. Adel Al-Tartir, personal interview, 24 October 2010.

27. Mahmoud Shqair, *Shu'un Filastiniyah*, no. 47 (July 1975).

28. Original recording in the possession of Emile Ashrawi, shared with me in August 2017.

29. As reported by Sameh Abboushey, personal interview, 11 January 2011.

30. Adel Al-Tartir, personal interview, 24 October 2010.

31. As explained by both Al-Tartir and Abboushey.

32. From the personal archive of Adel Al-Tartir. The manifesto was entitled *Masrah Baladna*. The company did not survive long enough to achieve all the goals in this manifesto.

33. Al-Tartir framed and hung those posters in the current location of Sundouq Al-ʿajab. The only manuscript I gained access to is *Nashrat Ahwal Al-Jaw*, which remains unpublished. Further research is needed on all other plays by Balalin.

34. Combined from three personal interviews: Majid Al-Mani, 13 October 2010; Adel Al-Tartir, 24 October 2010; and Emile Ashrawi, 11 January 2011.

35. Adel Al-Tartir, personal interview, 24 October 2010.

36. Reported by Abboushey, Ashrawi, Al-Tartir, and Al-Kurd in personal interviews.

37. *Nitsalaf* is a transliteration from Arabic. When reversed, the letters spell out the word *Falastin*, meaning Palestine. The equivalent reversal in English would be *Enitselap*.

38. *Nashrat Ahwal Al-Jaw*, 60. Unpublished script obtained from actor Adel Al-Tartir.

39. Sameh Abboushey, personal interview, 11 January 2011.

40. François Abu Salem memorial, 2011, Palestinian National Theatre, Jerusalem.

41. The full text of the speech, including the direct quotes cited here, is found in the François Abu Salem Archive in the Palestinian National Theatre, Jerusalem.

42. For example, Sameh Abboushey played a significant authorial role in the writing of *Al-ʿatma*, and Adel Al-Tartir's skills as a carpenter contributed significantly to the renovation of the municipal hall for the 1973 festival. Many individual contributions remain unidentified.

43. According to my informal discussions with his contemporaries, Abu Salem appears to have been influenced in the early seventies by Artaud's Theatre of Cruelty and the French avant-garde.

44. Former member Mohammad Anis reported all these reasons. See Anis, *Al-harakah Al-Masrahiyah Fi Al-Manatiq Al-Muhtallah*, 22–23.

45. Sahar Khalifeh, *Al-Ghadeer*, June 1973, 8.

46. As reported by Mahamid, who interviewed several company members including Emile Ashrawi and Walid Abdel Salam. See Mahamid, *Masirat Al-Harakah Al-Masrahiyah Fi Al-Diffah Al-Gharbiyah*, 32–33.

Chapter 4

1. See Yazid Sayigh, *Armed Struggle and the Search for State*, 271. He estimates the death toll to be over three thousand lives.

2. Ibrahim Jbail, personal interview, 24 January 2011.

3. Ibrahim Jbail, personal interview, 24 January 2011, and Jbail's handwritten description of his plays.

4. Ibrahim Jbail, personal interview, 24 January 2011.

5. Ibrahim Jbail, personal interview, 24 January 2011.

6. Theatre Committee, *The Association for Work and Development for the Arts* (booklet), 20–21.

7. Ibrahim Jbail, personal interview, 24 January 2011. Although membership in "outlawed" Palestinian parties was secretive and difficult to prove by the military governor's investigators, Jbail's association with the PFLP was a likely cause of Israel's refusal to allow him to continue leading Dababis.

8. Anis, *Al-harakah Al-Masrahiyah Fi Al-Manatiq Al-Muhtallah*, 76.

9. Ibrahim Jbail, personal interview, 24 January 2011.

10. Reconstruction from memory, Ibrahim Jbail, personal interview, 24 January 2011. In his summary statement, Jbail noted that soon after the production, fire stations were established in both Ramallah and El-Bireh.

11. Statistics reported by Mahamid, *Masirat Al-Harakah Al-Masrahiyah Fi Al-Diffah Al-Gharbiyah*, 55.

12. Mohammad Al-Thaher, personal interview, 26 January 2011.

13. See interview with Ahmad Abu Saloum by Bassam Al-Ka'bi, in Ka'bi, *Aswat Maqdisiya*, 9–25. Mohammad Al-Thaher, personal interview, 26 January 2011.

14. Mohammad Al-Thaher, personal interview, 26 January 2011.

15. Unpublished script obtained from the Mohammad Al-Thaher. Ahmad Abu Saloum described the play as one of the most significant productions in the 1970s in a personal interview, 13 January 2011.

16. Ka'bi, *Aswat Maqdisiya*, 19.

17. From a statement by Mohammad Al-Thaher received on 27 January 2011. It chronicles the history of the Palestinian Theatre.

18. Mahamid, *Masirat Al-Harakah Al-Masrahiyah Fi Al-Diffah Al-Gharbiyah*, 35. Mahamid discusses the troupe very briefly but does not provide specific details.

19. Anis, *Al-harakah Al-Masrahiyah Fi Al-Manatiq Al-Muhtallah*, 170.

20. Anis, *Al-harakah Al-Masrahiyah Fi Al-Manatiq Al-Muhtallah*, 219–220.

21. Ashrawi provides the date and translation of the name of this collective. Ashrawi, *Contemporary Palestinian Literature Under Occupation*, 8.

22. Quoted from an interview with Ahmad Abu Saloum in Ka'bi, *Aswat Maqdisiya*, 18.

23. Theater Committee, *The Association for Work and Development for the Arts*, 7.

24. Jbail's written summary statement, received 25 January 2011.

25. Jbail's written summary statement, received 25 January 2011. He noted that the play was presented in 1974, but the festival took place in February 1975. It is likely that the play was rehearsed in late 1974.

26. *Al-Masrah*, no. 1: 4.

27. *Al-Masrah*, no. 3: 43.

28. Al-Tartir reported that Al-Kurd joined the retreat at a later stage. Jackie Lubeck worked as a technician on the troupe's first show.

29. Adel Al-Tartir, personal interview, 24 October 2010.

30. Mustapha Al-Kurd, personal interview, 24 January 2011.

31. Mustapha Al-Kurd, personal interview, 26 January 2011. Similar performances of military power were seen in recent years at the Freedom Theatre in the Jenin Refugee Camp.

32. Based on the mandate's emergency laws, administrative detention is an arrest without evidence or trial. A 2012 Palestinian prisoners' hunger strike protested administrative detention and prison conditions.

33. The circumstances of Al-Kurd's release and departure, deportation, or exile remain undocumented in the public record.

34. Al-Kurd succeeded in reclaiming his residency with the help of a lawyer.

35. Theatre Committee, *The Association for Work and Development for the Arts*, 13.

36. Anis, *Al-harakah Al-Masrahiyah Fi Al-Manatiq Al-Muhtallah*, 76.

37. Ibrahim Jbail, personal interview, 24 January 2011.

38. All quotes are from Ibrahim Jbail, personal interview, 24 January 2011.

39. Mahmoud Shqair, *Shu'un Filastiniyah*, no. 47 (July 1975): 239.

40. Samara, "The Theatre of the Occupied Territories," *Al-Bayader*, 1976, 83.

Chapter 5

1. George Ibrahim, personal interview, 23 October 2023.

2. Mahmoud Shqair, *Shu'un Filastiniyah*, no. 47 (July 1975): 239.

3. Samara, "The Theatre of the Occupied Territories," *Al-Bayader*, 1976, 83.

4. The six founding members were Abu Salem, Lubeck, Muallem, Tarabsheh, Hammad, and Mahamid. Abu Salem retained the right to use El-Hakawati name as his own until his death. Upon leaving the ensemble, all the members who belonged to El-Hakawati at any given time stopped using the name. In 1990, the original ensemble officially disbanded after the unsuccessful production *In Search of Omar Al-Khayyam*.

5. Edward Muallem, personal interview, 26 October 2010.

6. Based on personal interviews or email exchanges with a number of artists including Jackie Lubeck (8 October 2012 and on Skype 30 July 2012), Adnan Tarabsheh (11 December 2010), and Edward Muallem (26 October 2010). On the first production, Wassef Dandis helped with set building.

7. As a prelude to the opening of the Nuzha Hakawati Theatre in 1984, the bylaws were written and the ensemble was officially incorporated.

8. All quotes from the articles of incorporation are drawn from Ziad Hamdan, "The Development of the Palestinian Theatre," 82–92, Appendix B.

9. El-Hakawati Press Archive, Ashtar Theatre.

10. El-Hakawati Press Archive, Ashtar Theatre.

11. Edward Muallem, "A Reading into El-Hakawati Theatre Ensemble," *Al-Nahar*, 1 April 1989.

12. Ilana DeBare and Lisa Blum, "Palestinian Theatre Takes Root," *In These*

Times, 17-23 October 1989; republished in *Journal of Palestine Studies*, 14, no. 2 (1985): 230-234.

13. Echoed in interviews with Edward Muallem (26 October 2010), Adnan Tarabsheh (11 December 2010), Iman Aoun (29 January 2011), and Jackie Lubeck (8 October 2012) and in my field notes from informal discussions with theater artists. See another description of the main characteristics of El-Hakawati Ensemble in Mahamid, *Masirat Al-Harakah Al-Masrahiyah Fi Al-Diffah Al-Gharbiyah*, 42-43.

14. Emphasizing the ensemble's focus on play development, Jackie Lubeck stated, "The plays were created by François and the company provided him with loads and loads of improvisations." Lubeck, email 31 July 2012. For the ensemble, play development was the priority.

15. See the interview with François Abu Salem in *Al-Sharq Al-Awsat*, Paris, 4 March 1986: "Our experience is distant from the Arab Experience. Our theatre is a Palestinian Cultural Center in Jerusalem." See also Mahamid, *Masirat Al-Harakah Al-Masrahiyah Fi Al-Diffah Al-Gharbiyah*, 40-54.

16. Jackie Lubeck, Skype interview, 30 July 2012, and personal interview, 8 October 2012. Abu Salem revived the play with the future El-Hakawati members at the end of 1977.

17. "Précisions et mises au point," *Le Monde*, 12 March 1977: 9. My translation.

18. Dates are based on company brochure in El-Hakawati Press Archive, Ashtar Theatre.

19. Quotes drawn from personal interviews with several ensemble members and Skype interview with Jackie Lubeck on 30 July 2012. Based on my field notes from formal and informal discussions, almost all Palestinian theater artists stated their intellectual sympathy with various political factions, but they insisted that their creative work remained independent.

20. I obtained this text from Edward Muallem. He preserved the play by recording it in writing. All summaries and analyses of plays in this chapter are based on El-Hakawati's unpublished scripts, period journalism, or video records. Dov Shinar's 1987 book *Palestinian Voices* provided snippets of information on El-Hakawati plays based on a brochure. See also Snir and Nassar, who cite Shinar as their main source on the plays.

21. Based on original text in manuscript form.

22. "Qadaya Al-Masrah Al-Mahali," *Al-Tali'a*, 16 November 1978, FAS Archive.

23. Ya'coub Ismail, "El-Hakawati Theater and Artistic Creativity," *Al-Tali'a*, 20 November 1978, FAS Archive.

24. Hatem Al-Dajani, "The Opinion of Hatem Al-Dajani of the Play B'ism Al-Ab, w Al-Um, w Al-Ibn," *Al-Tali'a*, 23 November 1978, FAS Archive.

25. Several newspaper clippings: "From Where and to Where?," *Al-Shira'*, n.d., FAS Archive; Mahmoud Radwan Al-Lamdani, "Spotlighting the Play: B'ism Al-Ab, Wal-Um, Wal-Ibn," *Al-Ghadeer*, 22-26 November 1978, FAS Archive; Amin Mohammad Al-Basha, "El-Hakawati Theater and Truthful Assessment: The Play B'ism Al-Ab, w Al-Um, w Al-Ibn," *Al-Shira'*, 15 December 1978.

26. Adnan Tarabsheh, personal interview, 11 December 2010.

27. Based on interviews with Edward Muallem (26 October 2010) and Adnan Tarabsheh (11 December 2010) as well as several exchanges with Jackie Lubeck (Skype and email in July and August 2012 and personal interview 8 October 2012).

28. Several clippings in the FAS Archive: Marius Schattner, "Les hommes sont des cochons: sur la pièce du groupe 'El Hakawati,'" *Bulletin d'information sur la Palestine occupée et la société israélienne*, November–December 1978; "Palästinensertheater aus Jerusalem," *Basler Zeitung*, 43; D. K. "Bilder. Podium: El Hakawati aus Westjordanien," *Badische Zeitung*, 18 June 1980; Fiore, Enrico. "La Palestina in lotta di "El Hakawati," *Paese Sera*, 12 June 1980.

29. Hussam Abu Esheh as interviewed by Mahamid. Al-Thaher. Abu Saloum, and Abu Esheh all expressed admiration for each other's work. Abu Esheh and Al-Thaher suggested that personal and political reasons played a role in the division. Mohammad Al-Thaher, personal interview, 26 January 2011; Hussam Abu Esheh, personal interview, 20 November 2011.

30. Kanafani, *'a'id Ila Hayfa*, 57. For a translation, see Kanafani, *Palestine's Children*, 128.

31. Kanafani, *'a'id Ila Hayfa*, 76. For a translation, see Kanafani, *Palestine's Children*, 138.

32. Hussam Abu Esheh, personal interview, 20 November 2011.

33. Ahmad Abu Saloum, personal interview, 13 January 2011.

34. Hussam Abu Esheh, personal interview, 20 November 2011.

35. Imad Mitwalli, personal interview, 12 January 2011.

36. Hillal Masha'leh and Kamal Nasser, "A View Point on the Production of Man Is a Cause by Sanabel People's Theatre," *Al-Tali'a Weekly*, 17 April 1980.

37. As reported by Jamil Al-Salhout in *Al-Katib*, 90. The clipping obtained from Abu Saloum does not have a date; Abu Saloum confirmed these accounts in a personal interview, 13 January 2011.

38. Ahmad Abu Saloum, personal interview, 13 January 2011.

39. The assassination took place on 8 July 1972. See Nasr, "Black September vs Mossad," 58–76, in *Arab and Israeli Terrorism*, for an account of this period and a report on Kanafani's assassination (65–67).

40. Ahmad Abu Saloum, personal interviews, 13 January 2011 and 7 December 2010.

41. Hussam Abu Esheh, personal interview, 20 November 2011.

42. Scrap of a newspaper article in Ahmad Abu Saloum's personal archive. Likely in reference to the 1980 arrests, this published article was not dated, but it mentions the name of the actors and includes a picture of Abu Saloum. This arrest was the initial cause of the ensemble's four-year hiatus in 1980. Abu Saloum (personal interview, 13 January 2011) noted that the arrest of ensemble members took place in July 1980, shortly after the production.

43. See Jamil Al-Salhout's article in *Al-Katib*, n.d., 90 (cited in note 37).

44. In Al-Thaher's words, "The Israeli Authorities threatened the schools,

El-Mutran, Frère, and others, to not give out their spaces to theatre artists . . . These school headmasters, of course, want to survive, so they stopped renting out. Things froze . . . no halls to perform in. Some attempts took place at worker's unions to build spaces, taking matters in our own hands, but it was too difficult." I learned about the efforts of Al-Amal Al-Sha'bi Ensemble (People's Hope) in a personal interview with Rajai Sundoka, 13 November 2011. Ahmad Abu Saloum provides a similar narrative in his interview with Al-Ka'bi in Ka'bi, *Aswat Maqdisiya*, 19. On this period, Abu Saloum said that whenever possible, the ensemble's activities thrived underground. For example, they performed an adaptation of Ghassan Kanafani's *Um Sad* at the home of ensemble member Ibrahim 'laywat. Ahmad Abu Saloum, personal interview, 13 January 2011.

45. Al-Thaher, *Masrahiyatan: Al-Lu'ba/Al-Mawlid*, 91.

46. Al-Thaher, *Masrahiyatan: Al-Lu'ba/Al-Mawlid*, 95.

47. Theatre Committee, *The Association for Work and Development for the Arts* (booklet), 17.

48. Nabil Al-Joulani, *Al-Bayader*, February–March 1981, 49.

49. This discussion is drawn directly from the first draft of the original initiative of the League of Palestinian Theatre Artists. The present league is an entirely different institution and was founded in 1989. George Ibrahim was elected as the first president of the existing league.

50. Mohammad Al-Thaher, personal interview, 26 January 2011.

51. George Ibrahim, personal interview, 23 October 2023.

52. Based on a combination of my field notes from informal discussions and recorded interviews with Mohammad Al-Thaher (26 January 2011), Ahmad Abu Saloum (7 December 2010), and Hussam Abu Esheh (20 November 2011).

53. Mohammad Al-Thaher, personal interview, 26 January 2011.

Chapter 6

1. *Mahjoub Mahjoub*, unpublished script, p. 1.

2. I obtained the text of *Mahjoub Mahjoub* from Edward Muallem. He preserved the play by recording it in writing. According to Jackie Lubeck, the production ended with Lily assisting Mahjoub, who blows himself up out of the coffin, and the rest of the characters return to the scene in bandages as they play musical instruments.

3. See Yasser Ibrahim Rajjal, "Jerusalem: Occupation and Challenges to Urban Identity," in *My Jerusalem: Essays, Reminisces, and Poems*, ed. Salma Khadra Al-Jayyusi and Zafar Ishaq Ansari (Interlink Group Pub., 2005).

4. Censorship file on *Mahjoub Mahjoub*, Israel State Archive. The committee signed off on the approval in a meeting dated 15 December 1980.

5. On 27 December 1980, *Al-Fajr* newspaper reported briefly on a performance in Me'lia, the hometown of Edward Muallem. It also published a critical review by Talal Abu Afifeh entitled "Al-Hakawati's play Mahjoub Mahjoub."

6. "After the Official Permit to Show the Play Mahjoub Mahjoub, Authori-

ties Return to Suppress and Stop Its Showing Arbitrarily," *Al-Itihad*, 20 January 1981. See also "Censors Ban Performance by Israeli-W. Bank Ensemble," *Jerusalem Post*, 18 January 1981.

7. For a journalistic account of the evening, see "After the Official Permit to Perform Mahjoub Mahjoub, the Oppressive Authorities Return and Stop Its Performance Arbitrarily," *Al-Itihad*, 20 January 1981. Habibi served in the Knesset from 1951 to 1959 and 1961 to 1972.

8. "After the Official Permit to Perform Mahjoub Mahjoub," *Al-Itihad*, 20 January 1981.

9. Edward Muallem, personal interview, 26 October 2010.

10. "After the Official Permit to Perform Mahjoub Mahjoub," *Al-Itihad*, 20 January 1981.

11. Mohammad Al-Batrawi, personal interview, 24 October 2010, in Ramallah. See also Nida Shoughry, "1976 Land Day," in her book *"Israeli-Arab" Political Mobilization: Between Acquiescence, Participation, and Resistance*. On 30 March 1976, Palestinian citizens of Israel declared a general strike and demonstrated in large numbers to protest Israel's expropriation of Palestinian lands. Protests and demonstrations extended to the West Bank, Gaza, and refugee camps in Lebanon.

12. See Snir, *The Palestinian Theatre*; and Nassar, *Palestinian Theatre: Between Origins and Visions*, 40-65, for the importance of the Communist Party to theatrical activity in the period 1948-1967. Scholar Leena Dallasheh discusses the political realities of Nazareth in her dissertation "Nazarenes in the Turbulent Tide of Citizenships: Nazareth from 1940 to 1966," NYU, 2012.

13. Letter in censorship file on *Mahjoub Mahjoub*, Israel State Archive. This letter and all subsequent letters are found in the censorship records in the Israel State Archive.

14. Correspondence in censorship file on *Mahjoub Mahjoub*, Israel State Archive. The article by journalist Ahmad Youssef was published in *La Gauche Arabe (Al-Yassar Al-Arabi)*, no. 29 (March 1981): 20-22. Youssef attributes the function of the theatrical movement to resisting the occupation.

15. See Kanafani's introduction in *Al-Adab Al-Falastinia Al-Muqawim Tahta Al-Ihtilal*, 9. As a member of the Popular Front for the Liberation of Palestine, Kanafani embraced both armed struggle and cultural resistance, together and separately.

16. For a detailed account of Palestinian armed resistance, see section 2, "Years of Revolution, 1967-1972," in Sayigh's *Armed Struggle*.

17. François Abu Salem, *Al-Hadaf*, 6 February 1982.

18. Newspaper article in censorship file on *Mahjoub Mahjoub*, Israel State Archive. The date and source of the article are not identified in the file.

19. "The Play Mahjoub Mahjoub: The Censorship Committee for Plays and Cinematic Films Lifts the Ban on It," *Al-Fajr*, 27 January 1981; "Ban Lifted on Israeli West Bank Play," *Jerusalem Post*, 30 January 1981,

20. "Palestinian El-Hakawati Ensemble to Radio Monte Carlo," *Filastin Al-Thawra*, 17 December 1981. Also see "The Play Mahjoub Mahjoub: El-Hakawati Ensemble Penetrates the Zionist Siege," *Al-Hadaf*, 30 December 1982.

21. *Al-Fajr* (English), 17–23 May 1981.

22. Edward Muallem, personal interview, 26 October 2010.

23. "El-Hakawati Theatre Ensemble Returns to Jerusalem," *Al-Fajr*, 1 January 1982. Also see "El-Hakawati's 61 Performances: Palestinian Theatre Successful in Europe," *Al-Fajr*, 15–21 January 1982.

24. Ned Chaillet, "Mahjoub, Mahjoub," *The Times*, 23 September 1981. Chaillet opens his article with a question on the idea of representation in Islam and suggests that El-Hakawati's artistic representation runs contrary to the traditional Islamic ban against representation.

25. "Arab Actors in London," *Jewish Chronicle*, 25 September 1981.

26. Rosalind Carne, "Mahjoub Mahjoub," *Financial Times*, 24 September 1981.

27. According to interviews with Edward Muallem, Jackie Lubeck, Adnan Tarabsheh, Radi Shehadeh, Iman Aoun, Imad Mitwalli, Amer Khalil, and other contemporaries, El-Hakawati did not function under the auspices of the PLO.

28. For a detailed historical account of the PLO's activities during this period, see Helena Cobban, *The Palestinian Liberation Organization: People, Power, and Politics* (Cambridge University Press, 1984).

29. Jonathan Keates, "Mahjoub Mahjoub," *The Guardian*, 26 September 1981.

30. Ned Chaillet, "Mahjoub, Mahjoub," *The Times*, 23 September 1981.

31. "Anti-Israel Play Comes to London," *Jewish Chronicle*, 28 August 1981.

32. "Laughs after a Frisking," *Brentford & Chiswick Times*, 25 September 1981.

33. "Laughs after a Frisking," *Brentford & Chiswick Times*, 25 September 1981.

34. "Arab Actors in London," *Jewish Chronicle*, 25 September 1981.

35. "Agressions contre la ensemble palestinienne 'El Hakawati,'" *Midi-Libre*, 27 November 1981.

36. In personal interviews and informal conversations, many Jerusalemite theater artists called El-Hakawati the leading Palestinian theater ensemble. For example, George Ibrahim stated: "I competed with El-Hakawati, not with anybody else, because they were good. . . . Every time I saw a good production, I wanted to do better" (personal interview, 23 October 2010).

37. "El-Hakawati Prepares to Perform Mahjoub Mahjoub in Tel Aviv," *Al-Fajr*, 19 February 1983.

38. "El-Hakawati Prepares to Perform Mahjoub Mahjoub in Tel Aviv." See also "Mahjoub Mahjoub Performed Next Tuesday in Tel Aviv," *Al-Quds*, 19 February 1983. Before the Oslo agreements and the building of the Wall, the movement against normalization and for cultural boycott were not yet defined or exercised en masse within Palestine. Although provocative in this period, many Palestinians considered playing in Israeli theaters to be a breakthrough.

39. *Filastin Al-Thawra*, 7 July 1984.

40. For more details, see Allyn Fisher's Associated Press article (not dated)

in El-Hakawati press archive in the possession of Edward Muallem, Dov, Shinar's summary, and *Al-Itihad*'s detailed critical review on 4 August 1983. Actors in the play: Radi Shehadeh, Edward Muallem, Jackie Lubeck, Adnan Tarabsheh, Ibrahim Khalayleh, Daoud Kuttab, Saqr Al-Salaymeh, Munira Shehadeh, Kamal Shahin, and Samir Shahin. Music by Mustapha Al-Kurd. Costumes by Jackie Lubeck. Set by Francine Gáspár. The review in *Al-Itihad*, 4 February 1983, reported the production credits.

41. *Le Provençal* (Istres), 9 June 1982; *La Marseillaise* 8 June 1982.

42. *Al-Watan Al-Arabi*, no. 277 (4-10 June 1982). This report on the Montpellier incident is short and does not mention George Frêche by name. For a clear statement on Frêche's position and involvement, see a French language article dated July 1982 by Philippe Dauma in El-Hakawati Archive (the name of the publication is not legible). Georges Frêche (1938-2010) governed Montpellier for twenty-seven years and regularly announced his unwavering support for the State of Israel and close public friendships with Israeli officials, including heads of state.

43. Radi Shehadeh, personal interview, 21 August 2017.

44. Adnan Tarabsheh, *Al-Kashef Wal-Masrah Wal-48*, 87.

45. Radi Shehadeh, *Sirat Hakawati Min Falastin*, 111.

46. "At narme sig historien," 2 July 1982 (newspaper name is not on the clipping), El-Hakawati Press Archive.

47. *Al-Fajr* (English), 3-9 September 1983 (this article includes a complete English language translation of the *Politiken* review). *Al-Fajr* (Arabic), 21 August 1982.

48. For example, see reviews by Antwan Shalhat in *Al-Itihad*, 4 February 1983; Ghassan Abdallah in the December issue of *Al-Fajr Al-Adabi*; and Edward Grossman in *Jerusalem Post*, 24 December 1982.

49. According to the evaluation form and the permit in the censorship file at the Israel State Archive, the main censor evaluated the play on 5 September 1982. The permit was printed on 28 September 1982. The script reasonably represented the plot but not the politics.

50. As confirmed by *Al-Fajr* (Arabic) on 18 June 1983. The report does not name the author.

51. According to Lubeck, personal interview, 30 July 2012, the set was transported in an eighteen-wheel truck and required two days to set up. For reports on these performances, see the following articles in El-Hakawati Press Archive: *Al-Bayader*, 20 July-20 October 1982; *Al-Itihad*, 3 December 1982; and *Jerusalem Post*, 24 December 1982. The Sakhnin performances were reported in a short article in one of the Arabic language newspapers but does not have publication info.

52. Edward Grossman, "A Story-teller and his Message," *Jerusalem Post*, 24 December 1982.

53. For the two reviews by Ghassan Abdallah and Rustom Dawood, see *Al-Fajr Al-Adabi*, December 1982, 108-118.

54. Letter in censorship file on *Ali the Galilean*, Israeli State Archive. The title of the play used in the submission was *Ali*. This quote is a translation based on the censorship script submitted by the ensemble.

55. "After 18-Month Ban: Hakawati Takes 'Ali' To Jericho," *Al-Fajr* (English), 21 December 1984. The article describes the application to the military government, the presence of the French film crew, and the outcome of the event.

56. Jackie Lubeck, personal interview, 8 October 2012.

57. "After 18-Month Ban: Hakawati Takes 'Ali' To Jericho," *Al-Fajr* (English), 21 December 1984.

58. Ghassan Abdallah, "El-Hakawati . . . and the Single View," *Al-Fajr* (Arabic), 5 October 1983; Antoine Shalhat, "Suddenly . . . the Show Remained Like Minefield of a Puzzle," *Al-Itihad* (Arabic), 13 September 1985, 6; Moatassem Sundouqah, "*Jalilee Ya Ali* Too," *Al-Fajr* (Arabic), 29 September 1983.

59. Nabil Ezzat Ghaith, "Jalilee Ya Ali," *Al-Quds*, 7 November 1983 (Arabic). Mohammad Abu Salah, "Theater Makers Among the Audience," *Al-Quds*, 13 January 1985 (Arabic). "El-Hakwati Theatrical Ensemble Continues to Show Its Play Jalilee Ya Ali in the Galilee and the Triangle," *Al-Itihad*, 12 August 1983 (Arabic).

60. Edward Grossman, "A Story-Teller and His Message," *Jerusalem Post*, 24 December 1982.

61. "Palestinian Arts Cause Stir in Tel Aviv," *Al-Fajr* (English), 8 July 1983; "Palestinian Culture Week Opens Today," *Jerusalem Post*, 28 June 1983.

62. Judy Siegel, "New Guidelines for Military Reporters Being Kept Secret," *Jerusalem Post*, 5 July 1983. The article quotes Authority chairman Reuven Yaron.

63. Briel Strassman, "The Stone Age in Neve Tsedek," *Ma'ariv*, 5 July 1983 (Hebrew).

64. Shosh Avigal, "Don't Arabs Have Eyes?," *Koteret Rashit*, 6 July 1983 (Hebrew).

65. Michael Handelzalts, "Another Theater," *Haaretz*, 5 July 1983 (Hebrew).

66. "Palestinian Arts Cause Stir in Tel Aviv," *Al-Fajr* (English), 8 July 1983 and "Israeli Theatergoers Applaud Palestinian Play," *New York Times*, 27 August 1985.

Chapter 7

1. Ahmad Amer, *Al-Sabah*, 28 July 1982, 13.

2. See Arabic-language version of all these laws at http://muqtafi.birzeit.edu/. All translations are mine unless noted otherwise.

3. Imad Samara, personal interview, 13 November 2010.

4. Edward Muallem, video interview, Jerusalem, 11 August 2017. The cover photograph of this book depicts the state of the building when El-Hakawati rented it.

5. Jackie Lubeck, personal interviews, 10 September 2012 and 8 October 2012.

6. The account of the film, the opening, and the direct quotes are drawn from "Jesus Film Used For Propaganda," *Al-Fajr* (English), 15 February 1984. Quotes on the poster included capital letters as relayed here. See www.inspirationalfilms.com for further information on the film.

7. Tribute by Jackie Lubeck, "On François," *This Week in Palestine*, no. 163 (November 2011).

8. "El-Hakawati Theatre: A Voice for Palestine." *Al-Awdah* (magazine), 12 April 1984, 12.

9. Edward Muallem, video interview, Jerusalem, 11 August 2017.

10. "Lijan Al-Shabiba Al-Maqdisiya," *Al-Sha'b*, 4 June 1984, reported on nine different days, when Jerusalemite youth committees assisted in clean-up, removal of rubble, and pouring cement to build the auditorium.

11. Tsipi Kuper, "Palestinian Theatre Launched," *Jerusalem Post*, 18 May 1984.

12. "First Palestinian Theatre and Arts Centre to Open," *Al-Fajr* (English), 4 May 1984; "Thousands Attend First Theatre Opening," *Al-Fajr* (English), 12 May 1984.

13. "First Palestinian Theatre and Arts Centre to Open," *Al-Fajr*), 4 May 1984; "Thousands Attend First Theatre Opening," *Al-Fajr*, 12 May 1984.

14. "El-Hakawati and Al-Layla Wa Layla in the Occupied Land: El-Hakawati Ensemble Opens Its Theater in Jerusalem," *Al-Itihad*, 22 May 1984. Jean-Pierre Langellier, "Schéhérazade et le gouverneur israélien," *Le Monde*, 28 May 1984, 6.

15. "Concrete Steps Towards a Theatre Center," *Al-Fajr* (English), 9 Dec 1983. "Artistic Center in Jerusalem: A Dream Come True . . . ," *Al-Quds* (Arabic), 30 Jan 1984, 4. On the thorny subject of volunteers: although there are many reports of many individuals and groups who assisted in the building project, their assistance was only occasional. The ensemble worked from sunrise to sunset six days a week for nearly seven months. Community members and groups assisted for hours or a day at a time, but it is crucial to recognize that the ensemble and their immediate supporters were mostly alone for the majority of the process, and without their consistent and invested efforts, this theater would not exist today.

16. "Hakawati-Lead Grilled on New Center," *Al-Fajr*, 18 May 1984.

17. "Hakawatis Beaten by Police Interrogators," *Al-Fajr*, 3 August 1984.

18. Personal interviews with Jackie Lubeck (8 October 2012 and Skype, 30 July 2012) and Edward Muallem (26 October 2010).

19. I obtained this text from Edward Muallem, who preserved the play by recording it in writing.

20. "Hakawati Harassed on Eve of Show," *Al-Fajr*, 1 March 1985. "The Show Must Go On," *Kol Ha'ir*, 22 February 1985.

21. Traditional Palestinian musical instrument like the flute.

22. Censorship file on *The Story of the Eye and the Tooth*, Israel State Archive.

23. Mohammad Abu Salah, "The Story of the Eye and the Tooth," *Al-Itihad*, 12 April 1985. "The Story of the Eye and the Tooth in El-Hakawati Theater," *Al-Quds*, 13 April 1985. This article contains opinions by several artists and intellectuals.

24. Nabil Al-Joulani, *Al-Mithaq*, 30 April 1985.

25. Radi Shehadeh, *Sirat Hakawati Min Falastin*, 171-200.

26. "Hakawati Demands Removal of Israeli Flag in Theatre," *Al-Fajr Weekly*, 4 October 1985.

27. "Hakawati Demands Removal of Israeli Flag in Theatre," *Al-Fajr Weekly*, 4 October 1985.

28. Edward Muallem, video interview, Jerusalem, 11 August 2017 and personal interview, 26 October 2010.

29. See Jamil Al-Salhout's article on Sanabel People's Theatre, *Al-Katib*, 86. Of note, Abu Esheh served a sentence of three years in Israeli prison.

30. Ahmad Abu Saloum, personal interview, 13 January 2011. See also Jamil Al-Salhout's article on Sanabel People's Theatre, *Al-Katib*, 86. The production was performed by Ahmad Abu Saloum, Hussam Abu Esheh, Nidal Abu Saloum (child actor), Ibrahim Othman Eliwat, Mahmoud Abu El-Sheikh, Akram Ashour, Hamdi El-Taweel, and Samir Safadi (child actor). I was unable to find the play text for this production.

31. Ahmad Abu Saloum, personal interview, 13 January 2011. See also Jamil Al-Salhout's article on Sanabel People's Theatre, *Al-Katib*, 86.

32. Censorship file on the Sanabel production of *The General Sir*, Israel State Archive.

33. This strategy was employed often by El-Hakawati Theatre Ensemble and most local ensembles in the 1970s and 1980s.

34. Performed by Hussam Abu Esheh, Imad Mize'ro, Ibrahim Eliwat, Iman Sarhan, Mahmoud El-Sheikh, Akram Kashour, and Ismail Jabel. Music by Sabreen, set by George Ibrahim, poster by Jamal Al-Moghrabi, and directed by Ahmad Abu Saloum.

35. Censorship file on the Sanabel production of *The General Sir*, Israel State Archive.

36. Mohammad Al-Thaher, personal interview, 26 January 2011. Copies of El-Hakawati's calendars are available in the archives of the Palestinian National Theatre.

37. Production program/brochure, Mustapha Al-Kurd Collection, Palestine Museum.

38. Calendars of events, Theater Archives, Palestinian National Theater/El-Hakawati, Jerusalem.

39. "Masseera Fanniya Kabirah," *Al-Quds*, 7 May 1986.

Chapter 8

1. Muhammad Al-Labadi, personal interview, Ramallah, 17 August 2023.

2. See Yazid Sayigh's chapters "Struggle Within, Struggle Without" (574–606) and "Intifada to the Rescue" (607–637) in *Armed Struggle and the Search for State* for a full picture of the period.

3. *Al-Nahar*, 7 November 1987; and *Al-Sha'b*, 17 October 1987. *Al-Bayader Al-Siyasi* published an article on El-Hakawati's position on 30 November 1985. These articles are found in El-Hakawati Press Archive.

4. Said al-Ghazali, "Is Hakawati Living Up to Its Goal," *Al-Fajr* (English), 4 July 1986.

5. Jonathan Kuttab, *Al-Fajr*, 5 December 1986.
6. Hussam Abu Esheh, personal interview, 20 November 2011.
7. Hussam Abu Esheh, personal interview, 20 November 2011.
8. *Natrin Faraj*, video recording, 1988.
9. *Natrin Faraj*, video recording, 1988.
10. Hayyan Ya'coub, *Al-Sharara*, 30 October 1987.
11. File on *Natrin Faraj*, Israel State Archive. See also *Tariq Al-Sharara*, 13 November 1987 in the personal archive of Ahmad Abu Saloum.
12. Hussam Abu Esheh, personal interview, 20 November 2011.
13. File on *Natrin Faraj*, Israel State Archive. Quote from letter, 2 November 1987, by Daniel Rossing, director of the Department of Christian Communities (sects) in the Ministry of Religious Affairs. Rossing was also the founder of the Jerusalem Center on Jewish Christian Relations.
14. Clergy and Laity Concerned (CALC), New York chapter, letter by Suzanne Ross, July 18, 1988. *Assanabil* is a transliteration of the Arabic name for Sanabel Theatre. Personal archive of Hussam Abu Esheh.
15. Jess Sullivan, "Critics Call It 'Anti-Israeli:' ASI Funds the People's Theatre Sanabel," *The State Hornet*, 16 September 1988. Personal archive of Ahmad Abu Saloum.
16. Sullivan, "Critics Call It 'Anti-Israeli.'"
17. Sullivan, "Critics Call It 'Anti-Israeli.'"
18. Pat McDonnell Twair, "Eerily Prescient Play Tours US," *Washington Report on Middle East Affairs*, December 1988, 51.
19. For a report on the incident, see *Media in Palestine: Between the Hammer of the Authority and the Anvil of Self-Censorship*, The Palestinian Human Rights Monitoring Group, http://www.phrmg.org/arabic/monitor1999/oct1999-4.htm (last accessed May 25, 2012; the website no longer exists). Abu Esheh discussed the meeting with heads of the churches in the personal interview, 20 November 2011.
20. Al-Kasaba Theatre, *30 Years: Al-Kasaba Theatre 1970–2000*, 31.
21. *Mazen Kamal Ghattas*, 25.
22. File on *Men Without Shadows* (in Arabic: *Mawta Bila Quboor*) by Jean Paul Sartre, Israel State Archive.
23. Based on viewing and analysis of an archival video of *Men Without Shadows* at Al-Kasaba Theatre, Ramallah.
24. Carl Vitalie, "Men Without Shadows Opens at Hakawati," *Al-Fajr* (English), 21 November 1988.
25. Muhammad Al-Labadi, personal interview, Ramallah, 17 August 2023.
26. Kamel Al-Basha, personal interviews, 18 September 2010 and October 4, 2023.
27. Original text in manuscript form provided by Jackie Lubeck. See also a summary of the play by Jackie Lubeck in *Al-Bayader Al-Siyasi (Arabic)*, 23 May 1987. El-Hakawati Press Archive.

28. File on *The Story of Kufur Shamma*, Israeli State Archive.
29. *Al-Itihad*, 6 October 1987, El-Hakawati Press Archive.
30. *Jerusalem Post*, 9 October 1987, El-Hakawati Press Archive.
31. David Drudge, "Added Police Expected at Acre Festival as Rival Demos Duel over Arab Play," *Jerusalem Post*, 9 October 1987. *Al-Fajr* (English), 4 October 1985, reported El-Hakawati's earlier refusal to perform *Ali the Galilean* until the Israeli flag was removed before an audience of 1,200 spectators. It also reported actor Ibrahim Khalayleh's ingenious publicity stunt of attaching a poster to the back of a roaming donkey in Acre (see chapter 7). According to *Al-Fajr*, the story was also reported by the Israeli newspaper *Yediot Aharonot*.
32. Drudge, "Added Police Expected at Acre Festival." According to novelist and playwright Salman Natour, the Likud party representative in Acre announced this vendetta of the flag on Israeli television.
33. *Al-Itihad*, 6 October 1987, El-Hakawati Press Archive.
34. *Al-Itihad*, 12 October 1987, El-Hakawati Press Archive.
35. Yousef Mousa. *Al-Itihad*, 14 October 1987. For more information on the Kahane Chai movement and its spiritual leader, the Brooklyn-born Rabbi Meir Kahane, see Martin and Kushner, *The Sage Encyclopedia of Terrorism*, 321-324.
36. Interview with Edward Muallem in *Al-Raya*, 16 October 1987, p. 2.
37. I transcribed and translated the speech from a video recording in the possession of Edward Muallem. Unless cited otherwise, the description is my observation as a viewer of this recording.
38. Quoted in *Al-Itihad*, 14 October 1987. "Pa'amim hufsaka hatzagat hate'atron 'El Hakawati' be-Festiv'al Akko," *Haaretz* (Hebrew), 13 October 1987, reported that six of these Kach members were detained for questioning after the incident over the flags. "Anshei Kahane 'pats'u' hatzagat hate'atron ha'aravi," *Yedioth Ahronoth* (Hebrew), 13 October 1987, also identified the individuals as Kahane Chai (Kach) members.
39. As per the report of *Al-Itihad*, 14 October 1987. My account of the events in Acre is reconstructed from interviews with Edward Muallem, Jackie Lubeck, Iman Aoun, Imad Mitwalli, and Amer Khalil.
40. Alisa Solomon, "At Papp's Public Theater, a Show of Arrogance," *New York Times*, 15 July 1989.
41. William B. Collins, "Denying Pressure, Joseph Papp Drops Play by Palestinian Troupe," *Philadelphia Inquirer*, 30 June 1989.
42. Collins, "Denying Pressure, Joseph Papp Drops Play by Palestinian Troupe."
43. Collins, "Denying Pressure, Joseph Papp Drops Play by Palestinian Troupe."
44. Based on reports in several articles. For example, see *Seattle Times*, 30 June 1989; Sylvie Drake, "Palestinian Play in N.Y., but No L.A. Booking Yet," *Los Angeles Times*, 27 July 1989; and *New York Times*, 25 July 1989. See the *New York Times'* attempt at balanced reporting on 15 July 1989 in two separate articles, one by

Andrew L. Yarrow, "Papp Cancels Palestinian Play," and one by Alisa Solomon, "At Papp's Public Theater, a Show of Arrogance." In her article, Solomon asked, "Why can't we see a Palestinian play?"

45. William B. Collins, "Palestinian Company Makes Debut at Painted Bride Center," *Philadelphia Inquirer*, 1 July 1989.

46. Collins, "Palestinian Company Makes Debut at Painted Bride Center."

47. Collins, "Denying Pressure, Joseph Papp Drops Play by Palestinian Troupe."

48. Collins, "Denying Pressure, Joseph Papp Drops Play by Palestinian Troupe."

49. Collins, "Palestinian Company Makes Debut at Painted Bride Center."

50. "The Suitcase Fund is New York Live Arts' international artist and cultural worker exchange program." See funding programs on www.newyorklivearts.org (last accessed 9 February 2013).

51. Wilborn Hampton, "An Odyssey of Refugees, in This Case Palestinian," *New York Times*, 28 July 1989.

52. Hampton, "An Odyssey of Refugees."

53. John Simon, "East Village/West Bank," *New York Magazine*, 7 August 1989, 45.

54. Simon, "East Village/West Bank," 45. For further reporting on El-Hakawati's North American tour, see Edward Muallem's concise summary in *Al-Itihad*, 20 November 1989; and "American Premier of 'Kufur Shamma' Is a Smash," *Seattle Times*, 18 August 1989.

55. Incidentally, the building that was being considered remains unfinished in 2023.

Chapter 9

1. "Masrah Al-Kasaba . . . intilaqah," *Al-Quds*, 1 August 1991, 13.

2. Unless otherwise stated, the narrative of the construction and development of Al-Kasaba throughout this chapter relies on my synthesis of personal interviews with George Ibrahim, Ramallah, 23 October 2010, 18 November 2010, 8 January 2011, 18 January 2011, and 27 October 2023. Additional useful context for Al-Kasaba emerged in my personal interviews with Hussam Abu Esheh (20 November 2011), Kamel El-Basha (18 September 2010 and 4 October 2023), and Mohammad Al-Batrawi (24 October 2010).

3. Personal interviews with George Ibrahim, 23 October 2010, 18 November 2010, 8 January 2011, 18 January 2011, and 27 October 2023.

4. Samih Al-Qassem, "Al-ghitha' w al-ghitha' Al-Rouhi," *Al-Itihad*, 19 July 1991.

5. Children's shows were often initially produced as "live action" and then remounted with puppets. For example, *Layla Al-Hamrah*'s puppet version was performed by Hussam Abu Esheh and Jackie Ayoub at Al-Kasaba Theatre and on tour, but initially, it played at Al-Omariyyeh and El-Hakawati. Al-Kasaba printed a brochure that cataloged thirty years of production from 1970–2000, which contains the cast names for almost all its productions. One of the notable

absences is *Romeo and Juliet*, a co-production between Al-Kasaba and the Khan Theatre in 1994-1995.

6. Unless otherwise stated, my narrative of this production relies on my synthesis of various interviews with members of El-Hakawati in Jerusalem, including Amer Khalil, Iman Aoun, Jackie Lubeck, and Edward Muallem (16-23 August 2017), production photographs, and my reading of the text.

7. Imad El-Din Abdelrazzak, "El-Hakawati Seeks to Drag the Past, Postponing Facing the Present," *Al-'arab*, 12 September 1991.

8. Kamel El-Basha, "Masrahiyat Ansar," *Al-Itihad*, 19 June 1990.

9. "The Palestinian Theater League Prepares to Open the First Jerusalem Festival from 27/11 to 20/12," *Al-Nahar* (Arabic), 31 October 1990; and "The Palestinian Theater League Begins Its Preparations for the First Palestinian Theater Festival," *Al-Rased*, 29 October 1990.

10. *Al-Sada* newspaper reported on this press briefing on 4 March 1993. Such press briefings were advertised regularly in newspapers, including *Al-Quds* newspaper on 8 March 1992, 14 April 1992, 27 May 1992, and 15 February 1993.

11. These unique events were all reported in *Al-Quds* newspaper on 7 December 1991, 13 January 1992, 4 March 1992, 12 April 1992, 22 April 1992, 3 June 1992, 29 July 1992, and 27 November 1992.

12. "Palestinian German Encounter at Al-Kasaba Theater," *Al Quds* (Arabic), 12 December 1991.

13. "The Council of Palestinian Culture and Media Hold a Cultural and Artistic Ceremony on the Anniversary of the Declaration of Independence," *Al-Manar* (Arabic), 23 November 1992.

14. Kamel El-Basha, personal interview, 18 September 2010.

15. Until her passing on 18 October 2023, Francine Gáspár held onto scripts and design sketches from this production. Jackie Lubeck and Jan Williams gifted me with the privilege of accompanying them to visit her in Paris in the summer of 2021.

16. "Jericho in the Year Zero," *Jerusalem Times*, 2 December 1994. The play starred Amer Khalil, Sylvia Wetz, Raeda Ghazaleh, Khitam Adelby, Adania Shebly, Mohammad Bakri, Akram Tillawi, Hussam Abu Esheh, and Ahmad Abu Saloum.

17. Fouad Awad, *A Theatrical Biography*, 113-130. Much of my account on this production relies on Awad's memoir. According to Awad, the Palestinian Ensemble included Mohammad Bakri, Khalifa Natour, Derar Suleiman, Bassam Zu'mot, Ghassan Abbas, George Ibrahim, Khitam Edlaby, Hussam Jowaylis, Maha Jowaylis, and Khalid El-Masou. The Israeli ensemble included Orna Katz, Alisa Rosen, Boris Achanov, Javiar Katz, Julie Goldstein, Aryeh Tcherner, Yoram Yossefberg, Ayal Sari, Ze'ev Shamshoni, Sal'eet Akhemryam, and Gilat Hadi.

18. Helen Kaye, "Love a Loathed Enemy," *Jerusalem Post*, 24 June 1994. Although I have not seen evidence for this, Varghese, *Palestinian Theatre in the West*

Bank, 36, notes that the international tour of the play was funded as a Hasbara project by the Israeli government.

19. Laura Blumenfeld, "Mideast Side Story: In Jerusalem's 'Romeo and Juliet,' the Real Drama Is Off the Stage," *Washington Post*, 30 June 1994. Additional previews: Dan Fesperman, "Arab-Israeli 'Romeo' Rings with Reality," *The Sun*, 15 June 1994; Vanessa Redgrave, "Peace, Plays, Politics: Vanessa Redgrave Was to Have Performed in Israel This Week. But the Lights Went Out Before the Curtain Went Up. She Explains Why," *The Guardian*, 22 July 1994.

20. Freddie Rokem, "Postcard from the Peace Process: Some Thoughts on the Palestinian-Israeli Coproduction of 'Romeo and Juliet,'" *Palestine Israel Journal* 2, no. 1 (1995): 112–117.

21. George Ibrahim, personal interview, 27 October 2023.

22. Fouad Awad, *A Theatrical Biography*, 124. Yael Munk refers to Anat Even's documentary film as subversive, in "'Dreamers Often Lie': On 'Compromise', the Subversive Documentation of an Israeli- Palestinian Political Adaptation of Shakespeare's Romeo and Juliet," *Altre Modernità: Rivista di Studi Letterari e Culturali*, no. 3 (2010): 174–181.

Conclusion

1. The largest city in the West Bank is Hebron at 74 square kilometers.

BIBLIOGRAPHY

'Abd, Allah A. A. *Waqi' Al-Sihafah Al-Filastiniyah Fi Al-Diffah Wa-Al-Qita', 1967-1987*. Dimashq: Da'irat al-Thaqafah, Munazzamat al-Tahrir al-Filastiniyah, 1989. (Arabic)

Ahmed, Seema S. "El Hakawati: Palestinian Theatre and the Politics of the Israeli Occupation: A Study of Political Culture and Political Socialization." BA thesis, University of Puget Sound, 1994.

Anis, Mohammad. *Al-harakah Al-Masrahiyah Fi Al-Manatiq Al-Muhtallah*. S.l.: Dar Jalilyu, 1979. (Arabic)

Armbrust, Walter. *Mass Mediations: New Approaches to Popular Culture in the Middle East and Beyond*. Berkeley: University of California Press, 2000.

Asadi, Jawad. *Al-masrah Wa-Al-Filastini Alladhi Fina*. Dimashq: al-Ahali lil-Tiba'ah wa-al-Nashr wa-al-Tawzi', 1992. (Arabic)

Ashrawi, Hanan M. "The Contemporary Literature of Palestine: Poetry and Fiction." PhD dissertation, University of Virginia, 1982.

Ashrawi, Hanan M. *Contemporary Palestinian Literature Under Occupation*. Ramallah: Birzeit University, 1976.

Ashrawi, Hanan M. "The Contemporary Palestinian Poetry of Occupation." *Journal of Palestine Studies* 7, no. 3 (1978): 77-101.

Ashrawi, Hanan M. *Our Jerusalem*. Jerusalem: Palestine-Israel Journal, 1995.

Awad, Fouad. *A Theatrical Biography: Three Decades of Life in the Theatre of the Palestinian Director Fouad Awad*. UK: Amazon Kindle, 2012.

Barakat, Rena. "Thawrat Al-Buraq in British Mandate Palestine: Jerusalem, Mass Mobilization and Colonial Politics, 1928-1930." PhD dissertation, University of Chicago, 2007.

Al-Batrawi, Mohammad. "Al-Thaqafa Al-Wataniyya Al-Filastiniyya wa Tashkiran Al-Intifada."

Ben-Zvi, Linda, ed. *Theatre in Israel*. Ann Arbor: University of Michigan Press, 1996.

Burke, Peter. *New Perspectives on Historical Writing.* University Park: Pennsylvania State University Press, 2001.
Censorship file on *Ali the Galilean.* Israel State Archive, Jerusalem.
Censorship file on *The General Sir.* Israel State Archive, Jerusalem.
Censorship file on *Mahjoob Mahjoob.* Israel State Archive, Jerusalem.
Censorship file on *Men Without Shadows.* Israel State Archive, Jerusalem.
Censorship file on *Natrin Faraj.* Israel State Archive, Jerusalem.
Censorship file on *The Story of the Eye and the Tooth.* Israel State Archive, Jerusalem.
Censorship file on *The Story of Kufur Shamma.* Israel State Archive, Jerusalem.
Cody, Gabrielle H., and Evert Sprinchorn, eds. *The Columbia Encyclopedia of Modern Drama.* New York: Columbia University Press, 2007.
Cohen, Hillel. *Good Arabs: The Israeli Security Agencies and the Israeli Arabs, 1948–1967.* Berkeley: University of California Press, 2010.
Cohen, Hillel. *The Israeli Security Agencies and the Israeli Arabs, 1948-1967.* Berkeley: University of California Press, 2009.
Darraj, Faysal. "Palestine." In *The World Encyclopedia of Contemporary Theatre: The Arab World.* Edited by Don Rubin, 186–197. London: Routledge, 1994.
DeBare, Ilana, Lisa Blum, and François A. Salem. "Palestinian Culture Takes Root." *Journal of Palestine Studies* 14, no. 2 (1985): 230–234.
Denning, Michael. *The Cultural Front: The Laboring of American Culture in the Twentieth Century.* London: Verso, 1998.
Essoulami, Saïd. *Cry for Change: Israeli Censorship in the Occupied Territories.* London: Article 19, 1992.
Fisher, Allyn. Associated Press article, n.d. El-Hakawati Press Archive.
François Abu Salem Archive. Palestinian National Theatre and El-Hakawati Archive.
Frisch, Hillel. *Countdown to Statehood: Palestinian State Formation in the West Bank and Gaza.* Albany: State University of New York Press, 1998.
Haddad, 'Abir Z. *Al-masrah Al-Filastini Fi Al-Jalil: Bahth Wa-Tahlil.* Nazareth: Wizarat al-Ma'arif wa-al-Thaqafah, Da'irat al-Thaqafah wa-al-Funun al-'Arabiyah, 1994. (Arabic)
El-Hakawati. Company brochure, n.d. El-Hakawati Archive.
El-Hakawati Press Archive. El-Hakawati Archive. Ashtar Theatre, Ramallah.
Hakim, Tawfiq. *Plays, Prefaces and Postscripts of Tawfiq Al-Hakim.* Translated by William M. Hutchins. Washington, DC: Three Continents Press, 1981.
Hamdan, Ziad M. "The Development of the Palestinian Theatre: Al-Hakawati Theatre Group." Master's thesis, University of Illinois at Chicago, Department of Communications and Theatre, 1989.
Jamal, Amal. *The Arab Public Sphere in Israel: Media Space and Cultural Resistance.* Bloomington: Indiana University Press, 2009.
Jawzi Nasri. *Tarikh Al-Idha'ah Al-Filasṭiniyah: Huna Al-Quds, 1936–1948.* Dimashq: Manshurat al-Hay'ah al-'Ammah al-Suriyah lil-Kitab, 2010. (Arabic)

Jawzi, Nasri. *Tarikh Al-Masrah Al-Filastini, 1918-1948*. Niqusiya, Qubrus: Sharq Briss, 1990. (Arabic)

Jayyusi, Salma K., and Roger Allen, eds. *Modern Arabic Drama: An Anthology*. Bloomington: Indiana University Press, 1995.

Jbail, Ibrahim. Author statement and handwritten description of his plays. January 25, 2011. (Arabic)

Ka'bi, Bassam Al-. *Aswat Maqdisiya* [Jerusalemite Voices]. Jerusalem: Palestine Red Crescent Society, 2009. (Arabic)

Kanafani, Ghassan. *Al-adab Al-Filastini Al-Muqawim Tahta Al-Ihtilal, 1948-1968*. Bayrut: Mu'assasat al-Dirasat al-Filastiniyah, 1968. (Arabic)

Kanafani, Ghassan. *'a'id Ila Hayfa* [Returning to Haifa]. Bayrut: Mu'assasat al-Abhath al-'Arabiyah, 2008. (Arabic)

Kanafani, Ghassan. *Palestine's Children: Returning to Haifa and Other Stories*. Translated by Barbara Harlow and Karen E. Riley. London: Heinemann, 1984.

Al-Kasaba Theatre. *30 Years: Al-Kasaba Theatre 1970-2000*. Ramallah: Al-Kasaba, 2000.

Khalidi, Rashid. *Palestinian Identity: The Construction of Modern National Consciousness*. New York: Columbia University Press, 1997.

King, Mary E. *A Quiet Revolution: The First Palestinian Intifada and Nonviolent Resistance*. New York: Nation Books, 2007.

League of Palestinian Theatre Artists. Unpublished draft of the original by-laws and regulations, 1982. (Arabic)

Lubeck, Jackie. "On François." *This Week in Palestine* 163 (2011).

Lustick, Ian. "Yerushalayim, al-Quds, and the Wizard of Oz: The Problem of 'Jerusalem' after Camp David II and the Aqsa Intifada." In *Jerusalem: Idea and Reality*. Edited by Tamar Mayer and Suleiman A. Mourad. London: Routledge, 2008.

Mahamid, Muhamad. *Masirat Al-Harakah Al-Masrahiyah Fi Al-Diffah Al-Gharbiyah, 1967-1987*. al-Tayyibah: Markaz Ihya' al-Turath al-'Arabi, 1989.

Madison, D. S. *Critical Ethnography: Method, Ethics, and Performance*. Thousand Oaks, CA: Sage, 2005.

Al-Mallah, Yasir I. *Safahat Matwiyat Min Tarikh Al-Masrah Al-Filastini: Dirasah Adabiyah*. al-Khalil: Jam'iyat al-'Anqa' al-Thaqafiyah, 2002.

Martin, Gus, and Harvey W. Kushner. *The Sage Encyclopedia of Terrorism*. Thousand Oaks, CA: Sage, 2011.

Masrah Balalin, assorted accouterments: tickets, Balalin posters, manifesto *Masrah Baladna*, a poster advertising a Ramadan evening performance, Sundouq Al'ajab in Ramallah.

Mayer, Tamar, and Suleiman A. Mourad. *Jerusalem: Idea and Reality*. London: Routledge, 2008.

Mazen Kamal Ghattas. Acre: Mazen Ghattas' Family and Al-Laz Theatre, 2006.

McKim, Linda Jo H. *The Presbyterian Hymnal Companion*. Louisville, KY: Westminster/John Knox Press, 1993. (Arabic)

Nasr, Kameel B. *Arab and Israeli Terrorism: The Causes and Effects of Political Violence 1936-1993.* Jefferson, NC: McFarland, 1997.

Nasrallah, Elias. "Matia Nassar: A Story That Must Be Told." Accessed April 21, 2010. http://www.palpeople.org/atemplate.php?id=2631. (Arabic)

Nassar, Hala Khamis. "Challenging the Walls—How Ashtar Theatre Delves into the Brutalities and Inequities of Palestinian Life. Plus: Al-Kasaba Theatre Comes to D.C." *American Theatre* 25 no. 5 (2008): 36.

Nassar, Hala Khamis. "Palestinian Theatre." In *The Columbia Encyclopedia of Modern Drama.* Edited by Gabrielle H. Cody and Evert Sprinchorn. New York: Columbia University Press, 2007.

Nassar, Hala Khamis. "Palestinian Theatre: Between Origins and Visions." PhD dissertation, Free University of Berlin, 2001.

Nassar, Hala Khamis. "Stories from Under Occupation: Performing the Palestinian Experience." *Theatre Journal* 58, no. 1 (2006): 15-37.

Nazım Hikmet. *Beyond the Walls: Selected Poems.* Translated by Richard McKane, C. R. Christie, and Talat Sait Halman. London: Anvil Press Poetry, 2002.

Pappé, Ilan. *The Forgotten Palestinians: A History of the Palestinians in Israel.* New Haven, CT: Yale University Press, 2011.

Poggioli, Renato. *The Theory of the Avant-Garde.* Cambridge, MA: Belknap Press of Harvard University Press, 1968.

Postlewait, Thomas. *The Cambridge Introduction to Theatre Historiography.* Cambridge: Cambridge University Press, 2009.

Qumsiyeh, Mazin B. *Popular Resistance in Palestine: A History of Hope and Empowerment.* London: Pluto Press, 2011.

Reich, Bernard. *An Historical Encyclopedia of the Arab-Israeli Conflict.* Westport, CT: Greenwood Press, 1996.

Reich, Bernard. *Political Leaders of the Contemporary Middle East and North Africa : A Biographical Dictionary.* New York: Greenwood Press, 1990.

Roy, Sara. "The Gaza Strip: A Case of Economic De-Development." *Journal of Palestine Studies* 17, no. 1 (1987): 56-88.

Rubin, Don. *The World Encyclopedia of Contemporary Theatre.* London: Routledge, 1994.

Rugh, William A. *Arab Mass Media: Newspapers, Radio, and Television in Arab Politics.* Westport, CT: Praeger, 2004.

Said, Edward. "Permission to Narrate." *Journal of Palestine Studies* 13 no. 3 (1984): 27-48.

Samara, Adel. "The Theatre of the Occupied Territories and the Horizon of Transformation from a Theatre of Resistance to a National Theatre." The Proceedings of the First National Festival of Palestinian Literature. Da'irat Al-Kitab, 1981.

Samara, Adel. "The Experience of Local Theater." *Al-Bayader* (Jerusalem), no. 1 (1976).

Samid Al-Iqtisadi: Samed. Bayrut: Mu'assasat Samid, Jam'iyat Ma'amil Abna' Shuhada' Filastin, v. 10, no. 74 (Oct./Nov./Dec. 1988).

Samuel, Edwin. *A Lifetime in Jerusalem: The Memoirs of the Second Viscount Samuel*. London: Vallentine Mitchell, 1970.

Sayigh, Yazid. *Armed Struggle and the Search for State: The Palestinian National Movement, 1949-1993*. Oxford: Clarendon Press, 1997.

Shehadeh, Radi. *Sirat Hakawati Min Falastin*. Edited by Samer Al-Saber. Amman: Al-Ahliyah, 2016.

Shehadeh, Raja. *Samed: Journal of a West Bank Palestinian*. New York: Adama Books, 1984.

Shihadah, Radi. *Al-masrah Al-Filastini Fi Filastin 48: Bayna Sira' Al-Baqa' Wa-Infisam Al-Huwiyah*. Ram Allah: Wizarat al-Thaqafah al-Filastiniyah, 1998.

Shoughry, Nida. *"Israeli-Arab" Political Mobilization: Between Acquiescence, Participation, and Resistance*. New York: Palgrave Macmillan, 2012.

Shu'un Filastiniyah. Bayrut: Markaz al-Abhath fi Munazzamat al-Tahrir al-Filastiniyah, 1971.

Shinar, Dov. *Palestinian Voices: Communication and Nation Building in the West Bank*. Boulder, CO: Lynne Rienner, 1987.

Slyomovics, Susan. "'To Put One's Fingers in the Bleeding Wound': Palestinian Theatre Under Israeli Censorship." *TDR/The Drama Review* 35, no. 2 (1991): 18-38.

Snir, Reuven. "The Emergence of Palestinian Professional Theatre After 1967: Al-Balalin's Self-Referential Play *Al-'atma* (The Darkness)." *Theatre Survey* 46, no. 1 (2005).

Snir, Reuven. "The Palestinian Al-Hakawati Theater: A Brief History." *The Arab Studies Journal* 6/7, no. 2/1 (1998): 57-71.

Snir, Reuven. *Palestinian Theatre*. Wiesbaden: Reichert, 2005.

Snir, Reuven. "Palestinian Theatre: Historical Development and Contemporary Distinctive Identity." *Contemporary Theatre Review* 3, no. 2 (1995): 29-73.

Stanton, Andrea L. *This Is Jerusalem Calling: State Radio in Mandate Palestine*. Austin: University of Texas Press, 2014.

Al-Thaher, Mohammad. "A Chronicle of the History of the Palestinian Theatre Troupe." Unpublished author statement. Received on 27 January 2011.

Al-Thaher, Mohammad. *Masrahiyatan: Al-Lu'ba/Al-Mawlid*. Jerusalem: Dar Al-Katib, 1980.

Theater Committee. *The Association for Work and Development for the Arts, Theatre Committee*. Unpublished booklet. 1979.

Urian, Dan. *Palestinians and Israelis in the Theatre*. Basel, Switzerland: Harwood Academic, 1995.

Varghese, Gabriel. *Palestinian Theatre in the West Bank: Our Human Faces*. London: Palgrave Macmillan, 2020.

Zuhur, Sherifa. *Colors of Enchantment: Theater, Dance, Music, and the Visual Arts of the Middle East*. Cairo: American University in Cairo Press, 2001.

Interviews and Personal Communications

Abboushey, Sameh. Personal interviews, 11 January 2011 and 24 August 2023.
Abu Esheh, Hussam. Personal interviews, 20 November 2011 and 18 September 2023.
Abu Saloum, Ahmad. Personal interviews, 13 January 2011 and 7 December 2010.
Ashrawi, Emile. Personal interviews, 11 January 2011, 17 August 2023, and 28 October 2023.
Al-Basha, Kamel. Personal interview, 18 September 2010.
Clergy and Laity Concerned (CALC). Unpublished letter in support of Sanabel's 1988 US tour, 18 July 1988.
Ibrahim, George. Personal interviews, 23 October 2010, 18 November 2010, 8 January 2011, 18 January 2011, 23 October 2023, and 27 October 2023.
Jbail, Ibrahim. Personal interview, 24 January 2011.
Khalil, Amer. Personal interviews, 29 October 2011, 3 September 2012, 2 February 2016, 17 August 2017, 14 August 2018, 11 September 2023, and 4 October 2023.
Kidan, Milad. Personal interview, 16 August 2017.
Al-Kurd, Mustapha. Personal interview, 24 January 2011, 26 January 2011, and 18 August 2017.
Al-Labadi, Mohammad. Personal interview, 17 August 2023.
Lubeck, Jackie. Personal interviews, 10 September 2012 and 8 October 2012; Skype 30 July 2012 and 15 August 2017.
Lubeck, Jackie. Email to author, 31 July 2012.
Al-Mani, Majid. Personal interview, 13 October 2010.
Mikhail, Nadia. Personal interview, 24 August 2023.
Mitwalli, Imad. Personal interviews, 12 January 2011 and 16 August 2017.
Muallem, Edward. Personal interviews, 26 October 2010 and 11 August 2017.
Natour, Salman. Personal interview, 4 October 2010.
Al-Qassem, Samih. Personal interview, 13 December 2010.
Samara, Imad. Personal interviews, 13 November 2010 and 16 August 2017.
Shehadeh, Radi. Personal interviews, 12 December 2010 and 12 August 2017.
Sheikh Qassem, Ramsey. Personal interviews, 23 November 2010 and 15 August 2017.
Sundoka, Rajai. Personal interview, 13 November 2011.
Tarabsheh, Adnan. Personal interviews, 11 December 2010 and 13 August 2017.
Al-Tartir, Adel. Email to author, 22 June 2012.
Al-Tartir, Adel. Personal interviews, 24 October 2010 and 26 December 2010.
Al-Thaher, Mohammad. Personal interview, 26 January 2011.

Scripts and Performance Videos

Balalin Theatre Troupe. *Nashrat Ahwal Al-Jaw* (*Weather Forecast*). Unpublished script, 1973. Supplied by Adel Al-Tartir.
El-Hakawati. *Ali the Galilean*. Unpublished video recording, 1985. Supplied by Edward Muallem.

El-Hakawati. *B'ism Al-Ab, w Al-Um, w Al-Ibn*. Unpublished script, 1977. Supplied by Edward Muallem.

El-Hakawati. *Jericho Year Zero*. Unpublished script, 1990. Supplied by Jackie Lubeck.

El-Hakawati. *In Search of Omar Al-Khayyam*. Unpublished script, 1990. Supplied by Jackie Lubeck.

El-Hakawati. *Jalilee Ya Ali*. Unpublished script, 1983. Supplied by Edward Muallem.

El-Hakawati. *Mahjoub Mahjoub*. Unpublished script, 1980. Supplied by Edward Muallem.

El-Hakawati. *Qissat Al-Ayn w Al-Sin*. Unpublished script, 1986. Supplied by Edward Muallem.

El-Hakawati. *Qissat Kufur Shamma*. Unpublished script, 1987. Supplied by Jackie Lubeck.

Ibrahim, George. *Adventure in Jerusalem*. Unpublished script, 1973. Supplied by George Ibrahim.

Ibrahim, George. *The City of Dreams*. Unpublished script, 1975. Supplied by George Ibrahim.

Ibrahim, George. *The Happy Shoemaker*. Unpublished script, 1977. Supplied by George Ibrahim.

Al-Kasaba. *Men Without Shadows*. Unpublished video recording, 1988. Supplied by George Ibrahim.

Sanabel Theatre. *Natrin Faraj*. Unpublished video recording, 1988. Supplied by Hussam Abu Esheh.

Sami and Susu. Unpublished video recording, 1970-1977. Supplied by George Ibrahim.

Al-Thaher, Mohammad. *The Priest and the Beautiful*. Unpublished script. Supplied by Mohammad Al-Thaher.

Al-Thaher, Mohammad. *When Necessary*. Unpublished script. Supplied by Mohammad Al-Thaher.

Al-Thaher, Mohammad. *Who's Barren?* Unpublished script. Supplied by Mohammad Al-Thaher.

Periodicals
Al-'alam
Al-Anba' (accessed in El-Hakawati Press Archive)
Al-Awdah
Al-Bayader
Al-Bayader Al-Siyasi
Al-Fajr Al-Adabi
Al-Fajr Daily
Al-Fajr Weekly
Filastin Al-Thawra

The Guardian
Al-Hadaf
Al-Hourriya
Al-Itihad
Jewish Chronicle
Jerusalem Post
Jerusalem Post Magazine
Al-Katib
La Gauche Arabe/Al-Yassar Al-Arabi
London Financial Times
Los Angeles Times
Al-Masrah, issues 1–4
Al-Nahar
New York Times
New York Magazine
New Yorker
Philadelphia Inquirer
Le Provençal
Al-Quds
Al-Raya (accessed in El-Hakawati Press Archive)
Al-Sabah (accessed in El-Hakawati Press Archive)
Seattle Times
Al-Sha'b
Al-Sharara (accessed in El-Hakawati Press Archive)
Al-Sharq Al-Awsat
State Hornet
Tariq Al-Sharara (accessed in El-Hakawati Press Archive)
This Week in Palestine
Washington Report on Middle Eastern Affairs
Al-Watan Al-Arabi

Web Sources
Btselem, www.btselem.org
Inspirational Films, www.inspirationalfilms.com
Jadaliyya, www.jadaliyya.com
Jerusalem Quarterly, www.jerusalemquarterly.org
al-Muqtafi Project, Birzeit University Institute of Law. http://muqtafi.birzeit.edu/
New York Live Arts, www.newyorklivearts.org
Pal People, www.palpeople.org (accessed 15 June 2010; this website no longer exists)
Palestinian Human Rights Monitoring Group (PHRMG), www.phrmg.org (accessed 25 May 2012; this website no longer exists)

INDEX

Abboud, Christina, 53
Abboushey, Sameh, 6, 60, 62, 63, 67-69, 71, 80
Abdallah, Ghassan, 160, 164, 165, 218, 243
Abdelnour, Yousef, 38
Abdel Salam, Walid, 110
Abd Rabbo, Yehya, 99, 236
Abedo, Abdel-Hamid, 238
Abna' Al-Balad (People of the Homeland) movement, 2, 117
'Aboud, Palestine, 101
Abrahamic College of Jerusalem, 164
Abu Afifeh, Talal, 147
Abu Ali/Daoud Hasaneine, 27, 142
Abu Esheh, Hussam, 217, 257; arrest of, 130; career of, 244; on *Man Is a Cause*, 127, 128; Palestinian Theatre and, 125, 131; with Sanabel, 6, 213, 216; in *Sayyidi Al-General*, 195; talents of, 196, 237-238; works on *Man Is a Cause*, 193; works with Ahmad Abu Saloum, 111, 258; works with George Ibrahim, 57
Abu Fareed, 45, 46
Abu Rahmeh, Tawfiq, 34
Abu Sabbah, Firas, 55
Abu Salem, Francine, 176

Abu Salem, François, 7f
Abu Shanab, Hani, 65
Abu Srour, Abdelfattah, 258
Abu Wardeh, Youssef, 10, 210
Acre, 159, 165, 192, 225, 286n31, 286n32; Auditorium Theatre, 224; Fringe Festival, 223; Theater of the Other, 246
Adventure in Jerusalem, 53
Africa, 40, 121, 132, 195, 222; South Africa, 212, 213; Tunisia, 26, 32, 169, 170, 178, 188, 205, 212, 226, 230
Ahl Al-Kahf (The People of the Cave), 24
Ahly Club, 159
Aida Refugee Camp, 15, 258
Akka, 129, 192
Aladdin, 56, 237
Al-Amal Al-Sha'bi (People's Hope) Ensemble, 130, 251, 266n9, 277-278n44
Al-Amal Troupe for Art and Theater, 202
Al-Am'ari Refugee Camp, 28, 86
Al-Aqsa Intifada. *See* Intifada, second (2000-2005)
Al-Aqsa mosque, 26

INDEX

Al-As'ad, As'ad, 34
Al-Ashekien (musical troupe), 220
Al-'atma (The Darkness), 67–74, 101, 273n42; curtain call, 67f; influence of, 83; legendary stature of, 259; plot, 79, 80; staging of, 78, 146
Al-Bahri, Jamil, 38
Al-Bakri, Fawzi, 65, 66, 93
Al-Bakri, Mohammad, 10, 136
Al-Bara'em (rock band), 61
Al-Barghouthi, Bashir, 50
Al-Barghouthi, Hussein, 34, 246
Al-Barghouthi, Mohammad Anis, 106
Al-Batrawi, Mohammad (Abu Khaled), 28–31, 33, 34, 35, 50, 65, 148, 187
Al-Bayadir (newspaper), 28, 34, 134
Al-Beit Al-Sakheb (The Turbulent House), 23, 51
Al-Bireh, Palestine, 19, 74, 86, 90, 166, 172, 254, 274n10
Al-Dabbagh, Ismail, 241–242, 244
Al-Dajani, Hatem, 122, 123
Al-Darse Al-Awwal (The First Lesson), 43, 44
Al-Dawaymeh, Palestine, 28
Al-Fahoom, Walid, 104
Al-Fajr Al-Adabi (newspaper), 151, 164, 182, 183, 243; Carl Vitale, 219; Ibrahim Jbail, 28; on *Jesus* film, 174, 179; Mattia Nassar, 34; publishes play reviews, 160; Said Al-Ghazali, 207; on speech *The Story of the Eye and the Tooth*, 185
Al-Fajr (magazine), 158
Al-Farafir ensemble, 179
Alf Leyleh w Leyleh. See *One Thousand and One Nights of the Stone Thrower (Alf Leyleh w Leyleh)*
Al-Frères School (Collège des Frères), 116
Al-Funoun El-Sha'biyyeh, 200
Al-Ghadeer (newspaper), 83
Al-Hadaf (newspaper), 59, 150

Al-Hakawati Theatre. *See* An-Nuzha-Hakawati Theatre
Al-Hakim, Tawfiq, 24, 52, 100
Al-Hambra Cinema, 127, 128, 172
Al-Haq 'al-Haq (Blame the Truth), 90
Al-Harah Al-Mukhtarah (The Chosen Neighborhood), 200, 202
Al-Haraka Al-Masrahiya (The Theatrical Movement), 1, 256, 257
Al-Hara Theatre, 10, 15
Al-Hashra, 13
Al-Hijjawi, Ali, 65, 110
Al-Husseini, Faisal, 207, 208, 230, 236, 243, 244
Al-Husseini, Haidar, 39
Al-'ibra (The Moral), 94
Ali El-Abbasi, Ahmad, 25, 26
Al-Intithar (Waiting), 98
Ali the Galilean (Jalilee Ya Ali), 156, 161–163, 165, 166, 168, 171, 183, 184; performance photo, 162f
Al-Itihad (newspaper), 21, 28, 29, 34, 48, 147, 148, 223, 225
Alive from Palestine, 255
Al-Jalazone Refugee Camp, 90
Al-Jamil, Anton, 39
Al-Jara'i, Radi, 244
Al-Jawal (Itinerant) Company, 202, 242, 244
Al-Jawzi family, 17, 38
Al-Jawzi, Nasri, 38
Al-Joulani, Nabil, 188
Al-Kasaba (The Marketplace) Theatre, 5, 9, 15, 22, 57, 234, 242; in the Intifada, 233, 235, 237, 238; *Layla Al-Hamrah*, 287–288n5; *Men Without Shadows*, 218f; opening of, 235f; *Romeo and Juliet*, 247f. See also El-Warsheh El-Fanniyeh (The Theater Arts Group)
Al-Kashkul (The Notebook) Ensemble, 98, 251, 266n9

Al-Katib (magazine), 34, 193
Al-Khatib, Nidal, 241–242
Al-Khayyam, Omar, 240. *See also In Search of Omar Al-Khayyam*
Al-Khil, Bshara, 238
Al-Kinz (The Treasure), 75
Al-Kurd, Mustapha, 6, 74, 101, 110, 257, 274n28; arrest/exile, 103, 104, 113, 115, 271n51; biography, 26–28; collaborates on Ramadan Nights, 196; composes for *Antara in the Courtyard*, 212; composes for *Free Wrestling*, 94; composes for *The City of Dreams*, 53; composes for *The Happy Shoemaker*, 55; composes for *The Story of the Walnut Tree and Lame Yunus*, 72; death, 259; performs "Bring on the Rail," 80; provides concert for El-Hakawati Theatre opening, 180; provides concerts for Festival of Covenant and Continuation, 244; provides musical ensemble for *The Chosen Neighborhood*, 202; provides musical lessons for El-Hakawati Theatre, 200; release, 275n33; returns from exile, 181, 275n34
Al-Labadi, Mohammed, 220
Al-Latrun, 22
Allenby Bridge, 24, 28
Al-Luʻba (The Toy), 131, 137
Al-Lyd, 152
Al-Mani, Majed, 110
Al-Masrah (The Theatre; magazine), 99–100
Al-Masri, Thafer, 177
Al-Mawlid (The Birth), 131, 137
Almeida Theater, 191
Al-Mghar, Palestine, 6, 100, 251
Almoravids, 2
Al-Muqataʼa, 28, 106
Al-Murabitoun, 2
Al-Musrara, Jerusalem, 45, 201, 213

Al-Mutran School (St. George's School), 40, 41, 61, 116, 138, 277–278n44
Al-Nabʻ Al-ʻali (The High Spring), 106
Al-Nuzha Cinema, 19, 128, 172, 174, 175, 177, 233
Al-Omariyyeh School. *See* El-Omariyyeh School
Al-Omariyyeh Theatre. *See* El-Omariyyeh Theatre
Al-Qaid, Yussef, 198
Al-Qaq, Anis, 207, 209
Al-Qassem, Samih, 31, 148, 220, 235, 236, 239; friendship with George Ibrahim, 50; Mohammad Al-Batrawi collects works of, 30; on Palestinian theater, 59–60; performs at El-Hakawati's opening, 180, 182; *Qaraqash*, 60, 62
Al-Qattan Foundation, 254
Al-Quds Cinema, 172, 204
Al-Quds (newspaper), 53, 65
Al-Rahala Theatre (The Travellers), 200, 206
Al-Rahhala, 242, 251
Al-Rajabi, Abdel-Aziz, 134, 135
Al-Ramleh, Palestine, 22, 239
Al-Raqqasseen (The Dancers), 92
Al-Rijal Lahom Ruʼus (Men Have Heads), 200
Al-Roʻat (TV station), 217
Al-Rowah, 242, 244, 251
Al-Rowwad Theater, 10, 15, 258
Al-Sabah (newspaper), 170
Al-Saber, Fathi, 43, 269n11
Al-Sadat, Anwar, 144, 147, 149
Al-Saʻdiyeh, 213
Al-Salaymeh, Saqer, 200, 242
Al-Salt, Jordan, 22
Al-Samaka Al-Thahabiya (The Golden Fish), 237
Al-Sayeh, Jameel, 238
Al-Seera Theater, 6, 251

Al-Shawk (The Spikes) Theatre, 57
Al-Tali'a (newspaper), 122, 129
Al-Tamri, Rehab, 44
Al-Tartir, Adel, 6, 110, 112, 257, 273n33, 273n42; in *Al-'atma*, 79; on Balalin, 74; founds Palestinian Theatre League, 134-135; Israeli military questions, 76; joins Theatre Family, 65; presents *Taghribat Sa'id Ben Fadel Allah*, 106; in Sundouq Al-'ajab, 101, 107, 112, 251, 258
Al-Tawil, Ibrahim, 90
Al-Thaher, Mohammad, 6, 94, 113, 206; disagrees with Theatre Committee, 134; on journalism, 92; in Palestinian Theatre Ensemble, 91; playwright for Palestinian theater, 110; publishes *Al-Mawlid* and *Al-Lu'ba*, 131; on schools hosting theater events, 130; on theatrical movement, 137, 138, 170; unpublished plays, 13; writes *La'nat 'atrees*, 197; writes *Who's Infertile?* and *The Scream*, 198
Al-Turshan (The Deaf Ones), 86, 88
Al-Yassar Al-Arabi (The Arab Left; newspaper), 150
Al-Yazijee, Khalil, 39
Al-Zubaidi, Jaber, 104
America. *See* United States (US)
American Colony, 128, 172, 234
Americans, 62, 121, 144, 179, 209; Arab-Americans, 216; Herbert Kenneth Carmichael, 40, 57, 60; Jackie Lubeck, 113, 146; Mrs. Samuels, 39
Amman Accords, 205
Amman, Jordan, 17, 18, 20, 28, 44, 45, 86, 173; George Ibrahim's life in, 22-25
Anani, Nabil, 44, 166
Anis, Mohammad, 3, 100, 101, 105, 106, 134

An-Nuzha-Hakawati Theatre, 5, 43, 187, 202f, 240; Ali Freitekh is proprietor of, 233; *Al-Mahrajan* (The Festival), 194; Anis Al-Qaq leads, 207; auditorium, 184f; becomes center for public assembly, 204; becomes hub for Jerusalem's theatrical community, 232; becomes Jerusalemite landmark, 193; becomes site for open political discussions, 243; board of directors of, 231; building before El-Hakawati, 172f; building of, 3, 176f, 203, 206, 230; celebratory parade for, 201; classified as third-class, 19; El-Hakawati and theater movement battle over, 13; El-Hakawati Theatre Ensemble renovates, 131, 175; establishment of, 181; *The Fire Raisers* and *Caligula* at, 199; lobby, 180f; Mustapha Al-Kurd's concert at, 104; new management of, 242; opening of, 179, 198, 275n7; productions presented at, 210, 211; as public institution, 239; renamed Theatre for Palestinian Culture and Arts, 241; surveillance of plays at, 183; symbolizes Palestinian theater golden age, 203; workshops held at, 200
Ansar, 241-242
Antara, 211
Antara in the Courtyard, 211-212
anti-colonialism, 15, 124, 153, 220
anti-Israeli sentiment, 153, 154, 216, 223
anti-Palestinian sentiment, 45, 124, 137, 157, 252
anti-Semitism, 155, 216
Aoun, Iman, 43, 55, 189, 210, 224, 257, 258; Ashtar Theatre, 251
Aqel, Abdel-Latif, 34, 244
Arab governments, 18, 42
Arabian Gulf, 18, 222

Arabian Nights, 57, 156
Arabic language, 20, 181-182, 217, 224, 238, 241; American speakers of, 216; *Beyond the Horizon*, 39; under censorship, 172; Christian cultural performances in, 41, 42, 43; classical, 219; communist writings in, 29; cultural event, 51; François Abu Salem's fluency in, 25; Hebrew University cultural event, 113; Israeli authorities prevent plays in, 138; *Khawaziq*, 105; Loránd Gáspár's poetry published in, 26; *Mahjoub Mahjoub*, 151; *The Merchant of Venice* and *Othello*, 23; Mohammad Al-Batrawi's collection of books in, 30; *Nashrat Ahwal Al-Jaw*, 73; newspapers, 21, 148, 155, 207, 223; performance for Hebrew-speaking audience, 166-168; preservation, 50; radio, 45, 46; *Returning to Haifa*, 126; reviews, 195; *Romeo and Juliet*, 246; "The Story of the Walnut Tree and Lame Yunus," 62; television, 47-49, 51; Theater of the Other, 223; translation of *The Exception and the Rule*, 100; *Une Tranche de Vie*, 61. *See also* Palestinian dialect
Arab-Israeli conflict, 11, 95, 187, 188, 205, 227, 228
Arab League, 145, 194, 205
Arab nationalism, 194
Arab National Movement, 22
Arab Palestinian Diaspora. *See* diaspora
Arab reactionism, 105
armed struggle, 2, 21, 44, 70, 94; *Alf Leyleh w Leyleh*, 160; François Abu Salem on, 59, 151; Ghassan Kanafani embraces, 150, 268n20, 279n15; *Hareeq Al-Jaheem*, 93; *Man Is a Cause*, 128; PFLP in, 31, 125

Asfour, Georgina, 233, 237, 238, 258
Asfour, Lily, 142
Ashrawi, Emile, 6, 33, 61, 70, 79, 110, 200, 257, 258
Ashrawi, Hanan, 4, 6, 20, 243, 268n37
Ashrawi, Ibrahim, 61, 63, 267n24
Ashtar Theater, 5, 10, 12, 15, 251, 252, 254, 255, 257, 258
Assanabil Ensemble, 215. *See also* Sanabel People's Theatre
Association for Work and Development for the Arts, 4, 98, 101, 107, 112, 134. *See also* Theatre Committee
Association of Palestinian Theatre, 17
At the Cross, 8, 24, 40-44, 52, 57; ensemble photo, 42f
Australia, 46, 47
avant-garde (movement), 60, 68, 73, 92, 158, 200, 273n43
Avigal, Shosh, 167
Awad, Barakeh, 178
Awad, Fouad, 10, 100, 211, 237, 245, 246, 248, 249, 250
Awad, Mahmoud, 56, 57
Awwal Manshur (First Leaflet), 113
Ayyoub, Jackie, 51, 52, 53, 55, 136
Azzam, Fateh, 200, 209, 212, 241

Bader, Issam, 44
Balalin, 7f, 75f; Festival Committee, 74; nationalism, 81
Baniel, Eran, 245-246, 248, 249
Bantustans, 255
Bar-Lev, David, 223
Bates, Dennis, 216
Bedouins, 44, 179
Beirut, Lebanon, 17, 150
Beit Anan Troupe, 200
Beit Jala, Palestine, 10, 15, 92, 251, 253
Beit Sahour, Palestine, 71, 92, 194
Belgium, 152
Ben Gurion Airport, 181, 214

Ben-Gurion, David, 18
Bethlehem, 172; Adnan Zubaidi, 212; Aida Refugee Camp, 15, 258; *Al-Mahrajan*, 194; Al-Ro'at (TV station), 217; Al-Rowwad, 10; Balalin, 71, 74, 75; boarding schools, 24; François Abu Salem's life in, 25; ghettoization of, 253; Inad Theater, 251; Laws of the Municipality of, 19; Palestinian Theatre Ensemble, 91; refugee camps, 165; residents of, 175; Sundouq Al-'ajab, 108, 112; theaters, 174; Theatre Family's evening of poetry, 67
Bible, 41, 43, 131, 184
Bila Lin (Without Leniency) ensemble, 5, 94, 96, 98, 101, 108, 112, 114, 256
Birds, The, 211
Birzeit, 3, 4, 5, 71; Birzeit Solidarity Committee, 155; Birzeit University, 63, 123; Palestine Museum, 266n10; Sanabel Singing Troupe, 200
B'ism Al-Ab w al-Um w Al-Ibn (In the Name of the Father, the Mother, and the Son), 112, 122, 141, 162-164; aesthetics vs. content, 191; George Ibrahim produces, 108-109, 116-118; in Hebrew, 120, 121; internationalizes theatrical activity, 137, 138; Nancy Festival declines, 157; Palestinian identity of ensemble, 124; performance in Galilee, 116, 123; performance in Jerusalem, 120f
Black September, 8, 32, 59, 60, 62, 86, 150, 153, 188
Blind and the Deaf, The, 107, 201, 206
Blithe Spirit, 39
Blumenfeld, Laura, 248
Boal, August, 255
Boulata, Kamal, 179

boycott, divestment, and sanctions (BDS) movement, 168
boycotts, 31, 50, 56, 137, 141, 168, 217, 239, 280n38
Brecht, Bertolt, 60, 78, 94, 100, 115, 158, 210, 258
Brentford & Chiswick Times (newspaper), 154
"Bring on the Rail" (song), 80
Britain. *See* United Kingdom
British Council, 254

Cairo, Egypt, 43
California State University in Sacramento, 215-216
Caligula, 199, 236
Camus, Albert, 52, 199, 236
Carmichael, Herbert Kenneth, 40-43, 57, 60, 61
Carmichael, Sue, 40, 41
Carne, Rosalind, 152, 153
Center of Middle East and African Studies, 100
Chaillet, Ned, 152, 154
Chekhov, Anton, 100, 210
children's theater, 6, 52, 53, 91, 111, 112, 199; innovations in, 237, 238; workshops, 200. *See also* puppet theater
China, 172
Chosen Neighborhood, The, 200, 202
Christians/Christianity, 39-43, 238-239, 267n10; *Al-Mawlid*, 133; Crusades, 240, 241; *The Darkness*, 78; *Eyes Upon the Cross*, 60; under Jerusalem Law, 145; Jesus, 41, 133, 215, 217; *Jesus* film, 174-175, 179; Lutheran Church, 23, 24, 61; *Natrin Faraj*, 213-217; in Ramallah, 9; *Sami and Susu*, 48; schools, 138; United Presbyterian Church U.S.A., 40
Christmas, 233, 238
Citizens Rights Movement, 223

City of Dreams, 53
Clergy and Laity Concerned (CALC), 215
Clowns, 179
Collins, William B., 228, 229
Comis, Jean-Pierre, 157
Commission on Ecumenical Mission and Relation, 40
Committee for the Arts, 203
Communist Party, 18, 20, 21, 30, 83, 117, 236; in Haifa, 50; of Israel, 148; Israeli, 239; leaders, 270n35; Palestine, 125
communists, 29, 80, 140, 259; Bashir Al-Barghouthi, 50; Communist Youth Union, 243; Daoud Hasaneine, 26, 27; Daoud Khouri, 34; Elias Nasrallah, 34; Emile Habibi, 28, 34; Emile Touma, 34; Ilias Nasrallah, 72; Mahmoud Shqair, 35, 111; Mohammad Al-Batrawi, 50, 187; newspapers, 129; Palestinian Theatre Ensemble, 125; Tawfiq Abu Rahmeh, 34; Tawfiq Zayyad, 34; underground, 33
Corneille, Pierre, 39
Corpse on the Pavement, 196
Coward, Noel, 39
Crosses of Silence, 198
Crusades, 240, 241
cultural resistance, 30, 31, 32, 33, 34, 148, 268n29; to Israeli hegemony, 93, 182; narratives of, 59, 72

Dababis (The Pins) ensemble, 13, 92, 98, 141; arrest of, 103, 259; Balalin and, 85, 89; exemplifies military against Palestinian theater, 104–106; formation of, 4; Ibrahim Jbail, 100, 274n7; leftism, 88; revives Theatre Committee, 134; as theater of resistance, 86–87; in theatrical movement, 256

dabkah (dance), 61, 72, 87, 98, 166, 179, 201
Daher, Wassif, 39, 40, 41, 42, 43
Da'irat Al-Khawf Al-Dababiyya (The Foggy Fear Circle), 87, 88
Damascus Gate, Jerusalem, 131, 201, 202, 213
Damascus, Syria, 17, 220
Damia Bridge, 45
Damouni, Sobhi, 38
Dance Theater Workshop (DTW), 228, 229
Dandis, Abed, 130
Dandis, Wassif, 179, 257, 275n6
Darini, Labiba, 47
Darkness, The (Al-'atma). See *Al-'atma (The Darkness)*
Darwish, Mahmoud, 30, 31, 148, 220
Dawood, Rustom, 161
Daw, Salim, 10
Democratic Front for the Liberation of Palestine (DFLP), 33, 83, 189, 204, 205, 220
Denham, Reginald, 39
Denmark, 157, 158
Development of the Arab Village in Israel in Ten Years, 18
diaspora, 17, 21, 33, 37, 214, 217; African, 222
Dickens, Charles, 24
Dictator, The, 195, 200
Dogs and Numbers, 196
Doueiri, Ziad, 245
Druze, 48

East Cooperative Press, 99
Easter, 41, 60
East Jerusalem, 5, 9, 10, 18, 44, 52, 57, 114; administrative control, 84; *Al-Fajr* (newspaper), 34; Al-Issawiyyeh village, 90; American Colony, 234; detached from West Bank, 253; El-Omariyyeh School,

East Jerusalem (*cont.*)
56, 69, 92; as emerging cultural center, 172; Israel's control over, 137, 145; Jordanian Education Law of 1955, 19; occupation of, 15, 128, 146, 213; old cinema houses, 68; as Palestinian capital, 232, 249; Ramallah area, 65, 123; replaced with *Israel*, 124; residents of, 144; schools, 53; Sheikh Jarrah neighborhood, 64, 175; society, 50; theater artists, 251; theater ensembles, 223; theater producers, 138; theaters, 197; theatrical movement in, 3, 4; US consulate, 215; YMCA, 92

Egypt/Egyptians, 17, 18, 22, 212; Abdel Ghaffar, 246; air force, 195; Al-Sheikh Imam, 13, 24; Cairo, 43; comedy, 163; film acting style, 159; films, 46, 172; Kamel El-Shinnawi, 45; Mohammed Tawfiq, 100; music, 27; obstructive politics, 165; Palestinians under rule of, 33, 39; plays, 43; poetry, 31; president, 144; Tawfiq Al-Hakim, 52, 100; Yussef Al-Qaid, 198

Egyptian Movement for Change/Kefaya (Enough), 2, 117

Eid, 239

Eid, Jamil, 113

El-Basha, Kamel, 55, 57, 220, 221, 233, 242, 244, 245, 257, 258

Electric Company, 214, 248

El Festival de Sitges, 191

El-Hakawati theater, 176f, 180f

Eliwat, Ibrahim Othman, 195

El-Janazir, Abu, 102, 206, 255

El-Masou, Khaled, 233, 248, 251, 258

El-Nashashibi, Amal, 177

El-Omariyyeh School, 53, 56, 69, 111; *Al-ʿatma*, 69, 74; *Al-Raqqasseen*, 92; *B'ism Al-Ab w al-Um w Al-Ibn*, 122; ceases renting to theatrical productions, 233; in El-Hakawati's touring circuit, 138, 198; *The Happy Shoemaker*, 54; Jerusalem theater festival, 98; *Lamma Injanina*, 103; *Layla Al-Hamrah*'s puppet version, 287-288n5; Mustapha Al-Kurd attends, 26; *A Slice of Life*, 65

El-Omariyyeh Theatre, 103, 287n5

El-Rayyes, Najib, 220

El-Sabbagh, Yousef, 179

El-Sharafeh, 89

El-Shinnawi, Kamel, 45

El-Tartir, Adel. *See* Al-Tartir, Adel

El-Warsheh El-Fanniyeh (The Theater Arts Group), 6, 57, 198-199, 206, 218, 221. *See also* Al-Kasaba (The Marketplace) Theatre

England. *See* United Kingdom

English language, 182, 216, 224, 238; *Al-ʿatma*, 147; audiences, 217; censorship of *Mahjoub Mahjoub*, 149; Christian plays in, 41, 42; El-Hakawati performs in, 223; Gáspár family, 25; George Ibrahim, 23, 24; Jackie Lubeck, 117, 146; of Palestinian actors, 228; Palestinian press in, 207; Palestinian theater scripts, 14; plays, 39, 40; *Story of Kufur Shamma* in, 227; translations to/from, 269-270n22

ethnography, 6, 11-14, 211

Europe, 14, 116, 132, 133, 135, 142, 249; audiences, 165, 192; Austria, 116, 191; avant-garde, 73; classic works, 6, 13, 137, 219; consulate, 57, 252; Copenhagen, Denmark, 158; countries of, 152; El-Hakawati Theatre tour in, 136, 155, 157, 170, 223, 229, 259; European Commission, 252; European Union, 252; festivals, 178; Germany, 104, 124, 180, 218, 219, 244, 246, 254; Italy,

124, 223; languages, 168; music, 25; Netherlands, 124, 153, 191; playwrights, 39; press, 13, 154, 159; Quatour group, 200; Spain, 191; Sweden, 252; Switzerland, 124, 150, 177; theater, 60; theatrical design, 248; United Kingdom, 23, 28, 32, 38, 45, 119, 153, 254. *See also* France/French
Even, Anat, 250
Exception and the Rule, The, 94, 100, 210, 245, 258
Executor and the Condemned, 52
expulsion, 15, 17, 26, 27, 28, 37, 90, 127, 153; of Jordanian governmental institutions, 59; of PLO, 8, 32, 169
Eyes Upon the Cross, 60

factionalism, 211; political, 83, 114, 125, 140, 188, 189, 205; within theater movement, 8, 60, 81, 210; West Bank's, 63
Farag, Alfred, 52
Farah, Najwa Qawar, 71
Farah, Yousef, 38, 52
Farraj, Hamdi, 130, 217, 243
Fasheh, Mounir, 63
Fateh (political party), 1, 31, 83, 140, 185, 189, 205, 220
fedayeen (movement), 33, 188
Festival of Covenant and Continuation, 244
Financial Times (newspaper), 152
Fire Raisers, 199, 199f, 206, 236
Firqat Al-Funoun Al-Masrahiyah (the Theatrical Artistic Group [TAG]), 5, 51, 52, 53, 57
Firqat Al-Funun Al-Sha'biya (Ensemble Folk Arts), 196
Firqat Dababis Lil-Funoun Al-Masrahiya (The Pins Troupe for Theatrical Arts). *See* Dababis (The Pins) ensemble

Firqat Zahrat Al-Mada'in, 200
First Jerusalem Festival, 242
Flayfel, Mohammed, 220
Fo, Dario, 210
Folklore Month, 74
Ford Foundation, 177, 208, 252
France/French, 26, 109, 116, 124, 152, 168, 245; colonial, 220; consulate, 81; El-Hakawati tours in, 170; François Abu Salem, 117; French-German Cultural Center, 254; French Resistance, 218, 219; Istres, 157, 181; Jérôme Savary, 156; Lille Festival, 246; media, 124; Montpellier, 155, 157, 281n42; Nancy Theatre Festival, 108, 109, 116, 124, 157; Paris, 26, 83, 191, 240; passports, 142; post-national viewpoint, 190; protests, 26, 64; Strasbourg, 26, 61, 114; television, 164
François Abu Salem Archive, 25
Frêche, Georges, 157, 281n42
Freedom Theatre, 10, 15, 275n31
Freij, Elias, 175
Freitekh, Ali, 172, 173, 233, 234
French-German Cultural Center, 254
French language, 25, 223
Friends Girls School, 179
Frisch, Max, 52, 199, 206, 237
Fugard, Athol, 212, 259

Galilee, 50, 129, 148, 239; *B'ism Al-Ab, w Al-Um, w Al-Ibn*, 116, 123; Edward Muallem and Adnan Tarabsheh, 113–115; El-Hakawati in, 6, 141, 152, 198; famous directors from, 10; foundation for theater in, 38; *Free Wrestling*, 95, 96; Green Line, 30; *Mahjoub Mahjoub*, 147; Palestinian poets and writers, 21; Radi Shehadeh, 209, 258; Sundouq Al-'ajab tours, 104. *See also Ali the Galilean* (Jalilee Ya Ali)

Galvin, Marjorie Noel, 46
Game of Love and Chance, 51
Garbageman, The, 242, 244
Gáspár, Francine, 25, 179, 245, 257
Gáspár, François (Abu Salem), 61, 114, 149, 150
Gáspár, Loránd, 25, 26
Gaza, 5, 17, 19, 48, 126, 251, 258; Al-Amal Troupe, 202; censorship/governance, 39; municipal elections, 94; occupation of, 32; Palestinian dignitaries, 177; Palestinians in, 29, 30; permanent Palestinian state in, 230; protests, 279n11; puppet shows, 237; schools, 18, 198; Theatre Day Productions, 10; workers, 211
General Union for Expressive Arts, 200
genre: absurdism, 206; comedic realism, 92; comedy, 43, 127, 163, 189, 196; magic realism, 206; melodrama, 163, 241; satirical comedy, 23; satirical orientalist fantasy, 158; situation comedy, 214; tragicomedy, 158. *See also* satire
Germany, 104, 124, 180, 218, 219, 244, 254; Land Nordrhein-Westphalia Festival, 246; West, 152
Ghattas, Mazin, 10, 218, 219
Ghazaleh, Raeda, 251
Ghosheh, Jamal, 209
Global South, 7, 195
Goethe Institute, 252, 254
Golan Heights, Syria, 30
Goldstein massacre, 246
Green Line, 18, 29, 30, 121, 140, 182, 239
Grossman, Edward, 159, 165
Grotowski, Jerzy, 115
Guardian, The (newspaper), 154
Gulf States, 18, 222

Haaretz (newspaper), 167
Habash, George Ibrahim, 23, 41, 46, 86, 150
Habibi, Emile, 29, 30, 31, 50, 148, 236, 239; as communist, 28, 34; in Knesset, 279n7
Haddad, 'Abir Z., 24, 46
Haifa, 48, 166; *Al-Itihad* (newspaper), 34; *B'ism Al-Ab, w Al-Um, w Al-Ibn*, 109; Communist Party, 50; George Ibrahim, 46; Khashabi Theater, 15; Masrah An-Nahid, 38. *See also* *Returning to Haifa* (novel/play)
Halim Hafez, Abdel, 27
Hammad, Talal, 108, 113, 116
Hampton, Wilborn, 229
Handelzalts, Michael, 167
Haniya, Akram, 166
Happy Shoemaker, 53, 54, 54f, 198
haraka (movement), 1
Hareeq Al-Jaheem (The Fire of Hell), 92–93
Hasan Ala' Al-Din, Mohammad, 17
Hasaneine, Daoud (Abu Ali), 27, 142
Hashemite Kingdom of Jordan, 17, 19, 20, 22–23, 39, 150, 172. *See also* Jordan
Hat and the Prophet, The, 107
Hawatmeh, Nayef, 150
Hebrew language, 24, 150, 182, 225; *Ali the Galilean*, 161; The Alternative Theater, 223; *Ansar*, 241; audiences, 165–168; *B'ism Al-Ab w al-Um w Al-Ibn*, 120, 121; depicted on Palestinian stage, 219; hegemony of, 248; *Jesus* film, 175; newspapers, 13, 151, 185, 210, 246; Palestinians learning, 255; radio programs, 50; *Sami and Susu*, 47, 48, 49; theater, 239; translations to/from, 269–270n22
Hebrew University, 76, 113, 120, 147, 149, 183

Hebron, 5, 10, 130, 202, 246, 251, 253, 258; size, 289n1
Hebron Daboya Operation, 130
Hendrix, Jimi, 61
Herut Party, 223
Hijazi, Sameh, 251
Hijjawi, Ali, 110
Hikmet, Nazim Ran, 62, 63, 72
Histadrut (General Federation of Laborers), 18, 144
historic Palestine, 6, 31, 38, 105, 128, 182, 193
Hodali, Christine, 55
Holland, 152
Horne, Kenneth, 39
Hussein (king of Jordan), 22, 24, 48

I'bilin, 149, 151
Imam, Al-Sheikh, 13
'imara Min Waraq (A Paper Building), 105
imperialism, 28, 95, 105, 132
improvisation, 165, 188; Antara in the Courtyard, 211; of Balalin, 69; B'ism Al-Ab, w Al-Um, w Al-Ibn, 116; of El-Hakawati, 115, 142, 276n14; François Abu Salem's production formula for, 163, 178; of Hussam Abu Esheh, 237-238; Mahjoub Mahjoub, 148, 149, 151; Palestinian Theatre, 93; Returning to Haifa, 213; The Story of Kufur Shamma, 210; The Story of the Eye and the Tooth, 189, 190
Improvisational Concert for the Sake of the Workers, 125
Inad Theater, 10, 251
'ind El-Luzoom (When Necessary), 93, 197
India, 172
In Search of Omar Al-Khayyam, 240, 241, 275n4

Institut Français du Proche-Orient (IFPO), 252
Insult, The, 245
International Arts Consultants, 227
International Film Festival, 245
internationalization, 117, 125, 137, 138
In the Name of the Father, the Mother, and the Son (B'ism Al-Ab w al-Um w Al-Ibn). See B'ism Al-Ab w al-Um w Al-Ibn (In the Name of the Father, the Mother, and the Son)
Intifada, first (1987-1993), 226; Al-Kasaba, 233, 235, 237, 238; children's stone throwing, 157, 230; At the Cross runs until, 40; Eran Baniel attempts collaboration, 246; feeling of potential statehood, 232, 242; George Ibrahim loses job, 270n25; mass popular organizing leads to, 32; Men Without Shadows, 218; nationalism, 268n30; Palestinian theater in cultural resistance, 5; Romeo and Juliet, 248; Sanabel People's Theatre, 213, 217; theater artists' memory of, 205; theatrical factionalism during, 210; theatrical productions decrease during, 171, 225, 234; "Ya Thalam Al-Sijn" (Arab anthem), 220
Intifada, second (2000-2005), 156, 238, 254
Iraq/Iraqis, 45, 240, 241
Is'eed, Jamal, 56, 57
Islam. See Muslims/Islam
Ismail, Ya'coub, 122, 200, 206, 242, 244, 245, 251
Israel Broadcast Authority, 166
Israel Defense Forces (IDF), 166, 167, 204
Israeli authorities, 129, 136; arrest/interrogate François Abu Salem, 182; Balalin avoids, 67; El-Hakawati's

Israeli authorities (*cont.*)
confrontations with, 170, 183, 192; George Ibrahim known to, 171; Mustapha Al-Kurd's return alarms, 181; pressure schools, 130; prevent plays in Arabic, 138; shut down plays, 204, 215; sponsor cultural activities in Arabic, 18; theater artists' struggle with, 6
Israeli Communist Youth Union, 243
Israeli flag, 192, 223, 224, 226, 249, 286n31
Israeli government, 18, 26, 49, 136, 145, 150, 223, 288–289n18
Israeli hegemony, 93, 182
Israeli Jerusalem Foundation, 246
Israeli Khan Theatre, 245, 246, 249
Israeli military, 128–129, 249; children throw stones at, 156, 159, 161; civil administration, 89; controls West Bank and Gaza, 32; *The Darkness*, 67; El-Hakawati pressures for permission, 164; force expands in Occupied Territories, 169; influence on quotidian life, 255; *Khawaziq*, 105; laws, 10, 30, 39, 86, 88; negatively influences Palestinian theater, 62; PFLP as enemy of, 150; questions Adel Al-Tartir, 76; repression, 64; rule, 18, 33; theater artists clash with, 205; violence of, 237
Israeli Ministry of Education, 56
Israeli occupation, 124, 249, 256; *Ansar* demonstrates, 242; Arab leaders beaten down by, 194; as challenge to theatrical movement, 84; greater capitalist enterprise and, 96; *Mahjoub Mahjoub* poses issues of, 147; no Palestinian ministry of culture under, 107, 111; resistance to, 58, 121; unions under, 211; US government supports, 216

Israeli television, 144; accessible to Palestinians and Israelis, 48; Arab section of, 49, 270n29; George Ibrahim in, 8, 47, 50–51, 108, 112, 171, 218, 221; George Ibrahim leaves, 56, 137, 138, 199; Salman Natour appears on, 286n32; *Song of Death*, 52
Israeli theaters, 155, 168, 249, 280n38
Israel State Archive, 6, 12, 67, 171, 184
Istres, France, 157, 181
Italy, 124, 223
It Matters Me, 50

Jabal Al-Mukabber, East Jerusalem, 17
Jaffa, 126, 142
Jaffa Gate, Jerusalem, 26
Jahshan, Adib, 38
Jahshan, Lavinia, 41
Jannanouny (They Made Me Crazy), 200
Japan, 212
Japanese Red Army, 150
Jbail, Ibrahim, 28, 86–91, 98, 100, 105, 106, 110, 134, 274n7
Jenin, Palestine, 19, 172, 253; Freedom Theatre, 10, 15; Refugee Camp, 275n31
Jericho, Palestine, 19, 26, 172, 253, 258; Jericho Cinema, 164; *Jericho Year Zero*, 245
Jerusalem Al-Jawal (Itinerant) Company, 200, 206
Jerusalemite theater, 13, 35, 199, 246, 271n46, 280n36
Jerusalem Law, 145
Jerusalem Players, 8, 39, 40, 43, 44, 57
Jerusalem Post (newspaper), 151, 155, 159, 165, 179, 223
Jerusalem-Ramallah area, 72; 1967 war of occupation, 33; Balalin well known in, 73; *B'ism Al-Ab, w Al-Um, w Al-Ibn*, 123; cultural

INDEX

production, 97; ensemble members considered foreign to, 136; Palestinian theater in, 169; performance permits from, 171; positionality in, 35; in post-Nakba context, 18; refugee camps in, 165; resistance in, 32, 205; *A Slice of Life*, 65; Sundouq Al-'ajab tours, 104; theater artists in, 38; theater community rift in, 56; theater companies in, 4, 5; theatrical activities in, 3, 138; theatrical spaces in, 258

Jerusalem theater festival, 98, 101

Jesus, 41, 133, 215, 217; *Jesus* (film), 174, 175, 179. *See also* Christians/Christianity

Jewish Chronicle (newspaper), 152, 154, 155

Jewish Community Relations Council, 215–216

Jewish Israelis, 47, 48, 104, 121, 161, 165, 167, 168, 192, 246; culture, 162; Leah Tsemel, 215

Jews, 45, 48, 50, 155, 190, 213, 227; Ashkenazi, 120, 121; as characters, 185, 188, 192; compared to Palestinians, 160; extremists, 248; settlers, 126; theatergoers, 116, 166, 221, 227, 228

Jordan, 17–24, 267n13, 269n11; armed struggle in, 151; Black September, 32, 188; George Ibrahim in, 28; government, 21, 59, 75; Hashemite Kingdom of, 17, 19, 20, 22–23, 39, 150, 172; Jerusalem under rule of, 39; Jordanian Army, 26, 27, 86; Jordanian Education Law, 19; media, 214; Mustapha Al-Kurd in, 104; nationalism, 19; Palestinian cultural intelligentsia in, 31; Palestinian resistance expelled from, 153; Palestinians under rule of, 33; PLO, 8, 205; police, 105, 143, 147; River Jordan, 44–45; Sundouq Al-'ajab tours, 106; television, 48

journalism/journalists, 18, 34, 98, 111, 135, 182, 193, 214, 215, 243; Daoud Kuttab, 166; European, 159; Ghassan Kanafani, 17, 30; Journalism League, 244; Mohammad Al-Batrawi/Fawzi Al-Bakri/Mahmoud Shqair, 65; Mohammad Al-Thaher on, 92; Najib El-Rayyes, 220; in *Natrin Faraj*, 212; period, 1, 11, 12, 13, 14, 276n20; Philippe Dauma, 157; Sahar Khalifeh, 83; tabloid, 92; Western, 153. *See also* media

Jowaylis, Hussam, 189

Jowhar, Ibrahim, 244

Kabul, 129, 165

Kach/Kahane Chai extremists, 223–224, 225, 286n38

Kanaaneh, Sharif, 164, 165

Kanafani, Ghassan, 107, 129, 268n29; assassination, 130, 244; *The Blind and the Deaf*, 201, 206; *Man Is a Cause*, 127, 128; in PFLP, 17, 30–31, 125, 150, 279n15; *Returning to Haifa*, 125, 126, 193, 255, 268n28; Sanabel's productions of, 259; *Um Sad*, 277–278n44

Karaman, Bushra, 108, 116

Katz, Orna, 248

Keates, Jonathan, 154

KGB, 150

Khalaf, Karim Hanna, 90

Khalayleh, Ibrahim, 162, 171, 201, 209, 210, 221; as leftist, 211; publicity stunt, 192, 286n31; questioned by Mascobiyya police, 183

Khaled, Leila, 150

Khalifeh, Sahar, 83, 232

Khalil Al-Sakakini Cultural Center, 254

Khalil, Amer, 12, 43, 176, 189, 210, 224, 240, 245, 254; El-Hakawati and, 258
Khamis, Juliano Mer, 239, 270n35
Khamis, Saliba, 50, 239, 270n35
Khashabi Theater, 15
Khawaziq (Shafts), 105
Khouri, Daoud, 34
Khoury, Makram, 10, 52, 136, 233
Kidan, Milad, 68, 70
Kiwan, Mohammad, 104
Knesset, 28, 29, 144, 145, 148, 279n7
Köhler, Hans-georg, 23
Kol Ha'ir (newspaper), 185
Kristeligt Dagblad (newspaper), 158
Kuttab, Daoud, 166, 173, 178
Kuttab, Jonathan, 158, 173, 179, 183
Kuwait, 90, 269n11

La Maison des Cultures du Monde, 191
Lamma Injanina (When We Went Crazy!), 102, 104, 113, 180
La'nat 'atrees (The Curse of Atrees), 197, 206
Land Day demonstrations, 140, 148
Land Nordrhein-Westphalia Festival of Germany, 246
Langar, Felicia, 104
Latakia, Syria, 17
Latif Aqel, Abdel, 244
Lawhat Mawlid Thair (Painting of Revolutionary Birth), 131
Laws of the Municipality of Bethlehem, 19
Layla Al-Hamra (Little Red Riding Hood), 56, 198, 237, 287-288n5
League of Palestinian Theatre Artists, 135, 237, 242, 278n49
League of Palestinian Visual Artists, 44
Lebanon/Lebanese, 17, 18, 32, 35, 104, 159, 180, 222; Al-Murabitoun, 2; camp wars, 205; civil war, 205, 230; invasion of, 130, 153, 169, 188, 230; 'issam Mahfouz, 195; Mohammed Flayfel, 220; refugee camps, 279n11; South, 119, 206
leftists/leftism, 6, 9, 27, 28, 31, 159, 225, 259, 268n37; *Al-Hadaf* (newspaper), 59; Balalin, 81; Dababis, 88; El-Hakawati, 117; Ghassan Kanafani, 30; Ibrahim Khalayleh, 211; Mustapha Al-Kurd, 80; Palestinian Theatre, 93; Salman Natour, 29; Tzavta, 155; writers, 33, 34
Le Grande Magic Circus, 156
Le Monde (newspaper), 116
Likud, 223, 224
Lille Festival, 246
London, UK, 152, 154, 155, 240; Almeida Theater, 191
Lubeck, Jackie, 257, 276n14; *Ali the Galilean*, 183; as American, 113, 146; *B'ism Al-Ab, w Al-Um, w Al-Ibn*, 109, 116, 164; costume design, 179, 212; El-Hakawati and, 141, 209, 210, 229, 275n4; as fundraiser, 177; investigation of, 149; on *Mahjoub Mahjoub*, 147, 278n2; on An-Nuzha Cinema, 174, 175; in Palestinian cultural production, 110; part of theatrical couple, 55; *In Search of Omar Al-Khayyam*, 240; skills of, 117; *The Story of Kufur of Shamma*, 221, 222, 224-225, 226; as technician, 274n28; Theater Day Productions, 251, 258; work on *One Thousand and One Nights*, 167
Lutheran Church, 23, 24, 61
Luxor Theater, 191

Ma'ariv, 166
Madfa'i, Walid, 51
Madrid negotiations, 243

INDEX

Mahamid, Muhamad, 5, 113, 116, 162; founds El-Hakawati, 275n4
Mahfouz, ʻIssam, 195
Mahjoub Mahjoub, 14, 142, 152–155, 159, 179, 183; in Arabic, 151; censorship of, 149; European tour of, 157, 170; performance photo, 143f; performed in Galilee, 147; radio in, 144, 149
Mahmoud, Mustapha, 195
Majd al-Kroom, 152, 165
Majmaʻ Al-Qabadayat (Gang of Toughs), 93
Makkawi, Abdel Ghaffar, 246
Man Is a Cause, 127, 193, 255
Manor, Ehud, 246
Mansour, Suleiman, 44, 166, 212
Maraia Theater, 6
Marakez Tafteesh (Search Centers/Checkpoints), 98
Marfaʼi, Walid, 23
Marivaux, Pierre Carlet de Chamblain de, 52
Marxism, 51, 125, 190. *See also* communists
Mascobiyya, 182, 183
Masrah Al-Seera theater, 6
Masrah Al-Shoke (Thorns Theater), 198
Masrah Al-Warsheh Al-Faniyyeh (The Arts Workshop Theatre), 6, 57, 198–199, 206, 218, 221
Masrah An-Nahid (The Rising Theatre), 38
Masrah El-Funnun (Theater Arts Company), 198
Massarweh, Riad, 10, 148
Mawta Bila Qubur (Men Without Shadows), 212, 218, 220, 232, 236–237, 242, 244; performance photo, 218f
Mazda Eclairage, 246
McDonnell, Pat, 216
media, 19, 20, 42, 90; Arab, 32; artistic, 6; international, 210; Israeli, 49, 51, 136, 155, 199, 214; Jordanian, 214; news, 11, 155; Palestinian, 51; Palestinian Council of Culture and Media, 244; social, 111, 258; television, 4; Western, 32. *See also* journalism/journalists
Merchant of Venice, 23
Messiah, 212–215
Middle East, 40, 95, 215, 228, 240
Midi-Libre (newspaper), 155
Mikhail, Nadia, 6, 41, 60, 71, 79, 257
Ministry of Information, 20
Ministry of Information Regulations, 20
Ministry of Religious Affairs, 215
Ministry of Social Affairs Law, 19
Ministry of the Interior (Israeli), 147, 185, 186
Ministry of the Interior (Palestinian Authority), 12, 149, 158, 217, 219
Mistero Buffo, 210
Mitwalli, Imad, 128, 179, 224, 225, 242, 257, 258–259
Mizero, Imad, 134, 225
Mnouchkine, Ariane, 26, 61, 83, 115
Molière, 39, 52
monitoring. *See* surveillance
monodramas, 241, 244
Montpellier, France, 155, 157, 281n42
Monty (Antwerp, Netherlands), 191
Mossad, 130
Mount Zion, Jerusalem, 257
movements, 1–5, 256–259; Abnaʼ Al-Balad, 2, 117; Al-Haraka Al-Masrahiya, 1, 256, 257; Al-Murabitoun, 2; Arab National, 22; boycott, divestment, and sanctions, 168; Citizens Rights, 223; Egyptian Movement for Change, 2, 117; labor, 133, 211; liberation, 31, 33, 34, 256; resistance, 15, 204; womenʼs, 125

Muallem, Edward, 12, 116, 179, 182, 209, 229, 258; *Ali the Galilean*, 162; El-Hakawati and, 114, 173–177, 240, 275n4; at François Abu Salem's funeral, 257; in Galilee, 113–115; *Mahjoub Mahjoub*, 152; part of theatrical couple, 55; play editing, 13; in *Qamar Al-Amira*, 237; questioned by police, 183; starts Aoun's Ashtar Theatre, 251; *The Story of Kufur Shamma*, 210

Munich Theater Festival, 191

Musara'a Hurra (Free Wrestling), 94, 95f, 97, 101, 112, 119

Muslims/Islam, 43, 48, 78, 124, 145, 213, 267n11; as anti-theatrical, 154, 155; ban against representation, 280n24; Quran, 26; schools, 138; Sufis, 27, 180, 201, 202; Sunnis, 214

Nabi Musa, 201

Nablus, Palestine, 75, 176, 222; Al-'idda Sufi Troupe, 202; cinema houses in, 19, 172; George Ibrahim in, 45; ghettoization of, 253; Mustapha Al-Kurd in, 26–27; Palestinian dignitaries of, 177; Sahar Khalifeh is from, 83

Najem, Ahmad Fouad, 61

Nakba (ethnic cleansing), 30, 37, 38, 205, 255; aftermath, 18–19, 39, 250; eviscerates cultural infrastructure, 15; George Ibrahim on, 22; leading artists as children of, 21; *Man Is a Cause*, 127; refugee life, 8; *The Story of Kufur Shamma*, 225

Naksa, 37, 59

Nancy Theatre Festival (France), 108, 109, 116, 124, 157

Naqara, Salwa, 10

Naserite movement, 2

Nashrat Ahwal Al-Jaw (Weather Forecast), 72, 75, 76, 79–80, 81, 118, 157

Nasrallah, Ilias, 72

Nasrallah, Israel Elias, 34

Nassar, Hala Khamis, 38

Nassar, Mattia, 34

Nassrallah, Elias, 34

National Front, 83, 232

national theater (of Palestine), 135, 230, 243, 255; Palestinian National Theatre, 15, 231, 243–246, 251–253, 257–258

Natour, Salman, 29

Natrin Faraj (Awaiting Salvation), 212–218

Nazarenes, 148, 200, 211

Nazareth, 100, 104, 123, 130, 147, 148, 155, 159

Netherlands, 124

Neve Tsedek, 166, 168, 170

New York, 157, 215, 227, 228, 229

New York Magazine, 229

New York Times (newspaper), 168, 229

New Zealand, 46

Night and the Mountain, The, 246

nihilism, 4, 21, 164, 206

non-governmental organizations (NGOs), 234, 252, 254

North America, 227, 252. *See also* United States (US)

Norway, 152

Nuzha-Hakawati Theatre. *See* An-Nuzha-Hakawati Theatre

occupation (1967), 30, 38; aftermath, 33; first Intifada follows, 226; Israel withdraws forces of, 230; *Man Is a Cause*, 127; *A Movement's Promise*, 9; Palestinian theater after, 98; Ramallah under Israeli military laws after, 10; *Returning to Haifa*, 125; shackles Palestinian cultural futurity, 15; theatrical movement and, 4, 8, 203

INDEX

Occupied Territories, 98, 105, 116; banning productions in, 171; creative movement throughout, 71; cultural producers in, 31; first Intifada arising in, 32; George Ibrahim on, 137; ghettoization in, 253; Israeli military expansion in, 169; Israel's Arabic-language programming in, 49; literature of resistance in, 268n30; *Men Without Shadows*, 219; Palestinian television/radio in, 83; Palestinian theater in, 101; policies of suppression in, 148; resistance in humanistic inquiry in, 59; theater standards in, 135; theatrical activity in, 5, 8; theatrical movement in, 84, 251; violence throughout, 226

October War, 95

Old City, Jerusalem, 75, 93, 107, 202, 213, 234, 236; Adel Al-Tartir in, 65; El-Omariyyeh School, 53, 54, 56, 198; El-Omariyyeh Theatre, 103; Mustapha Al-Kurd in, 25–27

O'Neill, Eugene, 39

One Thousand and One Nights, 14, 170, 244

One Thousand and One Nights in the Meat Market, 156, 158

One Thousand and One Nights of the Stone Thrower (Alf Leyleh w Leyleh), 156, 157, 160, 160f, 163, 165, 166, 167, 180

Open Society, 252

orientalism, 64, 73, 152, 153–155, 156, 158, 161, 217; motifs, 11, 124

Oslo Peace Accords, 257; Al-Muqata'a, 28, 217; children's theater, 238; failures of, 156; George Ibrahim, 52, 236; Israeli checkpoints, 254; *Jericho Year Zero*, 245; Jerusalemite vs. West Bank artists, 266n8; normalization, 168, 280n38; Palestinian National Theatre, 243, 244; *Romeo and Juliet*, 248–250; Samih Al-Qassem, 60; theater artists in period of, 5, 256; theater movement, 252

Othello, 23

Ottoman era, 31, 86, 87, 88, 220

Our Country's Theatre, 74

Painted Bride Art Center (US), 228

Palestine, historic, 6, 31, 38, 105, 128, 182, 193

Palestinian Art Week, 166, 168

Palestinian Authority, 1, 252, 255, 266n8; Al-Muqata'a, 28; Ministry of Culture, 13, 254; Ministry of the Interior, 12, 149, 158, 217, 219

Palestinian Broadcasting Station (PBS), 38, 39, 45

Palestinian cause, 205; Dababis, 87; El-Hakawati, 168; François Abu Salem's commitment to, 94; George Ibrahim, 58; Ibrahim Jbail on, 88; Israeli invasion of Lebanon affects, 169; journalists and, 92; liberation, 151; Mustapha Al-Kurd performs for, 180–181; PLO represents, 230; Radi Shehadeh on, 190; Sanabel, 194; students who believe in, 217; theater artists, 21; theater movement and, 206

Palestinian Council of Culture and Media, 244

Palestinian Cultural Center, 208

Palestinian Declaration of Independence, 197, 230, 244

Palestinian dialect, 4, 18, 46, 47, 52, 115, 146

Palestinian flag, 130, 144, 147, 149, 192, 249, 255, 257

Palestinian identity, 22; in *Al-'atma*, 79; in *Ali the Galilean*, 162; in *B'ism Al-Ab, w Al-Um, w Al-Ibn*, 124;

Palestinian identity (*cont.*)
constants of, 190; El-Hakawati attacked for, 158, 192; George Ibrahim maintains, 50; Jerusalem struggles to maintain, 203; legalized, 255; *Mahjoub Mahjoub*, 146; Mohammad Al-Thaher, 197; Nazarenes assert, 148; PFLP seeks to affirm, 151; suppression of, 15, 21, 33-34; theater committed to, 25
Palestinian Left, 6, 28, 29, 33, 140
Palestinian liberation, 31, 59, 70, 121, 122, 211, 252
Palestinian Liberation Organization (PLO), 248; El-Hakawati and, 280n27; expelled from Tunis, 169, 230; Fateh leads, 140; founds Association of Palestinian Theatre, 17; influence declines, 252; institutional independence of, 3; in Jordan, 8, 205-206; leads war of attrition, 31; in Lebanon, 159; *Mahjoub Mahjoub*, 153; *Majma' Al-Qabadayat* promotes, 93; militia forces exiled, 32; Palestinian Theatre under, 92; peace talks with State of Israel, 242, 243; political parties' involvement in, 1; reputation of, 150; in Tunis, 188, 226; Working Women's Association's celebratory convention, 185
Palestinian National Council, 140
Palestinian nationalism, 11, 31, 34, 142, 189, 196, 205, 259, 268n30; music, 216, 248
Palestinian National Theatre (PNT), 15, 231, 243-246, 251-253, 255, 257, 258
Palestinian People's Theatre, 4, 91, 125, 127, 130, 134, 193
Palestinian plays, 52, 82, 116, 168, 255
Palestinian revolution, 31, 33, 105
Palestinian television, 245

Palestinian Territories, 9, 218, 226, 230, 246, 253
Palestinian Theatre Ensemble, 6; competes with Balalin, 85; *Curse of Atrees*, 206; declines, 141, 198, 251; direct approach of, 218; division in, 4, 259; Hussam Abu Esheh and Ahmad Abu Saloum leave, 131; *Improvisational Concert for the Sake of the Workers*, 125; *'ind El-Luzoom*, 93, 196-197; in Jerusalem theater festival, 98; Mohammad Al-Thaher in, 91; opens, 74; promotes national unity, 92; in theater movement, 5; Theatre Committee splits from, 134
Palestinian Theatre League, 134, 237, 242, 244
Palestinian Theatre Troupe, 91
Palestinian Writer's Union, 244
pan-Arab nationalism, 19, 31, 100, 150
Pappé, Ilan, 49
Papp, Joseph, 227-229, 259
Paris, France, 26, 83, 191, 240
Patches, John I., 227, 228
patriarchy, 71, 77, 117, 119, 121, 122, 163
Pe'er, Edna, 50, 51
Percy, Edward, 39
Philadelphia Inquirer (newspaper), 227, 228, 229
Philadelphia, Pennsylvania, 227, 228
Poland, 152
Politiken (newspaper), 158
Popular Front for the Liberation of Palestine (PFLP), 22, 216; Ahmad Abu Saloum and Hussam Abu Esheh sympathize with, 193; airplane hijacking operations, 130; Balalin associated with, 83, 86, 89; Ghassan Kanafani in, 17, 30-31, 125, 150, 151, 268n29, 279n15; Ibrahim Jbail in, 274n7; Israeli

military against, 106; members imprisoned, 220; in Palestinian Left, 33; theoretical platform of, 117, 129; workers' unions led by, 189, 205
Press and Publication Law, 20
propaganda, 49, 51, 116, 152, 157, 175
protests/strikes, 105, 221, 223, 225; *Al-Mawlid*, 132; artist, 237; of Israel's expropriation of Palestinian lands, 279n11; labor, 226; leading to Intifada of 1987, 32; in *Mahjoub Mahjoub*, 148; prisoner, 275n32; in *In Search of Omar Al-Khayyam*, 241; student, 26, 64; of theatrical movement, 231
Public Theater (New York), 227, 228
puppet theater, 202; *Adventure in Jerusalem*, 53; by George Ibrahim, 200, 237, 238; *Layla Al-Hamrah*, 287n5; *Sami and Susu*, 8, 46–49, 51, 52, 56, 198; *Sharshouh*, 202. See also children's theater

Qafila Theatre, 258–259
Qalandia Checkpoint, 266n8
Qalqilia, 253
Qamar Al-Amira (Princess Moon), 56, 237
Qara'een, Ibrahim, 244
Qaraqash, 60, 62
Qit'at Hayat, 74
Quran, 26

Rabbat, Antoine, 39
Racine, Jean, 39
radio, 17, 102, 127, 241; Christian, 39; George Ibrahim, 49, 51, 56; Israeli, 45, 50, 51, 56, 93, 136; Jordanian, 23, 24, 45; for mind control, 79, 103; Ministry of Information, 20; Palestinian, 42, 83, 92; Palestinian Broadcasting Station, 38, 39, 45; use in *Mahjoub Mahjoub*, 144, 149; Voice of Israel, 46
Radwan, Fathi, 52
Rafe', Ali, 104
Ramadan, 239
Ramadan Nights, 196, 201, 272n20
Ramallah-Birzeit area, 3, 4, 5
Ramallah Cultural Palace, 254
Ramallah-Jerusalem area. See Jerusalem-Ramallah area
Ramallah Municipality building, 75f
Ramallah prison, 28
Ramallah Teacher's College, 61, 94
Ras Roos (One Head, Many Heads), 106
Red Cross, 237
Red Line (organization), 243
refugee camps, 88, 165; Aida Refugee Camp, 15; Al-Amari Refugee Camp, 28, 86; in *Al-Haq 'al-Haq*, 90; Al-Jalazone Refugee Camp, 90; Al-Wehdat Refugee Camp, 86; in *The Story of Kufur of Shamma*, 222, 229; United Nations, 18
refugees, 8, 19, 228; of 1948, 33; domestic concerns, 127; George Ibrahim Habash, 22; Mustapha Al-Kurd, 26; rights, 97, 214; UN Relief and Works Agency for Palestinian Refugees in the Near East, 18
Resistance to Communism Law, 20, 267n10
Returning to Haifa (novel/play), 30, 125–127, 129, 130, 193, 212, 255, 268n28
Reuven, Snir, 49, 266n5
Revolution of the Dead, 86
right of return, 140, 214, 249
River Jordan, 44
Rokem, Freddie, 248
Romeo and Juliet, 9, 191, 245, 246, 247f, 249, 250, 253, 259, 287–288n5
Rosa Luxemburg, 252

Rushdi, Muhammad, 27
Russian school of realism, 137

Saba, Emile, 258
Saba, Ibrahim, 43, 44, 61
Sabina, 51
Sabra massacre, 206
Sabrin musical ensemble, 196
Saidi, Gholam Hussein, 195
Sakhnin, 129, 159, 165
Salah Ed-Din (publishing house), 34
Salah El-Din Street, 202, 233
Saleh, Antoine, 10, 46–47, 52, 269n17
Salem, Estafan, 17
Salhout, Jamil, 193
Samara, Adel, 34, 107, 108, 111, 112
Samara, Imad, 173, 178, 179
Sami and Susu, 8, 46–49, 51, 52, 56, 198
Sanabel Ensemble, 5, 194
Sanabel People's Singing Troupe, 200
Sanabel People's Theatre, 131, 195, 221, 224; Ahmad Abu Saloum and Husam Abu Esheh in, 111, 193, 244; "Al-Haraka Al-Masrahiyya," 256; American tour, 216; censored, 215; first Intifada and, 217; *The General Sir*, 206; George Ibrahim's work in, 218; Ghassan Kanafani with, 259; Hussam Abu Esheh with, 6, 213, 216; *Man Is a Cause*, 255; Palestinian theater movement, 5; performances in Jerusalem, 91; Ramadan Nights, 196; support PFLP, 129; *Woza Albert!* 212
Sanabel's Cause, 8
Sartre, Jean-Paul, 52, 218, 237
satire, 206; *Al-'atma*, 146; *Al-Harah Al-Mukhtarah*, 200; *Ali the Galilean*, 165; *B'ism Al-Ab, w Al-Um, w Al-Ibn*, 121; comedy, 23; *Free Wrestling*, 95, 119; *Mahjoub Mahjoub*, 145, 152; *Natrin Faraj*, 213, 214, 215; *One Thousand and One Nights in the Meat Market*, 156; political, 159; *Slaves Go West*, 211. See also genre
Saudi Arabia, 269n11
Savary, Jérôme, 156, 157
Sayigh, Yazid, 31
Sayyidi Al-General (The General Sir), 194–195, 206
Scream, The, 198
1789, 72–73, 79
Shahin, Zakaria, 72, 74, 80
Shakespeare, William, 24, 39, 46, 60, 191, 245, 250
Shalhat, Antwan, 165
Shamandour (Great God), 73, 76, 77
Shammas, Anton, 47, 269–270n22
Sharaf El-Teeby Dabke Troupen, 200
Sharshouh, 202, 210
Shatila massacre, 206
Shaw, George Bernard, 39
Shawqi, Ahmad, 39
Shehadeh, Mounira, 55, 171, 176, 212
Shehadeh, Radi, 185, 190, 257; in *Ali the Galilean*, 162; in Al-Mghar, 100; Al-Seera Theater, 251; *Antara in the Courtyard*, 211; biography, 171, 258; in El-Hakawati, 189; in Galilee, 209; in *One Thousand and One Nights in the Meat Market*, 156; owns production company, 6; part of theatrical couple, 55; questioned by Mascobiyya police, 183; *Sharshouh*, 202, 210; *Slaves Go West*, 211; on *sumud*, 32; in *Weather Forecast*, 158; works as individual, 221; works in children's theater, 210
Sheikh Jarrah, East Jerusalem, 25, 62, 63, 64, 72, 171, 175, 230, 234
Shqair, Mahmoud, 34, 35, 65, 107, 111
Shu'fat, Jerusalem, 99
Shyoukhi, Raed, 258
Simon, John, 229

INDEX

Sinai Peninsula, Egypt, 30
Sirriyat Ramallah (cultural center), 106
Slaves Go West, 211
Souq Okath, 201
South Africa, 212, 213
Spain, 191
Statue of Liberty, 132, 133, 146
St. George's Cathedral, 24, 42f, 43, 116
Stiftung Mercator, 252
Story of Kufur of Shamma (The Story of the Village of Shamma), 13, 14, 210, 212, 221-229, 222f, 240, 244
Story of the Eye and the Tooth, The, 184, 184f, 185, 188, 189, 191, 206, 209, 210, 249
"Story of the Walnut Tree and Lame Yunus," 62-63, 72
Strasbourg, France, 26, 61, 114
Strassman, Briel, 166
Suez Canal, 95
sumud (steadfastness), 32, 33, 34, 47, 93, 132, 253
Sundouqah, Moatassem, 165
Sundouq Al-ʿajab (Box of Wonder) ensemble, 106-108, 255; Adel Al-Tartir in, 101, 107, 112, 251, 258, 272n15, 273n33; Al-Haraka Al-Masrahiyya, 256; *The Blind and the Deaf*, 201, 206; El-Hakawati and, 114; formation of, 4; François Abu Salem founds, 5; *Lamma Injanina*, 102, 180; revives Theatre Committee, 134; tours in Galilee, 104
suppression, 6, 20, 78; of Palestinian identity, 21, 33; policies of, 148; of revolutionary sentiments, 79; of theater movement, 138
surveillance, 103, 151, 184, 252, 253, 255
Sweden, 152
Swedish International Development Cooperation Agency (SIDA), 252
Switzerland, 124, 150, 177
Syria/Syrians, 17, 23, 26, 31, 51, 205, 220

Taghribat Saʿid Ben Fadel Allah (The Exile of Said, Son of Fadel Allah), 106
Taha, Al-Motawakel, 244
Talhami, Reem, 55
Tamari, Vera, 6, 60, 257
Tantura Theatre, 241
Tarabsheh, Adnan, 6, 113, 116, 123, 143, 157, 162, 171, 258
Teacher's Training Center (Dar Al-Muallemeen), 43
Tel Aviv, 51, 155, 156, 161, 166, 167, 168, 207, 214; Palestinian Art Week, 168; Tel Aviv University, 100, 248
Tempest, The, 245, 246
Tempodrom, 191
terrorism, 32, 51, 158; accusations in *Mahjoub Mahjoub*, 144, 151, 152; Ghassan Kanafani accused of, 130; PFLP, 150; of PLO, 153
Thawb Al-Imbrator (The Emperor's New Clothes), 75, 198
Theater Day Productions, 5, 10, 251, 252, 258
Theater of the Oppressed, 255
Theater of the Other, 223, 246, 249
Theatre Committee, 98, 107, 108, 112, 134. *See also* Association for Work and Development for the Arts
Théâtre de l'Olivier, 156-157
Théâtre de Soleil, 26, 61, 72, 78, 83, 115
Theatre Family, 41, 60, 61, 62, 63, 67
Theatre for Palestinian Culture and Arts, 241, 242
Theatrical Artistic Group. *See* Firqat Al-Funoun Al-Masrahiyah (the Theatrical Artistic Group [TAG])

There Is a Limit (organization), 243
Third World, 132, 195
Thorns of Peace, 52
Thousand and One Nights. See One Thousand and One Nights
Thousand and One Nights in the Meat Market. See One Thousand and One Nights in the Meat Market
Thousand and One Nights of the Stone Thrower. See One Thousand and One Nights of the Stone Thrower (Alf Leyleh w Leyleh)
Times (newspaper), 152
Toubi, Asma,' 17
Touma, Emile, 34
Tragedy of the Poor Molasses Seller, The, 196
Triangle area, 104, 108, 112, 123, 129, 152, 159, 165
Tsemel, Leah, 104, 181, 215
Tulkarem, 29, 253
Tunisia, 205, 212; Tunis, 26, 32, 169, 170, 178, 188, 226, 230
Turbulent House (Al-Beit Al-Sakheb), 23, 51
Tzavta, 155

Um Al-Fahem, 104, 113, 130
Um Sad, 277–278n44
Une Tranche de Vie (A Slice of Life), 61, 63, 65, 66
Union of Palestinian Working Women Committee, 243
United Kingdom, 152, 153; British Council, 254; British Mandate, 32, 38, 45; London, 152, 154, 155, 191, 240; occupation of Palestine, 28; phosphate company, 23; television, 119
United National Front, 83, 232
United Nations, 18. See also Green Line

United Presbyterian Church U.S.A., 40
United States (US), 9, 68, 116, 121, 133, 215; *Al-Mawlid*, 132; Commission on Ecumenical Mission and Relations of the United Presbyterian Church U.S.A., 40; El-Hakawati Theatre tour in, 1, 14, 223, 226, 227, 229, 259; funding organizations, 177; immigration to, 149; International Agency for Development, 252; *Mahjoub Mahjoub*, 144; orientalism of, 217; Palestinian theater in, 215, 216, 228; Sanabel People's Theatre tours, 216; Statue of Liberty, 132, 133, 146; *The Story of Kufur Shamma*, 222, 226; USAID (United States International Agency for Development), 252. See also Americans
UNRWA (UN Relief and Works Agency for Palestinian Refugees in the Near East), 18
Usrat Al-Masrah (The Theatre Family), 41, 60, 61, 62, 63, 67

VHS Hietzing, 191
Vienna, Austria, 116, 191
Visual Artists' League, 244
Vitale, Carl, 219
Voice of Israel, 45, 46

Wadi Al-Joz, Jerusalem, 159
Wahhab, Abdel, 27
Wall, Israeli, 253, 266n8, 280n38; *The Wall*, 255
Wannous, Sa'dallah, 196
War of 1948, 17, 18, 19, 21, 22, 28
War of 1967, 6, 8, 21, 24–25, 27, 33, 44, 144, 173, 205
Washington Report on Middle East Affairs, 216

Welfare Foundation, 177, 208
West Bank, 29, 51, 80, 94, 148, 164, 172, 201; activist cultural production in, 21; artists, 266n8; Balalin in, 64; censorship in, 17, 39, 158, 159, 171; communists, 50; East Jerusalem and Ramallah reflect context, 18; East Jerusalem detached from, 253; El-Hakawati in, 182, 198, 233; Hebron, 289n1; Inad Theater, 251; Israeli military controls, 32; *Mahjoub Mahjoub*, 152; military authorities arrests/interrogations, 30, 104, 141; Mounir Fasheh strengthens community of, 63; occupation of, 44; Palestinian Art Week, 166; possibility of Palestinian state in, 230; protests, 279n11; puppet shows in, 237; *Returning to Haifa*, 126–128; Salah Ed-Din (publishing house) in, 34; theater ensembles emerge in, 4; theater makers of, 10, 239; theater movement in, 5, 35; theaters in public life, 19; use of identity cards in, 254
Westerners, 60, 68, 73, 123, 163, 190, 207, 209; audiences, 116; civilization, 132; directing, 123; Don Quixote, 212; fairy tales, 57; hegemony, 194; journalists, 153; media, 32; music, 46, 120; philosophy, 189; plays, 61; repertoires, 24, 52; theater tradition, 219
West Jerusalem, 171, 217, 236, 246; under civil censorship laws, 10; educational control in, 56; George Ibrahim in, 141, 198; municipal elections, 147; Mustapha Al-Kurd in, 26; occupation of, 145; Palestine Broadcasting Station in, 45
Who's Infertile?, 198
Williams, Jan, 240, 251, 258
Women in Black, 243
Working Women's Association, 185
World War II, 18, 199, 218, 219
Woza Albert!, 212

Ya'coub, Hayyan Al-Ju'beh, 194, 195, 213, 214, 216, 251
"Ya Thalam Al-Sijn" ("Oh, Darkness of Prison"), 220
Yes Theater, 10, 258
YMCA, 40, 41, 42, 43, 60, 61, 116, 147, 149; Balalin, 88; East Jerusalem, 92; Ramallah, 62
Yoya, 210

Zahdeh, Ihab, 10
Zarqa, Jordan, 18
Zayyad, Tawfiq, 30, 34, 50, 148, 220, 239
Zilzal Fi Al-Ard (Earthquake on Earth), 200
Zionism/t, 11, 15, 105, 126, 185, 189; anti-, 216; armed militias, 226; colonizers, 188, 192; Entity, 31; Holocaust survivors, 128; liberal sensibility, 159; music, 190; outlaws, 129; political agenda, 136; propaganda, 116; Youssef Salameh, 186, 187
Zubaidi, Adnan, 212
Zu'bi, Nizar, 258
Zu'mot, Bassam, 41, 56